Sermons On The Gospel Readings

Series II

Cycle C

Gary L. Carver
Tom M. Garrison
Donald Charles Lacy
David R. Cartwright
Ron Lavin
John Wayne Clarke

CSS Publishing Company, Inc., Lima, Ohio

Copyright © 2006 by
CSS Publishing Company, Inc.
Lima, Ohio

Some scripture quotations are from the New Revised Standard Version of the Bible, copyright 1989 by the Division of Christian Education of the National Council of the Churches
of Christ in the USA. Used by permission.

Some scripture quotations are from the King James Version of the Bible, in the public
domain.

Some scripture quotations are from the Holy Bible, New International Version. Copyright
© 1973, 1978, 1984 International Bible Society. Used by permission of Zondervan Bible
Publishers. All rights reserved.

Library of Congress Cataloging-in-Publication Data

Sermons on the Gospel readings : series II, cycle C / Gary L. Carver ... [et al.].
  p. m.
  ISBN 0-7880-2399-3 (perfect bound : alk. paper)
  1. Bible. N.T. Gospels—Homiletical use. 2. Lectionary preaching. I. Carver, Gary L.,
1946- II. Title.

  BS2555.54.S4711 2006
  252'.6—dc22

2006011184

For more information about CSS Publishing Company resources, visit our website at
www.csspub.com or e-mail us at custserv@csspub.com or call (800) 241-4056.

Cover design by Barbara Spencer
ISBN 0-7880-2399-3   PRINTED IN U.S.A.

Table Of Contents

Sermons For Sundays
In Advent, Christmas, And Epiphany
Building A Victorious Life
by Gary L. Carver and Tom M. Garrison

Foreword   **15**

Advent 1   **17**
First Things First
Luke 21:25-36

Advent 2   **23**
Repentance Is Relationship!
Luke 3:1-6

Advent 3   **29**
What Shall We Become?
Luke 3:7-18

Advent 4   **35**
Mary's Magnificat
Luke 1:39-55

Christmas Eve/Christmas Day   **41**
Bethlehem: Where Extremes Meet
Luke 2:1-14 (15-20)

Christmas 1   **49**
Our Task: Acceptance And Challenge
Luke 2:41-52

The Epiphany Of Our Lord   **57**
    What Gift Do You Bring?
    Matthew 2:1-12

The Baptism Of Our Lord   **63**
Epiphany 1
Ordinary Time 1
    The Baptism Of The Lord
    Luke 3:15-17, 21-22

Epiphany 2   **67**
Ordinary Time 2
    Wedding Day
    John 2:1-11

Epiphany 3   **71**
Ordinary Time 3
    Prophet Or Profit?
    Luke 4:14-21

Epiphany 4   **77**
Ordinary Time 4
    The Bible: Head And Heart
    Luke 4:21-30

Epiphany 5   **83**
Ordinary Time 5
    Leaving Before The Invitation
    Luke 5:1-11

Epiphany 6   **89**
Ordinary Time 6
    Woe To The Blessed
    Luke 6:17-26

Epiphany 7   **95**
Ordinary Time 7
    Taking The First Step
    Luke 6:27-38

Epiphany 8   **101**
Ordinary Time 8
    Building A Victorious Life
    Luke 6:39-49

The Transfiguration Of Our Lord   **109**
(Last Sunday After The Epiphany)
    Back To The Future
    Luke 9:28-36 (37-43)

Sermons For Sundays
In Lent And Easter
The Glory Of It All!
by Donald Charles Lacy

Preface   **117**

Ash Wednesday   **119**
    The Hard Sell
    Matthew 6:1-6, 16-21

Lent 1   **127**
    Testing Time
    Luke 4:1-13

Lent 2   **135**
    No Intimidation
    Luke 13:31-35

Lent 3   **143**
    More Time
    Luke 13:1-9

Lent 4   149
    The Two Prodigals
    Luke 15:1-3, 11b-32

Lent 5   157
    Holy Extravagance
    John 12:1-8

Sunday Of The Passion/   165
Palm Sunday
(Lent 6)
    History Hangs In The Balance
    Luke 23:1-49

Good Friday   173
    A Frightening Friday
    John 18:1—19:42

The Resurrection Of Our Lord/   181
Easter Day
    Mary Magdalene's Day
    John 20:1-18

Easter 2   189
    Those Who Doubt
    John 20:19-31

Easter 3   197
    Fish And Sheep
    John 21:1-19

Easter 4   205
    So, Are You The Messiah?
    John 10:22-30

Easter 5   211
    Recognizing His Disciples
    John 13:31-35

Easter 6   **217**
Keeping His Word
John 14:23-29

The Ascension Of Our Lord   **223**
A Good-bye Topping All Others
Luke 24:44-53

Easter 7   **231**
Call To Oneness
John 17:20-26

**Sermons For Sundays
After Pentecost (First Third)**
Guided By The Spirit
by David R. Cartwright

The Day Of Pentecost   **241**
A New Continuing
John 14:8-17, 25-27

The Holy Trinity   **247**
Guided By The Spirit
John 16:12-15

Proper 4   **255**
Pentecost 2
Ordinary Time 9
What Outsiders Can Teach Us
Luke 7:1-10

Proper 5   **261**
Pentecost 3
Ordinary Time 10
Compassion Can Do More Than You May Think
Luke 7:11-17

Proper 6   **267**
Pentecost 4
Ordinary Time 11
    The Extravagance Of Love
    Luke 7:36—8:3

Proper 7   **273**
Pentecost 5
Ordinary Time 12
    What Happens When You're Not Prepared
    For What Happens
    Luke 8:26-39

Proper 8   **279**
Pentecost 6
Ordinary Time 13
    Reactions To Rejection
    Luke 9:51-62

Proper 9   **285**
Pentecost 7
Ordinary Time 14
    Ministering When You're Not Welcome
    Luke 10:1-11, 16-20

Proper 10   **291**
Pentecost 8
Ordinary Time 15
    A Samaritan Took Care Of Him
    Luke 10:25-37

Proper 11   **299**
Pentecost 9
Ordinary Time 16
    How Not To Become Distracted
    Luke 10:38-42

Sermons For Sundays
After Pentecost (Middle Third)
Only The Lonely
by Ron Lavin

Foreword   **309**
    By Rod Anderson

Preface   **311**

Proper 12   **319**
Pentecost 10
Ordinary Time 17
    Abba, Your Kingdom Come
    Luke 11:1-13

Proper 13   **327**
Pentecost 11
Ordinary Time 18
    You Fool!
    Luke 12:13-21

Proper 14   **333**
Pentecost 12
Ordinary Time 19
    Ready Or Not, Here I Come
    Luke 12:32-40

Proper 15   **339**
Pentecost 13
Ordinary Time 20
    Family Ties And Good-byes
    Luke 12:49-56

Proper 16   **349**
Pentecost 14
Ordinary Time 21
    Cured Cripples And Crabby Critics
    Luke 13:10-17

Proper 17   357
Pentecost 15
Ordinary Time 22
    Only The Lonely
    Luke 14:1, 7-14

Proper 18   365
Pentecost 16
Ordinary Time 23
    Counting The Cost Of Discipleship
    Luke 14:25-33

Proper 19   373
Pentecost 17
Ordinary Time 24
    Only The Lost And The Least
    Luke 15:1-10

Proper 20   381
Pentecost 18
Ordinary Time 25
    A Puzzling Parable With A Sharp Point
    Luke 16:1-13

Proper 21   389
Pentecost 19
Ordinary Time 26
    Welcome, Rich And Poor
    Luke 16:19-31

Proper 22   397
Pentecost 20
Ordinary Time 27
    Faithquakes
    Luke 17:5-10

Sermons For Sundays
After Pentecost (Last Third)
Father, Forgive Them
by John Wayne Clarke

Proper 23   405

Pentecost 21

Ordinary Time 28

Gratitude — A State Of Mind

Luke 17:11-19

Proper 24   411

Pentecost 22

Ordinary Time 29

Lean On Me

Luke 18:1-8

Proper 25   419

Pentecost 23

Ordinary Time 30

Prayer — What's In It For You?

Luke 18:9-14

Proper 26   425

Pentecost 24

Ordinary Time 31

A Tax Collector Becomes Rich

Luke 19:1-10

Proper 27   431

Pentecost 25

Ordinary Time 32

Putting Eternity To The Test

Luke 20:27-38

Proper 28   437

Pentecost 26

Ordinary Time 33

The End Of Time

Luke 21:5-19

Reformation Sunday   445
    The Freedom To Interpret
    John 8:31-36

All Saints   451
    What Price Must We Pay?
    Luke 6:20-31

Christ The King   457
    Father, Forgive Them!
    Luke 23:33-43

Thanksgiving Day   463
    A Breadbasket Full Of Goodies
    John 6:25-35

Lectionary Preaching After Pentecost   469

U.S./Canadian Lectionary Comparison   471

About The Authors   473

Sermons On The Gospel Readings

For Sundays In Advent, Christmas, And Epiphany

Building A Victorious Life

**Gary L. Carver
and Tom M. Garrison**

Dedicated to the most wonderful person in this world,
Who knows how to bring the spirit of goodness into my life.
Who stands beside me in brightest day and the darkest night
To my sweetheart, Renata

Acknowledgments

To my partner in the faith
and co-writer of these sermons:
Reverend Dr. Gary L. Carver

To my church family who showed more love through tough
times than I could ever have imagined:
Sun Lakes United Church of Christ, Sun Lakes, Arizona

To my dad:
Johnny H. Garrison

To my sister:
Linda Garrison Brown

Foreword

A few years ago, I was sitting in a worship service at Saint George's Chapel in Windsor, England. The passage for the day was Paul's writings from Romans 8, it is the strange sounding scripture "all things work together for good for those who love the Lord." I recall the priest that day turning the scripture upside down and sideways trying to make sense of it, because it is hard to see that all things do work together for good for those who love the Lord. I do not remember now if the good Anglican priest ever came to a comfortable place with the text, but I think I have.

There is more good in the badness than we can realize. When I was putting these sermons together it seemed like one obstacle after another prevented me from completing the book. The greatest of all the obstacles was what seemed to me to be the worst. I became sick and after many tests, I received the diagnosis of lung cancer. It didn't seem right or fair. How would or could this happen since I wasn't a smoker? Besides struggling with this life-changing diagnosis I was still gathering sermons I had written for this book. However, my energy was not in a new sermon book.

Then it happened, my good friend of nearly twenty years, one who has written several books for CSS, made the scripture "all things work together for good for those who love the Lord" come alive. He wanted to take the stress off me and so we decided to do the book together. What you will find in this book are sermons by the Reverend Dr. Gary L. Carver, of Chattanooga, Tennessee, edited by me and sermons that I had written for the book, also. Each sermon will be designated as to the author. This turned out to be a work of love.

Thank you, Gary!

First Things First

No moment in the life of a parent is more awesome than when a child leaves home for the first time and as you watch them walk away, you wonder: "Have I prepared this one adequately for all he or she will face?" Because none of us complete the parenting task perfectly, it is not unusual that sooner or later those same children come back and ask: "Why did you not tell me thus and so? I never heard a word about that growing up — why did you not warn me?"

This happens to ministers, as well as parents, in relation to religious and moral questions. I remember a bright, young college freshman in Texas coming to see me during the Christmas break and wanting to know about the Second Coming of Christ. She had grown up in our church where the subject of eschatology was rarely mentioned, but that fall she had gotten into a group that was reading Hal Lindsey's bestseller, *The Late Great Planet Earth*. She was all confused. She claimed that eighteen years of Sunday school with us had given her no tools whatsoever to handle this issue intelligently. I had to do what any parent figure in such a situation must do; namely, to ask her forgiveness and then move as quickly as possible "to fill in the gaps" and catch up as best I could. I had a similar experience recently with another college student. It led me to wondering when from this pulpit the issue of "The Last Things" had been addressed. I have no idea what level of interest some of you bring to this subject, but because it is very much in the air — Hal Lindsey's book has been made into a commercial movie — and the subject is often discussed on television, I decided to share with all of you some of what I shared with those concerned college

17

students about this whole issue of the end of the world and the speculations that cluster around it.

The first thing I said to these folk was that the concept of Jesus' return to earth at the end of history was not only explicitly set forth in the Bible, but is also consistent with the overall vision of history that you find there. After all, creation is depicted from beginning to end as a purposeful endeavor. It was begun like a drama with a specific idea in mind. Creation did not just happen — it was grounded in what Rollo May calls "intentionality," which means there is a plot, a beginning, middle, and an ending to the drama of history. C. S. Lewis said that when the author appears on the stage, you know the play is over. This is how he understands the doctrine of the Second Coming of our Lord. It means that he who has begun a good work will bring it to the best conclusion of which he is capable. After all, no one has ever claimed that this planet earth was intended to exist forever. In what is called by scientists "the second law of thermodynamics," it is clearly predicted that the energy supply of this planet will eventually come to an end, which means that a conclusion of life as we know it here is inevitable. The concept of the Second Coming merely affirms that such a conclusion will be purposeful. The drama of history is not going to just fizzle out or end in a whimper! It is going to come to the kind of climax that he who conceived the drama wants for it. Therefore, the first thing I said to these folk was that the doctrine is consistent with the whole biblical vision of history. To be born into this world is not to enter a process of utter chaos. There is a plot to it all, and for there to be a plot, there must be a fitting climax.

The second thing I noted, however, was that we mortals have no way of knowing precisely when this event would take place. With the same forthrightness that Jesus predicted that he would come again to earth, he also said: "But of that day and hour no one knows, not even the angels of heaven, not the Son, but the Father only" (Matthew 24:36). Alongside this flat acknowledgment of ignorance are innumerable parables of Jesus that underline the note of uncertainty and challenge human beings to be eternally vigilant and prepared at all times. "Watch," Jesus says again and again, "for you do not know what day your Lord is coming. The Son of

Man is coming at an hour you do not expect." Coupled with the definite certainty of Jesus' return is the clear uncertainty as to when this will take place.

In light of such obvious teaching, it really is amazing that conservative Bible-believing people invest so much energy in speculating about "The End Times." I spent considerable time with these college students trying to account for this seeming contradiction. I have my own hunch at this point. Again and again in history, when events get unusually complex or threatening, the tendency has been to turn to millennial speculation out of a sense of total powerlessness. They feel that things are in such a mess that only the intervention of God himself is capable of undoing what has been done. Then, too, the role of passive dependency is always easier than a stance of responsible involvement. Who has not, like a little child, wanted to gather up all the broken things and take them to Daddy to fix? The impulse to let someone else come in and solve all our difficulties is very strong; in fact, it is the classic infantile reaction to any problem, and who can deny that speculating abstractly about the future is less demanding than trying to serve lovingly and sacrificially in the present?

Here, in my judgment, is one of the subtlest temptations that faces any Christian in any era, and it leads to the third thing I tried to say. If we are not careful, we can get diverted here from what Christ has called us to do in this present age. This happened in Thessalonica not twenty years after Jesus died, and Saint Paul met the issue head on. Some of the folk there got so caught up in expecting and predicting the imminent return of the Lord that they had ceased to do any work and degenerated into idle busybodies who prattled only about the future (2 Thessalonians 3:11). Paul rebuked this tendency to let an over-interest in "the last things" divert us from faithfulness to "the first things." It was exactly the temptation to which Simon Peter succumbed in the text from John's Gospel.

Here is one of the tenderest scenes in all the New Testament. After Jesus had arisen from the grave and appeared to his disciples and to many other followers, he returned to Galilee, where some of

19

his disciples were fishing and early one morning prepared breakfast for that inner circle. After they had eaten, he singled out Simon Peter, and three times, once for each of the denials, he asked him simply: "Simon, do you love me?" This time, the old arrogance was gone. Simon did not say anything about loving Christ more than all the others. He simply whispered gently: "Lord, you know that I love you." And three times, Jesus said to Simon: "Feed my sheep ... tend my lambs ... feed my sheep." It was a reissuing of the original invitation to follow Christ and it climaxed the reconciliation of these two. However, right after this high moment of "getting back together," Simon looked over at John, "the beloved disciple," and proceeded to indulge in speculation about what the future held for him. Remember, Simon had just been given his own commission for the present, yet here he was wondering what was going to happen to this other man out in the future. I imagine there was a real note of harshness in the voice of Jesus when he said: "Simon, if it be my will that this one remain until I come, what is that to you? Follow thou me." In other words, he was saying, "Simon, mind your own business. First things first. I have given you a task to do, and the important thing is for you to be faithful at that point, not to spend your energies in speculation about something else." Faithfulness in the present, not curiosity about the future — this was the call of Christ to Simon Peter in that moment.

And unless I am badly mistaken, this is the call of Christ for us, as well. We, too, are to put "first things first." But what are the first things? To commit ourselves unreservedly to the Lordship of Christ — putting ourselves totally in his hand, receiving his love, and letting him teach us how to love the Lord our God with all our hearts and minds and souls and strength and how to love our neighbor and how to love ourselves. This is the great commandment according to Jesus. When we are willing to be fed by him and to join him in feeding others, then we are being faithful stewards.

This really is what we are to focus on in the present moment — letting ourselves be loved by God and letting that love flow through us to those who need it most. It occurred to me one day as I reflected on Jesus' great parable of the final judgment, that in a sense, the Second Coming has already occurred. Not the Final

Coming, mind you, but a Second Coming where Christ identifies himself with the last and the least of the human procession. Did he not say when they asked, "When did we see you hungry and thirsty and naked and in prison?" those awesome words: "In as much as you did it not to one of the least of these, my brethren, you did it not to me"? I repeat, in a sense Christ has returned already, and he is now exactly where he spent his life — among those who need him the most. To join him there and do what we can for these struggling brothers and sisters, this is our true calling as Christians, not to speculate about the future.

Here, then, is how I tried "to catch these college students up" at a place where our religious education has failed them. I apologized to them, for in a day when fanatical fundamentalism is on the rise everywhere, we do our children no service at all to send them out like sheep among wolves with no interpretive tools whatsoever. I hope what I belatedly shared with them helped some, and I hope this sharing has served to clarify and enlighten you about this concern.

There is something to the doctrine of the Second Coming — something very crucial. It is part of a vision of reality that says that creation is not a meaningless accident, but a drama with a plot — with a beginning, middle, and an end. There is an author behind all of history and seeing him step out on the stage will signal the end of the play. But as to when this will happen, ah — that is in God's hands alone. Not even the angels or the Son himself was in on that secret. It will come when you do not expect it, "like a thief in the night," Jesus said. And what are we to do in the meantime? Like Simon Peter, we are to let Christ feed us as he did those disciples there by the lake that morning, and then go out "to feed and tend others," especially those who need it most. First things first, is what Jesus would say, and that involves being loved and loving in the present rather than speculating about the future.

There is an old story about a warrior who was struck one day by a poisonous arrow. This man happened to be a speculative sort of person, so as he lay on the ground he mused to himself: "I wonder what kind of wood this arrow is made of? What sort of birds, do you suppose, the feathers come from? I wonder what type of man shot this arrow — tall or short, dark or light." His comrades, who saw his plight, could bear it no longer, but cried out in frustration: "For God's sake, man! Stop speculating and pull out the arrow!"

Need I say more?

— Gary L. Carver

Repentance Is Relationship!

Repentance is relationship. Nathaniel Hawthorne wrote a short story titled, *The Birthmark*. It is a story about a man who married a very beautiful woman who had a birthmark on her left cheek. She had always thought of it as a beauty spot, but her husband saw the birthmark to be a sign of imperfection, a flaw. It began wearing on him so much that all he could see was that birthmark. He could not see her beauty, her graciousness, or her great personality. He could only focus on what he perceived to be a flaw. He hounded her until she finally submitted to surgery to remove the so-called flaw. The birthmark eventually faded and so did she. In Hawthorne's mind, that birthmark was tied to her identity and shortly thereafter she died. A man who sought perfection ended up with nothing.

That is not the God and Father of our Lord and Savior Jesus Christ. That is not the God that we come to worship today. Nevertheless, when we think about Lent and hear words like "repentance" and "perfection," many times we get negative connotations in our minds. It conjures up negative images in our memories. From my own background, when I hear the word, "repent," I picture a preacher standing red faced, a loud voice, veins popping on his neck, pounding the Bible, pointing a finger, sweating profusely like a politician without a vote proclaiming, "Repent! Repent!" In other words, God is going to zap you if you do not repent. If you are bad, God is going to zap you. Not stated but implied is that if you are good, God will protect you.

It was exactly that kind of theology that Jesus blew out of the water. There were some who came to Jesus and mentioned the

23

Galileans who had lost their lives at worship when Pilate turned loose his soldiers upon them. As they were making sacrifices, they were murdered right on the spot so that their blood mingled with the blood of their sacrifices. And Jesus said, "Do you think they were worse sinners than anybody else and that is the reason they died? I tell you, 'No!' It just isn't so." Jesus said, "Unless you repent you shall also perish."

Jesus made a comparison with natural evil when he said, "What about those eighteen who died when the tower of Siloam fell upon them? Do you think they were the worst sinners of the lot? Do you think they were worse sinners than the rest of the people living in Jerusalem? I tell you, 'No!' It just isn't so. But I will tell you this, 'Unless you repent, you too, shall perish.' " Jesus is saying it is easy sitting around asking ourselves questions for which there are no answers because it allows us to evade the very things we can do. Jesus is saying that we are not to sit around trying to answer those questions. He is saying, "There are some things you can do and one thing you can do is repent."

In our text today is a very clear call to repentance. What does the word "repent" mean? It might fill your mind as it sometimes does mine with, "Just what is it we are to do?" What is repentance? Well, first of all, repentance is not the fear of God. I talked to an individual once and he said, "Well, sure, I'm scared of the old man," meaning God. So what! Repentance is not conviction of sin. I was witnessing to a person on one occasion and this person said, "Well, I'm sorry but I know it." So what! Fear of God and knowledge of sin is not repentance. Fear of God and knowledge of sin is essential, but not the essence of repentance. Repentance is not remorse. You can break a stone and that stone does not change its nature. It is still the same stone. It is just in smaller pieces. It is not just enough to be broken. It is not just enough to be contrite. It is not just enough to turn over a new leaf to mess up a clean page.

What is repentance? It is more than turning over our lives. It is more than just feeling sorry for our sins. Repentance means to change the direction of your life. It means to stop walking toward selfishness, self-centeredness, and a life that is centered upon what the self desires. It means to make a 180-degree turn, start walking toward God, his vision, his aim, and his goal for your life.

When Jesus came into the world, the dominant view of sin was going through one of God's red lights. Sin was doing something wrong. But Jesus helped us to see that sin was more than just doing bad things and not doing good things. Sin is missing the mark, missing God's purpose, goal, and ambition for your life. You are a dream in the mind of God and to be in sin means to be out of God's purpose for your life. It means not going in the direction that God would have you to go. To repent means to turn from your sinfulness and turn toward the life that God has for you. There is definitely a clear call to repentance in our text for today.

Also in our text is a warning that the time can be short. Notice the parable of the fig tree. A man had a fig tree planted in his vineyard. He went again to the tree looking for fruit but did not find any. He said to the man that tended the vineyard, "For three years I have come seeking fruit on this fig tree, and have found none: cut it down." By the third year, fig trees are supposed to bear fruit. That's why you have a fig tree. Bearing fruit is the nature of a fig tree. By the third year, none! He said, "Cut it down!" Cut it down — strong words of judgment. It is not fulfilling its purpose. Chop it!

It has been said that W. C. Fields was reading the Bible on his death bed when someone asked him why he was doing that. He answered, "I'm looking for loopholes." There are none! I'm reminded of the individual who said, "I have misjudged two things in life. I have misjudged the brevity of life and I have misjudged the breadth of eternity." We're all going to die. For some the time is shorter than for others. A clear call that time is running out. Christian, bear Christian fruit! That's what Jesus is talking about. Is that not what we are to do as Christians? That's why we are called Christians. We are to bear Christian fruit. We are to live a life that exudes Christlikeness.

A story is told by Alexander Whyte of a man by the name of Rigby. Mr. Rigby was a traveling salesman, and every time he traveled through the city of Edinburgh, he would attend worship services on Sunday night. He would always bring someone from the boarding house where he stayed to the services. On a particular

Sunday night, he brought a young man who made a profession of faith. He made Jesus his Lord and Savior. The next day, Rigby passed by the house of Alexander Whyte, the preacher, and decided to stop and share with him the decision this young man made. The preacher said, "Thank you. I really thought I made a mess of last night's sermon and this really helps me to hear what happened. By the way, what is your name?" The man said, "My name is Rigby." Alexander Whyte said, "What?" He said, "My name is Rigby." Whyte said, "Man, I've been looking for you for years." He went into a nearby room and came back with a stack of twelve letters. Those letters were from individuals whom Rigby had brought to the evening worship services and all twelve had accepted Jesus Christ as their Lord and Savior and two of those twelve had already entered the ministry. What did he do? He invited others to Christ. He brought people to church with him. That is a Christlike quality.

We are called to produce Christlike fruit in our lives. It is a clear call to repentance, and it is a warning that the time could be short. How many of us are guaranteed tomorrow? Today is the day, yet this parable ends on a note of grace because the man who tended the tree said, "Give me one more year. I will dig around the tree and fertilize the tree. Just give me one more year and if at the end of that year the tree does not produce fruit, then we will cut it down." This is a parable of mercy! This is a parable of grace! This is a parable of delayed judgment to give us time to repent! For you see, the Bible explicitly says God does not demand moral perfection. God knew we couldn't; God knew we wouldn't and that is why he sent his Son. God does not demand from us moral perfection! It is impossible! God knew we would sin! He knew we could not be perfect!

The book of Numbers, chapter 19, has an interesting passage beginning with verse 1. The priest was told to take a red heifer that was without blemish or spot, literally a heifer that was perfect, and he was to kill the heifer. How strange. Why would you take a heifer that was perfect, spotless, blameless, without blemish or flaw and kill it? Does that mean in some way that perfection does not belong in this world? There has only been one who was perfect. The rest of us, every single one of us, have flaws and blemishes. We are imperfect. God never expects us to be morally perfect. It is impossible for us to be morally perfect and that is why repentance is the nature of relationship with God.

Every day is a day of repentance. Every day is a day of turning toward God. God doesn't demand moral perfection, but he does demand a continual personal relationship to him; whereby we continually repent of our sins and turn toward him every day, sometimes every hour. God has not given up on failures. Thank God!

In 1986, an outstanding young man by the name of Donnie Moore was a major league baseball pitcher. He was pitching in the championship series and all he had to do was get one more out. Just one out and the California Angels would be in the World Series. Donnie Moore surrendered a homerun and his team lost. They did not make it to the World Series because of Donnie Moore's one mistake! A Cy Young Award winner — great athlete — one mistake — never got over it. A few years later, Donnie Moore took his own life.

A few years ago, in this thing we call March Madness, there was a nineteen-year-old forward for the University of Michigan Wolverines by the name of Chris Webber. They were playing for the national championship. Seconds were winding down in a very close game when Chris Webber got the ball and called time out. Only one thing wrong. They didn't have any more time outs. The ball went to the other team, and Michigan lost the national championship because of Chris Webber's mistake. He didn't dwell on it. He didn't let it defeat him. In fact, the very next year he was NBA rookie of the year.

Now, let me ask you a personal question. Which one was more in the will of God? The one who made a mistake and despairingly took his life or the one who made a mistake, found forgiveness, went on, and lived life? Which one? God has not given up on failures. God does not demand, nor does he expect, moral perfection. We are incapable of moral perfection, but we are capable of a life that is characterized by continual repentance as we live life in his presence.

The book of Genesis says that God created our world and he said, "It is good! Everything about this world is good!" The best thing about this world is *you*. You are the zenith, the apex, and the climax of God's creation. You are the very best that God can do. Man and woman are the height of creation! God created us good. We are not bad people. We are good people who do bad. When we do bad, we need to turn back to God and repent of our sins. When we repent, a bunch of wonderful things happen: God restores us to life, he restores us to health, he restores us to a relationship with him and with others, and he clears the air. The greatest joy in life is to be forgiven and to walk in grace and mercy knowing that God loves and cares for you. God gave to us a way to deal with our sinfulness by Jesus' death on the cross. The Bible says that there is more joy in heaven over one sinner's repentance than over 99 people who have no need to repent.

What a special day I had this past week. I was walking out of a restaurant when a little girl ran up to me and hugged my leg and her little eyes were just dancing. She said, "I've decided to ask Jesus to come into my life." She had decided to repent and I'll tell you what, the angels in heaven rejoiced! All of heaven rejoiced! I hope all of heaven will be rejoicing because of the decision you make today.

— Gary L. Carver

28

What Shall We Become?

Almost thirty years ago a play titled, *Mourning Pictures*, opened off-Broadway. Written by Honor Moore, it is the moving account of the last six months of her mother's life. Jenny Moore was no ordinary human being. She was the wife of the Episcopal Bishop of New York and the mother of nine vivacious children and an author in her own right. About a year before her death, she was in an automobile accident that led to a partial nervous breakdown, and just when she was about to recover from this ordeal, she was found to have cancer of the liver and colon, and this is what finally took her life, slowly, painfully, inch-by-inch. Her daughter, Honor, was with her during most of those last months, and after she died she began to write poems based on a journal that she had kept during this period. These became the basis of the play that tells the story of this particular human ending.

The drama begins as Honor recounts her first efforts to share with the audience the pain of this tragedy. Here are her words: "Ladies and gentlemen, my mother is dying. You say, 'Everyone's mother dies.' I bow to you, and smile. Ladies and gentlemen, my mother is dying. She has cancer. You say, 'Many people die of cancer.' I scratch my head. Gentle ladies, gentle men, my mother has cancer, and short of a miracle, she will die. You say, 'This has happened many times before.' You say, 'Death is something which repeats itself.' I bow. Ladies and gentlemen, my mother has cancer all through her. She will die unless there is a miracle. You shrug. You gave up on religion years ago, Marxism, too. You don't

29

believe in anything anymore. One step forward. One last time, ladies and gentlemen, my mother is dying. I haven't got another."

Hearing those words again, I found myself wondering how many times some burdened soul had tried to reach out and found a world so insensitive, so preoccupied, so caught up in one's own pursuit of happiness that no real effort was made to reach back to share. These responses that were made to Honor — were generalizations that said in effect: "I do not want to get involved. I have no time for you. I've got troubles enough of my own. Don't bother me with your burdens."

A famous English preacher, Alexander Whyte, was very disturbed one night because his closest friend in the ministry was at the point of death. Whyte was praying earnestly to God that this man might be spared when suddenly a voice said to him, "How serious are you about this one's survival? Would you be willing to divide with him the number of years you have left to live upon this earth?" With that, Whyte reports getting up off his knees in a cold sweat for, suddenly, intercession had become more than a matter of words. Now it was the precious substance of his own life that was at stake. He pondered this question very deliberately for a while and then dropped back to his knees and said, "Yes! I hereby relinquish half of the time I have left, if this will enable my friend to survive." He got up off his knees with no idea of what the ultimate outcome of this agreement would be. This little episode sets into sharper focus the issue I found myself facing with this scripture.

According to John the Baptist, as well as Jesus, this is by no means an idle question, for the basic secret of human fulfillment is to be found at precisely this point. The most important thing said about us human beings in scripture is that we are to become as the one that came in a very subtle way. This concept is put forward as John's response to these direct and maybe harsh teachings. The question comes, "What shall we do?" The answers John gave to those seekers address the inequities and injustices of that society: food and clothing are to be shared with those who have none; taxes are not to be based on the insatiable greed of the powerful; and the military must stop victimizing the public by threat, intimidation, and blackmail. It is clear from listening to John that the one for which he was preparing the way was Jesus. The advent of God is the kind of image that's only fulfillment lies down the road of giving ourselves away.

This point is not only true in the advent of God through the teaching of John the Baptist, but becomes the focal message of Jesus himself. We may recall the day a lawyer came up and asked Jesus almost the same question: "What must I do to inherit eternal life?" This was the lawyer's way of asking the fundamental question. "What do I do as a person so that my potential can be felt by others?" Jesus answered and said: "Thou shall love the Lord your God with all your heart and mind and soul and strength," or to put it another way, "Thou shall love your neighbor as yourself." The question quickly came: "Who is my neighbor?" Jesus then moved the audience to see the advent of God in their lives. He told what may be his most famous parable, the parable of the good Samaritan.

He began with a character that was not described specifically at all. We do not know whether he was a Jew or a Gentile, good or bad, rich or poor. His was simply described as "a man," a person making his way down that steep descent from Jerusalem to Jericho. It was known as the "bloody pass" because so much violence had taken place there. This man fell among robbers who left him penniless and half-dead by the roadside. Three people came along one by one, of which Jesus described specifically. The first was a priest, one who was charged with preserving the traditions of Israel. The second was a Levite, who was a chorister on the temple staff in Jerusalem. The third was a Samaritan, a racial half-breed in the eyes of the Jews, who was looked down upon with contempt.

Surprisingly, in the light of the tradition they were supposed to represent, the first two did nothing for the man. They looked at him and passed by on the other side, denying the advent of God and choosing not to give any of themselves to this man's misfortune. Indeed, even more surprisingly, the Samaritan acted differently. He not only saw the man and had compassion; he put himself out considerably to make some of his resources available to this needy man.

It requires a moment of reflection to fully realize what Jesus did in this famous story. The question the lawyer asks about one's

31

neighbor was by no means a new one. It became obvious that this is the central movement of God in the world. It is not unusual that John the Baptist would call on those of that day to be presented in a way that had not been traditional.

It is also the core of why, at Advent, we have a passage like Luke 3 before us. The way God moves us is to make ourselves more accepting, loving, and giving. This is how we, "inherit eternal life," or to put it in another context, how we fulfill our nature as human beings and come to completely understand the joy we are meant to have.

The story is told that when C. S. Lewis was a bachelor, he awoke one night and could not go back to sleep. It was a dark, cloudy night, so there was nothing to see, and the stillness that surrounded him was absolute. Lewis said he had never felt so alone and cut off in all his life, and, suddenly, he sat upright in a cold sweat when it occurred to him that such a condition was the logical end of a self-centered life! "What," he found himself asking, "if we finally get in eternity what we have lived for in time — no more, no less? This means if we have invested ourselves in God and other people, we will get the whole network of relationship, but if we have lived only for ourselves, this is what we get and nothing more." Lewis realized why solitary confinement is such a dreaded punishment. It denies a basic need of ours as social creatures. This is the consequence of a life led denying the image of God within and spending all energies on oneself. We get in eternity what we have lived for in life, no more, no less, which underlines the importance of the question that was posed to John the Baptist, "What must we do?" It is a question deeper than offering a coat, bread, or even treating someone in the right way.

There is an old parable of the man who dreamed he was transported into the next life and allowed to glimpse the places called heaven and hell. The man's guide explained that the one difference between people here and the people on earth was their elbows were stiffened. The man was taken first to the lower regions and what he saw was a scene of chaos, literally, "weeping and wailing and gnashing of teeth." The people of this area had loaves of bread, but because their elbows were stiff, they could not get the food to their mouths and they were thrashing around, striking each other in total frustration. It was the utmost of emptiness and misery. The man then was taken to heaven. The spirit of that place was totally different. Here there was harmony, creativity, and joy. Here the people also had food in their hands and stiff elbows, but because the people were paired off, intent on feeding another, and, in the process, they were being fed themselves.

This is a wonderful parable of the one truth I am hoping that you hear today. The truth of John the Baptist compels us to give of ourselves, in some small way, for God's presence to be made known in all our lives. The advent of God is made known not through the getting, but in the giving.

— Tom M. Garrison

Mary's Magnificat

Christmas songs have a way of staying with us from childhood. In fact, if you were to ask someone their favorite Christmas song it may range from, "Silent Night" to "I Saw Mommy Kissing Santa Claus." Many Christmas songs do carry the element of the holy in their lyrics and sometimes in the melody. Most of all, though, Christmas stands alone from all other holidays by the fact that it carries its own genre of music. The message of this season can be sung as well as spoken. The world has come to know the all-important story of Jesus, perhaps more due to the tunes, than the spoken word or reading of messages.

I have experienced the power of the secular and religious Christmas song. A few years ago, my wife, an Austrian, and I visited friends in Purgstall, Austria. We stayed at our friends' *kneippkurhaus* (inn and spa). One evening, we were sitting around a large table in the kitchen. The word had gotten around that an American was staying a few days (Purgstall is not on the tourist trail) and one of the longtime guests, a retired school teacher, wanted to meet me. She also wanted me to hear her sing. She brought her guitar and played folk songs from Hungary, Germany, and Austria. Before she left, she wanted to sing an American song, and since everyone's native language, except mine, was German, we had to put some thought into what could be sung in English. The one song that everyone knew was a most unlikely tune, "Jingle Bells." Soon we were off dashing through the snow in the middle of September. I was reminded how powerful our songs, seasonal or religious, really are. On this trip to Austria, I was reminded that "Silent Night" was translated into English, having been written by an Austrian priest. It is clear to me that in all cultures there is a history and tradition of our Christmas songs which is cherished.

There is a song that is maybe the best known in the world, and we call this song, "Mary's Magnificat." It is also clear that most of our exposure to this song is found sometime during the Advent season. If we have time we may even include it in our Christmas Eve service. It has a holy and almost mysterious sound. What do you do with Mary's Magnificat?

The Magnificat is the great New Testament song of liberation — personal, social, moral, and economic — a revolutionary document of intense conflict and victory. It leads to everything we would learn about Jesus himself. This is truly magnificent when viewed not only from the birth story, but also the death story.

Through this song of Mary we feel her expressing her faith and vision, and asking the right questions. In an old biography of Francis of Assisi, the story is told of a night he spent in the castle of an Italian nobleman. The host was curious as to the secret of Francis' remarkable vitality, so he arranged to have Francis spend the night in the chamber adjacent to his own. As soon as they retired, the nobleman watched to see what Francis would do, and it turned out to be quite simple. He knelt by his bed and prayed over and over again, "O Lord, who art thou, and who am I? Who art thou and who am I? Who art thou and who am I?" The biographer concludes that this is one of the clues of Francis' greatness. All his life he continued to ask the right questions, he never tired of trying to penetrate ever more deeply into the core of our existence. After all, the God-question and self-question are the ultimate realities. If we would grow in spiritual intensity, here are two frontiers on which the Magnificat is built.

The telling of the Magnificat can be of great help to us. In what transpired long ago we get a telling insight, not only into the nature of God, but also into human nature and how the two interact together so that great creativity can result. Here one can discover illuminating answers to the question: "Who art thou, O Lord, and who am I?"

As we ponder Mary's song we cannot forget the struggle Mary is going through. God had asked this young woman to do the impossible, to give birth without a man, and this pregnancy would bring the redemption of the world. This scandal would bring true righteousness. On the outset, Mary's song seems like it is out of place. God may have found favor in Mary, but what does God ask her to do? He asked her to risk her body, her marriage, her reputation, and even her life. Mary must have thought to herself: "What a strange kind of God this Yahweh is! What on earth is important enough to him to warrant this kind of sacrifice? What objective is there sufficient enough to justify such an endeavor?"

I am afraid that we have heard the song of deliverance and the love of God so often that "the wonder of it all" has worn off. This must never happen. I enjoy the Christmas poster which describes the season as the time, "when God cared enough to send the very best!" This message out of the Magnificat comes to express the very best on behalf of the very worst. Where else in the world do you see this kind of exchange, when the best people are asked to sacrifice on behalf of the worst? In our culture it is usually the other way around. The worst of humanity are sacrificed in order to preserve the best. With God, it is the opposite. The best, such as Mary and Jesus, are asked to sacrifice and suffer so that those who least deserve it are granted another opportunity to be helped.

This is the meaning of Mary's response to the momentous proposal. To be sure, a great deal was asked of her, but look at what was being offered to her! A chance to share with God in the most exciting adventure of — the adventure of changing enemies into friends, of turning darkness into light, and transforming a death-wish into the will to live again. This enterprise of restoring and finishing the creation is one to which all are invited, in fact you can hear Mary's song if you listen closely.

The good news of the Magnificat is that it is not too late to find the salvation of which Mary spoke. A relationship that comes not with an overpowering force, but a relationship that comes with a change of heart, a change that leads us to spiritual awakening. It was one of those moments that changed the life of Augustine. He was struggling with his own soul, searching for something more in

37

life and how the whole thing could have meaning. He was reading his Bible one day, when a strong breeze suddenly opened it to Romans 8. He began to read the very thing of which Mary sang. Down through the ages, those who would become influential servants of God have told their stories over and over again. I recall the story of the Baptist preacher, D. L. Moody. He said: "I heard an evangelist one night: This century has yet to see what God could do with one person wholly committed to his will." Moody said in his heart of hearts, "By the grace of God, I'll be that person." He emerged from the obscurity of selling shoes into an influence that effected a great portion of a nation. It is obvious from Mary's song that we can participate in the miracle of his kingdom coming and his will being done on earth as it is in heaven.

Here is why Mary's Magnificat is relevant to the growing edge of our spiritual lives. Saint Francis never stopped asking, "Who art thou, O Lord, and who am I?" As he came to know the song by the young Jewish woman engaged to Joseph, his words came clearly, "He is the one who made all things and who loves everything he has made. It is not the will of this Father that any should perish, but that all should be won back to life." To this end, our God still reminds us of the wondrous event we call Christmas when we hear Mary's Magnificat.

As you think of Mary this day, the question arises: Could there be a higher challenge than receiving a vision as she did, then responding in the timeless song? Mary challenges us with her words:

> *My soul glorifies the Lord, and my spirit rejoices in God my Savior, for he has been mindful of the humble state of his servant. From now on all generations will call me blessed for the Mighty One has done great things for me — holy is his name. His mercy extends to those who fear him, from generation to generation. He has performed mighty deeds with his arm, he has scattered those who are proud in their innermost thoughts. He has brought down rulers from their thrones, but has lifted up the humble; he has filled the hungry with good things, but has sent the rich away empty. He has*

helped his servant Israel, remembering to be merciful
to Abraham and his descendents forever, even as he
said to our fathers.   — Luke 1:47-55

It is enough that we sing our way though this Advent season and remember a song that lifts our hearts during Christmas.

— Tom M. Garrison

Bethlehem:
Where Extremes Meet

Every year at this particular season, I am amazed all over again at the impact that the old, old story of Christmas has on people. In light of how "fad-conscious" we tend to be in this country, it is a wonder to me that we have not grown weary of this ancient story and the figures of the babe and the manger and the shepherds and all the rest. After 2,000 years of exhaustive repetition, why do you suppose the events of Bethlehem still lay hold of our depths and continue to intrigue us? Is this simply the momentum of a long-established tradition, or is there another secret to this incredible vitality? In my judgment, there is more at work here than "the twitching of the dead hand of the past."

Now, to be sure, the power of tradition is present here, but alongside this, I sense another force that is much more potent; namely, a simplicity that is rooted in bottomless profundity. What you have in the Christmas story is a classic example of a reality that is at once known and yet not fully known. Here is something that can be grasped immediately and concretely by the youngest and the most profound of minds. As I have suggested in the sermon title, Bethlehem is a place where extremes meet — a coming to-gether of opposites — and this is at least one explanation of its fantastic appeal. If either side of the matter were not present, the Christmas story would not be what it is and has been. For example, if it were only a thing of profundity and depth, little children and the great mass of people would not be affected by it, for they would not understand it.

There is no great popular devotion to Einstein's theory of relativity; for the simple reason that it is beyond the capacities of most of us to comprehend its abstractness. Profundity, without simplicity, will always be limited in its appeal. By the same token, simplicity without profundity has a relatively short life span of interest. If something can be understood completely and entirely, it soon loses its power to fascinate and intrigue. Human curiosity is ever moving on toward what it does not know and unless there is something inexhaustible in simplicity, it is bound to fade in time.

My contention is that the Christmas story is a perfect balance of these two essential factors. Call it what you will — a simple profundity or a profound simplicity — it holds in tension the immediate and the inexhaustible, the certainty of the known and the beckoning of the unknown; and this is one of the secrets of its power. Bethlehem continues to attract and to astound for the simple reason that it is the place where extremes meet, the coming together of opposites that both satisfy and intrigue. It is from this vantage point that I want us to view this morning the miracle of Bethlehem. In terms of what led up to it, the event itself, and the responses that followed it, the power of Bethlehem lies in the simplicity and profundity that come together there in an intriguing blend.

First of all, let us focus on what led up to the first Christmas, on why Mary and Joseph were in Bethlehem at all, and why the birth took place in a stable. If you look deeply into these events, what you see is the coming together of human harshness and human kindness. Both extremes were there. Most of you will probably remember that both Mary and Joseph were from Nazareth, a nondescript hill town in Galilee, some eighty or ninety miles north of Bethlehem. Why then, in those days of torturous travel, had they journeyed so far from home?

The ostensible reason was a Roman census that was being taken, which required that each man return to the place of his birth. However, this in itself does not account for why Mary was along, especially in light of her maternal condition. The census was strictly a male affair. Rome was only interested in the head of the household and his property, which included his wife, so Joseph easily could have made the journey to Bethlehem alone — in fact, most assuredly would have, if it had not been for other reasons. This brings us to what had happened months before that had set this whole chain of events into motion.

The angel Gabriel had appeared to Mary and proposed that she would be the mother of the Messiah and this would be accomplished without the agency of a human father. Just as the Spirit of God had once overshadowed the formless deep and called forth creation in the beginning (Genesis 1:1), so once again that Spirit would overshadow Mary and call forth out of her empty womb a child to be called Jesus, the Son of the Most High. This is what actually occurred, but at the time, Mary was legally engaged to Joseph but not yet married, and you can imagine the whispers that began to circulate around Nazareth as the months rolled on.

People can be cruel, you know, especially in this kind of situation, and it is not unthinkable at all that to spare Mary further embarrassment, Joseph who had himself been convinced of this story through a dream, took the occasion of the census to move her to Bethlehem and get her away from the wagging tongues of Nazareth. It was not an easy choice, for birth in that day was essentially a family and a womanly enterprise. The older women of the village, both kinspeople and friends, were the ones to be with a mother at this time, and by having to flee like a refugee to Bethlehem, Mary was thus called upon to face alone — without feminine help — her descent into the valley of the shadows of birth. She had only a man and some animals to help her. There is real pathos, then, in the fact that the event took place in Bethlehem — far away from the home out of which Mary had been driven by the harshness of people.

Yet, the fact that it took place in a stable represents the other extreme that comes together in the Bethlehem scene; namely, an act of human kindness. I am indebted to Dr. William Hull at this point, for some years ago he preached a magnificent Christmas sermon in which he challenged the traditional interpretation of that verse: "There was no room for them in the inn." Dr. Hull noted several salient facts. First, Mary and Joseph probably had been living in Bethlehem for several weeks or even months before the birth of Jesus. Luke says, "While they were there, the time came for her to be delivered" (Luke 2:6). Joseph had a trade that could be practiced anywhere, so they may well have been staying all this time in a public inn, which was a far cry from the kind of motels we have today. For one thing, there was absolutely no privacy in Palestinian hostelries. They consisted of an open courtyard where the animals and baggage stayed. Off this courtyard were little stalls where the people slept, and this was obviously a poor place for something like a birth to occur.

Dr. Hull suggests that our familiar verse ought to read: "There was no appropriate place for them in the inn," and further suggests that the innkeeper must have realized this fact and took it on himself to scout out a cave that shepherds used in the winter months to house their sheep. At this time, of course, the shepherds were "out in the fields with their flocks," so an unused cave or stable would be a place of privacy where Mary could give birth to her child in dignity. Instead of being maligned, as he has so often been in Christmas sermons, Dr. Hull suggests that the innkeeper should be praised for going out of his way to help this refugee couple in their time of need.

I find this reconstruction both intriguing and convincing, and coupled with Joseph's sensitivity to Mary, it is a blessed contrast to the harshness of Nazareth. Here, leading up to the great event of Bethlehem itself, is a meeting place of extremes — human harshness and human kindness. Human beings' inhumanity to other human beings can be great at times; yet at the same time, human beings can be very good to each other as well. How typical this is of life itself — goodness and badness, pain and pleasure, insensitivity and care, all bound up together. In Bethlehem, both the shadows and the light came together. The fact that they were there and not in Nazareth is a reminder of human harshness, but the fact that it took place in a stable, not in the inn, is a reminder of human kindness.

But let us move on now to the event itself, for here is an even greater paradox to boggle our minds and imaginations. If *where* all this took place can be called a meeting of extremes, the same thing can be said of *what* took place, only raised to infinite proportions. For here is the most startling claim ever made for any event in history; namely, *that God became a human being*; that divinity put on flesh and blood, that for a period of time, the invisible Creator of all things came to live on earth as a human being among human beings. G. K. Chesterton is right in calling this an "enormous exception" and something absolutely unique.

To be sure, most men had always inferred that there was some kind of Creator behind the world and they believed they had messages from him and intimations of him. But to say that he had come, himself, as a human being and lived in Palestine during the days of the Roman Empire — this was without parallel. All that other religions had ever intimated was that the Creator was present at creation. Never anywhere else had it ever been hinted that the one invisible maker of all things became a human being and dwelt on earth, but this is what Christianity claims for the event at Bethlehem!

You talk about the coming together of extremes — this is it at the ultimate level! That omnipotence would take the form of helplessness, in which the hands that made the world would become hands too small to reach beyond a crib; this staggers the imagination and confounds the mind. Yet, this is the miracle of Bethlehem, and because of it, we have that mysterious balance of knowing and yet not knowing in relation to God that is so appealing.

For you see, deep down, human beings have always longed to know the shape of the ultimate and to see the face of mystery himself; yet how could they, being mortal, limited, finite creatures that they are? How can a tiny ant begin to understand a human being in all his complexity? He simply does not have the capacity to comprehend that which is so utterly different from himself. Yet, the gap between human beings and God is even wider and more uncrossable than that between an ant and a man, for God is the uncreated one, the ultimate originator of all things, unlike us not only in complexity but also as a painter is unlike a painting. How, then, could a human being ever know that unutterable otherness called God? The truth is, on our own, we never could; we do not have the capacities.

But what if God should move from the other side? What if he, out of grace and mercy, should decide to put himself into a form we could understand? This would make God-knowledge possible, and this is exactly what happened on the first Christmas night. From the loftiest heights of unknowableness, God moved down "the stairway of the stars" and entered history in the form of a little baby. He became what we are, that we might understand what he is. He graciously put himself into a form that we humans could comprehend. The extremes met that night; divinity became humanity; and of his fullness we received, grace upon grace and truth upon truth!

There is actually no analogy for such an event; it is *the* paradox of all paradoxes. However, perhaps you can sense its outline a little more clearly if I compare it to one of the familiar processes of our day. By this time, we all have become accustomed to television, and you perhaps no longer even reflect on the miracle of this process. In simplest terms, what happens is that a television station sends out a signal all over the countryside, yet, it is in the form that our eyes and ears cannot pick up.

Right now in this room, at least six different types of television signals are all about us, yet we are unaware of any of them. However, if we had a television set here at the front and plugged it in and set the dials just right, a miracle of perception would take place right before our eyes. Suddenly, we would begin to see images and hear sounds. Why? Because that set was able to take those inaudible soundwaves and convert them into sounds our ears could hear. It also could take those invisible image rays and transpose them into images our eyes could see. In short, by virtue of what the television set can do, what was hitherto before unavailable and inaccessible, becomes available and accessible.

Now let me say reverently and yet quite seriously that what a television set does for those inaudible, invisible television waves, *the Man Jesus does for God!* He is the medium by which divinity becomes knowable to humanity. He converts "the God-signal" into signals we humans can comprehend. He transposes the mystery of godness into the frequency of humanity. He became what we are, that we might understand what he is. Yes, the extremes met in Bethlehem that night, and now we have an answer to the question: "What is God like?" This is something that humans have always asked, and because of Bethlehem, we can say: "God is like Jesus."

46

For, incredible as it may sound, this man was God — "God-come-to-us," "God-in-a-form-that-we-can-understand." And one of the reasons the story of Christmas lives on in perennial freshness is that here is an assertion that never grows old. The simplest one among us can grasp something of its meaning; the wisest among us can never exhaust it. Here the extremes meet, simplicity rooted in profundity.

But, there is one other aspect of the mystery of Christmas, and that is the response that followed the event. Phillips Brooks describes it beautifully in the words of his famous Christmas carol, "O Little Town Of Bethlehem." "The hopes and fears of all the years are met in thee tonight." This is a kind of double reaction that occurred centuries ago to the coming of God in Christ. There was delirious joy both in heaven among the angels and on earth among the simple folk, like the shepherds in the field and old Anna and Simeon in the temple. One of the deepest dreams of the people had come true — that we might know what God is like and that he is with us and for us.

Yet, alongside this reaction of joy, there was a response of terror also, particularly in the regal palace of Herod the king. Something deep in the heart of this tyrant stirred that night, as if a threat to his security had arisen. When the Wise Men of the East appeared, his frenzy grew and expressed itself in a bloodbath of all the infants in Judea. The same event that carried the shepherds to the heights of joy carried Herod to the depths of fear, and this is not too hard to understand. For after all, are not each one of us ambiguous in our deepest feelings about God? We are at once attracted to him and yet repulsed by him. Part of us wants to know him — and to be guided by his truth; yet other parts of us rebel against his authority and realize that if he enters our lives, we will have to change and be judged by him and live in a different way. There is in each one of us, I think, something akin to both the heart of the shepherds and the heart of King Herod.

C. S. Lewis acknowledges this quite openly in his spiritual autobiography. On the one hand, he traces how all through his life he thirsted after the Ultimate. He wanted to know God, to learn the

47

secret of life, to possess that supernatural joy that comes from being at one with the Father. Yet, when the real God began to make himself clearer and clearer in Christ, Lewis found himself resisting. He wanted to be left alone, to remain free to do as he pleased, to live life on his own terms. He knew instinctively that if God really entered his life, he would come as Lord, and Lewis could not remain as he had been. And so the dilemma mounted, as at one and the same time he both wanted and yet did not want. At times he felt like saying: "Oh, I hope Christ is the truth about God, and I am afraid he is not." At other times he felt like saying: "I am afraid Christ is the truth about God, but I hope he is not." So is the ambivalence of the human heart — we hunger to be in touch with the mystery of Godness, yet at the same time we fear such ultimacy. Phillips Brooks was right about Bethlehem: "The hopes and fears of all the years are met in thee tonight."

And this is as good a place as I know to leave you with the Christmas story. It does have incredible power over human life, because here is where the extremes meet, where the mystery that both satisfies and intrigues is born. Here in the midst of human harshness and human kindness, God became a human being for us humans and our salvation. He became what we are — moved infinitely close — so that we could understand what he is. I wonder then: How do you react to this event? In joy or in fear? Are you like the shepherds, who found in Christ the true shepherd of their souls and were fulfilled? Or are you like King Herod, who in Christ rejected his true king and fought back? After all is said and done, this is the question posed every year at Christmas: How do you react to this God who came one night to that "little town of Bethlehem"?

Well...?

— Tom M. Garrison

Our Task:
Acceptance And Challenge

What do our children need of us really, as adults, as parents, and as the community of faith called the church? I found myself asking that question when the newborn infants of this congregation were brought before us and both the parents and our Sunday school teachers were gathered here at the front. The children looked so tiny — none of them able to walk or feed themselves or do hardly anything. If they are to become fully functioning human beings, obviously many things are going to have to be done for them and with them. What are they? I am sure there are many answers that could be given to such a question, but let me sum up my own thinking on the subject in two words; namely, acceptance and challenge.

What do I mean by these? Well, first of all, by the use of the word *acceptance*, I am referring to that crucial task of communicating to each child that his or her very existence in this world is something of enormous value. I think it is fair to surmise that the moment a child comes out of the womb and enters the realm of time and space, the little one begins to send out all kinds of questions into this environment. The infant wants to know: What kind of realm is this? What about my needs? Will I be provided for as well as I was back in the womb? And what about my presence here? Am I welcomed or resented? Am I regarded with esteem and delight, or looked down upon as an intruder or a burden?

Now, to be sure, I do not claim the newborn infant comes into this world framing these very words intellectually, but the little organism has its own ways of sending out these probing inquiries, and according to the way "the big people" proceed to relate to this one, certain answers begin to be formed at the deepest level of consciousness. The way a tiny infant is held and spoken to and cared for in those earliest days is tremendously important, but the process continues in one form or another all during our life journey. We never really stop asking the primal questions, such as: What is the world like? Is it well that I be here? And this underlines the importance of the relational feedback that we get from others. I agree with Myron Madden — nothing is more creative to the formation of a positive self-image than to have someone "to sparkle on you"; that is, to see a twinkle in another's eye when you come around that conveys: "Hey, I am glad you exist! That you are, what you are — the whole kit-and-caboodle that constitutes your individuality — is a value I celebrate."

Erik Erikson says the first developmental challenge in any relationship is deciding between trust and mistrust, and nothing is more helpful here than a delight-giver, be that person a biological parent or aunt or uncle or Sunday school teacher or whomever.

Let me tell you how the term "delight" came to be so meaningful in my thinking at this point. I learned it from a motivational speaker, Sam Keen, and what he said to his own father as his father lay dying. Sam had flown out to be with his father at this time, and one afternoon just the two of them were together in the hospital room. Sam said, "I don't know how you feel about everything you have done with your life, but I want you to know that as a parent, I think you have been a huge success. As far back as I can remember," Sam continued, "you never once let any of us children down at a crucial junction of our lives, and what is more, you did the finest single thing a parent can do for his child: namely, *you took delight in us.* You always made us feel that you were glad that we had been born, that you were delighted that we had come into your world, and for that one gift, I shall be forever in your debt."

Sam is right, I think. Delight is the finest single gift we can bequeath to any human being and while I am not sure about a lot of things in this area, of this I am confident — the little children you see here and all the children of the world need our acceptance and sheer delight that they exist in this world at all.

But, important as that is, acceptance is not all they need. In addition, these same children also need an authentic sense of challenge that they were put into this world for a purpose, that part of the value of their "being here" is what they can contribute to the ongoing drama of creation. The writer of the book of Ephesians says that we are "God's workmanship, created in Christ Jesus unto good works" (Ephesians 2:10). The Greek word here for "workmanship" could also be translated "poem"; that is, we are poetic creations; there is a rhyme and reason for the structure of our particular being. I am a key that has been fashioned to fit certain locks, which means that in addition to my being of value in this world, I can also give value to the very processes that have birthed me. We need, I think, to underline this aspect of humanness just now, for the great emphasis seems to be on what one can get rather than what one could give. Jurgen Moultmann said that Narcissus rather than Prometheus was the god of the decade of the '70s, and this represents a "falling short of the glory" of what our species was meant to be.

Back in the early days of this century, Albert Schweitzer shocked all of his academic contemporaries by resigning his professional post to enter medical school with the thought in mind of going to be a missionary in Africa. When asked why he was doing this, he replied, simply, that he had received so much from Western civilization that it was unthinkable he not give back into the stream that had so nourished him. Thus began one of the most influential careers of the twentieth century. As much as our children need a sense of acceptance, they also need this understanding of their reason for being here. According to the Bible, creation is not finished yet. We humans, who were not in on the ultimate beginning of things, have been given the privilege of participating with God in the completion of his great venture, and not to know that and recognize our identities as co-creators with God is to miss an important aspect of our human uniqueness.

I am saying, then, that our children need both of these things from us — acceptance and challenge, and let me acknowledge that it is genuinely difficult to keep a proper balance between these two. It is far easier to emphasize one to the exclusion of the other;

51

in fact, this seems to me to be the problem Jesus began to experience in today's passage. He was twelve years old at the time, which means he was not regarded as "a son of the law," and thus was eligible to go up with the other pilgrims to the Feast of the Passover in Jerusalem. How exciting this must have been to a peasant lad who had never traveled more than a few miles from home before! And to get to see Jerusalem for himself for the first time! The experience was actually so enthralling that Jesus lost all track of time, and when the people from Nazareth started home, he was not with them.

I have always thought there was a measure of neglect here on the part of his parents. How could you leave and walk for a whole day and not notice that your twelve-year-old was not with you? However, this is probably an unfair criticism. I read recently that because they walk more slowly, women pilgrims often left several hours before the men with some designated place to rendezvous at night. It is possible, then, that Mary assumed that Jesus was with Joseph and Joseph assumed that Jesus was with Mary, and so it was not until they got together that they realized that he was not there at all.

At any rate, when they retraced their steps and got back to Jerusalem, there they found him, unharmed, sitting in the temple enthralled by the discussion of the Law that went on there all the time. Mary could not contain her frustration. She spoke harshly to Jesus, out of that side of her maternal love that wanted to protect him from all harm. After all, Mary had paid a dear price in terms of shame and reputation to bring Jesus into the world, and there was much in her that was anxious to surround this special one from God with total protectiveness. However, when she spoke as she did, Jesus answered very earnestly, "Why did you even have to wonder where I was? Did you not realize that I must be about my Father's business?"

Here was the first inkling that Jesus felt a calling in himself that even his mother was not going to be able to understand. Already stirring within him was that sense of mission that would one day sweep him out of the carpenter's shop and into places and experiences that were utterly beyond Mary's peasant expectations.

The working out of his own special destiny under God is what one sees beginning here in Jesus' experience, and this was not to be the only time he would be caught between the protectiveness of his mother's love and the calling of his Father's business.

What is at work here, of course, are these primal realities of acceptance and challenge and these do, at times, seem to pull in opposite directions. Mary, both here and later on, seemed willing to sacrifice to the challenge Jesus was feeling in order to maintain the security where she could continue to lavish delight on Jesus. By the same token, Jesus was tempted by the devil to throw caution to the wind and attempt to accomplish his Father's business by jumping off the pinnacle of the temple and that would have been equally disastrous. The truth is — both mother's love and Father's business have a legitimate place, and what our children need from us most is the wisdom to recognize this fact and then somehow learn to balance these two appropriately without either absorbing or excluding the other.

We all have seen what happens when children get nothing but acceptance and no challenge. They grow up to be spoiled, flabby, and largely unproductive human beings. Paul Tournier has pointed out that, ironically, the overly protective parent winds up doing the very opposite of what he or she intends; namely, bringing harm to the life of the child. He says that the overly protected and pampered child goes into the world defenseless. The way a person builds up immunities of any kind is through some kind of exposure. If a child is hermetically sealed off from any kind of suffering or challenge, he or she never develops the strength to cope with those realities and because a parent is unable to remain with the child always, there eventually are encounters which the child cannot handle, and what is worse, what strengths that child possesses are never put to work in the task of finishing creation. We do not do our children, or the whole of creation, a favor when we meet all their challenges for them. Acceptance without challenge is demoralizing indeed.

By the same token, challenge without acceptance can hurt people just as well. All too often, I fear, the acceptance that is so crucial to self-esteem is made a conditional thing, tied to the accomplishment of a certain goal. I once knew a person whose parents were extraordinarily ambitious for him. In fact, his whole existence was a pressure cooker of challenge. He brought home a report card one day and his mother flew into rage and said: "Get one thing straight, young man — *C's are not acceptable in this household.* Get this grade up or else." Needless to say, such challenge had a terrifying impact on his emerging psyche. He was also told something by his father that must have been a common saying of the day, because I have heard it repeated in many other places. It was this: "Should you ever think that you have succeeded, realize that you have set your goals too low."

Talk about a formula that dooms one to non-fulfillment — that is it, if I have ever heard one! How could you ever come to feel a sense of satisfaction about anything if that was the kind of expectation that was laid upon you? What I am suggesting is that while acceptance without challenge leads to a flabby, underdeveloped kind of person, challenge without acceptance tends to crush a person unmercifully. This man about whom I spoke wound up an alcoholic and finally took his own life in despair. That, too, is "falling short of the glory" that we were meant to attain.

I come back then to where this all started. What do children need of us, as adults, as parents, as members of the community of faith called the church? To be sure, they need many things and we must never fall into the illusion that we will perform the raising task perfectly. But for me, two words — acceptance and challenge — sum up our task. By acceptance, I mean communication to these little ones that their very presence here is a great value, that they do belong, that they are the objects of our delight. To accept is "to sparkle on another" with the twinkling of the eye. That is so important, but just as crucial, I think, is the sense of challenge that helps the child see that he or she is here for a purpose — they really are "God's workmanship — his poems, created in Christ Jesus unto good works." It is never easy to balance properly both of these tasks, as the life of Jesus so clearly illustrates. But it is necessary.

Thus, to that task — awesome as it may be, I invite you all just now "to sparkle on our children" and to help them sense the part of the Father's business that is their business — this is our challenge as adults. Our text says: "Jesus increased in wisdom and in stature and in favor of God and man." My prayer is: "So may our children grow ... please?"

— Tom M. Garrison

What Gift Do You Bring?

I remember watching a football game between Kansas State and Ohio State. Kansas State was evidently favored to win because they had clobbered Oklahoma just a few weeks earlier, but they were not doing very well. In fact, they were behind by quite a bit and then in the last half they mounted a comeback and midway through the fourth quarter they were doing quite well. They were only behind fourteen points and were deep in Ohio State territory. Then it happened — a senseless, silly, stupid penalty. It was a personal foul penalty that cost them fifteen yards and set them back so far they did not get a touchdown nor were they able to get a field goal. They lost the game by seven points. Ohio State won.

A silly penalty! An action or a reaction! A decision! An impulse! And that one decision probably changed the outcome of the ballgame. Someone might say, "Well, he was probably hit and was only responding to what someone did to him." It doesn't matter! It doesn't matter if he acted or reacted. He still had the decision to make as to what he would do. He chose to make the play, and it affected the outcome of the ballgame. Well, somebody else might say, "Well, one play does not a ballgame make." And that is true in some cases, but in some cases it is exactly true. One decision, an impulse, or reaction, can actually change the outcome of the event. It can change the outcome of a life. It can change the outcome of history. One event. One action. One reaction. One decision. One impulse.

After the Revolutionary War, a British soldier said that during the war he actually had General George Washington in his sights

57

but could not pull the trigger out of respect for the man. One wonders what would have happened if General Washington had been killed in the middle of the war. There are also those who said that if the Japanese had decided to do so, they could have not only run through Pearl Harbor, but on into Los Angeles as well. One wonders if that would have altered in some way the outcome of the war. Some historians are quite adamant that Hitler would have gone not only through Europe, but on into Britain if he had not paused to go on military parade. One wonders! A small decision. A large decision. Sometimes seemingly insignificant decisions, but yet these decisions are the essence of life. Life is made of a series of decisions that we make that can alter the outcome of our lives. An event? Yes, even history itself. We have the freedom of choice to choose how we will act or react, how we will respond to any single event.

We have some people in our text today that chose to respond in different ways to the coming of Christ — to Christmas. Some responded out of fear. Some responded out of detachment or avoidance and yet others responded with worship and gratitude. The Bible tells us that when Herod, King of the Jews, heard about the Christmas event, he was afraid and all of Jerusalem with him. How could you be afraid of Christmas? Christmas is the time of joy and happiness. It is the greatest news ever spoken. How could anyone respond except out of joy and gladness? But it is true. Some respond to Christmas in a negative way.

In 1644, Oliver Cromwell, who was the Puritan leader of the nation of England, actually banned the celebration of Christmas. In 1659, in the new world, in the state of Massachusetts, it was declared that if people were caught celebrating Christmas, they would be subject to being fined. Even in Boston, schools were open on Christmas Day until 1870. Do you want to resurrect that law? The teachers' union probably would not let us do that today. Not everybody is happy with Christmas. Not everyone responds to Christmas with joy and happiness. Some even respond like Herod.

This is the first Herod that we find in the New Testament — commonly called Herod the Great. He was a man who had been born into his position through treachery, lies, deceit, and even the murder of members of his own family. Here was an individual who

58

was so insecure, feeling so inferior, that the crown upon his head rested so uneasily, that he was threatened by any kind of rival. Even the arrival of a baby — a tiny baby had been born and it created in him much insecurity and fear. Not everyone responds to Christmas with happiness and joy. Some respond out of fear and disturbance. Others respond out of avoidance or detachment. "Well, it's going on but I just don't want to be a part of it. I will not make a commitment to it."

That was the story of the scholars, the chief priest, the scribes to whom Herod went when he inquired, "Where is this birth taking place?" They had their answer. Give them that. They knew their Bible, the Old Testament. Immediately, they quoted Bethlehem, Bethlehem of Judea. That is where it is. They knew their Bible. They knew the scriptures. They had probably memorized scripture — item for item. They just missed Christmas.

They knew the Bible. They missed the gospel. They knew the scriptures. They missed Jesus. Because one knows the scriptures does not necessarily mean they know the God of the scriptures. It has to be more than that. The scripture is very, very important because in our story today you see a wonderful interplay between nature and scripture. Nature and scripture! Because it was in nature that they found the Messiah had been born, but it was only in the Bible that they found out where the Messiah had been born. There is this marvelous interplay here.

You see it is true today. All over our society there are stars in the "East" — in signs, in experiences, in history, in the news, that point to the mystery and awesomeness of God. They point to the existence of God. But without the Bible to define and clarify the meaning of those experiences, the picture of God remains unclear. We see them every day: the unfolding of a rose, the birth of a baby, the falling of the Berlin wall. What does it mean? The grandeur of the Grand Canyons. Signs are all around us that point to the mystery and awesomeness of God.

We wonder what it means. We find out when we go to the Bible. It is in scripture that the revelation of God in nature is defined and clarified and given its spiritual meaning. But there has to be more to it than that because Herod knew the scriptures. The

59

chief priest knew the scriptures, but they missed Christmas because neither Herod nor the scholars went to Bethlehem. They were willing to take someone else's word for it. They accepted secondhand information. They were not willing to get involved personally. We can know all about the Savior. We can have scriptures memorized, but unless we have a personal relationship to the Lord Jesus Christ, we miss Christmas. We miss it altogether.

It is only out of that personal relationship, characterized by discipline and prayer and worship that we are able to understand what Christmas is all about. We can know about Christmas, but to know Christmas, to define Christmas, to experience God in Christmas, we do so only through a personal relationship to the Lord Jesus Christ. You see some responded to Christmas out of fear. Some responded out of avoidance. Keep our distance. Let's not get committed. Let's not make anything personal about it. Yet, the Bible says there were some who experienced the Christ Child in a personal way and they responded not with fear or avoidance but with gratitude. They went personally to see it. How many there were, we don't know. It was probably a rather large group because this was hostile territory. Two or three did not travel alone in this territory. Who were they? We really don't know. They are called Magi. Some people said they were astrologers. Some say they were astronomers. Others have said they were magicians. Some even said they were priests of the court of the religion Zoroastrianism. We won't know. We don't know. Except we know they were seekers.

They were seekers. Something was missing within their lives. They had sought in other places and then they saw a sign. They knew not what. They came in their ignorance. They came through hostile territory. They were subject to lies, to corrupt politicians, to theologians who were misinformed and not involved; yet, they were seeking. And they persevered and found; and when they found, they responded with gratitude.

The Bible says that they bowed down and worshiped the Christ Child and then gave him gifts. Is that not why we give God our gifts? Is that not why we give to God our tithes and offerings? Is that not why we give to God our money, our talents, our time, our energy — the very essence of our lives? We do so out of the wonder and awesomeness of God. We do so out of searching hearts. We do so out of gratitude because he has come into the world and has come into our lives. So we give! We give out of hearts of generosity, out of gratitude, out of thankfulness. What else can you do in the presence of the holy? What else can you do when scriptures indicate as truthfully as it can, "This is the one before whom we bow"?

We don't know who they were. We know they were seekers and we know they were Gentiles. They were not Jews. Matthew wants you to know in the second chapter of his book that this gospel is for everybody. It is not just for a select group. It is not just for the "in" crowd. It is not just for those who think and have all the answers. It is not just for the religious elite. It is for everybody! Gentile and Jews! Men and women! Boys and girls! Black and white! It does not matter! It is for everyone. Why do you think Matthew ends his gospel by saying, "Go ye therefore into all the world and all nations carrying this gospel"? It is for everybody.

The great irony in our story is that those on the inside are on the outside because they don't get it. Those on the outside are on the inside because they do. Wonder how? How are they able to do so? It is worth thinking about.

I recently read something about mountain climbing. I am not a mountain climber, but I read some interesting information. There are fourteen peaks in the world that are considered major challenges for mountain climbers. Fourteen peaks over 26,000 feet, which is about five miles. These are the major challenges for mountain climbers. These are the peaks that one must supposedly use oxygen to be able to climb to the top. There is only one individual living that has climbed all fourteen peaks. His name is Reinhold Messner. He is a resident of northern Italy. He has been the object of scientific inquiry to understand why he and he alone has been able to do what he has done. It is truly amazing. They looked at his technology. He had no more technology than anyone else. In fact, they say that he didn't use as many ropes or ladders or technology that others did. In fact, he used no oxygen at all. They said, "Well, it must be something about his physical ability." And they looked and said, "He was no more athletically gifted than another million people in our world. He looked like a marathon runner and that probably helped." But here was an individual who had been able to do what nobody else had ever been able to do. They asked the question, "How?" One of his friends, another alpine climber by the name of Chris Bonington, said, "Here is an individual who is able to use creative innovation."

I am not sure what that means. I do know that Reinhold Messner was able to use extra-imaginative drive. I think that means this. You see all of us experience those times in life when we come to a wall, whether we say to ourselves or the world says to us, "This is impossible. You can go no further." But yet, people like Reinhold Messner say, "I am going on." And he does so. He does not let failure detour him. He is not put off when people say, "You can't!" He continues to go on. He finds a way. He pursues. He perseveres. He persists.

It is somewhat like a bunch of wise guys 2,000 ago who marched through hostile territory, not knowing exactly that for which they were looking. They were subject to lies, deceit, corruption, and theological ineptitude, but they kept on until they found God, the very same God who was looking for them.

He is looking for you and you can find him.

— Gary L. Carver

The Baptism Of Our Lord
Epiphany 1
Ordinary Time 1
Luke 3:15-17, 21-22

The Baptism Of The Lord

This text invites us to listen as John the Baptist tells the people that there is one who is coming to give a greater baptism than he will ever give. Baptism, from the outset in the gospels, becomes very important and moves very quickly to the baptism of Jesus. This seems to set the importance of baptism initially, and the significance is fortified in Acts. However, as important as baptism is, we do not find any instruction for how we are to behave at a baptism, possibly every baptismal occasion tends to create its own atmosphere. It also modifies the behavior of people involved in an appropriate way.

For example, if you attend a funeral, even if it is the first funeral you have ever attended, no instruction is needed. We simply know and understand the behavioral guidelines, even the inevitable socializing does not detour our thoughts from the magnitude of the event.

The entrance of the family focuses our attention on the reality of this event. A family now faces life without a beloved member and the changes that this has brought about. There is something about the moment that gives its own instruction. You do not need instruction on how to behave. The occasion modifies and sweetens the disposition.

It is the same way with a wedding — before the wedding there is laughing, talking, stale jokes, shaving cream all over the windshield, and tin cans tied to the bumper. When the moment arrives, announced by the sound of music, and the bride walks slowly down

63

the aisle, our attention shifts from the social to the sacred. There is no need for instruction, the occasion modifies the behavior.

It is the same manner in which we celebrate a baptism. As the minister states, "in the name of the Father, Son, and Holy Spirit ... Amen," the sacredness of the moment guides us into reverential silence. There is no instructional material, not even in scripture, as to how to behave.

Baptism is the living example of the baptism of Jesus of Nazareth. I am sure this is surprising to many who expect Jesus to be exempt from baptism. It seems natural that Jesus would stand on the bank and view others while they are baptized. Baptism is for everyone, especially:

- all of those who have wandered away from the path known to them as children;
- those who have stumbled into trouble over and over again;
- those who, not by accident, but intent, have turned their backs on God; and
- those full of greed who finally understand there is no place else to go.

Luke phrases it so simply, "When all the people were being baptized, Jesus was baptized, too."

Why was one so pure cleansed in the water?

Was it that at the age of thirty, as Luke tells us, he began his public ministry?

In the synagogue one day, did Christ realize the readings were really for him, that more than anything else he was to serve God? Did there exist a special meaning in life for himself and for humanity?

Following a long day in the carpenter's shop was he walking and encountered his own destiny?

Was he mindful of that fateful day that he was finally allowed to worship God in the temple as a boy of twelve? Could it be he remembered the encounter with the elders of the people and the scribes?

The questions are all good, but we have no adequate answer. What we do know is there came a day that he folded his carpenter's apron, having shaken the shavings out of it, and placed it on the bench. He bid his mother, brother, and sisters, "Good-bye." He did not go and command an audience with the emperor or even with the governor, but instead he makes his way to where the people have assembled. It is there he aligns with everyone else at the Jordan River and is baptized.

It was Martin Luther who wrote, "Remember your baptism," and what he meant by this was to claim for yourself all that is reserved for you as a child of God. In fact, still wet from his own baptism, according to Luke's account, Jesus is immediately reminded by his Father of the relationship with him: "You are my Son, whom I love; with you I am well pleased."

That passage speaks of the relationships of Jesus, not only with the Father, but also with those who are in need. Our relationship with Jesus shines brightest when we learn that it is a multi-relationship. The human need that is filled is not only ours, but whomever we touch.

I recall a story that Fred Craddock told about the southwestern Oklahoma community with which he was very familiar. The village had a population of 450 and four churches. All the churches were Christian denominations and they all shared the people of the town. Sometimes attendance was up and sometimes it was down. However, there was a cafe in town whose attendance always stayed the same. Many of the parishioners of the cafe never went to any of the four churches. The father of the faithful at the little cafe was Frank, a man of 77, who declared, "I have no need for church — I take care of my family, I work hard, everything else is just fluff." One day, a local minister in town saw Frank on the street. He introduced himself and Frank told him he wasn't looking for a church.

One day, to everyone's surprise, Frank not only showed up for church, but was baptized at 78. Talk started in town "Frank must be sick. He certainly is getting older." There were all kinds of stories. The preacher and Frank became friends. Finally, a few months later, the minister got up enough courage to ask the question that had been bothering him since Frank's attendance that day. "Frank, do you remember when I baptized you?" Frank answered slowly, "Yes, I recall." The minister paused for a moment then asked the question so long on his mind. "I am sure you still work hard and take care of your family." "That's right," Frank nodded in agreement. "Well then," the minister said with a bit of caution, "what made you do it?"

Frank cleared his throat. "I didn't know before what my business was; you see I thought it only included my work and my family, but I learned it was to serve God and human need."

It is at those moments when the heavens open and you can almost hear the voice of God: "This is my Son; with him I am well pleased."

— Tom M. Garrison

Epiphany 2
Ordinary Time 2
John 2:1-11

Wedding Day

It had been a standard practice, in years past, that the most popular month for weddings was June. The idea of someone being a June bride was without doubt not just normal, but expected. As our society has moved in so many directions, it has become the case that June no longer holds the fascination as it once did. We do know that weddings are always the source of much anticipation and, at times, problems.

In fact, the people who deal with weddings, such as florists, caterers, mothers of the bride, and, yes ministers, all know a shared truth. The secret truth; if there is a wedding, something is bound to go wrong.

It may be small:

- like the best man getting ready at the church realizes that the pants to his tuxedo are a foot too long, and an inventive best man would borrow the office stapler and fix the pants himself; or
- like the ushers lighting the candles and inadvertantly lighting the unity candle as well as the other candles.

It could be large:

- like the bride arriving 45 minutes late, not even dressed for the wedding; or
- like the wedding in a small chapel where someone realized fifteen minutes before the wedding that all the flowers were

still at the bride's home, forty minutes away, forcing the guests to listen to the organist play the same five songs she knew over and over again until the flowers were retrieved.

It is not a matter of *if* something will go wrong, but will it be small or large? Will it be that the photographer overexposed the pictures, or the father of the bride comes having had a little too much celebratory drink before the wedding?

The rule of thumb is that if the rehearsal goes with great precision then watch out for what will happen at the wedding. If something does not happen at the wedding proper there is a good chance it will happen at the reception.

The fact of this should let us breathe a little easier, knowing with all our human frailty that there will certainly be some surprises. So it should not be a big surprise when we attend a wedding and see the ring bearer go screaming out the side door just as the couple recites their vows.

Knowing all these things can, and do, happen, it should not surprise us that at the one wedding recorded in scripture, that Jesus attended, something went wrong. It was not the vows or the best man's robe being six sizes too small. It was at the reception. The problem seemed to be that the wine ran out before the receiving line ran out. The Bordeaux was served but not for those in the back of the hall ... they would have to settle for Kool-Aid®.

Jesus, his mother, and the disciples are in attendance. The writer of John lets us in on the little secret of not just the wine becoming another on the list of those things that go wrong at a wedding. What happens is that the writer allows us to overhear the conversation between Mary and Jesus.

Mary says, "Look they are out of wine."

Jesus replies, not with a loving kindness you would expect from him, but with a bit of an irritation, "Dear woman, why do you involve me? My time has not yet come."

Jesus instructs the waiters: "Fill the stone jars with water."

Mary advises the servants to do exactly as he asks. They, of course, follow his instructions. He then continues, "Draw some out and take it to your master." The reaction from the master is focused on the bridegroom, thinking that he has saved the best wine until the last.

As we look at the stories in John, our imagination is allowed to grow. This gospel lets us overhear the direction of the reason a story is told. When the story begins there is the discussion from Mary that she was expecting Jesus to attend to the need at hand. It is here the writer makes it clear in Jesus' words the direction Jesus would take throughout this gospel.

"My time has not yet come," says Jesus. The best way to say this is that, "timing is everything."

- It happens in life that if we had only waited another two weeks to sell the stock we would have tripled our money.
- In the movie, *Serendipity*, which is based on the premise of narrow misses, much of the pleasure of the film is the search a couple conducts looking for each other and the near misses that ensue.
- Being at the right place at the right time makes all the difference in the world.
- It is also true that the Son of Man, Jesus himself, makes it clear to his mother that the timing in his life has not come to a point that it is, "his time."

There is not only an emphasis on timing for Jesus, but it had to take into account the difference between that timing and our timing. It resounds in the way we look at ourselves, those around us, and the world.

Only recently, I was reminded of something I was told as a boy. I would never have a problem too big for God if only I would seek the way to the answer in God's plan. What that meant was that God and yes, Jesus, has a time set out with teaching and solutions.

I was reminded again of this recently when I spoke to someone that I have known for years. You see, I had called to talk to them about someone I knew they cared about who had been hospitalized. The problem was that they had not spoken to each other for several years. Encouragement was given to visit this person in the hospital. Knowing they were devout in their denomination I appealed to the teaching of Jesus, to love without restriction and to go the second mile. The reply came back, "I know what Jesus says but...."

It seems that the time of Jesus is not necessarily our time. It is just too hard to accept that God's ways are to be ours. It is beyond comprehension to think that the time for true renewal is in this time, and not just in the time of Jesus. I don't know if you noticed that there were some things about this wedding that were beyond the problem of the low quantity of wine. There are other key elements that carry us away from a wedding and to an understanding.

- Did you notice that this wedding took place on the third day? Sounds familiar doesn't it? We know the phrase, "On the third day he was raised from the dead." We can see this if we only know the time has come.
- Note also that on that day we could watch the transformation of Mary from mother to disciple, "Whatever he tells you do it."

There are times when we witness firsthand that his time has come. It was a night much like all other spring nights in the south, the only difference was my youth minister called me to accompany him to the Greyhound bus station on the back side of the old train station in the heart of the worst part of town. He briefed me as we made our way through areas I normally would not go. On this night, a young girl needed help. On that night, somebody needed the two of us. We found her, a young girl, all of sixteen, looking for a way out. As we sat and talked with her, it was plain that $20 was not what she needed, her greatest need wasn't even food. What she needed the most that night, was to know someone had the time for another human being, whether it was at the Greyhound bus station or the country club. Someone saw the need and filled the jars, and then waited to see how God works.

The next time you go to a wedding don't be surprised if you come to realize, "It is his time."

— Tom M. Garrison

70

Epiphany 3
Ordinary Time 3
Luke 4:14-21

Prophet Or Profit?

I shall never forget the night that Mae June came to church. Mae June was a working woman who, in our little community, was often seen in the late hours of the night in some of the darker places of our little town.

The rumor circulating over breakfast every morning at the city cafe, was that Mae June had a male companion. Mae June had a boyfriend. They were seen quite often, not only at night, but in the daytime and on the streets of the little city. Then came the night that Mae June came to the church where I served as pastor. She and her male companion came and sat down near the front. The church had what was known as a prayer rail with cushions all across the front of the sanctuary. When we offered the invitation at the conclusion of the service, Mae June came and knelt at the prayer rail and prayed. When she finished her prayer she turned and began talking to the congregation. She asked the congregation if they would pray for her friend. We prayed with Mae June.

I was interested in seeing how the church would respond at the end of the service. It was a good crowd for a Sunday night. If I remember correctly, I think the mayor, the district judge, and a county commissioner were there along with a lot of mothers and fathers. Out of all of those people no one — no one — shunned Mae June. They talked with her. They prayed with her. They accepted her. It was like the church was acting like a church.

Jesus went to church one time and they tried to kill him. His home church in his hometown accepted him at first. He became popular in other areas, but when he came to his hometown church, they accepted him quickly. He is Joe Carpenter's son. Isn't that Mary's son over there? Everything was fine until Jesus said something that made them all mad. It made them so mad that they literally tried to kill him. In his hometown! What could he have said that could have been so provoking? It might have been that Jesus was a prophet.

In the New Testament, a prophet is not someone who forecasts hundreds of thousands of years in the future, but someone who looks at today and says, "This is the way things are." Then the prophet says, "Unless things change this is the way things are going to be." The prophet goes beyond that. The prophet not only says this is the way things are, a prophet will say if you do change; these are the way things could be. A prophet! If you change. There are some in Jesus' day who did not want to change. They were out for profit, the status quo. The status quo! You remember, Ronald Reagan said, "It's the mess we are in." The status quo. The ones who were living their lives for profit were content with the way things were and they did not want this prophet upsetting the applecart so they tried to kill him.

I think the real reason they tried to kill Jesus was that he said, "Today the scripture is fulfilled in your ears." I am it! Me! The Lord has appointed me, sent me, anointed me; and they couldn't stand that Jesus was one who was willing to stand in the gap between the way things are and the way things can be. Jesus was willing to stand in the Great Divide and to be the bridge over which people could travel from the way things are and the way things could be. How was he able to do that? How are we?

First of all, Jesus just felt a definite calling from God. It is very simple and plain in the scripture. The Bible says that Jesus returned to Galilee in the power of the Holy Spirit. Jesus had been on a forty-day spiritual retreat struggling with the temptation of his life and how to go about his ministry. He was spiritually disciplined and ready to carry out his ministry, equipped to do what God would have him to do. He was ready to fulfill his calling. If we are to fulfill our calling to do what God would have us to do and to stand in the gap between the way things are and the way things can be, then we must be as spiritually disciplined as Jesus. We do this by doing the things that Jesus did: going on spiritual retreats, prayer, solitude, in communion with the Father, in the power of the Holy Spirit, immersed, absorbed in the Word.

It is not by accident that he went into the synagogue and began in a worship service and read from God's Word. He did it quite often. It was not accidental that he chose this passage of scripture, the great reading from the Old Testament prophet about a time similar to the one in which Jesus found himself. Jesus was careful to show them by scripture that the tension that existed between them was not between the people of Nazareth and Jesus, himself. The tension that existed was between the people of Nazareth and their very own Bible. Their very own Bible told them that they were called of God to be missionaries to the entire world, and that they were to embody servanthood. You know we are never so angry as when we are shown by the Bible that we are wrong.

How do you argue with the Bible? You cannot argue with the Bible. You either have to accept the Bible and live by the Bible or reject the Bible, deny the Bible, and respond in anger and violence and that is what they did. Knowing they were wrong, condemned by their own scriptures, they responded in violence and literally attempted to kill Jesus.

It was Jesus immersing himself in scriptures that allowed him to be able to project a vision of hope. A vision! Jesus came and said, "God has sent me. He has anointed me to preach the gospel to the poor." There will be a time when the poor hear the gospel, when the prisoners are released, when the captives are set free, when they who are spiritually and physically blind, are able to see and God's grace and God is proclaimed. This was the great vision that he posited before them and called them to hear what their lives could be. Jesus was no Pollyanna. He was not filled with naiveté. He was not just idealistically dreaming. Jesus knew in a harsh and ruthless way the way things were. He could look around himself. He knew that they were in an occupied territory. He knew that there were poor people, homeless people, and sick people everywhere. He knew that taxes were sky high. He could see the Roman soldiers and he could see that the very worst of the lot were the poor people. They were on the bottom rung of the ladder. They were the ones who were paying the price and Jesus said the most wonderful thing, "The poor people will be able to hear the gospel and will be able to respond." Jesus knew the way things were and so do we when we open our eyes.

A woman in Nicaragua gets eleven cents for sewing together a pair of blue jeans that are sold by an American company for $14.95. That company made 566 million dollars in profits on those jeans in one year. One out of every five Ugandan children will not live to age five because they do not have simple, primary health care. That is not just in Nicaragua. This is not just in Uganda. There are hurts to heal in our cities. There are poor people here. There are home-less people here. There are addicted people here. There are lonely people here. There are oppressed and captive people here. There are hurts that need to be healed! And you ask, "What can I do? Is there anything I can do? Can I be one who stands in the gap be-tween the way things are and the way things can be? Can I be a bridge over which other people can travel in that journey from the way things are and the way things can be?"

We can expect controversy. Not everyone is going to under-stand. They did not understand in Nazareth. They knew and loved Jesus, but did not understand him. Change is a difficult thing and very often elicits hostility. But we can be that kind of individual who embodies the promise as did Jesus. First of all, simply find something that we like to do and do it. Find something we do well and do it for the glory of God. One single person, one individual, one congregation, one group of people can make a difference.

One average-sized church in Brooklyn, New York, decided that it would fight a popular clothing company and, in doing so, ended the sweat shops in El Salvador. It was just an average-sized church that stood up and said we are against the exploitation of children. The Faith Network of Children decided that it would conduct a campaign and close the sweat shop in El Camino, California, where 72 people from Thailand, behind barbed wire, were being paid $1.60 an hour and working eighteen hours a day. Somebody stood up and said, "Wait a minute! We are against the exploitation of women."

In 1977, both Jews and Christians marched in a silent march during Holy Week. Christians and Jews marched silently during

Holy Week in an effort to protest against the most luxurious hotels of California, and particularly Los Angeles, because they were paying slave labor wages to the people who were making their guests feel luxurious. Some of them had been working there over twenty years and still had no benefits or any health care. Because they got some peoples' attention, fourteen of the most luxurious hotels in Los Angeles banded together and signed a commitment that they would pay their employees a livable wage and try to provide for them benefits that would be an example for hotels all over the world to follow. This happened because Christians and Jews marched silently during Holy Week.

James Wallace said that he is now seeing those who are pro-life and those who are pro-choice coming together in an effort to see what they have in common and somehow stem the tide of 1.5 million abortions performed in the United States every year by concentrating on positive things: combating teen pregnancy, giving other alternatives for women, and reforming adoption laws. People can make a difference!

People make a difference at First Baptist Church in Chattanooga, Tennessee, every day of the week. This church is involved in over twenty ministries in downtown Chattanooga. People build houses for Habitat for Humanity. People teach English as a second language. People fight racism through the Westside Development Project. People fight drug addiction and alcohol addiction through Teen Challenge and it goes on and on. People can, and do, make a difference right here in Chattanooga, Tennessee. Will you make a difference? It only takes one! It only takes one person to start. One person can influence a church to make a difference!

Bill was 37 years old. He awoke one morning, drunk as usual. His doctor had told him, "Bill, you are either going to go crazy or you are going to die of alcoholism." In his despair, he cried out in a prayer and said, "Oh, God, if you are there, let me know it!" And God did! Bill never took another drink. Bill then wrote twelve steps by which others could combat their disease and, as a result, over two million people now live productive, happy lives combating their disease of alcoholism. One person!

75

In 1835, Elijah saw a man lynched. It changed his life. He cut back on his career as a Presbyterian pastor and as a school teacher. He went back to his earlier training as a newspaper editor and began to write anti-slavery tracts. He delivered speeches and aroused hostility. People persecuted him, beat him, and finally burned him out of his home. He was injured in combating the fire, and after only two years, he was killed. Elijah P. Lovejoy, a life cut short. A young attorney in Elijah's home state of Illinois read Elijah P. Lovejoy's materials and was deeply influenced, and 26 years later, that young attorney signed the Emancipation Proclamation. One person! One! Will you be one?

Where are you in the text today? Are you up reading the scriptures like Jesus? Or, are you just bystanders listening? Are you one of those who are protesting — "We don't want change" — or are you one of the others saying, "I want to be one of his disciples. I want what he has. I am willing to do whatever it takes. I want to be like him"? They were all there and we are all here. Where are you today? Will you be one to stand in the gap?

By accident, a fellow wandered into a Quaker meeting. No one was saying anything. It was quiet. Everyone was sitting there listening. Silence. He sat a while. He did not know what was happening. Finally, he gathered up the courage and he nudged the guy sitting near him and said, "Pardon me. When does the service begin?" And the man responded, "When we leave."

— Gary L. Carver

The Bible:
Head And Heart

"With Jesus in your heart, you just can't hate anybody." That is our destination, but sometimes the journey is just as important as the destination. I want to take you on a journey through the text for today. As we continue to preach on the life of our Lord Jesus, we will basically arrive at the same destination: "With Jesus in your heart, you just can't hate anybody." This is a wonderful text, a dense text that is chock full. It's almost like a good hamburger with all that good stuff hanging over the sides and juice dripping everywhere.

Hear the story again. The village of Nazareth was in a buzz. Everyone was so excited because they heard that Jesus was coming home. He had been serving in Capernaum for a period of time teaching, preaching, healing, and performing great miracles and enjoying immense popularity with the people. Crowds were following him everywhere and now the "home boy" was coming home. There was great excitement. Everyone went to hear the "home boy" that had made good. The synagogue was packed. The biggest crowd in years. Jesus stood to read the Word of God. "The Spirit of the Lord is upon me, because he has anointed me to preach the good news to the poor. He sent me to proclaim freedom for the prisoners and recover sight for the blind, release the oppressed and proclaim the year of the Lord's favor."

Jesus then handed the scroll to the attendant. The Bible says that the eyes of everyone were fastened upon him as he said, "Today this scripture is fulfilled in your hearing." The people spoke well of him. They all were amazed at his gracious words and they

77

said to each other, "Is this not Joseph's son?" You can just see two "good ole" boys sitting on the back pew; one punches the other and says, "I always knew that boy would do good. I tell you what, I could see it in him even as a young child." "Yeah, he used to come by my shop and I would give him a word or two of advice. I always knew he was destined for great things. In fact, I remember when I used to teach him in synagogue school. We're mighty proud of him."

As Jesus continued his lesson, he said, "You will surely quote this Proverb to me, 'Physician, heal yourself.' Whatever we have heard done in Capernaum, do also here in your country." Jesus reminded them of their own scriptures. He told them about the days of Elijah when there were many, many widows but Elijah went only to the widow Zarephath in Gentile territory. He reminded them that there were many lepers in Israel in the days of Naaman but God only healed Naaman the Syrian, a Gentile. After speaking those words, the Bible says that the people were furious. The congregation so quick to worship was now furious. The same two "good ole" boys sitting on the back pew are saying, "Who is this? Who does he think he is? Why is he saying all of this about us? What a shame upon this synagogue and the people of this town. Who does he think he is?" "Well, you remember the circumstances under which he was born...." And with that, the whole congregation reached out to try and kill Jesus. One moment he is the grandest thing in the world since sliced bread and the next moment they're ready to kill him. What happened? How could someone be favored one moment and in such disfavor the next? What did Jesus do to make his hometown want to kill him?

Was he just too familiar to them? Familiarity does breed contempt. "Well, that's Mary and Joseph's boy. We know his brothers and sisters. I can't believe he is talking like this. We watched him grow up." Maybe they were just too familiar with Jesus. Sometimes being familiar with someone can make us think they are less capable. The Bible says that Jesus' brothers did not believe in him.

I think just the opposite is true, in a sense. When people who know you best, love you and care for you, that can be a true indication of your real nature. For example: One of the greatest testimonies to the life that Jesus lived, to his deity and to his resurrection was his brother, James. The Bible definitely says that, before the resurrection, James did not believe in his brother, but after the resurrection, James became the pastor of the Jerusalem church. What a turn around! Why? Because Jesus was exactly who he said he was and one who knew him best believed it. What a testimony about the nature and life of our Lord Jesus! Just too familiar? Was that the reason they turned on him?

Or maybe it went a little deeper than being too familiar. They were not at war with Jesus the person; they were at war with the nature of his ministry. Jesus was saying, "I am going beyond Israel. I am going to the Gentiles," and with that one statement, he destroyed their notion of privilege. In speaking to them, he tore down all of their officially sanctioned walls and barriers of hatred. "We're God's special people so that gives to us special privileges and it also gives to us the ability to exclude anyone who is not one of us." Jesus destroyed that and they responded in anger.

We can understand a little of how they felt. They were God's chosen people. They had been persecuted all of their lives because they maintained God's Word and kept up the Jewish customs. They built the temples and tried to live as God would have them live because they were God's people. They had taken a stand and were persecuted for it. It is true that when you are a persecuted people you have to develop a sense of pride merely to survive. But the real danger is when that pride becomes exclusive. It's hard for persecuted people to hear that others will be included in the same grace that they will know and feel they have deserved.

It's hard for us, also. It's okay as long as food is delivered to our door, but what about when grace is extended to our neighbor? It's hard for us, as a denomination, to accept the fact that we're not the biggest and the best any more and that missionaries are now being sent to the United States to try and convert us to their beliefs. The white American male has dominated, but that is rapidly declining. It's hard for us to admit that other countries are experiencing great revivals and other cities are knowing great growth in discipleship. It's hard for us to hear that other people are prospering in the Word of God.

We have to remember that God loves everybody. If we get to the point of excluding anyone, we will exclude, first of all, ourselves, because the Bible says that Jesus could not do any great work in Nazareth because of their unbelief. They would not accept the fact that he was going beyond them to the Gentiles, and because they could not accept the nature of his ministry, they could not receive his blessings and his miracles. By excluding the Gentiles, Nazareth excluded itself.

It could be that the conflict is not between Jesus and his familiarity or between Jesus and the nature of his ministry. Although, both certainly are contributing factors, but very possibly what this text is all about is that these people were at war with their own Bible. Jesus read to them from their Bible and they became angry. They already knew the Bible taught that the Word of God was for everyone. It was not the exclusive property of the Jews. Never! They already knew that the Bible said that Abraham would not only bless his people but through Abraham all the nations of the earth would be blessed. They already knew that Exodus 19 said that God had chosen the Jews to be a nation of missionaries. They had already heard the story of Elijah. They had already heard the story of Elisha. They had already heard the story of Amos when he said that God had not only delivered the Israelites from Egyptian bondage but delivered the Syrians and Philistines as well. God had been working with a lot of different people, not just the Jews. They knew all of that because their Bible said so. But it was difficult for them to hear those words.

We hear it with our heads and we know it to be true, but to hear it with our hearts, believe it, and do it, that is something quite different. The longest journey you will ever make will be the journey from your head to your heart. We've read the Bible over and over again and we know it in our heads, but to know it in our hearts is quite another thing entirely. We know that men and women ought to be treated equally in the work place because the Bible says so. But we say, "Don't take it out of my paycheck!" We know that everyone ought to be given equal housing, but we say, "Don't move into my neighborhood and cause my property value to go down!" We know that God cares and loves everybody and gives to us the

80

ministry to love and care for everybody — the homeless, the poor, those with AIDS, but we say, "Don't make me touch one of them!"

We know in our heads, but to know in our hearts is completely different. Jesus was trying to give to them a new version of reality. Jesus was trying to enter into their imagination and help them see a different world. Things did not have to be the way they were. Jesus was trying to help them see a new vision of reality, a new vision of how the world could be because that's the way behavior is changed. Behavior is changed through imagination.

In order for an addict to be changed, they have to envision themselves as being clean. People who are unforgiven have to envision themselves as being forgiven. Those full of hatred have to envision themselves as being loving people to ever rid themselves of hate. Behavior is changed through imagination. It is changed through the acceptance of another vision of life. It is changed when we accept that God is making us into something that is new and different.

God wants to remake us in the Spirit of God with Christ living within us and holiness at the core of our being and neighborliness the practice of our everyday lives. We are a new people because God has made us new and there is something new in our heart because God's presence lives there. We relate to our brothers and sisters out of true neighborliness because he says we are to love our neighbor.

Jesus was trying to help them envision a new world. When we see that vision and truly hear his Word, we have one of two choices. We can accept it or we can reject it. In Jesus' day there were those who accepted his Word and became a part of the kingdom of God, followed him, and gave birth to the most powerful movement in the history of the world — the Christian church.

And there were those who said, "No! I don't believe it. I don't accept it, go on your way!" The decision is ours. We can accept his will and way for our lives or we can say, "I don't want to have anything to do with it." I think sometimes we make the decision to reject his Word because we just don't want to get involved; life is too crowded as it is. "Don't bother me with any more of those details. I may be in a rut but it's my rut and I like it."

Then there are those who would love to change and have this new vision of a new reality in their lives but they just don't think they can do it. Well, let me tell you something. You can't! Not on your own power. It can only come about through the power and the presence of the living God within your life. The question is this and it is a matter of faith: Do you believe that God has the power to make you into the person he wants you to be? Do you believe that?

I saw a Walt Disney movie on television recently. It was a wonderful movie titled, *Ruby Bridges*. It was the story of Ruby Bridges, a six-year-old African-American girl, who was the first person to integrate the schools in New Orleans. Every day the federal marshals escorted her into the school house because both sides of the sidewalk would be lined with people who were screaming threats. Robert Coles, a noted Harvard psychiatrist, volunteered his time to work with young Ruby. Every day he would talk with her, trying to help her weather the crisis. On the news one night, he noticed her walking up the sidewalk and the people were screaming and throwing things, but suddenly she stopped and said something and started backing down the sidewalk. Then the marshals picked her up and took her into the building. That night, Cole asked her what she said to the marshals. She said, "I was not talking to the marshals." He said, "Yes, you were. I saw you on the news. I saw your lips moving. You were talking to the marshals." She said, "I was not talking to the marshals." He said, "Well, what were you doing?" She said, "I was praying for those people who were hollering at me. I had forgotten to pray and I was trying to go back and pray for them as I walked to the school building." Cole shook his head and said, "You were praying for the people who were screaming at you?" She said, "Yes, my mama taught me that when people speak mean of you, you pray for them just like Jesus prayed for the people who spoke mean of him."

You see, when Jesus lives in your heart, you just can't hate anybody.

— Gary L. Carver

82

Epiphany 5
Ordinary Time 5
Luke 5:1-11

Leaving Before The Invitation

John and Mary have been married for about twenty years. These are good days for Mary as she looks at her life with a sense of satisfaction and joy. She worked long and hard to help put John through medical school. Now that the schooling debts are almost paid off, they have a nice home, a savings account, and she has been able to quit work. Johnny and Susie, sixteen and fourteen, are happy in their school and neighborhood. Many of the things for which Mary has dreamed and worked all of her life are finally coming true for her. Life is good. John's medical practice is becoming firmly established. These are good days.

John has called a meeting of the family, and Mary has in the back of her mind an idea of what it's all about. She feels that John is going to announce that he has made preparations for a long-awaited vacation to Europe — a full month! Mary has dreamed of a vacation in Europe all of her life. The children will never forget it. She is so excited.

John stands and says, "Well, family, I have an announcement to make. I feel that God is calling me to be a missionary. If we watch our pennies, I can resign my medical practice and go to seminary. Oh, I know there will be sacrifices and I know that our parents are getting older, but God is in this. I truly believe that God is going to take care of them as he will take care of us. Now, Johnny and Susie, you may have to take part-time jobs to help with your college education. And, Mary, just think how wonderful it will be and the joy we will have as I live out God's calling in my life. Everybody happy?"

Sometimes we fail to remember that Jesus' calling of the disciples was a calling to a second career. Lives were firmly established, families had deep roots, and all of a sudden here comes this preacher, Jesus, and he turns things upside-down. Think about Simon Peter. Simon Peter probably had parents that needed care. We know that his wife had a mother with a history of illness. What about the children? They probably came bounding in from school asking, "Where is Daddy?" "He's gone again! He's out running around the countryside with that itinerant preacher." Think about Simon's wife. She fell in love and married a successful fisherman, and all of a sudden, she's the preacher's wife. What happened? Did I miss something? Think about that. Second career — fruit basket turnover.

No wonder people are tempted to leave before the invitation. No wonder people are tempted to just come to Sunday school. "We don't go to worship. We don't stay for the invitation." No wonder people are tempted. Why risk it? Why become vulnerable to an experience that could change your very life? Why become vulnerable to an experience that could affect the way you spend your time, energy, and money? Why be vulnerable to an experience that will cause you to reorder your priorities? Why stay for the invitation? Why listen to the call of God? It is one thing hearing the call of God, but it's an awesome experience accepting the call of God.

It was an awesome experience for Simon Peter. He had been fishing all night and had not caught a single fish. Jesus said, "Go back, put your net out." Jesus was telling them to do that during the daytime! You can just imagine Simon Peter nudging one of his buddies and saying, "Can you believe this? We're professional fisherman, and he is a carpenter. Probably has never wet a hook in his life and he is giving me advice about fishing." Simon Peter responded, "Nevertheless, if you say so, Master, that's what I will do." He did what Jesus told him to do and lo and behold, he caught more fish than he had ever seen before! He got his business partners to help load both boats until they were ready to sink. That was a miraculous experience and it happened in the ordinary experiences of life. God does that you know.

God takes the initiative and comes to us in the everyday experiences of life and calls to us. It happened to Moses as he was wandering around in the Judean countryside. He had been dead spiritually for forty years and all of a sudden in the common experience of tending sheep God called. God called David in the den of his father's house. He had no idea why they had summoned him in from tending sheep. God called Gideon while he was out farming. God called Paul when he was out rounding up troublemakers. God called Isaiah when he went to the house of God to worship, and God called Simon Peter when he was out fishing. In the common everyday experiences of life, God calls to us. Why? Could it be that God is concerned about us and cares about the everyday happenings in our lives? Could that really be true?

In the spring of 1978, the film, *Oh God!* was given an award. It was a film that portrayed the message that God cares about people, that God comes to people, and he wants people to be happy. Do you know the award that film received? "Best Fantasy Film of the Year." To some people, it is a fantasy that God cares for us; that God loves us and comes to us in the ordinary affairs of our life. To some, it is a fantasy! Why? If we truly believe that God comes to us, speaks to us, calls out to us, then we, too, have to put our nets where he tells us. We, too, have to place the net where he tells us in spite of the fact that we think we know better. That is what this church is trying to do.

The task force is meeting and seeking answers to questions like: "Where are we going to expend our resources, our money, our time, our talents, and our gifts? How can we reach people for Christ? Where are we going to put our nets?" Right now we don't know, but we do know this: It is not in the way we have been putting our nets. We do know that. Things are changing and we have to change and present a never-changing gospel to an ever-changing world. It is an awesome thing to be called by God. It is a humbling and revealing experience. When Simon saw the miracle and stood face-to-face with the miracle worker, he fell and said, "Get away from me! I am unclean! Get away from me! I am a sinful man! I am unworthy to be in your presence." Simon was not only humbled but it revealed to him, just like Isaiah of old, that he was a sinful man.

Notice that Jesus did not reject Simon. Jesus already knew that Simon was unworthy, but that had nothing to do with it whatsoever. What made the difference was that Simon became aware of his unworthiness. It was Simon's awareness of his unworthiness that fit him for service, not the fact that he was a sinner or not a sinner, not the fact that he had great gifts or that he was an emotional person. Simon's awareness of his own unworthiness equipped him to be a servant and that drove him to his knees as a sinner lifted up and as a servant of the Christ.

Several years ago, two land surveyors were sent from a large city in Wales to survey the mountains in North Wales. For a week, they stayed in an isolated cabin in shepherd country. Every day they went out with maps, compasses, and charts checking the countryside and the valleys. Several days into the first week, an old shepherd came up to them and said, "Might be best if I go with you tomorrow." They said, "No, there's no need for that. We have our maps and charts. We'll be fine. We have everything we need." The old shepherd said again, "It might be best if I went with you tomorrow." "No, we have our maps and charts. We know these hills just like you. We'll be okay." And the old shepherd said, "You may have your maps, but the fog is not on the maps."

There come times in our lives when all the charts, maps, and other resources are insufficient. There come times when we can only do God's work in his power and in his strength. It is an awesome, humbling, and revealing experience to stand before the miracle worker as he reaches out and calls us. We realize, first of all, that we can't do it in our own strength and in our own power, but it is through his power that we can do it.

It is not only an awesome and revealing experience, but it is a humbling experience. It is a joyful and progressive experience. Notice that after being lifted up, leaving everything and following Jesus, it wasn't over. It continued. It is a lifelong experience of obedience and joyfully growing.

I love the story that is told of a sophomore who worked in the library at Princeton to earn money to help with his education. One night about closing time, he was walking around the empty halls of the library when he noticed in the very back corner amid an old stack of books, an old man reading and taking notes furiously. The old man was very intent. The librarian became a little curious so he went back to the old man and said, "My, what are you studying so intently?" The old man looked up long enough to say, "Well, I'm a student of physics." The young librarian said, "Well, last year I took a course in physics and I think I have all I need for an understanding of physics." He then turned and walked back to his desk. You can imagine his chagrin a few minutes later when the old man checked out some books, and on his library card was the name Albert Einstein. It is a calling to a process. It is a calling to a life-long process of obedience and service and growing more like Jesus. There is nothing in the world more joyful than that. There is nothing in the world more challenging.

You may say, "Well, I've never met Albert Einstein and I've never stood in the face of a miracle. I've never stood knee-deep in fish in the middle of a boat on the Sea of Gennesaret." That may be true. How do I know God is calling me and then how do I know that God is calling me in a particular direction? That's a good question. Let me try to answer it this way: You may not know what you are supposed to do tomorrow, but do what you know to do today. Do what you know to do. Do what makes you happy. I'm sure every person in this house of God knows that there is something you are to do for God today. Do what you know to do. Do what fulfills you as a person and as a Christian.

William Bausch tells the story of a nun who received some extra grant money. She worked as a chaplain in a women's prison in Chicago. She went to the women and said, "I have some money that I want to spend on you and I'm going to give you some options: 1) I can hire an attorney to come and talk with you on how you can shorten your sentences, 2) I can hire a welder to come in and teach you to weld so that you can have a marketable skill when you leave the prison, or 3) I can hire a dancer and a painter to teach you how to dance and how to paint." Ninety-five percent chose the dancer and the painter because, as they said, "They always wanted to express themselves, but never had the chance."

That puts God's calling where it should be and that is in a positive light. The most fulfilling, the most expressive, the most

87

joyful experience you will ever know in your life is walking in the middle of God's will for your life. Hear the invitation, and say, "Oh God, here am I, send me. Send me!"

— Gary L. Carver

Woe To The Blessed

One of my all-time favorite television programs was *M*A*S*H*. In the early episodes, Frank Burns and Hot Lips Houlihan were an item. Often they were pitted against Trapper John and Hawkeye. In one such episode, Frank and Hot Lips had been trying to "do-in" Hawkeye but had failed. Hawkeye now had the upper hand, and Radar said, "Why don't you do to them what they were trying to do to you?" Hawkeye said, "Look at them! They're each just one-half of a person and when they come together, they barely make a whole person. They have enough troubles of their own."

When I was pastoring in another state, I became acquainted with a very prominent religious leader whom I had admired for a long time. As we worked together and as I got closer to him, I became disillusioned because he did not seem to be the person that I had envisioned him to be. In fact, he was petty, self-centered, and manipulative. He used people for his own selfish ends. If you ever crossed him, you were off his list forever. I was speaking to my dear friend at that time, Hudson Baggett, who was then editor of the *Alabama Baptist*, about this individual, and in poetic language, once a teacher of preachers, he said, "What a shame it is that so big a man is so little. How tragic it is that such a large man cast such a small shadow."

Half-people — casting small shadows. In our text for today, Jesus is talking about people who are half-persons becoming whole persons. Jesus is talking about people who don't get life. They just don't get it, but Jesus says that they can get life. It started as most everything starts in the Gospel of Luke, with Jesus in prayer. Verse

89

12 says that Jesus spent all night on the mountainside praying to the Father trying to ascertain the Father's values, the Father's views, and the Father's will. After spending the night in prayer, he chose his disciples. Luke is speaking with theological geography in that Jesus came down from the mountain on a level plain with the people. He was with the people. Emmanuel — God with us.

As he came down from the mountain, he was teaching, preaching, and healing. The crowds closed in around him when Jesus stopped and said, "Wait!" And he uttered these words, "Blessed are you who hunger, blessed are you who are poor, blessed are you who cry, blessed are you when people exclude you, and blessed are you who jump for joy when people reject you." And then he said, "Woe to those who are rich, woe to those who are well fed, woe to those who laugh, and woe to those whom everyone speaks well of." These words shocked them out of their theology of favoritism. They looked at each other and said, "What in the world is he talking about? He has just turned our entire world upside-down. What could he mean by all of this?"

And we ask ourselves, "What does he mean?" I don't know about you but this text makes me a little bit uncomfortable. When I read this text, I feel uneasy because what I hear just might change my life. What does he mean? Does he mean that God hates the rich or that God hates the so-called blessed of our society? Of course not! God loves everyone! What he may be saying is that if our lives are centered around our possessions and the pleasing of ourselves by our resources, we may already have our reward. The word "reward" here means "paid in full." Isn't it ironic that in a day in which we supposedly have the finest economy in years, there is a yearning in the heart and soul of the American people for spirituality? Now I'm not talking about a spirituality that is always found in churches, but a hunger for spirituality. It is as if the entire nation is saying, "There's got to be more!" Perhaps Jesus is saying that if our lives are centered around only that which pleases us then we have all that's coming.

Jesus said, "To whom much is given, much is required." So often we forget that everything we have been given, life itself, our possessions, our resources, and our finances are given to us by

God as a gift to be given to others. We are just a channel through which our energies and resources are funneled to others. That is the purpose of the church. The church is to give us structure and discipline so that we may not only be ministered unto but we can minister and give our talents, resources, and gifts to others making their lives better. The church budget is a structure to teach us to tithe and to give of our resources so that other lives may be enriched. "To whom much is given, much shall be required," Jesus said.

Or, maybe Jesus is talking to those who are so blessed and reminding us that success is much harder to handle than failure. Ask Leon Spinks. Several years ago, he shocked the boxing world when he upset Mohammed Ali, the heavyweight champion of the world. The year after Leon Spinks became heavyweight champion of the world, the world for Leon Spinks was total chaos. The night he went in to face Ali for the rematch, over thirty people were in his entourage as he made his way into the ring, but after defeat he sat in his dressing room alone.

Ask Oskana Baiul who, just a few short years ago, stunned the Olympic world with her beautiful figure skating, but success was hard to handle. Now she fights to regain a fraction of her former abilities. Ask the Boston Red Sox player. I forget his name but they say he makes over two million dollars a year and he just filed for bankruptcy. Ask Mike Tyson. He made $147 million in 27 months and his accountant told him recently that he was broke. Success is hard to handle.

I love the *Peanuts* comic strip where Lucy is chiding Charlie Brown. In the first frame she says, "I have just examined my character and I find it to be without flaw." Next frame, "What I am going to do is hold a ceremony and give myself a medal." Next frame, "And then I'm going to give a wonderful speech." Next frame, "I am going to receive myself and congratulate myself in the receiving line." In the last frame she says, "You know, when you're a saint you have to do everything for yourself." I don't know if I would agree with her definition of a saint, but I can hear the loneliness. There has to be more.

Rabbi Kushner tells the story of being shown a caterpillar in South Wales. The caterpillar makes itself into a moth that has no mouth and no digestive system. That is all the caterpillar does. The moth then lays its eggs and dies. It has no other reason for living. There's got to be more to life than show up, further the species, and die!

Maybe Jesus is saying that he loves the poor. This is not Matthew. Jesus is not talking about poor in spirit; he is talking about people who are poverty stricken. He is talking about people who do not have enough to eat or wear and he is saying that God loves the poor. His own Son knew what it was to be poor. His own Son knew what it was to be hungry. His own Son knew what it was to walk as you and I walk, suffering all the trials and afflictions of this life. His own Son knew what it was like to be rejected. His own Son knew what it was to be overwhelmed by the enormity of life. His own Son knew everything that you know. His own Son knew what poverty was. God wants it better for those who are poor, for those who weep, and for those who are excluded. Could it be that one reason God loves the poor is because they come to him in their poverty and brokenness and say, "God, this is all I have"? Sometimes those who have a lot try to buy God off. Sometimes those that are well fed don't feel the need for God. Sometimes we who laugh say, "You know life is going pretty well," and sometimes we who are spoken well of think, "Well, I'm popular so everything must be all right. I must deserve all of this."

Sometimes when we have everything, we simply don't feel the need for God. Those who are poor come to him with empty hands saying, "Oh, God, we have no one but you and you can have all that we have, which is nothing." Maybe Jesus is talking about making God the center of our existence. We come to God not in what we have, but in what we have not. We come to God not in what we are, but what we are not. We place it before him and say, "Oh, God, here am I. I am yours completely! You are the center of my life. All of my life is centered around my relationship to you. You are at the center of my thoughts and actions. You are the purpose and direction of my resources. Here I am, God. Everything I have and everything that I don't have, everything that I am and everything that I am not, I bring to you."

And you say, "Preacher, that sounds great, but I can't enter a convent. I can't join a monastery. I have bills to pay, a family to support, and a life to live! Don't talk to me about that kind of stuff. I can't live up to it. Life is not meant to be a joyless parade," and you are exactly right. In fact, the Talmud, a commentary on Jewish Scriptures, says, "We will be brought in judgment to God for every good thing that he put upon this earth that we refuse to enjoy." You say, "Now, preacher, you've got me more confused than ever. Are we supposed to be joyful or are we supposed to be poor? I don't understand." I think he means that we are to put God at the very center of our lives. We are to put our personal relationship to the Lord Jesus Christ at the very center of our existence. It is the most precious gift that we have.

Every thought and every action we extend is centered around our personal relationship to the living Lord, Jesus Christ. I think it means this: In our best of days when everything seems to be going well, we ought to enjoy life with fullness, joyfulness, exuberance, and extravagance. We ought to enjoy the marvelous life that God has placed before us, always mindful that there is a great danger when we center our lives around what we have. That can become a distraction to our relationship with God.

I also think it means that in our worst of days when nothing seems to be going right we must remember that the final accounting has not occurred and we do not need to be weary in well doing because God rewards his faithful. I don't know about you, but sometimes I get tired of structure. I get tired of discipline. I get tired of poring over sermons late at night, but Jesus says, "It is all worth it!" That is not just some "pie in the sky" statement. Jesus is saying that it is not only worth it then, it is all worth it now! A life surrendered to Jesus is the very best of all lives, and that will work in the best of your days and in the worst of your days.

I love the story that is told of a factory that was having problems with employees stealing. The company hired a security firm to help with the problem. They had guards posted at all exits and they were to check each employee as they left for the day. They searched their clothing and lunch boxes to make sure they were not taking anything out. Every day one guy came by with a wheelbarrow full of junk. Every day they stopped him and plowed through all of the junk and garbage that was in the wheelbarrow. It took several minutes every day to search through the junk. Every day the same thing — nothing but junk in the wheelbarrow. Finally, the security person said, "Look, fellow, I know something is going on. Every day you come through here and all we find in the wheelbarrow is junk. If you promise to tell me exactly what is going on, I promise not to turn you in. Tell me what is going on." The fellow grinned and said, "I'm stealing wheelbarrows."

That story has two truths that I want to leave with you: 1) Things may not always be what they seem to be, at least on the outside, and 2) Don't go looking in junk and garbage for the most obvious answer to the meaning and essence of life. It's found in God's Word. It's found in your heart. As you give your heart and life to Jesus Christ, as you center your entire existence around him, oh, the blissful joy and happiness that is yours. Are you one of his? How can you answer that without a smile on your face?

— Gary L. Carver

Taking The First Step

Create in your minds, if you will, a scene where the people are gathering at a small church for worship. They are drifting in one by one. One man storms in, unaware that his entry is causing a disturbance. He's angry! He's mad! He's fuming! As he sits down, his mind begins to recall the events of the day. Someone he thought was his best friend took an idea of his, lied to him, lied about him, and gave the idea to the boss. Now, this so-called friend will probably get the advancement that should have been his. He feels cheated, mistreated, and betrayed.

Another person slips in and sits in the back with her head covered, and her outer garment pulled up around her face. She is hoping that no one will notice the bruises on her face and the darkness under her eyes. As she sits down, she recalls the recent events. Her husband hit her for the first time. He has such a temper. As she is sitting there in silence before the service, she begins to pray, "Lord, what am I going to do? What can I do? What if he hits the baby? What am I to do, Lord?"

The convener of the worship service stands up and says, "Thank you for coming. Let me remind you that next week at this same time, we will meet at Lydia's house. Before we have our scripture, I have a prayer request. Let's all pray for Jonas. He was arrested yesterday by the Romans because he spoke to someone about Jesus.

"We have a special guest for our worship service today. Our dear brother, Theophilus, has come for worship and he will read the scripture for us." As Theophilus stands and unrolls the scroll, he says, "I have the words that were written to me, as you all know, from the beloved physician, Luke. These are words of our Lord Jesus. Words that are very appropriate for these very troubled times. Would you hear the words of Jesus as recorded by Luke?"

> *But I tell you who hear me: Love your enemies, do good to those who hate you, bless those who curse you, pray for those who mistreat you. If someone strikes you on one cheek, turn to him the other also. If someone takes your cloak, do not stop him from taking your tunic. Give to everyone who asks you, and if anyone takes what belongs to you, do not demand it back. Do to others as you would have them do to you.*
>
> *If you love those who love you, what credit is that to you? Even "sinners" love those who love them. And if you do good to those who are good to you, what credit is that to you? Even "sinners" do that. And if you lend to those from whom you expect repayment, what credit is that to you? Even "sinners" lend to "sinners" expecting to be repaid in full. But love your enemies, do good to them, and lend to them without expecting to get anything back. Then your reward will be great, and you will become the sons of the Most High, because he is kind to the ungrateful and to the wicked. Be merciful, just as your Father is merciful.*
>
> *Do not judge and you will not be judged. Do not condemn, and you will not be condemned. Forgive, and you will be forgiven. Give, and it will be given to you. A good measure, pressed down, shaken together and running over, will be poured into your lap. For with the measure you use, it will be measured to you.*

What do those words mean? What do those words mean to the young man who has been lied to and lied about? What do those words mean to a woman who has been abused? What do those words mean to you? Some of you have been lied to and lied about. Some of you have been cheated and mistreated. Some of you have been misinterpreted. Some of you are bruised emotionally and possibly physically. What do these words mean to you? Is it just some idealistic dreaming, something that sounds good, but impossible to put into practice? What is Jesus saying?

I believe Jesus is saying to us, in verses 27-31, that we are to never, never retaliate. We are to never seek revenge, we are to never practice an "eye for an eye," and we are never to exchange evil for evil. Jesus uses the imperative here. He is saying you do this. You are to be different. You are mine, and you are to love your enemies, you're to do good to those who hate you, bless those who curse you, pray for those who mistreat you, and turn the other cheek. Give to everyone who asks of you. You're to go the second mile. You're to do unto others as you wish they would do to *you.*

Jesus has no word here for the victimizer, but he has a strong word for the victim. Jesus just naturally assumes that kind of behavior does not belong in the kingdom of God, and that kind of behavior is not practiced by a child of God. He doesn't have to tell us not to do that. That is so completely foreign to the Spirit and work of Jesus Christ. He doesn't address the victimizer, but addresses those who are children of God who may be victims. The days in which these words were recorded, the church was a victim, very often abused. He is saying that you have the option to choose not to be a victim. You have the choice to determine ahead of time how *you* are going to respond when something happens to you. You have the ability and the power through Jesus our Lord not to respond in kind, and you have the power to take the first step and to respond in love. We have the ability through Christ to take the initiative and when abuse comes our way to respond in love, in kindness, in blessings, and in prayer.

Recently, our church hosted a reception for some members. I had walked the honored guests to their car about 9:30 and as I started back into the church, someone began hollering at me. I stopped, and he said, "I need help." He had a wonderful story, and it was a logical one. He needed $10 or $12 to buy a spare tire. He was in desperate need and had to have it right then. I gave him the money, and as I walked back to the church, I thought to myself, he took you, you're a sucker, and you swallowed that bait hook, line, and sinker. He lied. I found out later that he definitely did lie. He was one of the regulars that we have at church all the time. I began

97

to berate myself and then I thought, "No, no, no that's not right. Jesus says that if you perceive there is a need, respond with love and generosity. If the other person is lying, that's his problem. I am to treat people as I would like to be treated if I were in their situation."

We're not to take how we respond to life from those who mistreat us. Notice the next few verses. Jesus said just the opposite is true as well. He said that if you love those who love you, what credit is that? Everybody does that. If you lend to those from whom you expect repayment, what good is that? Even sinners do that. What Jesus is saying here is that we do not take our cue on how we respond to life from what life does to us. We respond out of the love of God that is in our heart, and in whose name we are assembled here today.

Jesus said, "Love your enemies and do good to them. Then your reward will be great and you will be the sons of the Most High, because God is kind to the ungrateful and wicked. Be merciful. Just as your Father is merciful." We are to take our cue for life from God. He loves indiscriminately. He loves everybody — the good and bad. He is gracious and his work in us is to make us gracious as well.

I have a friend who is a man about whom much has been said, and not all of it true. Some have taken his remarks out of context and misinterpreted them. He has been accused of many things of which he is not guilty. Yet, he took a stand and told me of a commitment that has been made at Southern Seminary to minister to everyone who comes through the doors no matter who they may be. A commitment has been made to give them the best possible theological education possible. No matter what! Because our first commitment is to Jesus, our Lord, and it is out of our love and commitment to him that we treat everyone else. Amen, amen.

As children of the kingdom, we are not to take our cue from the world whether it be friend or foe. We are to take our cue from our loving Heavenly Father, and it is out of his love and graciousness that we take the initiative and respond to life. He says in verses 37-38 that the child of the kingdom is not to judge or condemn. That's God's business. As his children, we are to give and forgive.

Maybe the old Negro-spiritual prayer says it best: "You can talk about me all you please, but I will talk about you when I get on my knees." What do Jesus' words mean? What does it mean to a man who is sitting in a worship service that has been lied about and lied to, cheated and mistreated? Maybe it will help him to face his anger toward the person who has wronged him and give him the power not to respond in kind, and to take the initiative and respond in love and seek reconciliation.

What does it mean to a woman who has been abused by her life's partner? Hopefully, it will enable her not to blame herself, not to see herself as deserving of abuse, not to take blame and not, in some perverted way, enjoy the abuse. Hopefully, it will enable her to not respond in kind, but to seek help for herself and for the one abusing her and have the power through Christ to respond in love, though difficult it may be.

What do these words mean to you? How do they speak to you? How can they help you respond to what is happening this week or what happened last week? How can they help *you* to take the first step? You may say, "I can't love my enemies right now. Is there a step I can take beforehand? Is there an intermediate step, a half-step?"

Dr. E. V. Hill is an African-American preacher in Los Angeles. Several years ago, during the Watts riots, he and many others were threatened. Some were beaten and one was killed. The week before someone was killed, Dr. Hill got a telephone call. His wife could easily see that he was disturbed by the call. He put down the receiver and said nothing. She asked about the call and he said, "Nothing you need to know." She said, "Yes, I do need to know, if it affects you, it affects me. Who was that?" He said, "I don't know. All they said was, 'Do not be surprised if you find a bomb in your car.' " The next morning when Dr. Hill awoke, he looked around and did not see his wife. He put his robe on and ran out on the front porch and saw his car turning the corner. Driving up in the driveway was his wife. He asked, "Where in the world have you been?" She said, "Well, I thought if somebody is going to be killed, I'd rather it be me."

Maybe we cannot love our enemies today. Maybe it takes all of the love we have to simply love those around us, but that is a step. That's a half-step, but it's not the first step. Taking the first step is when we love Jesus and make a commitment to Jesus of Nazareth as our Lord and Savior. It is realizing that we are sinners. That we have done wrong. We may have been abused, but yet there have been times when we have abused as well. We may have been sinned against, but there have been times when we have sinned and our sin has hurt others. The first step is to realize our sin, to repent of that sin, and turn to God in faith, trusting in Jesus as our Lord and Savior. That's the first step.

Have you ever taken that first step — a commitment to the Lord Jesus Christ as your Savior? These words are impossible, and I promise, you cannot put them into affect without God, but with him, you can, and you will. Would you take the first step now?

— Gary L. Carver

Building A Victorious Life

J. Wallace Hamilton in his book, *What About Tomorrow?* tells the story of a wealthy builder who called his top assistant and said, "I am going away for ten months. While I am gone, I want you to oversee the building of my home. I am going to be retiring in a few years. I have these wonderful plans and an excellent lot by the lake and I want you to oversee the building of our home." As he left, the assistant said to himself, "He lives in luxury and has done very little for me. When he retires, what will I have?" So the assistant used every opportunity to feather his own nest. He hired an immoral builder, he used inferior products, he hired inferior workmen; and when the house was completed, it looked fine on the outside but its deficiencies in workmanship and materials would soon show as the tests of time came.

When the wealthy builder came back, he said, "Do you like the house?" The assistant replied, "Yes, I do." The builder asked, "Is it beautiful?" The assistant answered, "It certainly is." Then the builder said, "It is a surprise for you. I am retiring in a couple of years and I want you to be taken care of, as well. The house is yours."

We each live in the houses we are building. I was the pastor of a family who asked me to go talk to their son. He was a 21-year-old man, living at home, had no job, nor could he handle one if he did. His mind was literally fried from taking LSD. He could not carry on a coherent conversation. In fact, he told me that his older sister had a machine that she could turn on and drive intense pain through his head.

We live in the houses we build. A girl's parents told her to, "Leave that boy alone" — he was bad news. "But we are in love!" she said. He was older and more experienced. He took advantage of her inexperience, and later on, she became experienced and in trouble. He said he would take care of it, and he did. Now, she will never have her own child.

We live in the houses we build. For forty years, a man smoked three packs of cigarettes a day. Now, he cannot leave his house because of the emphysema and the asthma. He is a prisoner of his breathing apparatus and a prisoner of his own habit. Normally, he would be expected to live another fifteen to twenty years, but the odds are now that he won't make it through the next one. We live in the houses we build.

You know the old saying: "If I had known I was going to live this long, I would have taken better care of myself." All of us, to some extent, can share that sentiment, because it is true — we live in the houses we build. The frightening thing is *not* that we are going to die — that is a foregone conclusion. We all accept that. The most frightening thing is, we may *live*; and we may have to live for a long time in the houses we have built for ourselves.

That is part of what Jesus is saying. Jesus is also saying that the durability of our houses will depend upon their foundations. The Tower of Pisa was begun in 1173. Its original constructor worked twelve and one-half years, completed three and one-half stories and then it began to *lean* — so much so, that he deserted the project, and eighty years later another builder came. He thought he could correct the defect and he built the tiers even straighter, he thought; but that did not solve the problem. Ninety years later, another builder put the dome on its top, but still, every single year, that tower leans a fraction of an inch more. One day, even though it has stood for 800 years, that 14,500-ton tower is going to fall because the soft, watery sub-soil will not support its weight. It is simply on a faulty foundation. Many of us are living our lives on faulty foundations. Our society is seeking to build many lives on faulty foundations. One of those faulty foundations, I believe, is the foundation of self-sufficiency. This is the day of rugged individualism. This is the day when we are "to be our own person."

This is the day when we are to strike out and claim our own, develop our own potential, and seek to live in our own strength. None of us was ever meant to live in our own strength. It is simply an impossibility, and no matter how developed, intellectual, educated, or prosperous we may be — or how "macho" we think we are — none of us is self-sufficient.

Another faulty foundation is an effort to obtain the quick fix. The quick fix! We are supposed to have a pill or remedy, a solution for everything; and it is supposed to come quickly. I think that is part of the reason in our world that many people are running toward an easy religion, a religion that requires little, that allows one to sit home and "view the tube" and send in a dollar. Ours is a society that is looking toward "answer-man preachers" with simple answers to complex problems, when all we do is "do as they say." Every time they holler, we send a dollar! And everything will be fine. It is a society that runs after the quick fix of a cheap Christianity, ignoring the fact of what it cost Christ; ignoring the fact that it must cost us if it is to be authentic, life-changing, and have meaning both in our lives and in others. Life and faith cannot be built upon self-sufficiency or an effort to find the quick fix.

It was G. K. Chesterton who said, "There is nothing so weak for lasting results as this enormous importance attached to immediate victory ... There is nothing that fails like success." Immediate victory is so seldom found in life, and its search can develop a faulty and insecure foundation.

But there are true foundations. There are foundations upon which we can build our lives, and they will work. One of those foundations is what Jesus is talking about in our scripture lesson today. He is simply saying that, "He that heareth these words," — he that hears the Sermon on the Mount — embodies their principles, lives out their characteristics, and *doeth them*, is like a man who built his house upon a rock! When the storms of life assailed it, it stood and stood secure.

I go to the doctor every now and then when something is wrong, and that doctor will share, out of his or her wisdom, information with me about the ailment; and I will hear that. Then he or she will

103

take a piece of paper and, in writing I cannot understand, will write out a prescription. Now I have heard the word of the doctor. I looked in my desk drawer before I came into this service, and I have six prescriptions that have never been filled! It is amazing to me that those doctors' prescriptions have never done me any good at all! I knew what the problem was, and the medicine is prescribed accurately for the ailment; but somehow that medicine has never done me any good. I *heard* the word. The only thing worse than that, would be to go out and take every medicine available. "I have something wrong, so I will take this medicine, that medicine, and the other medicine. I will consult all my friends and they will tell me what is wrong with me; and they will share with me from *their* prescriptions."

We need to both *hear* the Word and *do* the Word. That is what Jesus is talking about. To hear the Word and to have only the Word is stale, dull, dry, barrenness. To do something without hearing the Word is fanaticism. Jesus is saying, "I want you to hear my Word and then translate my Word into action. I want *you* to put my intentions for *you* into application." "Be ye *doers* of the Word." That is what God calls us to do: Live lives that both hear God's Word and put God's Word into action, lives that are characterized by discipline and obedience.

It was Horace Greeley, the great newspaper editor, who once received a letter from a woman. The letter went something like this: "Can you give me some advice on saving our church? We are always in financial straits, and we have tried everything. We tried a bazaar, we tried a raffle, we had an oyster supper, we had a donkey party (what that is, I do not know!), we had a strawberry festival, and another festival. How can we save our church?" Greeley's advice was two words: "Try Christianity." "Try Christianity!"

Following our Lord has never been tried and found wanting. It has been found difficult and left untried. He calls us to a life of obedience, he calls us to a life of discipline, he calls us to a life of hearing his Word and doing his Word, and putting a "period" where God puts a "period." Then, as we discipline ourselves and as we follow him, as we try Christianity, it will solve many of the financial problems, many of the image problems, many of the internal problems that we have. Try God! Try Christianity! Try following Jesus Christ in discipline and obedience.

It was Ruskin who said, "Every duty we omit obscures some truth we might have known." What did he mean? He is simply saying this: Revelation follows action. When we do what we *know* to do, then God will give us something else to do and something else to learn. Until we get off point A and do what is required there, God is not going to progress us to point B. Revelation follows action, not vice versa. God will reveal his love, his will, his grace, his guidance, his leadership, and his depth to us when we do what we know to do.

Someone said, "I wish I were a better father." God says, "Do the things that good fathers do, and you will *be* a better father." "I wish I were a better wife." Do the things that good wives do, and you will be a better wife. "I wish I were a deeper Christian." Then do the things that deep Christians do, and you will be a better Christian. *Do* and then you will *be*. It is discipline. The foundation of our lives will determine the durability of the house we build, and that foundation is discipline in the way of and obedience to the Word of Jesus Christ. Because every house will be tested. Every home will have the ravages of nature to strike it. Every house we build will be tested, and what are we going to do then? What are we going to do when we have the temptation of sitting down to the table late at night, behind on our bills, and it is tax-figuring time; and we think, "I could just shave a figure here or there and cheat on my taxes"?

What do you do when you have the misfortune of planning and saving for a trip and just as you are to leave on the trip, the family vehicle breaks down and you are facing a $500 charge? What do you do when you have the sorrow of your last parent who has passed away and *you* are now the oldest person in your family — you are the matriarch or patriarch of your clan? What do you do when you get caught in a terrible illness and you happen to be in-between hospitalization plans? What happens when you are passed over for a promotion by a younger, better qualified person? What do you do when your teenager is in an accident while driving a car, and *you* have to pay the $500 deductible? What do you do?

105

What do you do when your mate lies, your friend betrays you, your boss will not support you, or reneges on his support of you? What do you do when you are praying and your prayers will not form? What do you do when the Bible seems to be dull words upon a page, the Spirit is not moving in your life, and you feel that neither God nor anyone else cares. What do you do when you go through the storm or the dark night of the soul? Every house is tested. What do you do, then, if your foundation is built on sand?

Beethoven said when he first learned of his illness and felt its coming effects on his hearing: "I will seize life by the throat!" Many biographers have said he was actually able to turn his deafness into a plus, that his lofty and beautiful music could only come as a compensation for that kind of loss. Here was a man who lived in silence and isolation and it was out of the silence and isolation that he brought beautiful harmony into the world.

What are *you* going to do when your house is beaten by the storms and the wind and the rain? In 1981, my family and I went to the Southern Baptist Convention in Los Angeles. On the way out, we stopped to see that wonderful wonder of the present world, the Hoover Dam. We learned of its construction. For 23 months, they poured concrete day and night into a base 660 feet thick into the solid granite wall of Black Canyon. This is what is called an arch gravity dam. It is an arch turned on its side and the result is this: The greater the pressure on that dam, the more the dam arches, or wedges, itself into Black Canyon. The greater the pressure, the stronger it becomes.

What about you? Do you have the foundation, the resources, so that you can say, "The greater the pressure, the stronger I become"? Life's troubles and storms bring out the best in some of us and the worst in some of us. Which is it with you? It depends a lot on the foundation on which we are standing. Sometimes we are able, as Beethoven said, "... to grab adversity and seize it by the throat." Sometimes we are able to take the pressures and storms of life and allow it to make us stronger. At other times, our needs are just a little bit more immediate. John Killinger, in his book, *Preaching*, tells the story of a gunner in a B-17 during World War II. They were coming in for a landing and the gunner was in the nose of the

106

plane. He saw that the airstrip on which they were about to land had a huge ditch in front of it and he knew for them it would be "curtains." He tried to get the attention of the pilot through the intercom system. Finally he did, and this is what he heard: "God, help me not to panic! God, help me not to panic! God, help me not to panic!" The pilot had seen the ditch, too, and the pilot was praying. Then miracle of miracles, that pilot was able to set the plane down right before the ditch, actually bounce over it and then go down the landing strip.

Sometimes, our prayer is simply, "God, help me not to panic." What is your prayer today? Upon which foundation are you building your life?

— Gary L. Carver

The Transfiguration Of Our Lord
(Last Sunday After The Epiphany)
Luke 9:28-36 (37-43)

Back To The Future

The experience in the ninth chapter of Luke is called "The Transfiguration Experience of our Lord Jesus," and is recorded in two other gospels — Matthew and Mark. Preachers, teachers, scholars, and theologians are all aware that something significant happened. I'll join with the ignorant and say like most of them that I don't know what happened, but something special and very unique made an indelible impression upon the minds of those who experienced it. It is as if there is almost a shroud of mystery surrounding this experience. What did it mean to Jesus? What did it mean to the disciples both then and later on? What did it mean to God who is the true actor in this scene?

Jesus had just told his disciples for the very first time that he was going to die. For the first time, they understood that he was not here to set up an earthly kingdom, but was here to die as a suffering servant for the sins of mankind. This threw the disciples' world into an upheaval — Jesus, the Son of God — die? "Wait a minute. Give me a moment or two to process that."

We talk a lot about what we are living for. Do we talk enough about what we are living from? We're living for this and for that — what are we living from? What is the source of our power and strength? For Jesus there was no question: He lived from his relationship to the Father. In every major experience in the Gospel of Luke, we find Jesus in prayer. Jesus was praying when this wonderful transfiguration experience occurred. He took three disciples with him. The leader, of course, was Simon Peter. It is interesting to just imagine in our minds, guided by the Holy Spirit, what this meant to Simon Peter. At first glance, it seemed to mean very little because he was asleep.

Now imagine this, God has brought from heaven both Elijah and Moses, the two greatest historical personages of the Old Testament, symbolic of the Law and the prophets. Elijah and Moses have been raised from the dead and the disciples are asleep. Are these folks dullards or what? They missed it completely. "As he was praying, the appearance of his face changed, and his clothes became as bright as a flash of lightning," and just as this situation was about to be over, Simon woke up and, realizing what was going on, responded in his usual over-emotional way and says, "Lord, this is great, this is fantastic. We ought to put up three tabernacles to commemorate what has happened here!"

Simon is the perfect example of the person who, when he doesn't know what to say, still speaks. Even Luke comments. Look at verse 33. Luke said that Peter knew not what he was saying. It's just Simon babbling again — open mouth, insert foot. We cannot confine God. We cannot freeze-dry life until we can come back and own it again. When the cloud appears, Simon is afraid. I could identify with that. Moses, Elijah, a cloud, and suddenly there's the voice of God: "This is my Son, whom I have chosen; listen to him." I would have been afraid. The disciples are just there and have no idea whatsoever what is going on, and they are told to keep it to themselves. First, they didn't understand it and second, it would be of special significance to them later. What did it mean to the disciples? Very little. What did it mean to God? Why did God do this? Why did God bring Moses and Elijah back from heaven and put them upon earth to go through this experience? I don't know, but maybe God in some way is like us. He was a proud parent. Is there anything more satisfying to a parent than to see your child whom you have prayed for and nourished and loved to be on their own and accomplishing exactly what you equipped them to do? Could God have been sharing some of those heavenly, parental feelings here? "This is my Son, whom I have chosen; and he is doing exactly what I want him to do."

When I was thirteen and fourteen years old, I played on a baseball team. One of the men who helped coach and train us in a

110

different and special way was R. L. Penland. We all called him "Snuffy." He was a wonderful man. He loved youth. His son, Greg, was the catcher on our team and was a great athlete. During that year, R. L. Penland died prematurely. The Emma Sansom High School in Gadsden, Alabama, gives an award every year, the R. L. Penland Memorial Trophy, to the most outstanding athlete of the school. One of the very first to receive that award was his son, Greg. All of that training, nourishing, and love was so concentrated into that young man by his father that he was carrying on just as if R. L. was there. Could God be the proud heavenly parent here? I think that could be true.

Very possibly, God is also realizing what a tremendous risk he has taken. He put his reputation on the line in Jesus. Think about that just a moment. I heard this statement this past week: "God bared his face in Jesus Christ." God said to an entire world, "If you want to know what I am like, look at Jesus." God risked his reputation on Jesus of Nazareth, and don't think for one minute Jesus did not have the choice to do otherwise, or else the temptations would have no meaning. In every situation, Jesus did exactly what the Father wanted him to do. No wonder God was proud.

What did it mean to Jesus? Understanding the mind of the Son of God is not the easiest thing in the world to do. First of all, we begin to understand that Jesus does very little here. Jesus is not the actor, God is the actor and Jesus is the one being acted upon, yet Jesus receives the benefits of the transfiguration experience. Here, in a moment of prayer and retreat, Jesus is encouraged and energized and receives the very hand of God upon his life and ministry.

Can you imagine what it meant for Jesus to hear the voice of the Father? The one he wanted to please most of all to say, "I am pleased with you. You're on the right track. You're doing what I want you to do. Go ahead and do it." I think that Jesus went back to the task of setting his face toward Jerusalem, of suffering and death and humiliation on the cross. The task had not changed, the circumstances had not changed, his mission and ministry had not changed, the hatred of the groups that were plotting against him had not changed. Nothing had changed, yet everything had changed, because now he was energized and invigorated and encouraged by the Father.

Several of us were at a WMU convention and others were at a minister's and spouse's retreat. This was a time of recharging the batteries, being energized and encouraged. It was a wonderful time of hearing speakers such as Dr. Paul Simmons and Dr. Fred Craddock. It was great not being an actor, but being acted upon, and, for just a few moments, letting someone else take care of our spiritual needs. If Jesus of Nazareth, the sinless, perfect, Son of God, had to have a time of retreat and prayer and revitalization and encouragement, how much more do we need that? Jesus went from this experience encouraged and energized by the Father.

Maybe we sold the disciples a little short. I really believe this was a meaningful experience to them. They possibly did not understand its significance then, but by the fact that it is recorded in three of our gospels shows that it made an unforgettable impression upon their minds. Why? They had seen the future. They had seen this man called Jesus of Nazareth being transformed by the very Spirit of God, to the point that his face shone with the glory of God and God spoke. He was transfigured. He was not only transfigured then, he would be transfigured later on. They had seen the future.

When a doctor reads the x-rays and has knowledge of the patient's future, he has a present responsibility to act upon that knowledge. A stockbroker gets advance knowledge that a company is about to be bought over by another company and he or she has to act responsibly. In light of that future knowledge in the present, the disciples had seen the future. They knew what was going to happen.

They knew that Jesus was going to be victorious over death, hell, and the grave. They knew that Jesus was the only begotten Son of God, full of the glory of God. They had seen the future, but they had responsibilities for it in the present. They had been privileged to be in a special moment never to be repeated in all of history. When we are on those mountaintop experiences and see the future, then we have a present responsibility to help others to see and understand.

112

Later, when Jesus was transfigured, it all fit together. "Let me tell you about it. Let me tell you what Moses said. Let me tell you what Elijah said." They understood it as Jesus was preparing to go to Jerusalem and die. "Let me tell you about the future. We know what is going to happen."

It is our responsibility as Christians to see that others know about Jesus and understand about him as much as possible. We know the future belongs to Jesus. We know he will be victorious. Sometimes it doesn't seem that way — there are troubles, problems, temptations, worries, anxieties, conflicts, and hostilities. And we say victory?

I am a very poor golfer. When I'm playing and the performance of three other people depends upon me, often I hear, "Carver, watch the ball. Get in the right position. Watch the ball." When I played baseball, people were always telling me to watch the ball. Tennis — same way. When I played football, on defense particularly, they would say, "Now you don't know what they're going to run. You don't know the play they're going to execute. What you've got to do is watch the ball. Stay focused, and watch the ball." I think that is the message that we have for the world. We don't know what play the opposition is going to run so we must stay focused upon Jesus. We must get ourselves first of all, in the right position, in the right stance, living from the Father as the source for our lives, and stay focused upon Jesus Christ. Watch the ball. Become disciplined. Become focused.

Just as God encouraged Jesus, it is our business to encourage others. Does the church have a more meaningful ministry than the ministry of encouragement? Just as Jesus was revitalized and invigorated and encouraged, is that not our ministry to a world that desperately needs a word of encouragement, a word of love, and of mercy?

Isn't it true that sometimes in the church we shoot our wounded, and the very people who need our help the most? We sometimes turn a cold shoulder to them. Just because someone has failed in one area of their life, what difference does it make? We may have failed in another area. We're all sinners. Could there be a greater ministry of the church than that of encouragement?

If Jesus, who never failed, needed encouragement, how much more do we who fail daily need a word of encouragement? "Hang in there. God is alive. God is with you even when you don't feel him." Some things are true, as Fred Craddock says, "Even when we're asleep. We have seen the future. We know. We've read the last page. We know where our world is going and we know in the end Jesus will be victorious."

In Rome in 1520, a young artist was dying at 37 years of age. He had just a few days left. How would he express himself as an artist in the last few days of his life? His name was Raphael. He chose to spend his dying hours painting *The Transfiguration*. He never finished, but he got one part completely finished and that was Jesus. The critics say that Jesus' garment is so white and glistening that no one could bleach it as white. Raphael stayed focused. He had seen the future and that future was a victorious Jesus. His way of telling the world was through his painting.

What's your way of telling the world about the victory of Jesus? When people see your life, will they see a victorious resurrected Jesus Christ? Are we helping others to understand that one day the dwelling place of God will be with men and he will live with them and they will be his people and he will be their God? He will wipe away every tear from their eyes. There will be no more death, no more mourning, crying, or pain; for the old order of things has passed away and behold all things have become new.

— Gary L. Carver

Sermons On The Gospel Readings

For Sundays In
Lent And Easter

*The Glory
Of It All!*

Donald Charles Lacy

Dedicated to the
High Street United Methodist Church
of Muncie, Indiana,
where I was baptized
and received into the church
in the spring of 1954

Preface

What is better than preaching, writing, and listening to sermons? Well, not much! All these events are opportunities for growth given to us by the Holy Spirit. The laity and clergy across our land are very privileged.

The holy season of Lent and Easter is a remarkably glorious time for professing Christians to celebrate. In fact, without this blessed time we have a mere philosophy of life and not a victorious faith!

These sermons have all been written after calling upon the Holy Spirit. Guidance was sought that the Word of God would be presented in all its magnificence and practicality, despite the imperfections of the writer and preacher.

Prayers are given that each comes alive from the printed page. In truth, the Holy Spirit makes or breaks our sermons! Nearly fifty years of preaching have taught me we are merely instruments and/or vehicles of God's Word.

Please read these sermons with serious joy. Preaching is a noble, spiritual art. Our faith is one which is never ultimately defeated and in our depths we know this beyond doubt. Always give thanks for the crucified and resurrected Christ.

A special word of thanks goes to Judy Marsh, an administrative secretary, committed to excellence.

Donald Charles Lacy

The Hard Sell

Our blessed Lord presses the issue. Do you or do you not want to be my disciple? If you do not, then it is with great sadness that your Savior must move on with those who are willing to fully commit themselves.

In our lives, each and every one of us receives Christ's invitation of discipline and abandonment of the world. No longer are we getting acquainted. We are being asked to come into a relationship at once glorious and painful. Yes, it comes to all of us — sooner or later.

It is like moving from an introductory offer, which we explore, and then deciding whether or not to buy into the entire program. There is a host of witnesses that function, I like to think, like a cheerleading team. They want us and plead with you and me to come into the most blessed fold of all.

There is nothing academic or even philosophical about all of this. It is more a matter of, "Do you or don't you?" — so much depends upon our answers. To avoid and evade over a period of time, perhaps years, is to say, "No." Are there regrets in this experience? You bet there are! We must be realistic.

Our Lord commands us to do that which is against our natural tendencies. After all, why shouldn't we show off our good deeds? Dear Jesus, you have called us to witness and others must see our splendid work! Surely we waste our time and energy by not displaying the giving spirit in our lives! If others don't know about these wonderful acts of discipleship, how can the world be expected to believe? Well, yes, that is you and me — at least — upon some occasions. Isn't it interesting and irritating how the problem seems to recur all during our lifetimes? Some of us may even have secret diaries that resemble *Saint Augustine's Confessions.*

The world says show off your achievements. The dear Lord says do your ministries in the quietude and holy secrecy that best serves his purpose. The world says we must not hide our good deeds and the more they are seen, the better. The world says don't restrain your natural tendencies of wanting others to see and especially reward, your accomplishments. Yes, the world keeps right on insisting that we are to look at how others view our expressed goodness, even if we have to hire a publicist! But our dear Lord has other plans and they are intended for the saving of our eternal souls. Often, this is a more clear-cut choice than we would like to admit.

There are those popular philosophers and theologians who believe in the innate goodness of man. They will tell you that at birth we are totally clean and rightly motivated. Whatever we do is simply a means to enhance a goodness we have had from the very beginning. In fact, serious religion of any variety may be an obstruction to our naturally intended growth. How do we answer this? If they are right, then the Adam and Eve story has no validity. Even more importantly, the coming of a Savior to right our wrongs — indeed, forgive our sins — is mostly hogwash. Granted, our Lord's request can be a "hard sell."

In all honesty, the "back to nature" theme and method of living can have its solidly desirable and suitable points. Who can argue with the promotion of clean air and pure water? Who can seriously challenge the call to relieve us of the pollution in our lives? In an environment which raises many crucial questions, we know the truth of this rightful quest. At the same time what would the most purified environment look like without the internal and very personal cleansing of Jesus Christ? It does not seem the proponents of pristine living conditions know quite what to do with that momentous and essential inquiry. Perhaps professing Christians have not spent enough time looking at and praying for our natural surroundings. Granted, but never at Jesus' expense!

Our Lord calls us to a depth the world does not know. To be an alien in this life has become a rather popular theme and topic in recent years. Of course, this is nothing new. The New Testament apprises us of this. While living out our lives among others, we are continually reminded of this state of affairs. In short, there is a difference — even qualitative — between committed followers of Christ and those who are minimally interested or not interested at all. Those of us who listen carefully to his voice have a struggle with this and it has a lot more to do with our lives than on Ash Wednesday once each year! We must learn to be content with our "alien" status.

The Master told his disciples it would be that way. He tells you and me — sometimes frequently — that's the way it is. We are on different wavelengths. We discover that our assumptions about life and even our most cherished beliefs do not strike a significant chord with those seemingly content to live as the world directs. Our best mode of behavior is to succumb to the blessed reality, in our case, that all is well with us because we have seen a great light in the darkness. Forbid we feel superior! Forbid we overlook the necessary Christlike compassion that is a beacon to an otherwise lost and dying world. Yes, our work (ministry) is cut out for us. It is an old/new battle.

One of the dangers that strangely poses itself in taking Saint Matthew's words with supreme seriousness is the subtle temptation of "self-elevation." How often we have seen the finest and best be virtually annulled by an attitude of thinking of ourselves too highly. To be separate and distinct as holy people somehow gets translated into "I am better than you are." The devil is much at work (and play) here! His twists and turns seem never to stop, as he persistently seeks to trick us into becoming more abomination than blessing. We are never truly big enough within ourselves to handle these fabrications and machinations. The Holy Spirit must be present.

It is always wise to remember that wherever the greatest spiritual success comes into being, there is likewise the greatest opportunity for the evil one to derail the highest and best we know. Pause

121

for a time and recollect the moments in your lives this has happened. We forget our common humanity and believe we are more than sinners saved by the grace of God! It is a slippery slope. We are called to invigorating celebration but can end up in debilitating frustration. Indeed, the vast majority of us are not called to hibernate in prayer on a faraway island. Our Lord instills within us the motivation and equips us to live out our days victoriously among other people. Some are saintly and some not so saintly! How fortunate we are.

Our Lord wants us to be "low profile" for the benefit of all. Virtually every word tells us exactly that in our text. Be a braggadocio if you must — but that is not the way of Christ. Sound the trumpets and call attention to your giving but don't label that Christ's way of doing things. Some of us have this ongoing itch to let others in on our good deeds, so they can — at least — smile with affirmation. If someone doesn't scratch it for us, we do it ourselves! Some might call this unfair and even unjust but for the moment let's be brutally honest. If we seek to stand out before others and take unlimited bows, how in the name of high heaven can we benefit anyone?

We are led by the Holy Spirit to benefit others. Why? For the simple reason that this is the behavior our Master lays before us and urges us to accept. Don't let others know you are fasting for them. If the Holy Spirit causes them to learn this precious thing is taking or has taken place, so be it. Most of us on such a journey know this happens from time to time. It is God's doing and not ours. His will and ways are always to have priority. Christ sets the pattern and we are to emulate him, come what may. So, the message is crystal clear — or is it? Again, there is this fallen nature that rears its ugly and sinister head. It says that if we do something good, others should know.

You may say, "But, pastor, we all have the need to be praised by others." If that is our basic motivation, then as the scripture says — we have received our reward. How can we possibly serve others by constantly demanding attention and thanks in our own ways? The answer to that is obvious. We can't. Among our cumulative experiences, there must be dozens and even hundreds of good people we have known who insist on being given credit for their good deeds, monetary or otherwise. Really, is it praise or sincere affirmation from others we need? Ponder that for a time and you will see the chasm separating the two. The most affirming person in the universe is our Lord!

Treasures on earth are often summed up in property and money. We can't seem to keep from putting price tags on everyone and everything. Who and what are you to a world that is immersed in such a mentality? We even put a monetary sticker on those in our sacred ordained ministry! Just maybe, on judgment day our Lord will implement "the last shall be first and the first shall be last"! Then, the worldly label of dollar bills on each head will run amuck and he will have a free-for-all on his hands because we could never think in any other way. Perhaps we will then come begging to enter the heavenly gates, being freed from our secular mindset. Is this an excursion into a fanciful and unrealistic world? Frankly, that is doubtful and it is time for clergy to confess.

Our Lord gives a glimpse of where lasting riches are. It comes down to a choice, doesn't it? If we but look carefully at our passage of holy scripture, the obvious is before us. If we choose to play psychological games and attempt to rationalize our human nature into something of pure beauty, we have missed this lofty Ash Wednesday message. As we know, such a choice is continually before us. It is not a matter of a one-time answer set in cement. If we fail to get it the first time, it is still there. Even if we fail many times, it is in the recesses of our souls. To have once received and implemented it is no guarantee we live by its wisdom.

Every so-called secular or worldly accomplishment in our world can be taken from us. Who knows the amount of money, time, and energy that goes into the print or other media to explain away someone's good deeds? Those sorts of shenanigans appear to go on all the time. The calculated deceit in today's world stretches our imaginations! Only what we have done for Christ and consequently stored up in heaven is free from such onslaughts. It is a simple, spiritual truth but human nature is often hell-bent on discrediting it. Our saved souls yearn for permanent treasures. Only by living Christ's ways can they be there at our death.

123

If we place our hearts in this world's treasures, we have a big problem. It is going to evaporate or worse! The titans of today and the past have all had to deal with it. The little folks, like you and me, also have to deal with it. We can condemn such people and even — in our own minds — send them to hell, but that by no means indicates that they are going there. Some of us have laid up treasures in heaven and we are not so concerned about who has the biggest treasure, but that what we do have is safe and secure. Yes, that is the way it is for those of us, who in our many sins of omission and commission, have sought to conquer, with the Holy Spirit's full assistance, our fallen nature.

To trust any human being totally and completely — almost without exception — is a big mistake, perhaps catastrophic. Not to trust God totally and completely is a mistake we cannot afford to make. If he is wrong, there is no hope for anyone. If he is right through his Son, Jesus Christ — and he always is — even our lowly common sense tells us to pay close attention! To be sure, we are in an arena taxing our hearts and minds. Our perceptions and perspectives can be outlandishly wrong. But we certainly do have a glimpse, don't we? We are not blind beggars with no shepherd and physician. The Holy Spirit is among us and the law of the Savior's love pursues us, seeking our healing submission.

At the beginning of Lent, it is time to move beyond our convenient and well-accepted Christian practice. It is time to move boldly (or humbly) away from showing others we belong to Christ and to please watch what we do! Away with worship attendance mostly to be seen. Away with prayers having more to do with others hearing our perfectly spoken words. Away with giving all of our money in checks, so there is an accurate record for the church and the IRS. Away with ushering and greeting to show we are active in the church. Bring on the anonymity for which our blessed Lord calls! Bring on the blessedness wrought by not letting the left hand know what the right hand is doing!

The world has an ongoing lust for security. How can we keep our stocks and bonds from slipping away from us? How can we keep our popularity and have others always think well of us? How can we secure a place for ourselves in history forever and ever? In all cases, we are living in quicksand, which may devour us at any-time and most any place. As committed Christians, we know our treasures can be sealed in heaven, where neither moth nor rust consumes. We also know our treasures can be safe, where thieves do not break in and steal. It is a call for tears of joy because we have found the "pearl of great price." The Lord holds our treasures and will present them to us on that great day!

Testing Time

To live the Christian life is to be tested. As day follows night and night follows day, we experience it all of our days. The deeper we go, the more testing comes upon us. So, there is nothing unique about all of this. If we expect our daily walk with Christ to be any different, we are guilty of self-deception.

Sometimes it is really severe and we wonder about its cessation. Patience becomes virtually non-existent. Strength seems to go out the window and we languish not only in pain but borderline disillusionment. They are not fun times! The sooner such episodes go on their way, we are greatly relieved.

As we attempt to survey the ages of church history, aren't we strengthened to know there are many similar experiences? It is our common lot but let us not be content to stop there. It is not only Christians who face these times, all of humanity finds it omnipresent. That is the way it is!

Before we begin on a non-productive negative binge, let's recount the times our testing has led to blessings untold. Our Lord has not abandoned us and, in fact, he makes a point of reminding us of the harshness of his own testing that came upon him as God's earthly Son.

Are we able to live by bread alone? To live in this world is to be engulfed in the material side of it. To be hungry is to be hungry! Yes, our dear Lord must have been famished. It would not take nearly forty days for you and me to reach that stage. Could we even go one week or ten days? In the depths of our souls we have,

127

at least, some answers. It sure would be "tough stuff." Imagine all of the hunger pangs to be experienced. Visualize all the days of good cooking that we could not enjoy. It begins to be not only a potentially inconvenient experience, but one of honest-to-goodness discomfort.

We know what our Lord's point is, don't we? He wants us to shift our fixation on "bread and potatoes" to something that transcends the necessities of this world. Come on now, disciple, let's get serious about things beyond our favorite restaurants and church dinners. Granted, the food industry seemingly at every turn tries to persuade us it's time to eat or drink. Do you get the idea we are expected to get up eating and drinking and retire at night still filling our mouths? Maybe it is not quite that bad but expand it to include an array of things we are supposed to purchase. Advertising can be so disarming. The devil can be so slick and not be close to a wilderness.

Some decidedly spiritual souls have learned that the more they deny themselves of food and drink, the more they sense the closeness of Jesus, their Christ. Those who have gone to their beds from sheer exhaustion must truly be receiving accolades in heaven. The stories are many and reliable sources convey to us their validity. Church history is punctuated by those dear and precious ones who know firsthand the truthful reality our Master presents. Praise God for these jewels who keep on sparkling in our midst! What is the secret to their impact? They simply and responsibly have taken the Man of Galilee seriously. Are you and I among them? What has the Holy Spirit said to you about this?

The materialism of America is widely — yes, universally — known. For all of our goodness and attempted good deeds, there is a shadow bringing question marks. Perhaps, underlying our witness is the fear of not living by bread alone. Our lives have become so saturated by consumerism, we are hardly able to think outside of such a mentality. The late Pope John Paul II spoke to our spiritual deficiency charitably but firmly. Like most instances, we need to pay attention to his teachings — both Catholic and non-Catholic. Being familiar with actual deprivation and practicing holy disciplines, his message is of one healing our depths and not our surfaces. Our automobiles, homes, clothes, food, and drink are no substitutes for something far more precious.

Are we able to live without worldly power? Isn't power downright fascinating? It cuts across every segment of society and finds its way into even the most humble situations. Every pastor — after some years in the ministry — knows he/she does not have any real choice; it is built into the fabric of who and what we are. To refuse to deal with it is to deal with it in ways not likely to be fruitful. The finest people in our churches, rightly motivated, deal with it. When they are mature and spiritually oriented, they are great assets to pastors. They can make potentially disastrous situations turn into things of great beauty.

But remember, Jesus was promised all the kingdoms of the world, provided he worshiped the devil. It is also wise for you and me to remember that the devil is not likely to promise us nearly as much! Yet, the temptation to the wrong kind of power or the exercise of it is much with us. Never underestimate the evil in our midst; it comes to us in forms of goodness but, in reality, demonic excesses are waiting to destroy. To believe we can escape the sly and usually hidden agendas of evil is to be guilty of self-deception. Our Achilles' heel is often over something or someone, seemingly insignificant. Is there paranoia at work? Maybe. However, just because we are paranoid doesn't mean the devil isn't after us!

The rightful exercise of power is what the world always needs and — to be sure — what our churches always need. The devil was coming at our Lord for all the wrong reasons. To be brief, our Lord was pressured to back away from his calling and become an earthly dictator. Don't the lowly like you and I discover that likewise this can be our plight? As long as we sell our souls to Satan, we can have power in abundance for our own exaltation. You want control over the official board or trustees — the devil can make it happen! Is that overstating our case? Perhaps — but don't deny that we often teach the concept of unconditional acceptance. The church could do so much good — if I had complete control of the board!

There is such a mixing of worldly and spiritual power, it's hard to know the difference. Our answer to the quandary is found in abandonment to the Holy Spirit. The scriptures tell us that as our sure and certain guide. As we give ourselves, pastor and people, to the Lord without conditions attached, good and evil begin to separate before our Spirit-infused eyes. It is not for us to know all the whereofs and wherefores. It is humbling, but always true, you and I cannot know everything there is to know about people, places, and things! Our love can be "patient and kind" but that does not mean we know all the details of any situation. Our love can be free of arrogance and rudeness, but that does not mean we are filled with genius.

Are we able to live in the absence of physical miracles? If we are sons and daughters of the living God, why don't we just test him by showing unbelievers that we shall be miraculously rescued? Maybe we could make a trip to the Sears Tower and announce in advance we are going to jump from more than 100 stories. Then, we will be quick to point out that God always comes to the aid of his children. The angels will drop from the heavens and we will be unscathed. Does that sound like the beginning of a profitable Hollywood movie? Well, it is a way of putting you and me — to some extent — in Jesus' place. Maybe we should have picked out the very top of the tallest spire at one of the world's great cathedrals.

Indeed, it is testing time for that Jewish fellow barely into his ministry. As usual, the devil is crafty and insinuates that it's time the Son of God prove to the world that no one can hurt him. This could turn out to be quite a media event! It could even be promoted in such a way that gamblers would have their odds and people across the globe would have their eyes glued to the tubes. Human nature is drawn to physical miracles. We like it right there before our eyes. If Jesus takes the bait, then his Father will certainly see to it that he is not crushed and — in fact — not even scratched. It is a melodramatic scene and some still ponder, "What if Jesus had tried it?"

We have all known those precious people who seem to be waiting on a sign from heaven that involves a physical miracle. It is never enough to note and appreciate two people who formerly hated one another now loving one another. This is the wrong kind of miracle and doesn't sell much! They will insist the real test, where Christians must succeed, is physical especially before crowds who can attest to authenticity. The folks in Jesus' time were much like

130

that. You are God's Son, well, that's fine; now let's see you perform and, if you are successful, we will believe. Credibility is always necessary in these matters. Flamboyance is not. Showing off one's special relationship to God that can even manipulate, my friends, is a bit too much.

Faith healers always seem to be — sooner or later — a mixed bag. Maybe we want them to perform so desperately, we will cut some corners to prove physical miracles. In the name of God, pray to him that is not the case! "With God all things are possible" is so hopeful and many of us believe just that. Yet, as the saying goes, "Not all things are prudent." God's will is invariably the best and fruitful in ways we can only imagine. While the holy scriptures speak of great changes physically in certain passages, this was true only in a few cases. Thousands received ministry but, apparently, only a few were healed in a physical way. Only God knows for sure.

Are we able to live in continual watchfulness? Note that the devil has finished every test and departs but only until an opportune time. That's ominous and even scary! Saint Luke makes it quite clear: The great deceiver is not at all finished. Imagine the trash talk that Jesus heard and most likely during his most trying moments. The underlying message is present and it speaks volumes about our blessed Lord's authenticity: He was a human being tested, only more so, so no one could prove he was merely going through the actions. If he had been solely fabricating his temptations how could he even remotely be considered the Savior? If the devil was programmed not to win, have we been dealt a crooked hand?

Where the most significant and relevant point comes into play is in our willingness to be watchful at all times. Lent teaches us many wonderful and most helpful things and certainly this is one of them. It's a good and marvelous state of affairs to be happy in the Lord. It is also a required attitude of heart and mind to know that such bliss is never all the time; days (and nights) of temptation and testing are sure to come. Will we be ready? It mostly depends upon our spiritual adaptability. We never assume Satan is through

131

testing us. Our best assumption is that he will be back again and again.

But how do we keep from falling prey to incessantly looking under rocks and behind doors? Who can be ready for the guy who has been deceiving precious people since the beginning of time? Those are questions that must be asked. They are deeply spiritual, regardless of how they are phrased. The host of witnesses and those now living on this earth help us. They have traveled and are traveling the road. Have you and I been tempted more than anyone else? Are we being picked on? Why is it that some days the devil is a lot closer than God? Yes, most of us know the feeling and it doesn't do much for our self-image!

The good book tells us the fruit of the Spirit includes faithfulness, humility, and self-control. Now, we are onto how we can live a victorious Christian life and deal with temptations of various sorts day in and day out. "All things are possible with God" is not a cliché we bring out and brag about periodically. There is a harmony with the Holy Spirit which makes this true beyond all doubts. We are not losers, except in the world's sight, going to and fro wondering about God's presence. The only sure thing in life (and death) is the Father, Son, and Holy Spirit. All else pales in insignificance and eventual powerlessness. Tell the devil he can't have you. But be sure you do so by telling him God makes this possible and you don't. To know our acquired spiritual strength is to become weak ... and honest.

Three temptations that are a part of our spiritual memories need to be re-evaluated and studied to aid us in our walk with the Lord. At each juncture the testing is a grave matter. The devil is attempting to come at him at his greatest vulnerability. Does he need — desperately so — food and drink? Yes. Does he need to show the world — as the Jewish Messiah — the kingdoms all belong to him because he is God's Son? One could certainly make a case for that. Does he need to do something spectacular, especially of a physical nature, to illustrate control over the laws the Father had originally set in place? Well, that would help his case in the eyes of a lot of searching human beings.

Regardless of the persistent poignancy of our Lord's time of rough and tough testing, the experience comes down to you and me. What have we learned from his horrendous battle with the enemy of every person? As we prepare to celebrate the resurrection of the Christ, Lent becomes that fertile period of self-denial — perhaps of temptations of our own choosing. Ours is a costly discipleship that says we shall not be defeated by the one who would delight in sending us to hell. The purpose of testing is to make us spiritually strong and steadfast. Praises be to God we are his people and he will be with us in all our trials and tribulations. Count it a privilege to experience them!

Lent 2
Luke 13:31-35

No Intimidation

Boldness is necessary to accomplish ministry, especially that which is prophetic and points to judgment. Our dear Lord is boldly assertive and wants there to be no doubt about what his Father has sent him to accomplish. He provides both a lesson and model for us.

Our timidity in the face of odds is not becoming to those who profess to follow Christ. Only when it covers a determined soul for the faith is it in keeping with our commitment. Let's face it, some of the most timid souls in church can be downright raucous at athletic events!

We are called always to learn from the Man of Galilee and sometimes that is among the most simple style of living. He was not a milquetoast kind of guy! All of his heart, mind, soul, and strength were set in motion to fulfill his destiny, as directed by his Father in heaven.

If we are looking for fearless leadership, we have found it. He is daring and will not be denied. Some of us would like to see ourselves cut from that fabric and, praise God, sometimes we see miracles happen. The grace of God is allowed to work and a powerful love becomes there for all to view.

It was a time of poking serious fun at Herod Antipas. A pastor taught me long ago nothing succeeds quite like well-placed and intense humor. There is a real art to this strategy of ministry. One who is not skilled in this area and out of step with the Holy Spirit most likely will find he/she is on the agenda to be ousted! Acquiring such a method, hopefully on your knees, is truly valuable. We

135

are prevented from becoming doormats for a good reason. If your superior wants you to rethink your style and, perhaps, crawl back to the parsonage or rectory in submission, simply point to Jesus' precedent.

In a way, it is somewhat out of character for our Lord. From one point of view, it looks like Herod is being unnecessarily baited, even negatively provoked, but that may be a way of backing away from a style that causes great discomfort. Some will quickly say that people have enough frustration in this world and why cause them any more? Well, we can be apologetic and even appeasing without initially recognizing it for what it is. Frequently, blunt honesty is what it takes in a world caught up in half-truths and outright lies. Praise be to our Savior and Lord, we don't have to be buried in a casket before our time.

There is the temptation to be a "smart mouth" and tell people off. That's why maturity and the guidance of the Holy Spirit are mandatory. We have all known those who have used the technique to tell off our enemies and ridicule them, even in public. Doing this deed may make you feel better for the moment, but what about tomorrow, even a year from now? There is a saying in some of our denominations: We had better watch what we say to a colleague; he/she may turn out to be our boss. Some of us who have been around a long time have seen exactly that happen. What does all of this do for Christ and the church?

We can't help but admire the way our Lord gets in the face of some of the Pharisees, as well as Herod. Are we willing to take that admiration and implement it, separate and apart from our preconceived agendas and outright prejudices? So much depends on how close Christ is to us and whether or not we are willing to be obedient. His expectations and ours may be something quite different. At any rate, there is nothing quite like throwing down the gauntlet in the face of those who would cause our ministries to falter or much worse. How much goes unaccomplished because we simply are not bold! There is no good reason to complicate the matter. We serve a risen Lord whose forthrightness always challenges. Aren't we fortunate?

It is a moment of putting well-meaning Pharisees in their place. As some thinkers have indicated in recent years, the Pharisees were much misunderstood. It seems, until current scholarship came along, we didn't know there was more than one kind or variety. For centuries, there was the general acceptance of their hypocrisy and strong opposition to Jesus. While we cannot know for sure their motives in warning him, we can't but wonder just maybe it was out of the goodness of their hearts they did not want to see him seriously injured or killed. We have learned to be "pharisaic" but that does not of necessity point to odious self-righteousness.

Whether they actually took Jesus' message or not, remains an open question. What we most significantly know is his answer to those who appear to be protective. He was not going to be intimidated. He gave them understanding in a language which could not be misunderstood there was no way "that fox" was going to get in the way of his mission. If he did and in a way he did, then he best know the "Jesus express" would, nevertheless, be on schedule and accomplish its purpose. Thereby, the influence of these Pharisees would not be one allowing for retreat of the Son of God. We might conjecture as to what would have happened had he listened to them and sought a more diplomatic approach.

Don't we have to do the same thing Jesus did? Aren't there times that well-meaning people have to be put in their place in order for us to get our work done? If pastors blink in some circumstances, they may very well lose their credibility. If pastors pander to those who want them to avoid conflict at all cost, have they not compromised their ministries? Granted, some are confrontational and angry enough to shoot off a cannon to kill a horsefly. Such pastors usually need time away on a regular basis for solitude and regaining perspective. Yes, those of us who have been around for many years know what this is all about! We must be certain we are attuned to the Holy Spirit.

We are counseled by the Holy Spirit to be very careful differentiating between our Lord's dictates and our personal, questionable agendas. Human nature can tell us to call down fire from heaven on most anyone who disagrees with us! That layman/laywoman trying to run the church might be sincerely looking out for everyone concerned. So, it is often a delicate matter and one that bears our best-inspired judgment. Perhaps pastoring churches, like no other calling, tests our quality of compassion and strength of decision making. It seems some pastors are invariably in trouble in their parishes and for the right reasons. In my experience, in-depth growth in the parish is sooner or later closely related to our unwillingness to be intimidated.

It was a prophetic declaration of what was to come. Our Lord was not trying to slip up on anyone! It was as though he was pointing out, "Here it is, folks. Pay attention to what I am saying because this is the way it is going to be. You may not believe it or be able to fill in the blank spaces, but this is the way it is going to be." If you are like me, that draws upon the deepest resources in my soul and produces respect for him par excellence. We worship a Lord who is mystical by his very nature but not esoterically removed from us. While we must not make the error of reducing him to our levels, likewise we must not push him so far into the clouds that we lose touch.

What an incomparable faith we have! It absolutely refuses to be intimidated and put on a level where compromises crowd out its essential nature. Of course, this is what we learn or relearn during the purifying and nourishing season of Lent. In a sense, today we appear to be returning to the ancient world with its countless numbers of gods and goddesses. All about us are major religions that have broken into numerous facets and — perhaps more importantly — pagan systems and behaviors across the globe. The number of Protestant denominations no longer has a monopoly on this! Yet, towering above it all there is the revelation of our Savior and Lord who told the world 2,000 years ago what he was going to do and then he did it.

The field of prophecy is an area of study, at least for one veteran pastor, remaining something of an enigma. Who knows the precious people who have been led astray by those on an ego trip contrived by Satan or disastrously, innocently wrong? Intimidation almost always seems to have a part in a sometimes-gross monster, spiritually killing and maiming. When it comes to this field,

138

we are nudged to keep in mind that even Jesus admits only his Father knows when the Second Coming will occur. Praise God from whom all blessings flow Jesus the Christ reveals to us all we need. His ministry was announced and consummated. We are not among the most privileged people — we *are* the most privileged people!

Jesus is set on finishing his work or ministry. Are we set on finishing ours? It is an inquiry of colossal proportions. It speaks to our destiny and the understanding of it. We may not like it, but we have it before us in some form every day of our lives. When we come into a right relationship with the Father through his Son, Jesus Christ, our needed workload begins to unfold. We are shown directions, aspects, and categories on the horizon. As Saint Paul learned, we do not see them always clearly and distinctly — if ever. We are to finish well and that means spiritual success abounding in great joy. The Lamb of God who takes away the sins of the world grants us mercy and then lasting peace.

It is a death knell for those whose rejection is generations old. The disclosure of disclosures comes before the world for all to behold. First it comes to the Jewish people — God's chosen people. It begins the gathering of pulling his people together. It is as though a hen is gathering her brood under her wings and there are the reluctant chicks who refuse to come all the way. The fight against what is intended for them is underway and continues to this very moment. Many Gentiles find their way and join the blessed congregation of the redeemed. His own people rejected him and, to a large extent, do so even now. The picture is that of God Almighty dutifully beckoning his children to come home and they refuse.

Let us not become borderline anti-Jewish and bewail their missed opportunities. We have enough to do to handle our own! Generation after generation has had witnesses for much of the world. Indeed, there have been and are innumerable disciples of the Christ — imperfect though they be — who have paraded their Christian virtues before our very eyes. Some keep wondering when the Jews by and large are going to accept their Messiah. This is God's business! When are we going to receive our Messiah with completeness and finality? Such an inquiry is placed squarely before us. We all have families in which the rejection is generations old and growing. Lent calls us to take inventory.

"Blessed is the one who comes in the name of the Lord." We knew him by way of the blessed Virgin Mary, John the Baptist, his apostles, crucifixion, and resurrection. Each segment is there for you and me to study. Each is there also for our gratitude and ongoing direction. It seems that if we have missed something or someone essential, it is our fault. Our belligerence and pride are present in ways that should humble us, bringing to us the probability of salvation. What shall a man or woman present in exchange for his/her soul? So, our Lord was not intimidated; therefore, why should we be? These are superb questions during the challenging days before crucifixion/resurrection!

Rejection is such a nasty word. We deal with it on racial, ethnic, gender, social, and political bases. It is a universal trait to be recognized: No one wants to be rejected. Then, cutting across all these categories and more, too, we discover rearing its ugly head is the rejection of Jesus Christ. This is the supreme refusal! But, dear friends, it does not have to be that way. In our depths, we know it does not have to be that way. Again and again, far too many times to count, our Savior and Lord calls and woos us to come to him and, in time, enjoy eternity with him. He finished his work centuries ago and it is there for all to see. Is there a justifiable reason to die without him? If there is, please share it with some of us!

Our Lord would not be run over by the political boss in the area. You can be sure Herod Antipas sought only to hurt, compromise, or kill him. How refreshing and brave for our hero to stand up to him, indicating he was on a mission and no one was going to stop him. Our Lord was meek and mild in some ways but never one to back away from his mission, which meant the horrors of the cross. He is the standard whereby you and I are measured. Are we willing to die for others, especially those we don't even know? He was obedient to the very end. Placed before us is a gargantuan order of bravery and courage.

It is said many times and places that everyone has a price. In other words, we can be intimidated in the right situation by the right person. Well, that includes you and me! Often this comes

140

about by threats to our families, specifically our spouses and children. Every married pastor knows the reality of such a state of affairs in the parishes. We can be pushed in different directions because our loved ones will suffer — if we don't knuckle under. A devout person said that's the best case for celibacy! Give that suggestion some thought and be reminded as the Holy Spirit blows wherever it chooses, perhaps in our day and time even more so, we must be open to forms of ministry never thought viable. It is truly a great day to do ministry!

More Time

Who can speak of "justice" in any long-standing and helpful way? It is a subject that fits many who write commentaries but we discover in most cases they are woefully inadequate. You and I, lay and clergy, deal with it almost daily and much of the time when we would rather not do so.

It is a theme seemingly as old as history itself. Indeed, when did we not speak and write about it? The Old Testament (Hebrew Scripture) has numerous references to our topic. In that classic verse of Micah, he reminds us "to do justice." Our civilization has been much influenced by the Judeo-Christian viewpoints.

Our legal systems, both civil and religious, provide ways of knowing what is expected of us in behavior. The scales, sooner or later, are always there to do the weighing. In recent years it seems religious courts have become more important. After all, it is a trying time of sorting out the guilty and innocent.

While our preaching may seek to avoid or limit it, we discover that is hardly the case. Our intentions are aboveboard but the reality of living causes our concerns to come into the picture. So we do the best we possibly can.

Fortunately, justice was, is, and shall be in God's hands. There is a safety net here, isn't there? To classify those who are worse sinners than others or decide who has had enough time to be fruitful ultimately is in the Almighty's hands and not ours. For many of us such truth is consoling and gives us reason to look at today and the future both humbly and positively. Sometimes during periods of special stress, we are summoned in love to become patient and wait on God. How good this truly is! How difficult it may turn out to be! In these relationships we can gain strength.

Jesus warns us over and over again not to be judgmental. For one thing, he points out our utter lack of ability. For another, it poisons the people of stature, who can at times forget their relationship to God and others. In brief, we can be rightly motivated and still not get the message. How often we have experienced this in the life of the church! Assessing fines in parishes may not help us at all in regard to calling where God wants us to go, however, not to apply church discipline can be more than scandalous; it may very well be hypocritically disgraceful. Wow, what a can of odious worms we can open.

You and I need to know and openly admit that God sees our frailty and inadequacy. The concept we are speaking of tends to land us, at least, on two different sides. Perhaps, we wish with all our hearts that was not so but it certainly is. There are situations when the sides are so many, we can end up in a kind of nihilism. Nevertheless, this is our lot for the world in which we live.

Can you think of a time when you did not want God in charge of justice? Probably, we all can and that is when it involves a loved one or some figure in whom we have great confidence. Our salvation, so to speak, is found in remembering God has no beginning or end. He always has been and always will be. So, justice at the moment may be seen in time as either good or bad. But, as the saying goes "don't move to judgment too soon." Only our Creator and Redeemer has the wherewithal to handle such a heavy and complicated matter. Fairness is what God says it is. It may not appear so, but try peeking into the next century and the one after that. Remember, oh man and woman, you are dust and to dust you shall return!

Mercifully, we have today to remedy a faulty relationship with God. These words are another way of saying, "Today is the day of salvation." If this has become a cliché, it is a very good one. We have learned in our day and time how important relationships are. We may have even gone overboard in elevating the necessity of human interaction. If that is the case, we still have a lot of work to do in relationship with the Father, Son, and Holy Spirit! Mind you,

144

these are not three gods but one perfectly united and working in total harmony. Grant we would never be confused in this classic understanding of who and what God is.

So, how is it in our relationship with God? It is an inquiry always on the table. Why? Because our entire lives and deaths are directly linked to it. There may not be tomorrow but there is always today. The finest people I have known have patterned their spiritual goings and comings in this context. They followed our blessed Lord's advice to let tomorrow take care of tomorrow. There is an undeniable and always urgent closeness here. There may or may not be opportunities to straighten out our relationship to God in the hereafter. While the ancient church, along with some of our Christian friends believe so, there is pause for all of us. If the opportunity is here, why wait? According to reputable teachers, spurning the Holy Spirit is unforgivable.

Attempt to count the times the Spirit of the living God is present, urging us to make peace with him who is all and in all. Grant mercy to us, oh, God, and we beg of you to apply justice mercifully! Some things are so basic to us and only by deliberate avoidance do we move from the truly good things intended for us. Brothers and sisters, that is for you and me. We are not speaking of heavy theology and extended periods of dialogue. Yes, and who needs a whole series of retreats and seminars to tell us what we already know? While quality events such as these are helpful for some people, who does not already perceive God in his/her life? Indeed, our needs may be decidedly more social than theological.

Spiritual direction has become very important in the last two generations. It has cut across all denominational boundaries and most all of us are in favor of it. So much spiritual growth appears to have come from it. But, let's ask some questions. Have some become virtually dependent on it? Do some have to consult their director before action or no action all the time? Can it become so all encompassing we must consult our director, even to tell us simple things we innately know? These questions are not in any sense to be taken as cynical. They are to elevate the most priceless connection of all: our personal relationship with Jesus Christ, Savior and Lord.

Gratefully, our lives and deaths must be seen in opportunities. We admit there are just so many opportunities and we are correct, at least, as far as we can determine. We have an ongoing impediment of being finite! Yet, this truly is a good and wholesome way of coping with life and death. As affluent Americans, many of us know what it is to have ample financial resources. Many retirees have time and reasonably good health. Indeed, some of them work wonders and do much-needed ministry. We are indebted to them over and over. When we are able to add some goodness to another's life, every day can become a beautiful thing to behold.

It is amazing — yes, even fascinating — to observe our lives and others, as they relate to opportunities. Some of us are truly grateful and can hardly wait to get up every morning to see what the day brings. Woven into all of that, of course, is God's justice. We are called to perceive and utilize each and every opportunity. Pastors are privileged in the highest and best sense. For example, people trust us with their weddings and funerals. Usually, we are paid a sum of money. Not everyone thinks we should take it but many of us do because we can take whatever amount it is and give it away, hopefully in cash and anonymously. These can be unique and heaven-sent events!

As we minister to people in the parishes, occasionally we come across those who are near death's door and claim they have missed too many opportunities. Their entire stream of thought and conversation is one of allowing so much of life to escape unfulfilled. It can be a dreary time of sadness and heartbreak. Sensitive pastors and laity struggle with what to say to them. After all, if they are eighty years of age, what do we say to them? Do we suggest they pray for more time? Do they pray God's justice will be greatly tempered by his mercy? Do we pressure them to confess their sins and start anew? The list of questions can go on and on. Most of all, we must impress upon them that God still loves them.

One of the paramount lessons we can teach our children and grandchildren is to spot opportunities that will not only benefit them, but others as well. To put it in media is one thing but to give firsthand illustrations is quite another. Of course, it is not an either/or situation; it is a both/and full opportunity. We can be highly

146

selective. That might play well at first. Then, we can move to showing them to live in our world is to have continual chances for doing good to others and for ourselves. Granted, the wrong mindset can grab for doing evil and implementing bad things. However, why even introduce them to such negativity? As they become older, they will rather quickly see the downside to opportunities.

Magnetically, we know there is a solution in our yearning. Justice is always and forever in God's hands. Our limitations will not allow us to see all of this to its end. Only God will be presiding now and forevermore. But there is a certain magnetism, isn't there? The Holy Spirit draws us to what is right and profitable. We do so knowing love is patient and kind; furthermore, it is not jealous or boastful. Those who have grown up in religious families know these truisms better than most. Give thanks for family trees that cultivated religious principles now and set in motion for the future.

We love our blessed Lord's kingdom and we are drawn to it. In worship, study, and prayer we sense these are ways not only to come to his kingdom but to stay in it all our days. It is a magnificent scene that never ever loses its magnetism. The lure of its lovely gardens and luscious fruit remains intact. Only the subtle temptations of the devil and sometimes horrific onslaughts he sends cloud our days and give nearly overwhelming darkness to our nights. The best of all is that the completion of our journey will find us safe and sound in his kingdom, never to be threatened again. Why be downcast, except temporarily? The king of the universe is on his throne and no one — not even all the devils in hell — can change that.

Lent places before us more than a time of preparation to celebrate the resurrection of our Christ and God. It speaks to us about justice the year around and how seasons come and go but his justice abides forever. While it is a portion of the church year, it influences everything else we do because the crucifixion/resurrection event is the primary basis upon which our holy faith is built. The solution to our yearning is there in blazing and blissful truth that seeks to draw others to its forever-living message. Yes, we are to do more than politely go through the motions of Lent and its disciplines! Can worldly and secular powers offer us anything approximating this? Absolutely not.

Count your blessings and name them one by one. Well, that is simple and yet profound at the same time. While it would take a long time to count all of them, the gospel communicates one blessing we must not forget. God does not leave us like beggars with no spiritual food or drink. It is there for the taking and to top it off we are drawn to it. Regardless of what befalls us, God's justice reigns and rules. Why refuse the magnetic impulses that come to us? We are his sheep and lambs. The Shepherd invites us to stay close by. Near him we will not spiritually want for anything. Our restless hearts find his abode to be exactly what we need. Indeed, so much for so little because, after all, it is all a gift from whom all blessings come.

Our Lord tells us that unless we repent we will perish. He also wants us to know, after a time, we are to bear fruit or cease to exist. Prominently brought into play is a troublesome, but always present, meaning of justice. We have our doubts about people and situations. Did they get what they deserve? Go back as far as you like in our Judeo-Christian tradition and the always challenging phenomenon is with humankind. Our text succinctly moves to the forefront the issue for all who call themselves followers of the Christ. In a tidy scriptural passage we have problems proposed and solutions given. We are not without light!

Especially as we move along in years, we are drawn to what the Lord expects of us. In fact, it may take the form of his expectations years ago. Have we done our repenting and made use of our opportunities? Is there time for healing and reconciliation not only with God but our brothers and sisters, both Christian and non-Christian? Yes, there is just so much time in this life. We must treat every day as a gift from God. Each second that ticks away belongs to us and it does not return. We do not strive for perfection as much as holiness of heart which insists we make use of every moment in serving Christ and his church in the broadest sense. So, if you haven't done so, repent. Then, make sure you bear fruit the remainder of your life.

The Two Prodigals

The relationship between and among siblings is a study both intriguing and challenging. Many of us know the truth here first-hand from the experience of growing up in families. Even if one happens to be an only child, we are brought in touch with brothers and sisters in other families.

A great deal is made of the birth order in a family. For example, the oldest son has traditionally been known as the child who is to make his mark in the world and, in some cases, look after parents and those siblings who are younger. Frequently, the youngest child is seen as "the baby," who gets special privileges.

Oh, yes, we know the dynamics, don't we? Joys and sorrows abound. Successes and failures come and go. Tragedy and triumph are there to see. Who is the most successful? Who does mother/father love the best? Don't tarnish the family name! Close ranks for the sake of family unity.

When we read the stories of the so-called great of this world, often some of the most captivating accounts involve siblings. On the current scene the Bush and Kennedy families receive lots of attention. In a sense we only need to look inside our own to note our curiosity.

The younger son went out and brazenly sowed his wild oats. Was he bored or just wanted to stretch his wings? Perhaps, neither one nor the other is the right answer but the two do point to causes that get people in trouble — regardless of age or station in life. Haven't we all been there and done that? We just get tired of the "same old same old" and decide that there has to be a better way to

149

live in this world of ours. Boredom over an extended period of time can be almost maddening for enterprising people. Then, doesn't everyone have the right to seek growth situations? We are here to stretch and not atrophy.

How long did it take him to squander his inheritance in sordid living — days, weeks, months, or years? Apparently, no answer is to be found in the holy scriptures. Frankly, it sounds like it might have taken quite a while. There are similar situations all around us. Who among us cannot cite the young man or woman who headed out with Dad's (or Mom's) money in hand to some exciting place to have a really good time? Perhaps, like the younger son, the venture ends up being experiences of sex, booze, drugs, and the like. Then, it comes time — broken and downtrodden — for him/her to come home. The most terribly sad tales are of those who never came home and died in squalor.

The whole idea of sowing wild oats has been deeply ingrained in our culture for generations. It was thought necessary and even a rite of passage, especially for youthful males. For some years, we have witnessed the acceptance of young women also entering into this experience. While our reaction may be negative to both, something far more sinister has come into the picture of today's living. Sowing wild oats may very well continue for a lifetime! Morally, there is no settling in and becoming a decent contributing member of society. Some seem to spend all their days moving from one relationship to another and rationalize it by noting its charm and practicality. Yes, it is past time for us to cry out to God for help!

To die of hunger is a tragedy far beyond what most of us can understand. The media sometimes gives us graphic pictures and more details than suits our temperaments. The younger son is dying of hunger and lives on a level much lower than his father's hired hands. We observe the interplay of both material and spiritual hunger. To the benefit of many, we have learned the two are really closely related. Our blessed Lord tells us to be spiritually right with him is to feed the hungry and he doesn't say just to pass out attractive Bibles! The message is clear and is not always easy for some of us to accept the clarity of it immediately. We can be so engrossed in writing sermons or some other worthy venture, the truth escapes us!

The elder son was consistent, hard working, and faithful. He must have been the epitome of what the firstborn son should do and be. We can look upon him and note that he is likely holding up the good name of the family. He is probably picking up after the mistakes of an aged father and had formerly worked around the younger fellow, who likely had never earned his weight. He was solid as a rock and gave the whole family a sense of stability and security, especially as the father grew older. We don't ask our sons and daughters to emulate the younger son. We say become like the elder son.

So, what is our experience along this line? Perhaps, one of us is the oldest in the family and senses the pressures to be close to perfect for the sake of the family name and ours. It is not an easy role, at least for those known to me. Expectations are high and maybe even impossible in a real world. Those who are conscientious deserve our respect and maybe even our admiration. Some family units owe nearly their entire success to such people. This may be less true today than in yesteryear, but it is still true to some extent. We have known those who earned our sympathy. They tried their best to measure up but just could not do it. Their faltering was more noticeable because, after all, they were supposed to succeed for themselves and others.

When the young wastrel returned, it was reported to the older son. How appropriate! He was out working in the field, just as he had been all his adult years. You could set your clock by a fellow like that and not be disappointed. No doubt the neighbors praised his work ethic and loyalty to his father. We all want children like that, sons or daughters. Yes, it is a matter of pride but also the sense of seeing fulfillment for good in the family. We thank God for them and sing their praises, usually to others. Maybe in this case there just weren't enough open signs of approval. In fact, it sounds like he was being taken for granted. He didn't mind being faithful but why give recognition to his brother, who turned out to be a first-class bum?

Initially, as we read the story, aren't we on the side of the elder son? Early on, it seems mostly an open and shut case of who is right and who is wrong. One fellow is head and shoulders above the other. There is no contest and little or no debate. One keeps the home fires burning and the other shows us his nature is that of a parasite. One knows that when the going gets tough, the tough get going. The other is so morally soft he winds up eating with pigs. There is so much to be said positively about the elder one. In the other case, it is difficult to find something remotely resembling anything positive! Our hats go off to the superior son.

The younger son came into an awareness and did the right thing. He admitted to himself the party was over. It is possible he was so emaciated he was hard to recognize. Maybe that's when he truly came to himself and did so remembering with great fondness and exhilarating appreciation his former life. It had been quite a time of planting pernicious seed and now the harvest was being grievously gathered. He had learned internally and externally that whatever we do in life has a result to it. Yes, he was reaping what he had sown. There was nothing pretty about the picture but there was hope. Why? Because he knew what fatherly goodness was and prepared to go back to it.

In a way, his story is one of all of us. We may not have been promiscuous, sexually or otherwise, but we were far from knowing Jesus as Savior and Lord. There was a void of major proportions. Christ may not have been berated or declared inconsequential, but he may very well have been totally ignored. Yes, and can't we do this in the most marvelously, socially approved ways? We may be eating high-priced steak and drinking fine wine, but somehow cannot get through our heads we need to come home to the Father! It seems to me that Christ is especially concerned about such types because they remain blind and too proud to cry out to the Father.

As he repented and declared that he was no longer worthy to be a son, the angels and all the heavenly hosts must have sung songs of jubilation. Ah, what a time to celebrate a lost son being found! The father is overjoyed and tears must have been streaming down those once sorrowful cheeks. Nothing would be too good for this young prodigal who had been to the far country and now had returned. He was beaten up badly and probably smelled like the pigs that may have been the closest thing to friends he had. A gala event would mark the return of him who had thrown away not only his material resources but himself as well.

So, we have placed before us the story, most likely ours as well, of one who trampled on his inheritance and the good will of his father. We can relate to that! Despite our civilized and sometimes sophisticated ways, you and I are prodigals. The only difference among us is that some have returned home and others have not. It is much like saying all are sinners, some are saved by the grace of God and others are not. To come to oneself in the highest and best sense is a remarkable gift which God enables to happen. It takes humility, sincerity, and honesty to admit our dependent place before God, doesn't it? The prodigal trudges from a foul-smelling pigpen to his father's front yard with flowers blooming, birds singing, and the aroma of forgiveness in the air.

The elder son belittled his brother and did the wrong thing. What's all this music and dancing about? Maybe my father has finally noticed what a good boy I am! Maybe my pet sheep has brought the highest price ever at the livestock market! Maybe my name will appear at last on our biggest grain barn! Maybe my father is presenting me with all that is his and no one else will even be considered! Well, that isn't very complimentary, is it? Is it realistic? Sorry to say, most likely it is because we can perceive his mindset, cold heart, and unforgiving spirit. He had been found out. He was simply being himself.

Obviously, he is not a prodigal and yet he is far from the virtues necessary to forgive his once-decadent brother. But, wait a minute. Wouldn't you be angry, too? Dumb-dumb little brother threw away what his family had accumulated for him. He displayed disdain for the very people, especially his father, who had loved him and supported him. What does anyone owe this degenerate? Oh, yes, unquestionably yes, there is a legitimate point provided here. It would take many adjectives with strong negative tones to describe this guy. When we apply a common standard of fair play, this hedonistic son is a real loser. Who is more justified than the elder in taking offense at the stupidities of a wayward brother?

With the attitude and tone of "Mr. Perfect," the father's heart must be breaking. Yet, he manages to reiterate that his son, who was dead has now come to life. He also affirms the elder son and wants him to know he remains a very important son, who shares in all the father has. The father, even in the face of impudence and unbelievable jealousy, does not reprimand him or even indicate his totally selfish behavior. Are we listening? There really are two prodigals and in our time we are called to live the Christian life in full realization that that's the way things are. Our Heavenly Father pleads with us to learn, and learn well, lessons presented.

Much of the commentary over the generations and even centuries tend to come down on the side of one prodigal son who lived despicably and then revived triumphantly. The elder brother is either something of a nonfactor or a misunderstood fellow caught in unpopular circumstances. Truly, he is also a prodigal and we hope and pray the parable is not the complete story. A more inspiring conclusion would discover he repented of his arrogance and lack of mercy. Furthermore, we long to hear him tell his father that he is grateful for all that has been given him. It would be an inspirational appendage and appear to fulfill a gospel narrative we have known from our earliest days in Sunday school or other forms of Christian education. But we are not authorized to write holy writ!

Two sons and their father are forever with us in seriously living out the faith. Despite the majority viewpoint, both are prodigals. One has returned home and the other is physically home, but not spiritually home. What a story! These fellows have all kinds, sizes, and shapes of problems. One has the humility and sincerity to seek honest solutions. The other wonders why his younger brother can do what he did and get by with it. The difference, of course, is the grace of God. One accepts it and the other doesn't. There is so much of you and me in these fellows. Perhaps we understand ourselves to be above them. Well, look again!

Truly, dear friends, the message is quite clear. Both are in need of the salvation of our Savior and Lord, Jesus Christ. Now, let's include ourselves and the rest of humankind. To be prodigal sons and daughters is no disgrace. To continue to be — even when the Holy Spirit pleads with us — is the major problem of every precious human being. Lent is an exceptional time to fall on our knees

154

and unhurriedly seek the riches of the Christian message, delivered long ago. Yes, softly and tenderly Jesus is calling us home. Yes, oh, gentle Savior, pass me not and hear my humble cry. Yes, he touched me and made me whole. Our days are numbered but praises be to the living God there is today and maybe tomorrow.

Holy Extravagance

In our spiritual voyages, surprises — sometimes outlandishly — come to us. We scratch our heads and wonder if what we are experiencing is fact or fiction. It may or may not be a time of inspiration. However, it may be one of instruction, as we view it in retrospect. You and I are to remember that every occurrence may very well be a teaching event.

Mary's act near the time of Jesus' crucifixion is a scene mostly outside of our expectations and predictions. It catches us off guard and the same may have been true for those actually there long ago. Perhaps she caught them at an off moment and they quietly gasped in near horror.

Are we surprised by religious experiences today? In truth there are so many expressions it would take something quite bizarre to make us stand up and actually notice. Of course, when we leave that broadening field of what we define as "Christian," there is a far greater chance of being astonished. Yes, and that may not be all bad!

The Lenten season is well on its way to being over and we are summoned to take a close look at its happenings, some were bizarre and yet were expressing strong love and commitment. Who would not want to have been there? Seeing no hands go up, we are urged to continue.

We are taught that the presence of Jesus is what really counts. When we get up every morning, that should be our theme song. He walks with us and talks with us in our joys and sorrows all day long. There is a blessed fragrance that fills the air. We don't know

157

if it is costly or not and it doesn't seem to be important one way or the other. As we move about, it moves with us. Who can put a price tag on this? In dollar bills, we know no one can. In the context of his immense suffering for us, you and I kneel before his sacrifice. Then, we praise God the Father for the love shown us in his Son, Jesus Christ, forever and ever.

When we go to bed at night, we say, "Thank you" several times. We do that more for ourselves than for him. To be sure, he desires our full compliance. On our pillows and in our beds there is this fragrance. After a time we are not shocked. We come to expect it. If we are truly in tune with the Holy Spirit, every night is memorable because we ask him to take care of us and he does. Perhaps you have found that special prayers — yes, even holy communion — are a preliminary to a night of solid sleep and relaxation. We are not only loved, we are protected by one who knows us best! Dear ones that is comforting!

The house was filled with his fragrance. Are our homes or residences also filled with this blessed aroma? Fathers and mothers, if that is not the case, then why not? Yes, there is the "hurry" button that continually gets pressed. Good parents have learned they have to fight for quality time together. They are willing to do so because they just love the aroma of Christ in them and about them! Take your own survey among those professing Jesus Christ as Savior and Lord. They desire more than anything else the precious and priceless perfume of him who died and arose again. The most brilliant of Frenchmen can neither produce it nor provide it. What a treasure Mary illustrates for us!

We reside in a world that is smelly in ways frequently offensive and, in fact, can cause us to vomit. It's the moral and ethical dimension, isn't it? Sordid politics, masking as do-good philosophy, is one we discover that especially frustrates and angers us. The plus sign is that we are able to recognize and name it for what it is. We are not helpless because the presence of Christ is about to come into the most rotten situations imaginable. How do we know? Simply, it has done it before. You and I know all things are possible with God. We are to trust and obey, for there is no other way to begin to right people and situations that are very wrong. Our confidence is nothing other than the good news being repeated and elevated.

We are taught that exuberance has a place in vital religious experience. Mary is a woman who is not going to be denied. She wasn't there to be passively watching for ways not to cause anyone a problem. Shocking others at a dinner party probably didn't interest her. If they were accepting or scandalized, all well and good. She wanted to make a point and she did. Like us, in special situations, she probably didn't have a clue as to the full impact of her actions. If poor Judas Iscariot didn't like it, maybe he should go elsewhere and lump it! The Christian faith has always needed people like her and we are better because of them. Not to feel comfortable may very well be what you and I need.

Tried and true religious behavior has a way of locking certain patterns in place. We can eventually go through the motions and little else. We can be frozen in place and become even immobilized to the point of reflecting "goodness gone to seed." Diminishing returns are all about us and, sadly, you and I may even become satisfied with our spiritual lives. Our need is for Mary or someone like her to come on the scene and into our nonproductive refrigerators to thaw us out! Then we have the possibility of spiritual good coming to us. Our pressing need for the fragrance only the Holy Spirit can provide can be met. It may be best not to ask questions but only savor the moment.

The very idea of Mary anointing Jesus' feet and wiping them with her hair was probably repugnant to others besides Judas Iscariot. There is, however, no record of their objections. To my knowledge, there is no precedent for it. She provided a shocker. Those outside of the faith today may question her sanity or perhaps pass it off as an excessively emotional woman who needed to do some odd deed to work off her frustration. It needs to be said that radically following Christ can lead any one of us into conduct the world reports as off-the-wall. Those Christians just didn't make much sense to a pagan, ancient culture. Unconditional surrender to Christ in our day and time doesn't make much sense in ours, either.

159

Don't you just love Mary's gall? And to think we are reading, studying, and preaching about it today. Who would have thought the fathers of the church would include the story in holy scripture? Ah, but wait a minute, we have the answer to that one. The Holy Spirit ordained it and it was and is so! The Bible does not provide us with a take it or leave it posture. To be in the scriptures is to have credibility. We attempt to talk our way out of it and away from it at our own peril. Our correct response is appreciation, gratitude, and teachability. Our Lord says to come and learn from him because he is the way, the truth, and the life.

We are taught that those who pose for good are dangerous. Poor Judas Iscariot, but let's take him for what he is. Was he really thinking about people in poverty? That has already been answered for us. All of this perfume that could bring in tons of money and you waste it on Jesus' feet! Maybe if we didn't already know Jesus, we would have bought into the treasurer's comment. After all, he was an apostle and there were only twelve of them. Yes, he was posing for good and, if you didn't know him, he made quite a good impression. We know some people like that, don't we? Sometimes their posturing is a sight to behold!

You and I can be gullible. We focus our attention on people resembling the fellow in question. Apparently, he kept the common purse and used to steal from it. Talk about corruption in high places! But, there is a lesson here and God's people are urged to learn it as early as possible. Beware of those who tout their goodness. Every church and church organization, which have been in operation for any length of time, knows the embarrassment and even disillusionment going with this foul smell. The media frenzy eats up pages of print and expensive time on both radio and television.

Despite those who parade a philosophy of the natural goodness of humankind, original sin seems to be about as lethal as it ever was. Those well-meaning souls who think human nature is continuing to get better had best look again. This is not a pessimistic view. It is realistic and finds its source in holy scripture. Admittedly, we have come a long way in racial and gender equality. Yet, even then, we forget or refuse to admit that our primary goal is to accept the fact that everyone is equally important before God and

160

we are to treat one another with that in mind. It is not possible for human ingenuity to provide full equality for every man and woman, largely because the definition of "equality" is different for different people.

In a way, Judas Iscariot is unwittingly part of a positive family gathering, immersed in spiritual fragrance. Had we asked him, he certainly would never have allowed such holy extravagance! Maybe we are too harsh and should listen one more time to some scholars who insist he was predestined to do what he did. That is a bit of a stretch for some of us and, thank God, the truth is in his hands and beyond our puny comprehensions. The episode can grow complicated and a project for academics. In the meantime, you and I are inspired to live the Christian life. We know it is wrong to pose for good and our depths sense the hypocrisy gravitating to the forefront.

We are taught the cries of the poor must be heard, but Jesus comes first. Jesus orders Mary to be left alone. Furthermore, he says the costly perfume is to be used for the day of his burial. His strange statement indicates the poor will always be around but he won't. Our initial response may be along the lines of his primacy in our ministries and the fundamental reason we do them. Briefly, we feed and aid the poor because Jesus the Christ challenges us to do so. Our core for doing meaningful ministry is found in him and none other. Another way of looking at it is to show that there is only a short time left on earth for him and it is imperative he be placed first.

The centrality of Christ in the life of the church emerges originally because of his physical presence among us. Had our Lord just sent his ideas by way of Peter, James, John, and Paul, where would the Jesus movement be today? Likely, a well-developed theology and/or philosophy in books on the shelves of libraries would be its lot. It took flesh and blood! Indeed, it took his body and blood in the form of a sacrament to provide for a holy extravagance imparted to his friends. Had there been no physical Jesus literally walking and talking among us, the power of our religion would be so diminished that we could hardly visualize its relevance. He was God in the flesh.

161

The world needed a man who could see, hear, feel, taste, and smell. There were thousands of gods in the ancient culture in which our Lord entered. Not one of them was human in the real sense. Oh, there were the Caesars but so what? Ruthlessness character-ized most of them. There was very little compassion and they were not going to die for anyone. That is, they were not going to die for anyone if they could keep from it. The Father, it seems, asked, "So you want to see God?" Then, he added, "Well, don't go away, be-cause my only Son is being sent to you. Yes, dear people, he will live with you and die for you, Jesus is the supreme sacrifice. Be-yond him there is none other. So, come now, and enjoy the riches of the faith."

Do we need to know more? No, only that overarching burst of truth coming straight from the Father. Provision is made for us in all ways in a world known for its countless saviors. The Father announces Jesus is his Son and he is pleased with him. We are to receive him as Savior and Lord. In all ways, you and I are given the mandatory ingredients for being born again and inheriting eternal life. Why shouldn't Mary anoint his feet? We can take care of the poor, too! Oh, such completeness is ours as a gift from the living God. Indeed, what holy extravagance! The good news keeps com-ing to us in a myriad of ways. Celebrate today, tomorrow, and the next day. Our Lord will celebrate with us.

You and I, like others across the centuries, were invited to a dinner. The principal characters are Mary, Martha, Lazarus, and Judas Iscariot. It was a memorable gathering, as Mary anointed her Lord's feet with expensive perfume. The one who betrayed Jesus made quite an issue out of her act. He thought the money the perfume cost should have been used for the poor. The sad thing is, he was a thief and his do-gooder approach carried no weight. The Master affirmed Mary's generous act and indicated that the poor are always with us, yet he will not be with them much longer.

We learn there is a holy extravagance about the event. It is discovered in the presence of Christ bringing with it a singular fragrance the world can neither produce nor give away. The spiri-tuality of our Master makes for victory in all circumstances, mainly because we are teachable. Mary was not a loose cannon looking

162

for notoriety and an elevated place in Christ's kingdom. Her generous deed was one for the benefit of all concerned there and then, plus all those who followed and professed the Christ. Her selflessness and lack of fear continue to shine for all to view. How preciously beautiful all of it is! If the Father really calls us to step out of the humdrum of social relationships and do something extraordinary, may the Father, during this Lenten season, grant you the strength to do it.

History Hangs In The Balance

One would be hard pressed to find a historical event with so many ramifications equal to these words from Saint Luke's Gospel. In fact, for the devout Christian there is no other! It is a moment when the universe seems to come to a standstill and the angels watch in troubled awe.

You and I observe from afar, indeed, a great distance. Unless we figuratively or literally read the passage on our knees, we are not apt to catch this sublime, serious moment. Yes, and our appreciation may very well remain at surface level, more or less. It is not a moment of timidity but one of pure gratitude.

Historians and theologians record these events today. It is nearly impossible to do so without commentary that shows biases and that is not all bad! Our faith is based upon a few historical happenings that bring earth and heaven together. Explanations simply beg to be given.

While the gospels do not give identical accounts, we cannot miss the similarities. Our Lukan passage is straightforward and would appear not to sugarcoat anything. For that alone, our thanksgivings should be heard throughout the universe.

His innocence is emphasized but guilt prevails. Pilate kept saying over and over that there was not enough evidence to crucify him. The Roman prefect of Judea was the second-longest holder of the office, apparently for ten years or so. In a time of virtually omnipresent intrigue, he was a survivor. It was manifest that he wanted to do the right thing. There just was not enough evidence to convict Jesus for major crimes and have him put to death. Would or could Jesus be considered innocent until proven guilty? The mob would see to it that that would not happen. Innocence of serious charges was not relevant!

Perhaps some of us perceive a goodness and fairness in Pilate that is not allowed to carry the day. It certainly seems he is guided by a sense of justice and fairness. We are close to admiration and begin to wonder if he is an innocent party himself, caught in a web of power politics with a strong, religious overtone. Well, he does disappoint us and yields to the political realities at hand. A man in his position cannot allow substantial unrest in the area assigned to him by Caesar. When it comes to preserving number one and a place of power, we know who and what almost always wins.

The power structure among the Jews insists Jesus is guilty. It seeks no other verdict. It is time to be rid of this pesky fellow who stirs up the people and irritates the ruling Romans. This is not to maintain Jews were generally guilty then ... or now. We must be careful — even astute — in handling such a delicate matter. To do otherwise is not only to ask for criticism but to open ourselves to outright dishonesty and even flagrant anti-semitism. If we have stretched our ecumenical and interreligious wings, we know that Jewish people cannot only be friendly they can be friends and even comrades. That is cause for "hallelujahs"!

The hallmark of the situation shows the forces of sinful men colliding with one another and the mysteries of God working themselves out. Do the people responsible for our Lord's crucifixion desire to fight it out with God? Do they believe the will of God does not eventually prevail? Are they deliberately selecting and insisting upon an avenue of action opposed to their Creator? Maybe our answers to such inquiries are summed up in "of course not." The ferocious frenzy to declare him guilty, so crucifixion can take place, may be experienced by you and me as totally irrational and motivated solely by prejudice. But have we forgotten what mobs can do to the innocent? If we have, our memories should be jogged by the lynchings of thousands recorded in our nation.

His followers and friends objected but they are to be pitied. We know his disciples, as well as others, were not at all in agreement with this maddening spectacle. While mostly unrecorded, those

166

who could and did follow him must have said their piece. Since they, at that time, appeared to come mostly from those without significant place and power, what chance did they have in turning back the juggernaut? Let's be honest. The sobering answer is "very little — if any." Their objections fell on the deaf ears of those who controlled the situation. Who can blame them for their lack of bravery and courage? Are you and I ready to cast stones?

Isn't it amazing the success stories, especially all the healings recorded in Saint Luke's Gospel, have so quickly and unceremoniously gone down the tubes? The meteoric character of his career was there for many to witness. What went wrong? For 2,000 years we have probed this matter. We seem to keep trying to make the story turn out differently. Let's be honest and admit that we are stumped and so much doesn't make sense in the way we want! It isn't enough that our salvation is the outcome. We are tempted to keep on telling the story in a way which communicates that we think it should have happened some other way. In fact, just maybe we could have improved it.

Pity enters at the juncture of visualizing the faithful making little or no difference in the drama unfolding. Why are they so helpless? We suspect there is much cowardice at work. If there is, we would rather not observe it. After all, weren't the earliest of disciples the best and most determined to follow him of all? Shame on you people who objected so meekly and inconsequentially! He told you to be prepared to lay down your lives for your friends and he was the best friend you ever had. Our pity can lead almost instantaneously to a top-heavy judgmental attitude. In short, we accuse people of doing the very things we do.

For some, his unwillingness to save himself must have really irked them. Common sense said there was no good reason for this tragic event to occur. If you are who you say you are, why hesitate in throwing the cross in their faces and walk away victoriously? That's all it would take and the Romans would back down to keep the peace. The Jews, who opposed him, would be discredited and the Master could finish years of essential ministry. As usual with them, plus you and me, salvation history is being made and we refuse to recognize it. How true of our spiritual pilgrimages today!

The blessed Lord works in us and through us but we find fault with what is transpiring. Original sins just never seem to go away.

His detractors and enemies jeered but he called for forgiveness. Not only did they shout "crucify him," they sought to hurt and embarrass him at every opportunity. Just to take him out and kill him was not nearly enough. The Master had to undergo punishment after punishment. Most of us do not have the imaginations to get close to the reality of all of this. It was truly hell on earth for a man — believe it or not — who pleaded for them to be forgiven. Perhaps the closest we get to the sordid scene is the experience of some prisoners of war. Your captors want you to suffer in great pain before they kill you. The longer death can be put off, the better!

Sprinkled throughout church history are saints who enacted the Lord's call to forgive enemies. Those who hurt them the most were those they begged God to forgive. Can we speak a word about ourselves here? If the answer is in the affirmative, are we prepared to be guided by pristine honesty? We are mostly fair-weather Christians, aren't we? We relish being known for our regular worship attendance and tithing. Those disciplines alone put us above the average and we are self-satisfied. If everyone just did as much as we do, what a wonderful world it would be and how strong the churches would become! We may be tempted to think enough of that and walk on with heads held high, proclaiming our exemplary conduct.

Sometimes we hear serious-minded people saying they don't like God. Well, how can you like an eternal being who tells you to forgive those who harm, humiliate, and hate you in ways totally nonsensical? So, now we come into the area of the nature of God. If Jesus Christ is God in the flesh, then what he says must not only be true, but followed. That helps, doesn't it? We may not want to accept it. We may even find it repugnant. Nevertheless, to be true to our Savior and Lord, we have received our orders. Here we come to terms with what human nature prods us to do and what our Master summons us to do. It is an ongoing tension and with merely human feelings, a terrifying truth.

168

How can people want to destroy someone as well-meaning and pure as the Man of Galilee? What good or contribution is there in him being crucified? Here we enter the "unreasonable reasonableness" dimension of our salvation. An enigma is presented. A contradiction seemingly irreconcilable makes its way into our minds. Wouldn't it be better just to ignore or evade the guy? We are now getting someplace. Christ was so strong in person and message that people who were around him were pushed to be for or against him. His opposition had mounted. They absolutely refused to change, plus there were those who always wanted to please the power brokers. It is the same story told today across our planet.

His death brought supernatural happenings but the spectacle prevailed. The Lord's demise has brought us to the door of discovery. The criminal has been promised paradise and darkness has covered the land for three awful hours. Then, Jesus cries out to his Father, commending his Spirit to God. They were left with very mixed feelings and thoughts. Whom do we mean by "they"? The answers are many and it is not unlikely there was even something close to unanimity among his own followers. To be sure, the Lord's hardcore enemies must have been ecstatic and yet with the darkness, in particular, must have sensed a fear they had not experienced before. At the other extreme those who loved him deeply must have felt the best part of their lives was over.

The centurion perhaps said the only words that made sense. He praised God and called Jesus innocent or — better still — righteous. There was the crystal-clear recognition that this man, so maligned, was someone very special and God was much in the brutal and inhumane scene. It is as though the Roman officer perceived he had just witnessed an event never to be forgotten with God entering history in a supernatural way. We may take it to mean God has allowed the death of a righteous man for a purpose so meaningful and unforgettable that we have only seen the beginning of its import for generations to come. The everlasting and living God gives his gift.

To say the least, it was a spectacle at the moment no one could understand. However, there must be a sense — even with the prevailing spectacle — there was more of something to come. Did

169

anyone know what that something was? Who can know for sure but the answer appears almost 100 percent to be completely in the negative. Have we been there before in a much smaller and insignificant way? Perhaps it was during the time of a major tragedy or triumph. We knew, didn't we, that we had not heard the last of it? What we did not know was what was coming, but to be sure, something more was on the horizon. What did the Lord have in store for us? Time would tell.

Yes, as they walked home beating their breasts, and the Master's followers watched at a distance, a new day was at hand. Oh, it was not yet consummated but just wait and see! We believe Luke narrates the story well and reliably. Those present did not know whether or not the worst had come and gone. There were those who remembered. He said that death and resurrection were a part of the fabric of his mission. It would be the culmination of his ministry and all of humankind would be impacted. So much now was hanging in the balance. It was the "not yet" time in salvation history. We were not there but our blessed Lord through his Holy Spirit takes us there, and we are greatly humbled but inspired beyond words to exclaim the gift at hand.

With brilliant directors and actors, Hollywood could hardly produce the colossal event presented to us. It defies human ingenuity and creativity. We are witnesses, as Christians and non-Christians alike, to the unfolding drama prepared by the Father for his Son from the beginning. Man is in a fallen state and must be rescued. It is so bad only the Son by sacrificing himself can bring about a right relationship with the Father. Everyone and everything becomes a part of the supreme revelation to precious people, who are otherwise lost in their sins. It is a no-holds-barred moment in history and failure means eternal gloom and doom.

There is something about such a defining instant — brief in anyone's measurement — that penetrates our eternal souls. It is so personal we gasp for breath and hope in painful pangs, bordering on panic. The message is to you and me, isn't it? There is no need to look around and see to whom it applies. Brothers and sisters, we are the ones crying out for a salvation that conquers death, even the

170

worst kind. He had to die for you and me to live. He had to suffer in unconscionable agony for you and me. The ultimate price had been paid and the way was cleared for a victorious resurrection assuring others, including you and me, that there was hope only Jesus Christ could give.

A Frightening Friday

So much happening in so little time! We are left gasping for breath. We stagger under the weight of the mighty arm of historical occurrence. You and I praise God because we know the rest of the story. Those present did not know how things would turn out. They must have been like awestruck children nearing exasperation.

Those of us who have read and perhaps studied the great writers amazingly discover that Saint John tops them all. Shakespeare was truly brilliant but there is a peculiar demeanor about our lengthy passage that goes beyond his work. Dante and Milton — with others coming to mind — cause us to pause reverently in admiration but John causes us to kneel in adoration.

How can we even begin to digest all of this coming at us at one time? It is so imposing and it stretches us to limits that give us a glimpse of our immortal souls. We want to shout for everything to wait a minute or two, indeed, a year or two! Call in the wise men and women; let them brood for a time.

But now — just maybe — the Holy Spirit has provided us with enough love, faith, and hope to continue in genuine humility. Praises be to God, what an opportunity! We are privy to the unfolding and making of salvation history. It is a moment of our spirits being quickened.

Judas Iscariot betrayed his Lord. This whole business of betrayal is one which is gripping for us because we never know who will decide to sell us out. The drama of human beings relating to human beings is filled to overflowing with such nasty experiences.

173

Some move well into adulthood before finding out what has happened to them. Others learn in high school or even before. How about you and me? If it hasn't happened to us, it will! Yes, and not one of us has a desire to be labeled a "Judas." His name — all it conjures up — is an odious reminder of what is at hand.

How many times have we heard this man thoroughly castigated for his dastardly deed? We have probably lost track. His is an infamy that never goes away. It carries a singular stench. He betrayed our blessed Lord! He was a scoundrel and deserved the worst cell in hell. But many of us over time become more thoughtful, don't we? The scum of the earth who betrayed the greatest and most pure man to live among us is seen, at least, with some compassion and not a few questions. Was he really that bad and did he have a will of his own to prevent his name being remembered forever as the epitome of a traitor? You and I cannot condone what he did, and Christ tells us not to judge.

What are the motives behind his actions? Some say he was a Jewish patriot who wanted the hated Romans driven from the land. He was patient with Jesus for a time and began to see there was no hope for this to happen. Others maintain that he was a crook from the beginning and wanted only to handle the little band's money. He would then steal cleverly from that precious treasury to promote himself. Yes, it is even thought the devil so totally dominated his motives there was no other way for him to behave. Could he have been predestined? Haven't we seen people, who despite their apparent good intentions, never seem to come out on the right side of anything?

While you and I see ourselves, for the most part, as quite distant from his perfidy, are we really? If Christ and his church do not say what we want to hear, what is our response? Sometimes good people betray their pastors. Sometimes good pastors betray their people. To be sure, these are exceptions, but our personal stories cannot be told accurately from our internal struggles that are only known by us and God. To be more focused, we have all been tempted to betray somebody. The evil one tells us that is not the way something should be and we are led into a trap. To correct the situation, the evil spirit skillfully sells us on betraying someone we have loved and supported. So, the question becomes one of accepting or rejecting the bait made to look necessary for all concerned.

Simon Peter showed his cowardice. Peter invariably seemed to get the attention of the gospel writers. He was the dominant apostle, regardless of whether he was doing good or ill. He ran the gamut of cowardly bum to sacrificial saint. Of course, we would only see the latter after the resurrection and the day of Pentecost. He was the most unlikely of the twelve — except Judas Iscariot — to provide leadership for the ancient church. How could someone be such a bumbling idiot? His Lord had called him close different times, giving his insight into the future. It is as though he heard a different drummer. He had the close confidence of his Lord and worked overtime to negate that beloved relationship.

At this cataclysmic point in time, there just doesn't appear to be much hope for him. All he was capable of doing was slipping around on the fringes telling folks he doesn't know the Man of Galilee. After all that his Savior had seen him through, he was apparently scared out of his wits some people would connect him to the fellow about to be crucified. What a loser! It was indeed a frightening Friday and Peter was one of the biggest ducks in the puddle. He was so far removed from the imperative loyalty to lead the Jesus movement, we scratch and dig around to find something with which to defend him.

Just the simple word, "coward," causes many of us to shiver and shake. Is there ever anyone who wants to be described as one? Except in jest and playfulness, we don't like any part of that word. Oh, we might like it applied to someone else who strongly disagrees with us or does something we can't tolerate. Even then, it has a way of cluttering up our understanding of religious and moral perceptions. We would just as soon it not appear in our dictionaries and vocabularies. In a sober moment of pondering, we admit that if we took it out, we would have to find another word to define what certainly is a fact of life! Yes, history books indicate it is not an uncommon trait.

Peter's fate turned out to be infinitely better than that of Judas Iscariot. Who could tell at the time how things would turn out? It looked like a big zero was the answer. So, what is the difference?

Is it that God liked Peter a lot better than Judas? Needless to say, that is a stretch and mostly for those who want to do endless dialogue dynamics for the sake of exploring all possibilities. Perhaps the best way to understand his problem is to note that he recognized the Lord has chosen him for great things but he simply did not know what to do about it. So, he stumbled and fumbled with a generous amount of grumbles. Jesus was through with his betrayer but not his cowardly apostle.

Pilate performed his political duty. Good old Pontius Pilate! He seemed to do everything on schedule. He was a predictable politician. After apparently having such accurate and objective thoughts of God's Son, he progressively or regressively — depending on one's understanding — ended up defending what was near and dear to him: his position. To let things get out of hand was certainly to be demoted and possibly much worse. So, to survive and meet his own needs in his world, he caved in and opened the way for our Lord's hideous death. Sound familiar for politicians? You bet it does! He was right on schedule and we might even be tempted to inquire as to why he took so long.

Maybe we should inject the thought, which has much substance, that there are only two kinds of politics: good and bad. The good means most everybody wins in the highest and best sense. The bad means quite the reverse. Is Pilate reacting like most of us would react in that situation? Obviously, he was fascinated by the man whose guilt or innocence was in the balance. He had not been with Jesus in closed sessions like the apostles. He was known only at a distance. While fear and some sense of justice motivated him, he did the only thing that made sense at the time. What would you and I have done? Would we have been seriously interested in good politics? Each of us has to answer for himself or herself.

It must have been quite an ego trip to have Jesus before him and be able to convict or acquit this amazing fellow. It was an opportunity made in a pagan heaven, filled with idols and self-congratulatory weapons. He had, some would call, God in his presence, the power to destroy or release. Wow, that is something of a very special circumstance! What else could be so favorable for a man who wanted always to stay on the good side of Caesar, who

176

many considered a deity? Perhaps there is nothing so destructive in our world as pure, unadulterated egotism: witness the likes of Adolf Hitler and many others. It was a singular and demonic instant of glory.

Pilate has not only found his way into the holy scriptures, he appears as well in both the Apostles' and Nicene Creeds. We are not apt to forget him anytime soon! His is one of the few names having been perpetuated from the times our Lord walked and talked upon this earth. He made history and his name is there for all to see. Yes, one wonders about his select place — good, bad, or otherwise. He could be called a major player or actor but it was certainly the Father's stage and the Father, contrary to what some may say, was doing all of the directing. Yes, we see only in a mirror dimly but God has the total picture, which he sees perfectly and in its totality. The majority of Christian worshipers across the globe say Pilate's name.

Mary, his mother, was given to a trusted and loving apostle. Can we even begin to imagine Mary's thoughts and feelings during these hours? She watched her son undergo a humiliating death. There he was stark naked in agony, dying like any common, ordinary thief or seditionist. Her heart must have been ripped asunder and she may have even shouted at God because it was all so unjust and unfair. Try — for a fleeting moment — to put yourself in her place. She carried him inside her body like any other mother and gave birth to him. He was a part of her body and after the birth, when she could hold him in her arms, there was that powerful sense he belonged to her. In a way she died, too. Her baby, little boy, teenager, and adult man was gone.

She is the blessed Virgin Mary to much of Christendom. What an appealing and magnificent name! She was a sublimely favored one and full of grace. The Lord was with her. She was blessed among women. The fruit (Jesus) of her womb was blessed. She is defined as the mother or bearer of God. Many ask her to pray for them at their deaths. Wow, that really was and is some extra special lady! Why is it when we speak about feminist power and priorities, she seems invariably absent? To some extent, in our day and time

177

this is being answered and many Protestants have had their blinders lifted and she begins to move to her rightful place.

It is said on reliable authority that the apostle who received the honor or responsibility for her was John. Our Lord would look after his mother, like any good Jewish son, and so he gave her to one he must have trusted the most. It all happened just before he bowed his head and gave up his spirit. Exactly what occurs after that remains questionable, except for mention in the Acts of the Apostles. In reverential retrospect we view a son who refused to die before his mother received some security for the future. For an instant, motherhood is lifted to a new level because she bore the Son of the living God. The ages have spoken of such maternity. Catholics and Orthodox integrated her extraordinary place in the faith, centuries ago.

Hopefully, gone are the days of vitriolic arguments about her and where she belongs in our belief systems. Pope John Paul II, who spoke to many outside of the Roman Catholic church, has helped us immensely. The movement on the part of some of us in the Protestant churches has helped and is helping. Increasingly, we are experiencing evidence she is more — much more — than a woman in the right place at the right time! The healthy dialogue has caused some of us to shout praises to God, our Father, for the progress at hand. It did not come overnight but it has come to us under the guidance of the Holy Spirit. No feminine force can unite us as Christians the way Mary does. She may very well be the key to our unity.

The key players do what they do! Among them — along with Jesus — is Judas Iscariot, Simon Peter, Pontius Pilate, and the blessed Virgin Mary. How can the story of a frightening Friday be told without them? Yes, and it isn't over until it's over! The piercing of his side is not the end. The gentlemanly conduct of Joseph of Arimathea and Nicodemus, we soon learn, is not the end. We group the events together, as best we can, and wait in anticipation of the supreme victory song of salvation history. Those, centuries ago, had mixed feelings. Some thought the ignominious tailgate had come down and the Master had failed in a definitive fiasco.

The thing you and I must not do is to become lackadaisical which leads to a lackluster attitude toward Resurrection Sunday. Oh, dear Father of our Savior and Lord, please don't allow this to happen! We are reminded there is not the smallest amount of humdrum in what is taking place. We know beforehand that the gloom and doom gathers by the tons. We have to wait until a glorious victory is declared once and for all. Our brothers and sisters who were there join in an unending chorus of praise with us. Our spiritual ancestors plead with us to be vigilant and reexperience what Christ does for us. Kneel in prayerful tears of joy for atrocious events that changed our lives and deaths, now and forever. Amen.

Mary Magdalene's Day

Mary Magdalene may very well be the most enigmatic and controversial figure in the resurrection story. In a way the holy scriptures give us just enough information to excite our curiosity in regard to her personal relationship with the man she adored, Jesus of Nazareth. We still wonder what kind of person she was.

Fiction writers have had a field day, especially in recent years. Was she really married to Jesus and did they have children? Did they establish a bloodline that is with us today? Such inquiries, while they may border on blasphemy, need airing. That is not to assume our traditional revelation is in error.

Wherever we come down in our understanding of her, we are forced to admit that she was a major player in the story upon which the authenticity of our religion is based. In short, if there is no resurrected Christ, we have a philosophy and theology among others. It becomes neither unique nor especially powerful.

The debate between eastern (Orthodox) and western (Roman Catholic) Christianity shows views with some solid differences. When we enter the explanation of Protestants, we enter into an even wider and more complicated discussion. Nevertheless, there is agreement that she is someone with whom we must come to terms.

She cared deeply about Jesus. All accounts indicate there developed a strong and emotional relationship between the two. Did she love him? Of course, she did. It is that love which has provided fodder for both the believing and unbelieving grist mills. So, how is that different from countless other relationships adoring women

181

have with their "kings"? We can summon to our consciousness examples galore of some notables and others that are "down home" figures. The difference is seen in whom he claimed to be, especially in the understanding of the ancient church.

If we discovered reliable sources proving Mary Magdalene and Jesus were married and had children but otherwise his messiahship remained intact as recorded, how would you and I respond? For many this is not only an awkward inquiry but one causing us to vomit at the mere articulating of it. Jesus was celibate, perfect in all ways, and there is no reason to test — really test — it by thinking along the lines of marriage and family. The dialogue today is heated and may not go away any time soon. Opportunists are always with us and at times they can be quite convincing before we find them out. Surely open and free inquiry is imperative. In fact, this is the way Christianity has survived over the centuries.

We sure wished we knew more, don't we? It is much like parishioners who hear stories — perhaps even allegations — about their pastors and priests, except at a level of extreme importance. We know what the child abuse scandal has done to the Roman Catholic church. Whether by fact or pure supposition, the spotlight is placed on all priests. It just doesn't matter that substantiation may be no higher than three percent. She cared deeply for her Lord. On a strictly human level, those kind of relationships sooner or later cause the busybodies to come out in the open. Strong affection and great respect are not immune from Satan's clutches. The very best are tempted to become the very worst.

To notify Simon Peter first of all is to show not only that he was the leader of that faithful band of followers but her attempt to stay within the community of believers in loyalty. She could have gone to his enemies, Jewish and Roman. She seems unwilling to take credit for anything and apparently wants, first of all, to share her discovery with those within the fellowship of faith. Within itself, her approach is commendable. Her deepest thoughts must have been at the point of desiring to know if he was all right. He must have been her life in the spiritual sense. There is a message for you and me here. Our top priority is what our Savior and Lord means to us and not suspicions of so-called facts that sway our commitment.

She experienced the presence of angels. Simon Peter along with the other disciples surveyed the situation and returned to their homes. Not so with Mary! She stood outside the tomb weeping. Then, alone, she looked into the tomb and saw two angels in white. The gospel is specific in their location. One was at the head where he was lying and the other at the feet. The occasion gives rise to the skeptics who wonder why it is recorded that only she saw the angels. Was she building on her desire to have supernatural beings present? Perhaps her need to make the situation into more than it was caused angels to be seen. But don't those folks who are invariably doubting lose this one?

The conversation with the angels must have been brief; at least, that's what the record indicates. As we extend our thoughts, we discover a woman, perhaps in the grips of hysteria, who wants with all her heart to know where they have laid him. She wants to see him and probably touch him. He was her Lord. The price had been paid for our salvation and she was not about to run away. She knew firsthand what that salvation was. It was embodied in Jesus of Nazareth. Alive or dead, she wanted to know where they had laid him. Maybe it could be a sacred moment of relaying to him how much he meant to her. Surely, the crucifixion could not be the end for such a good man.

For some, the presence of angels may be very unusual. Yet, those who have studied the holy scriptures and read histories before and after Jesus' earthly existence know angels were almost commonplace. At certain points in one's life, especially birth and death, they put in an appearance. You and I may see this as mostly superstition and avoiding down-to-earth facts. But we didn't live in that world. Therefore, what is written down for future use must be taken seriously. Why quarrel with a source the universal church proclaims as integral to the revelation of our faith? Fortunately and mostly positively angels have made a serious comeback in our day and time. This may very well be a Holy Spirit reminder!

So, our dear lady, sometimes maligned and other times elevated to levels of the highest discipleship, comes to a moment of transition. Does she already know the answer is at hand? The narrative does not say so and it doesn't appear that even the angels have implied what has transpired. She must be all alone with none of the other disciples present. Others mentioned earlier have gone to their homes. What they are talking about we do not know but what we do know is Mary is alone with two angels in white. She must not have been afraid. Our suspicions are that she is not going to give up on finding the Man who must have meant more to her than life itself. She may have been the most dogged of the disciples who believed defeat was not defensible!

She recognized him by his voice. Not knowing who he was, she responded to his question of why she was weeping and for whom she was looking by supposing he was the gardener. She wanted to know where they had laid him. Then, she iterated words which bring about a multitude of questions. She says she will take him away. What right did she have to claim the body? Obviously, at that moment Mary thought he was dead. Was it because no one else wanted his broken body? Crucifixion leaves a body most ugly and, in his case, his side had been pierced. Who would want such a deformed, haggard, and discredited corpse? She did!

Ah, he says her name and she immediately knows who he is. She responds by calling him "teacher." What a meeting that must have been! Her anxious longing for her Master was gone. There he was! The man Mary expected to find in the form of a dead body was doing much more that that; he was talking to her. He had arisen from the dead, as he said he would. Other than her exclamation, we have no account of what was going through her mind. We can only guess. Would he be available for times of intimate conversation? Would everything be returned to where it was before his death? Where would he live and practice his ministry? Perhaps he would execute justice and take his killers to task by destroying them. So, there she is awaiting answers.

Does our dear Lord ever call you or me by name? We have known people who claimed as much. We are impressed by those who profess exactly that. Some build denominations and others followings which often are impressive. When we are called by our names, it makes a difference. By and large, we all like to hear them. The truth of the matter is, we not only like to hear our names but to sense a strong, even undeniable, urge. That's a normal course of life. In Mary's case it was so much more than having a relative, friend, or acquaintance blandly say the word. Our names are highly significant.

Jesus Christ reports to her that he will be ascending to his Father. But until it happens no one is to hold onto him. Just what the meaning is here has confused even the most brilliant and committed scholars. So, it is by faith and mystery we let his words rest and relax in our hearts, minds, and souls. Briefly, whatever the Lord is doing is fine with us. We know everything will come out well for those who love him and seek to follow him. There is nothing quite like putting faith in him and his ways. Mary is to tell his brothers. That within itself must have been quite innovative. Again, we encounter the relationship between the two. It means he trusts her! What higher badge or medal could she be presented? We underestimate Mary at our own peril.

She announced his resurrection. Our text says to us specifically that one of the disciples saw the empty tomb and believed. Yet, it also relates to us that they didn't understand the scripture that he must rise from the dead. So, there is no clear-cut announcement of the resurrection. It takes Mary Magdalene to do the announcing to the disciples. She reports, "I have seen the Lord." While we may get into heated conversations, it certainly sounds like she is the one who was willing to make it known. It also sounds as though she is the only one to whom he literally spoke. Indeed, it was "Mary Magdalene's Day"!

That, within itself, must have been quite a shocker. Women did not do such things then. This happening that would shake heaven and earth was an event so monumental that no one could possibly have considered that a woman would make the pronouncement. Well, there you have it again. Our Savior and Lord didn't follow protocol! She was presented an honor so profoundly marvelous that we look at her in awe. We must wonder why it was given to her. After all, there is a great deal of information saying she was a woman of questionable morals. Ah, but that was so like Jesus and his ways. Peter, James, John, and Paul would come to us as solid apostles. She would largely be in the background, smiling in glorious contentment and savoring her honor.

As is so frequently the case, the most germane inquiry is, "Have you and I seen the Lord?" Now, we have been thrilled by one of the most moving passages throughout the holy scriptures and there is this inquiry, refusing to go away. If we have not seen him, what good does it do to go on living with a miraculous affirmation and story never reenacted into our lives? It is a pressingly relevant way to get at religion, which is alive and well. Really, no other kind or variety is worth having. Not to have some conversion experience, regardless of how and when it comes about, may be the most sad void known to those who continually hear the gospel preached. Offering after offering is made through Word and sacrament. What's our response?

Don't you just love Mary Magdalene? A part of her fascination is the way she surfaces at the most crucial event in the history of Christianity. Any number of persons would likely have had it some other way. For example, surely Peter and John should have had the honors. Maybe they did more than the narrative says but we don't know that. What we assuredly know is this special woman must have been the first one to arrive at the tomb and even more significantly the one who presented the glorious information to the disciples. So, we thank her and acknowledge that God does whatever he chooses to do and with whomever he wishes. Grant that our wills be malleable and moldable for his touch.

Is it truly "Mary Magdalene's Day"? The evidence is there. The Gospels of Matthew, Mark, Luke, and, in particular, John differ. However, we learn that each of the four has a unique contribution. John's Gospel places before us a lovely story, featuring Mary Magdalene. It is immersed in emotion and we are recipients of the picture of a woman who loved and cared deeply about Jesus. He responded to her hurt and lostness. He called her by name and the heavens burst forth in songs of praises. Question what you will about her but here is a woman sold on her man. His name was Jesus and it would be known for more than 2,000 years, but so would hers.

A living relationship with the risen Jesus Christ is what counts, isn't it? Anything less will not enable us to live a victorious faith that others want. To be able to tell others we have seen the Lord and he lives in our hearts is the message the world always yearns to hear. To see his behavior in action with power and vitality makes even the hardest sinner sit up and take notice. Are we being too fundamental and, some would say, pietistic? Perhaps, but then we must discover new words to say essentially the same thing! The message of salvation delivered to humankind remains the same. We are called to be Easter or Resurrection Christians. The grave has been conquered. Heaven is a reality. What more can we ask?

Those Who Doubt

Christianity has always had its doubters. Sometimes it comes in open and public terms. Perhaps more often, despite our attempts at accurate measurements, are the doubters who speak only to intimate friends or not at all. When you and I doubt we are not alone. In the ancient world, our precious faith made little sense to most Jews or Gentiles.

Some great souls, even saints, have been born out of times of skepticism. We have always had our "doubting Thomases." Read the autobiographies and biographies of those stalwarts in church history. When the truth is fully uncovered, we discover some thoroughgoing doubters!

Well, how about you and me? In honesty and sincerity, we admit the message of Christ did not and does not always convince us. It is therapeutic and, perhaps above all, admirable to come to that place in our lives. Our pride is defeated and we admit we are not always 100 percent sure.

The Resurrection and Easter story is the one we may be tempted to water down or simply shrug our shoulders in polite disbelief. Of course, the virginal conception of our blessed Lord is another really big area of question marks! But let us not digress from our major consideration.

Thomas was very specific about his requirements for believing. Don't try to tell me you have seen the Lord, unless you have some real proof. Show me the mark of the nails, so my finger can be placed there. Yes, and my hand must touch his side. There will be no sentimental guessing and wishful thinking. There will be no misleading attempts to prove a point and pass it along to the world at large. The Master was much loved by all of us but we cannot claim too much for him and be dishonest with others, including those who need his message so desperately. Yes, it is hard to argue with our friend!

It is recorded that Jesus had already been among a select group of disciples. He showed them his hands and side. He spoke to them and breathed upon them the gift of the Holy Spirit. The forgiving and retention of sins is even placed upon them. What more could anyone possibly ask? Surely, here was proof enough for anyone who knew the Master intimately. What more needs to be said for verification of his appearance? Surely there was not a single soul who would lie about it. The Master had come and gone. He made his point with clarity. Many people would believe far less important things with a lot less evidence! Still, Thomas was a holdout.

Probably, by now we are beginning to have a real problem with this fellow. What else did he want and/or need? Well, we have to hand it to him; he was quite specific! Didn't he trust his comrades in the cause of Christ? Does he want to be difficult and like some little obstreperous child? Showing oneself to be an independent thinker is one thing. To challenge the witness of his brothers and sisters in Christ is quite something else. We may be motivated to tell him a thing or two. How dare you call into question such stalwarts as Peter, James, and John? Maybe he was one of those people who wished the resurrection was true but had many misgivings. On the other hand, maybe he was just egotistical.

Is it possible, realistically, to place you and me at the scene those twenty centuries ago? To do that kind of thing takes real effort. We would all like to do that, wouldn't we? Our assumption is that if we could really get back to the first century, things would be clarified and we would understand Thomas much better. Don't count on it! It seems to me about the only thing we can understand and accept is his insistence on complete accuracy by physically touching two places on the Master's body. He was unmovable and the history books remember him as someone who not only demanded proof but one who would become a prototype for all of us. Is there anyone you know who hasn't heard of "doubting Thomas"?

Thomas kept his end of the bargain and did not argue. We may not accept this in glowingly positive terms. In fact, this may be more of a deal with God than anything else! We all know or have heard of those stories. Maybe it was during a war and we promised God that if he would just spare us we would believe and go on to a lifetime of service for Christ. There are many accounts of such experiences coming out of the Second World War. Death was imminent and God was told that if he would just spare us, we would go home and live exemplary Christian lives. Some of those promises bore rich fruits for others. Perhaps that is not quite the same as a doubting Thomas but don't miss the similarity.

In a way, there is a childlike simplicity about Thomas. If you show me the goods, count on my acceptance of his resurrection! We might view him as a small boy who wants to be convinced but isn't. You say you can hit a ball out of the infield, well show me. You say you are good at flying a kite, well show me. There is an innocent quality to it, isn't there? Rather than being, at least, somewhat critical of him, we do well to show him some respect. You and I know the story. Had we been there we might have been a lot more difficult than he was. Even today, after all of the confirmation in people's lives, we can be downright demanding for signs of the genuineness of Christianity.

We all admit, in the privacy of our spiritual lives, it is not very helpful to get into an argument with God. Experience tells us again and again he always wins. Sometimes, however, there is solid progress that comes out of our moanings and groanings, indeed, our lack of gratitude and grace. The Old Testament (Hebrew Scriptures), especially, point to characters thoroughly upset with God, who proceed to tell him off! More relevantly, can we feel free to argue with the one who made us, that is, if we do it respectfully and in a worshipful mood? For many, the answer is, "Yes," isn't it? Maybe the most admirable characteristic of Thomas was that once his needs were met, he was totally sold.

You and I are counseled not to tempt God. To do so puts us in a worse position than being between a rock and a hard place! We are insolent to the point of being blasphemous. But we do not want to be too hard on ourselves. We can get our backs up for the right reasons and be purely motivated — like Thomas — which leads us into a newly discovered intimacy with the Father, Son, and Holy Spirit. Never underestimate the patience and mercy of God! While we may have communicated that our man is tempting God and we wonder how he got by with it, is that truly the case? We may not all agree about the answer. But keep in mind, as the text later shows, our Lord has a very important point to make for posterity and we are greatly helped by it. How like our Lord to show us the way!

Thomas was confronted by Jesus. After the Lord spoke, again, his words of peace, he directly addressed Thomas. This doubting fellow was on the hot seat! There, before his brothers and sisters, the Lord dealt with the situation. Let's use all of our ingenuity and imagination to bring the moment into focus. The risen Christ was looking at him with those loving and yet piercing eyes. They are eyes that do not miss the least little thing! One wonders if Thomas had the spiritual stamina to look into them more than an instant. More decisively, could you and I hold up under such pressure? We might be tempted to run but where would we go?

We do well to pursue the matter of Jesus' presence and our reaction. Not likely have many of us had an experience close to that of Thomas. That is not as relevant and timely as our under-standing that the Lord comes to us and spiritually shows us his nail prints and wounded side. It is closely akin to the reception of the body and blood of our crucified Savior during Holy Communion. He comes to us in those simple and plain elements. He has done so for centuries to countless millions, many on a regular Sunday basis and some on a daily encounter. In a way, the celebration of the Lord's Supper is a divine and holy confrontation. In effect, he says to us — indeed pleads with us — to receive him and enjoy the blessed event prepared for us.

Is our response to the Lord comparable to that of Thomas? As his body and blood are lovingly placed before us, what is our re-sponse? Recall our doubting friend exclaiming, "My Lord and my God!" Protestants have yet to come to terms in any far reaching way with the sacrament many call the Eucharist or thanksgiving. However, we should joyfully give thanks for the progress we have witnessed in the last thirty years. Increasingly, some of us are discovering something very similar to a blessed and assuredly precious confrontation. It is certainly not one of being hateful and seeking negative domination. It is one of invitation to abundant life with potentiality well beyond anything we can plan or orchestrate.

In a world that has become decidedly multicultural and religious, only the real thing shall see us through to victory, now and forevermore! In our nation, long considered a Christian nation, our way of life is becoming more and more altered — in some cases, radically so. Some thinkers, even theologians, tell us we were never a Christian nation. That may very well be true but try to communicate that to any number of people! The perception of being a new Israel with God's special blessing is alive and well. Doubtless we have been blessed and chosen but a new day calls for a new orientation to the realities of other religions, especially Islam. Regardless, Jesus Christ is always faithful to his people.

Thomas is to be commended but not imitated. Intriguingly, our Lord pays him a kind of backhanded or indirect compliment. It is as though he is saying *you are right* and *that's good you believe, but is it solely because you have seen me.* Is it because you touched the nail prints and my seriously injured side? If I had not come to you in person, what would you have done? In fact, what makes you think you are so special in requiring evidence the others didn't? Possibly we are depicting Thomas in terms never intended but one cannot help posing questions that appear to be much in order. It is well to remember Christ knew the future and he didn't.

You did a good thing, Thomas, but the days — indeed, centuries — will not bode well for those who demand proof in a certain way in order to believe the unrivaled story of salvation, delivered once and for all by Jesus the Christ. There we have it! We commend you friend but it is not the way of the future. Millions — even billions — of human beings will come and go. Precious few will have the high honor accorded to you. For the vast majority the Holy Spirit will carry the day and spiritual presence shall be the accepted means of conversion, leading to supernatural confidence and wholesome contribution. Praises be to the resurrected Lord Jesus, who neither forsakes nor leaves his people.

Don't be like Thomas and require of the Lord a specific sign! Our Savior is crystal clear that "blessed are those who have not seen and yet have come to believe." There is not much subtlety here! We honor and appreciate his likes but don't imitate him. The eyes of faith must prevail as the Father works and weaves his ways and will among precious people. What a glorious history it is, as you and I are recipients of the greatest story ever told. We are to see with spiritual vision. In the long run it is invariably superior to any other type of eyesight. Give thanks for the means of knowing Jesus Christ as Savior and Lord.

There seems always to be a significant place for a word of caution. In brief, don't slip back into a mode of requiring the Holy Spirit to speak to you in a certain way. Be reminded the Holy Spirit blows whenever and wherever he chooses. We might also add to whomever, whatever, and however! How supremely happy we ought to be and wondrously we should celebrate the Father's goodness. Seek the Lord day or night and in any place. Listen to the one who has a word of inspiration for you. Learn to cultivate and use any tool for spiritual growth provided. Be resilient to the methods and tools provided. Thomas, we love you and grant you honor. But you had your way and we have been given ours. He lives, Christ Jesus lives today!

Our text is the story of a man who refused to believe in Jesus' resurrection, unless the Lord appeared and provided proof. Furthermore, both his hands and side must be touched. We smile and sometimes wonder why our Lord went so far as to accommodate his demand. After all, who demands anything from God Almighty? Perhaps it is a uniquely special way God walks the second mile to reach a doubting child. Whatever the reason(s), we sense it is a teaching moment for all those who would come later. Learn not to demand a miracle in order to believe! Our Lord and God provides his presence in spiritual power and we are to believe.

Have we not all known those who insisted on proof that crushed all doubts? Perchance we know them because we are the guilty parties! A cardinal theological principle is that we are saved or converted by faith. We are given the gift and receive it in faith like children. The first Easter has long passed and Thomas remains a

194

topic of discussion. The heart of the lesson is there for all seekers to accept: We are to believe without physically touching his hands and side. His ongoing spiritual presence is the pearl of great price that gives us hope and direction for times that try our souls and those about us. It is not that so much is expected of us. It is that so little is expected! In the context of repentance and forgiveness simply accept him by faith.

Fish And Sheep

Don't you find this passage filled to overflowing with delightful descriptions? Only in the Gospel of Saint John do we discover such an appealing and even worshipful relationship between Simon Peter and his Savior and Lord. A feast is set before us and its attraction will last a lifetime for all those who profess the Christ.

As usual, the Master relates his will and ways through common and ordinary means. Who didn't know what a fish was? Yes, and who didn't know a sheep when he/she saw one? Additionally, the Psalm 23 was deeply engrained in those who called themselves religious Jews.

To have caught the scene(s) on videotape might be something all of us wished could have happened. Obviously, that didn't happen, at least, as we understand those things. Perhaps in heaven it will be played back to us in all its magnificence but there is no need to wait and see.

We are treated to a sublime and yet down-to-earth story, filled with meaning so profound that we continue to reflect and ponder. How privileged we are! We are more privileged than Abraham, Isaac, and Jacob. Yes, and add to that Moses, David, Isaiah, Jeremiah, and many others.

Peter failed and then succeeded at fishing. For some of us fishing has just never caught on as a pastime. We use our spare time in other diversions. For many it is golf or some other worthwhile activity. For those of us less participant oriented, watching baseball, basketball, football, and racing comes to mind. Perhaps it is best for us to notice then from the beginning, fishing — except for the rich — was a way of making a living and not much of a hobby. In that day and time, most everything had some connection to providing food, clothing, and shelter. Jesus was good at tapping into the fishing business for disciples!

Yes, we discover the Big Fisherman first failing and then succeeding. It seemed like that was the story of his life! The gospels again and again depict him as a bumbling sort of fellow who managed — at first — to botch most everything. Surely, a man who caught fish for a livelihood would have the good sense to try more than one side of the boat. Anyone with solid business skills knows one does not continue to spend time for very long in an area which is not profitable. But just maybe we should not be too hard on Christ's chosen leader. How often do you and I botch promising ventures? Do we need to elaborate further?

It sounds like it was quite a catch of fish. In fact, we are told there were 153 large fish. By today's standards, this may sound small and modest. Yes, and isn't it fascinating the actual number is given? It adds credence to the whole event, doesn't it? There are those who respond that it doesn't make a bit of difference and all that matters is that it was a good fishing trip. It succeeded, despite Peter's usual unintended buffoonery, and proved once again that Christ's favorite fellow was still just that. We might ask: "Why did God's Son continue to be patient with him?" To be honest, we can only conjecture.

He must have been some sight, because you remember he jumped into the water, after the disciple Jesus loved told Peter of the presence of the Lord. It even sounds like the other disciples were doing all the work in bringing the heavily loaded net to shore. This fellow designated as "the Rock" by many was certainly colorful but many, if not most of us, would not have made him first among equals in the college of the twelve apostles! Yet, the gospel story, not just in John but the other three, tells us he and the Lord had a very special relationship. After all, he was the one who recognized Jesus as the Christ. Some might add, in jest, Jesus had to call him to ministry before he went broke in the fishing business!

Peter had a memorable breakfast. The enormous catch was safely ashore. The Lord was waiting on the beach. He had some bread and was cooking fish over a charcoal fire. Jesus invited them to breakfast. Can you and I imagine having breakfast with Jesus? In our society and culture, we might want to visualize some well-to-do fellows, dressed in sport clothes, sitting in a restaurant. Our dear Lord looks much like them, except he has on a clerical collar! They have the works. There are eggs, pancakes, ham, sausage, bacon, toast, coffee, juice, and jelly. Far-fetched and amusing? Well, yes, because it bends the story so far it loses its majesty. It also has pork on their plates!

They all knew it was the Lord. Plates were not passed and he served them, which is significant. Do you get the idea that there is more than tasty fish and wholesome bread at work here? Do you also sense that there's a lot more to it than hungry, seedy fishermen devouring a tasty meal? It has a Eucharistic dimension, doesn't it? In a way, it is a fish story and yet in another it isn't at all. For one thing Jesus, according to the text, already has the table set. Not one of the 153 fish is needed or is it? It is reminiscent of the loaves and the fishes. There is both miracle and mystery at work here. So, as we attempt to decipher the meaning, food from the hands of the Master is put before us.

Man cannot live by bread alone, regardless of its freshness and delicious taste. It is in the spiritual sharing of our gifts that we are nourished and fulfilled. Our blessed Lord was always giving gifts and in doing so challenges us to do the same. His greatest gift is found in his undeniable presence, as the crucified and resurrected Lord, in the Holy Communion. While Peter and the others experience a memorable breakfast, the message is clear. He is the one who feeds us. We do not feed him. He will continue being the Christ, regardless of what we do or do not do. In our case, however, it is what he does for us that enables us to live the Christian life.

To have fellowship with the Master early in the day has long been a staple for those who are serious about living the Christian faith. To begin the day aright with him is to set in motion forces of good for the entire day. Early in the morning our song shall rise to you! When morning guilds the skies, we cry out that Jesus Christ be praised! While Protestants have tended to be more cerebral in their morning devotions, they have begun, at least in some cases, to learn the tremendous stabilizing influence of attending mass on the part of Roman Catholics. To receive his body and blood is to receive holy medicine from the living God! Of course, we can do Bible study, offer prayers of intercession and petition, receive the holy sacrament, and meditate, how thoroughly blessed we are!

Peter was greeted by three questions. It was only after breakfast that the Lord posed his trio of questions to Peter. The blessed event of both material and spiritual food had happened. Jesus had a plan, didn't he? The focus was now on his main man. The fellow whose track record was subject to criticism was now on the spot. We note it was one-on-one, with the others simply watching and listening. It was testing time and Peter was on trial. There are those who say Jesus was doing this grilling to be sure he had chosen the right man to lead his church. Suppose Peter had failed the test. Then, what would have happened? Yes, and how would a failing grade influence the history of the church?

We get the feeling the Lord wanted to have everything in place before he ascended into heaven. So, he kept pressing the issue and Peter must have felt the heat. Three consecutive times the questions were asked. There was no breathing space, so to speak, as the text presented a trilogy which will forever be imprinted in our Christian consciences. Peter was to love his Lord, tend his sheep, and feed his sheep. The recipient of the inquiries seemed to grow weary and, in impatience or hurt feelings, attempted to remind the Lord that he knew everything. It was a classic scene for all our spiritual ancestors and will remain so for all future generations, provided the Lord tarries.

We may want to suggest to Jesus that he take it a little easier on the poor fellow. As a matter of fact, we may even begin to feel sorry for him. Peter, the Lord really isn't angry at you, but he needs to be sure of your love and thorough commitment. Peter, the Christian movement cannot be tripped up by a vacillating attitude that compromises what the Lord has set out to accomplish. Peter, so much is being given to you in responsibility and authority. To fail is not just to fail yourself and the apostles. It is a matter of there being no room for negligence. Souls hang in the balance. Posterity counts on you perhaps like no other human being who was ever born.

In a small, but certainly similar way, we pastors know this holy routine. It is not secular questions and answers, like being interviewed or evaluated for a job in a bank. Some of us in years and even decades still hear our blessed Lord addressing us as a reminder. For the shepherd of the lambs and sheep to fail his/her boss is to set in motion more hurt than any of us can adequately imagine. It is sometimes scary, but necessarily so. Perhaps the hardest thing to understand is that just because the world labels us failures does not mean it is so. We may have to betray the world in order to serve our Master! The ordained ministry at its intended best is never a secular calling to a profession like other professions.

Peter caught a glimpse of his own death. Again, Jesus proceeded in what can be termed a logical progression. The all-important threesome was out of the way. Essential answers had been given. As Peter heard the words drop from his Master's lips, he must have trembled. Would he have to die for his faith? For a man like Peter to be taken where he didn't want to go, potentially was a very hard pill for him to swallow. When it happened, he was to be old and not have any actual say-so. His right of decision would have vanished but, best of all, is that it would glorify God! Some would say it was bad news so the good news could flourish.

While the holy scriptures do not mention the specific way he dies, well-received tradition has a word for us. Apparently, Christians were going through terrifying persecutions in Rome and it came time for Peter to be killed. This tradition said he was to be crucified like numerous others in the usual way. Peter said he was not worthy to die the same as his Master did, so he requested to be crucified head downward. What better way could he glorify God? It sounds like he received his fate with composure and fortitude. There is a certain divine aura about all of this and it makes us weep tears of both sadness and joy. However, as we reflect, joy comes to the forefront and wins.

Jesus' call to Peter to follow him must have been kept hero-ically in tact. To believe or not to believe in the papacy and the popes with Peter being first, tends to be a moot point for those of us who have sought to follow the ecumenical imperative. Perhaps it is because recent popes like John XXIII and John Paul II have shown us by example they could relate to Catholic and non-Catho-lic alike. Generally, our affection and respect for them has become a major unifying force for those confessing Jesus Christ as Savior and Lord. Both men were gifts to all of us and their charitable goodness lingers like the aroma of gorgeous flowers sent to us by the angels in heaven. We have witnessed centuries-old prejudices diminish and even die!

As you and I receive this powerfully relevant text into our very souls, we relearn the amazing genius of the holy scriptures. The Lord Jesus Christ tells us the truth and expects us to appropriate it in ways benefiting every life we touch. We walk by faith but, like Saint Peter, we are given a glimpse now and then. Those precious moments are signposts, making our pilgrimages somewhat easier. Our faith, how gloriously precious and indispensable to our well being it is! Stop tending to feel sorry for Peter and celebrate his life and death. His imperfections and betrayals were but stepping-stones for someone who, by the grace of God, finally grew up in Christ.

Simon Peter is the star "attraction." He is pictured again and again as the prime apostle to lead the ancient church. Our dear Lord just would not let loose of him! It is here that some of us reflect on voyages in our spiritual experiences which are best noted as hectic and perhaps earthshaking. But did the Master give up on us? The answer is in a resounding negative. We were not remotely close to what we should have been but the Lord clung tenaciously to us. We are not in the "star" category. Yet we know firsthand the power of Christ's persistence and his ways of spiritual formation. By the very nature of our calling, we pastors are fishermen and shepherds.

Praises be to God the Father through our Lord Jesus Christ we are told to follow him! All human beings at some time in our lives decide to follow someone. Indeed, there are those who change who they will follow a few or several times. Why not settle in with the Master in the early portion of our lives and live spiritually happy the rest of our days? Laity are also capable of being both fishermen and shepherds. Sometimes they are even better at it than those of us duly ordained by our denominations. Never underestimate the powerful love of God. Yes, and when he absolutely refuses to let you go, kneel in gratitude and thank him now and forever. Amen.

Easter 4
John 10:22-30

So, Are You The Messiah?

History shows that people are invariably looking for Messiahs or Christs. There is that special person who is to come among them and, in a sense, do for them what they cannot do for themselves. Even for years after our Lord arose from the dead and ascended — yes, and still at this moment — people are looking.

Our Jewish friends, in particular, have this long historical record of watching and waiting. There were, and are, many disappointments in all of this yearning. Indeed, before and after Christ there were those who claimed to be the anointed one of God. Again and again dreams and hopes were followed by disasters.

There seems to be something amiss in most everyone, until he or she has settled on the promised extra special one in their lives. Thinkers, pundits, and even theologians write of the apparently unending search for a great figure. It can be agonizing for some and supremely fulfilling for others.

Don't we wish we had full autobiographies from our friends and relatives telling the stories of their quests? Unquestionably, it would be revealing and some might even make the bestseller lists! Pause to ponder the life of a grandfather or grandmother and wonder about their search.

There are those seeking a clearly defined Messiah. We have a job description. Some said loudly in our Lord's time, "You don't fit what we had in mind!" Isn't such a response modern and don't we hear it every day or so? He or she is supposed to look like this. The perimeters are drawn. Anything outside of them will call into question his or her messiahship. What is expected is more or less set in cement. Deviation, even the lightest, will raise the thought that the one in question is merely posing and is not really the person sent by God.

When we move into political and economic philosophies, we experience much the same thing at work as that which occurs in religion. Quickly, communism and socialism appear on our radar screens. Yes, and there is the admission democracy and capitalism can be counted in much the same category. In America, we labor to keep things straight and not make our Lord an advocate of democracy and/or capitalism! It isn't always easy, is it? Sometimes we ask if he actually gave his approval to a specific political or economic philosophy. Furthermore, we are sometimes made uneasy by thoughts that the American way is not necessarily his way.

Some of the Jews were in suspense and obviously could not figure out whether he was the Messiah or not. He did not give them the answers they wanted. Often lurking in the background of such folks was the expectation that he would set out to defeat the despised Romans and restore their sovereignty. Charismatic military might was at the core of what they had formulated not only in their minds but in their hearts, as well. You and I are called upon to be compassionate and patient. There were genuinely good and certainly sincere people involved. It was not a situation nearly as clean-cut as some would have us believe!

On a more human level we discover, at least, some likeness among pastors and parishioners. That pastor is not at all what we expected and solid support will be very hard to come by! We might want to reverse the perspective and hear a pastor lament what is found in the parish! Laity and clergy alike, who are committed to Christ and his church, know the answer. If we never had those difficult moments in the lives of pastors and parishes, how can we expect to be stretched for greater good? It is frequently not an easy pill to swallow. You mean we are to accept and support this pastor, even though he/she doesn't measure up? Only spiritual maturity, especially sincerity and humility, can save the day.

There are those who have missed the signs of messiahship. It was the Feast of the Dedication — Hanukkah, and Jesus was walking in the temple. To be more specific, he was in the portico of

Solomon. There were those who thought it contained some of the remains of Solomon's temple. It is most likely he was being quizzed by an upper echelon of people, who included a generous number of Sadducees. They were prominent politicians. We might best delineate them as those who straddled the fence between their own countrymen and the Roman rulers.

So, the ruling class was pressuring him to make a statement. Would he please call a press conference? Would he level with them and say point-blank that he was the one they sought? The answers and the ways in which he was delivering them were not acceptable. His works are there for all to see. Of course, they probably wanted a private audience with him! Then, the innermost secrets could be shared. After all, they were the ones with the privileged places in the community and deserved to have the truth of God, separate and apart from others! We all know such people, don't we? Don't let the lesser ones know what we have been told and we will support and, above all, guide you.

We are confronted by something of an enigma. Jesus relates to them that they have missed the signs and yet also wants them to know they don't belong to his sheep. He has done works in his Father's name and they do not believe. Apparently, the Lord's understanding of God does not do a thing for them! Can't you imagine someone being that independent with the power brokers? We can only guess at the awful condescension filling the air. Jesus, we know your parents; they were not all that much and here you are trying to be somebody with little or no proof. The most hectic moment must have been at the instant he told them they didn't belong to his sheep!

Let's face it, you and I miss the signs, too. To celebrate and confess Jesus Christ as Savior and Lord is a powerfully inspiring statement. To be open to what the Holy Spirit is saying next may find us unsure and even faithless. Is what is coming across the screen a part of his messiahship? We thought we had this down pat and now we are confused by being urged to move out of our comfort zones. We must go back to the drawing boards and check this out! Indeed, we can be a great deal like the Sadducees and their fellow travelers and not notice. Then, in a repentant attitude we are urged to see and accept our Lord in a more expansive way. Is it painful? Probably. Is it growth producing? Most likely.

There are those who hear his voice and know him. The Messiah's people hear his voice and not only that, they also know him. Apparently the Jewish powerful elite heard his voice but didn't know him. That really hits home, doesn't it? It raises questions we all have heard so well. Across this world of ours, and a lot closer to home, his voice is heard. Those of us who have both heard and know him have probably lost track of the many dear people who admitted hearing but not knowing. The invitations were many and the avoidances or rejections come back to our memories with sadness.

To hear and to know is to follow. Oh, there are exceptions but that is beyond our very limited comprehensions. To know is to desire to follow now and for evermore. Yes, the roads can be bumpy, but to know him keeps us going because he is by our side encouraging us. Just think of it and give thanks: We are his sheep! Are we privileged and part of the elect? That's a loaded question but, as far as we can discern, the answer must be in the affirmative. It is never cause for smugness or anything resembling assurance produced by one's goodness. The grace of the living God has descended upon us. Christ belongs to us and we belong to him. Try to think of something more positive!

When we are in love with Jesus, we have heard his voice and know him. To know him is to love him! As we follow him in that love through the Holy Spirit, a sense of walking and talking with him fills our souls. Successes and failures come and go. Joys and sorrows make their appearances. Pain and pleasure greet us and return another day. High points and low points of spiritual experience are an ongoing adventure. Sing at the top of your voices that Christ has come. How do we know? We know because he lives in us! So, it is an old, old story of Jesus and his love. In countless forms, the ages confirm all that we have said. In a priceless and unbroken chain, Christian soldiers march on!

Our hope is summarized in a few words of the text. Gone are the days of rejection. Gone are the days of uncertainty. Gone are the days of cross-purpose. Gone are the days of empty living and fear of dying. You and I know beyond any shadow of doubt that we didn't earn any part of our salvation. It was a gift of the Father, who sent his Son to us as the Messiah. There is no waiting in suspense. He was and is here and that is that! Even in the face of defeat and sadness, there is still cause for jubilation. Why? Because we know that face will change and ultimate victory is ours. Regardless of how dark the clouds are, they are always lifted. The true, noble, and right emerge in all their glory.

There are those to whom eternal life is granted. This is very plain. He gives us eternal life and we will never perish. The promise is even underlined by indicating no one will snatch us out of his hand. Those cynical of our faith are apt to respond in derision and suggest the Messiah's promise is nothing more than wishful thinking. He/she would add that it is unverifiable and, in fact, cause for something resembling hilarity! Nevertheless, Christians can be a tough lot and that means we are ready to rise in righteous anger and illustrate our reasons for believing what we do. The Holy Spirit, that probably no one imbued with cynicism would concede, provides and abides.

Jesus proclaims that he and the Father are one. This was an outright anathema to those with whom he was conversing in our text. To the powers that be, it meant he was either God or equal with God. No wonder they insisted on his crucifixion. No one could be labeled God, especially outside of their power structure! Time and again we get the idea, unless they can name him the Messiah and give him their approval, he would always be deficient and not measure up. We may find a form of solace in their ways and even a form of comfort but let us look into our mirrors and be honest about our affinities.

Who can begin to define or depict eternal life? Well, we have a few indicators. To be on firm ground and on the safe side, all we truly need to do is accept the fact we are going to spend eternity with the Father, Son, and Holy Spirit. To try to fill in blank spaces with our so-called brilliance may only confuse the very people we are attempting to help. What more do we need to know? We are going to be with God forever, living in bliss and perfection. There

209

will be no end to our flawless and perfect existence. Time will have no bearing. The creator of time will be in charge and no one will be able to remove us from the Father's hand. What else can we seriously ask for?

Some of us have believed virtually all our lives that heaven or eternal life is built into the very fabric of our Christian existence. To be a Christian is to acknowledge and profess the reality of life after death with our blessed Lord. It does not make any sense to us to espouse a religion that says heaven is all right but we can take it or leave it. As we go about our witnessing, there is the firm pledge of heaven. As we pastors preach our sermons and celebrate Holy Communion, there is our Savior's Word that we are scheduled for heaven in due time. The evidence builds and certainty becomes second nature. We probe deeply into our souls and there is no disappointment. Heaven is ours!

It is a time of confrontation. The powers that be are pushing for Jesus to announce he is the Messiah. Jesus is even more determined to let them know that they have been missing the point all along. He has told them, mostly by his miraculous works, but that does not seem to register. In saber-like fashion, he sends a bullet to their breasts, which communicates a fact likely infuriating them: They do not belong to his sheep. The insiders are really the outsiders! Their need to be in control and dominate has left them on the outside looking in. Sometimes this predicament rings a bell about the institutional church, doesn't it?

Our Lord deals with them in candor, filled to overflowing with confidence, and causes their comfort zones to be rudely shaken. You and I find ourselves in circumstances not all that different upon occasion. We plant our feet, confess him as Savior and Lord, and prepare, if need be, to do spiritual battle. We deal with people on a daily basis who are not his sheep. Oh, they have heard his voice but have explained it away — sometimes in clever ways. They don't know him and are not interested in him because he is just not their idea of what a Messiah should be. But, praise God, we follow him in spirit and truth all the way to the pearly gates and he beckons to us to come on in.

Recognizing His Disciples

Recognition of people, places, and things is a fundamental pre-requisite of successful living. We count on signs to guide us. Most of us take it for granted. We move through life in various speeds and count on our powers to recognize who and what is about us. It is so simple and pervasive that we hardly notice.

The obvious is with us and yet is it so obvious? Our talents of interpretation and, yes, our prejudices are sometimes awkwardly there for all to see. We can never be quite sure how others will recognize what we do. Quickly, we can come up with example after example calling forth human distinctiveness — even eccentricity.

Even in the close relationships of our families, there are those differences in the ways we see our environment. On most occasions, we can allow for major and perhaps contradictory opinions. Sometimes a teenager will shock us and we react in bewilderment.

Humans must make for fascinating observation by aliens in outer space — that is, those aliens some declare are real and even visit planet earth! Until we can, in fact, prove they exist, maybe we should confine our energies to what we do know for sure.

Jesus was going to his Father. He was to be with his children only somewhat longer and a new sign must come among them. How like Saint John's writings to call us "little children"! It is a beautiful way to say many things. Among them is our dependency. Truthfully, we relate to people both inside and outside our churches who can't fathom the need to be dependent. Their philosophy is to go full speed ahead in daily living and not count on any strength but what can be seen and measured. Their view is one of being fully adult and mostly mature. Dependence is not only guaranteed to make you eventually fail, it is a handle for weaklings.

Isn't it intriguing how we can become so professional and self-sufficient, that our dear Lord appears to bring failure upon us? Of course, not everyone would agree with that! Doesn't God want us to succeed? Well, we are now in some murky water. My experience is that God is apt to do anything to make us grow, but the intended growth includes even greater dependency upon him. Jesus goes to his Father and, in a mysterious way, we sense a dependency on his Father. To be sure, theologians have kept such a topic for ongoing debate. They get into matters of the Trinity and its precedence — if it has one! We need not be baffled because who said the human mind has unlimited capacity?

We can only envision the love the Father has for the Son and vice versa. Maybe a more honest comment is that we pretend, as best as we can. At this interval, we might want to inquire about the relevance of such exploring in light of our discipleship, which most assuredly maintains that we are to love one another. Yes, and candor must rule. You and I can move into those deep waters of gender relationships. For fathers and sons to love one another or for men to love one another may very well produce a situation having great appeal to a certain mind-set. Gender wars are all about us and some are brazenly insistent on proving preconceived male/male or female/female relationships to establish gay/lesbian credibility.

If you and I had the opportunity to return to our fathers, would we do so? Perhaps there is a hiatus and he is deceased. The relationship just never worked out. We wished that were not the case but it is and we don't know what to do about it! Many have known only their mothers as the spiritual strength and voice in the family. Dad is gone. While it is not good riddance — because who would want to say that about one's own father — many have their questions and it has to do with their fathers. Countless men and women have ambivalent feelings. The Father/Son relationship at the spiritual and eternal level interlocked in love is one thing. At the human level it can be a vast wasteland.

Jesus lays before them a new standard for all the world to see. There is a sure sign for all of us to lay our claims, as Christians, before others. It is to be above and beyond everything the world has to offer. You and I may still be at a point in our lives where we accept this new commandment as strictly an ideal. But is that what Christ had in mind? We can talk back in well-phrased rationalizations and indicate Jesus really did not mean what he said in the strictest sense. It is one of those teachings when we say, "He meant well," but the reality is quite different. Therefore, we only attempt to live up to this lofty pattern of living.

In the profane and mundane ways of the world, we are tempted to scale back the highest and best virtue yet known to humankind. We do not ignore it really. We do place it on a shelf no one can reasonably reach. It is just beyond our fingertips as we stand on our tiptoes. Do we like it that way? Well, yes, we do, except for those who understand that Christ does not command us to do something without giving us the strength to do so. Lest we forget, our blessed Lord is conveying his marvelous message to those already within the fold. Not to practice it "within" is not likely to carry much weight "without."

The question always seems to arise in regard to whether we are claiming too much or too little. Some say all things are possible with God and others maintain it is best to go easy and not embarrass oneself! Suppose, for example, you decide to show others your love for someone in your church who has, by all measurements downright and outright, mistreated you. You tell others about the unseemly situation and point to a future moment of reconciliation. The time arrives and the household of faith watches your every movement. You kneel before the person and ask for forgiveness and healing in the context of however he/she experiences the circumstances. The person responds by saying get up and forget about it!

Can we occasionally confuse loving one another, as Christ taught us, with our unspoken need to force someone into an unhealthy plight? In other words, perhaps our practice of Christ's love is truly geared toward showing up the person and establishing our righteousness? Some may exclaim that this is an awful thought! Well, be reminded that we are to be wise as serpents — according to the Lord — and that clear pointer may make us reevaluate our

213

intended testimonial to illustrate his decree. Note the intensity the practice of Christianity can reach! We must count on the spiritual brilliance of the Holy Spirit to provide for us. It is sometimes in our own strength that we want to be and do things that can be hurtful.

Jesus sets the example for loving. His words are without complexity. Just as he has loved us, we are to love one another. We can even reduce this to commonsense teaching — in a sense — in any secular classroom in the country. He points out, "Look, I have done what I am commanding you to do." Isn't it great instruction? You bet it is and we are not left in the dark! Our Savior and Lord is so easy to follow, at times, that we can hardly believe it is him. His eternal brilliance can be lost in our wish that he was a distant lawgiver pronouncing theological dogmatic statements. May God be merciful! Lord Jesus, why do we expend time, energy, and intelligence to misunderstand you?

The everlasting benchmark of his love was and is shown in the crucifixion. He laid down, and continues to lay down, his life for his sheep and lambs. It is a sacrificial love, radiating throughout the universe. When the devils and demons of Satan unleash their godless fury in wars and pestilence, we cling to hope in the love shown us. When things are the darkest and all hell is breaking loose, there is the man on a cross praying that the culprits may be forgiven, for they know not what they do. But let us not be one-dimensional. When our affluence and spoiled ways call into question the authenticity of his love, he pleads on his cross for our renewal!

Why is it so hard to get Christians to accept and practice Jesus' example for living? We have been at it for twenty centuries. Many areas of the world, especially the United States and Europe, have promoted the Christian faith. In the USA, we have sought by both theory and practice to make it possible for his teaching to be implemented. True, we had our share of denominational wars and the testing of the church/state relationship. Nevertheless, we must admit that regardless of what measuring device we use, we have fallen woefully short. Maybe it is just too obvious. Maybe we have had it too easy and suspect things will run just as smoothly whether we take our Lord's summons to heart or kick it under the rug for now.

Those of us who seek to be the best we can be wonder about our children and grandchildren. What one characteristic of our lives can we leave with them to enhance their lives? We know the answer is the love of Jesus Christ. Our timidity gets in the way and our lack of depth spirituality exposes us. Our gift is real love and it is evidenced in the example perpetually set before us in the holy scriptures and is given life by the Holy Spirit. Some of us are so good to our grandchildren. To ask from us is to grant almost instantaneously their request. Do we spoil them? Most of us know that answer. Just maybe they catch more of the love of Christ in us than we know.

Jesus gives us our trademark. If we have his love for one another, everyone will know we are his disciples. That is our trademark. It isn't the great preachers of yesteryear and today. It isn't memorizing the creeds. It isn't giving our money to our churches in record numbers. It isn't putting up concrete memorials, so we will be properly remembered and appreciated. Again, we are driven to admit that it is a way of life filled with love for one another, especially within the household of faith. Our Lord's love practiced in the churches always has a way of moving beyond the walls, so the world can experience our trademark.

When we begin to grow old, we sense the Lord is still pleading for us to love one another, so the world will know we are his disciples, and it seems to become more preciously piercing. It is his way of letting us know he has not given up on his children. The message is the same. We cannot alter it and he refuses to grant an abridgement. The Christ of the ages keeps right on insisting in loving firmness. Long after we are gone, it will be the same. The forms that try to contain our religion will change and often succeed. The indispensable heart of the gospel — to love one another so others will know we are his followers — will absolutely not change.

Human proclivities, being what they are, would very much like to soften or even relegate the trademark to a secondary place. Why can't we just create categories and point to them as the legitimate way to know the power of our faith? For example, those who claim to be saved and sanctified are a category unto themselves where you can always see evidence of his supreme message. Perhaps we

215

could maintain that if we receive the Holy Eucharist every day, we have arrived, and nothing else needs to be mentioned. This love thing, as Jesus puts it, is not only a pesky and feisty command; it is written in indelible ink and refuses to be silenced by the most destructive computer virus!

Once we understand and fully accept that we have a living faith, we are on the way to coming to terms with our Lord's teaching. Saint Paul aids us in the brilliantly written passage of the way of love in 1 Corinthians chapter 13. He interprets, like no one else, his crucified Lord's divine indoctrination. When we are tempted to move the prime message of the ages for Christians over to the sidelines, we are blissfully beckoned to note the trademark that will just not go away. Try as we may, we are defeated by a stubborn and enduring command Christ says belongs to us. We object and evade at our own peril. It is a command we must obey so that others may know to whom we belong.

Both the Father and Son have been glorified. The earliest disciples of two thousand years ago belong to them as children. It is also just as true for you and me right now! A standard has been set in place to be permanent. The body of Christ will seek to practice it among themselves. The world will observe and survey. We hope and pray that our act of loving each other will be a divine program of salesmanship, leading to many conversions. Christ has set the example in stone and it shall neither be moved nor crushed by the forces of evil. Let the fury of hell be unleashed and witness his commandment, showing all its everlasting stability.

For centuries, the world has fixed a skeptical eye on the way it is to recognize his disciples. Sadly, his disciples have been wordy and vague about the reality of loving one another within the body of Christ. You and I have, far too often, sought a diversion or substitute for the actual working out of what he most certainly puts before us for implementation. Let's go watch baseball on television and deal with it some other time! Let's do a lot of Bible study in Psalm and Proverbs and lay aside our Master's lofty decree! Oh, we have our ways, don't we? Perhaps for a time we should remember that we are his "little children" and beg for help.

Keeping His Word

Keeping our word has a long and positive history in our nation. For generations, a man was known by whether or not he kept his word. His word was his bond. Deal after deal was made on that basis. The essentials of the business world found it always helpful and even necessary for commerce to run smoothly.

Some of us can remember vividly how these agreements functioned. Woe be unto that man who did not keep his word! If it happened more than once or twice and there were no extenuating circumstances, he was marked as a bad risk. Our fathers and grandfathers always knew instinctively what was at stake.

Our dear Lord points out to us without fanfare, "Those who love me will keep my word." He adds a whole new dimension to the business transactions, mostly of yesteryear, and the need of keeping one's word. He kept his word and now they (and we) are to keep ours. The prerequisite is love.

We get a firsthand preview into the dynamics of practicing the Christian faith. It sets in motion the way we are equipped to live in a conquering fashion among the foibles of human interactions. We are so blessed!

Our Savior and Lord prepares us for his physical absence. Many of his followers, according to holy scripture, witnessed him living, dying, and resurrected among them. If he would just stay as the risen Lord and minister to them, it would be a miraculous blessing! Don't you imagine there were many who not only wished for this but desperately hoped he would physically stay with them? All of them had already been through so much. Admittedly, not many

217

of them seem to entertain the notion that he would arise from the dead. But he did, so that all would be as it should be.

Some may have begged him to stay. What would you and I have done under those unique circumstances? We can't be sure, of course, but in all likelihood, we would reflect those same desires and yearnings. Jesus, you are going to put us through hell on earth and then you are leaving us! That might be somewhat of a stretch. Yet, knowing human nature, it may be almost exactly some of their thoughts and feelings. Spiritual electricity is in the air and the voltage is impossible to measure. Since John's Gospel is written more in a mystical and devotional fashion, it is hard to perceive the timing of the writing. Of one thing we can be certain, and that is that substantial change is in the air we breathe.

Like none of the other gospels, John keeps reminding them of the very close relationship between Jesus and the Father. It is as though he wants to be certain there is no misunderstanding. Jesus relates carefully that both he and the Father will come to them and make our home with them. He is doing the will of the Father and the Word they hear is not his but that of the Father. Jesus did not come to the earth by his own will, but by the Father, who sent him. So, all the preparation is being done in conjunction with the Father. Perhaps there is no more clear place in the gospels which illustrates the uniqueness of John's writing. However, this should not be a problem because many of us have learned that even the synoptics tell individualized stories!

Soon, Jesus will be gone from their midst. How on earth will they get along without him? It must have been a sad moment drenched with apprehension and uncertainty. If they have on their listening ears, provision is being made for them. Something will come into their lives that may even make them wonder why there was any sadness whatsoever! The key is to love their Lord. Otherwise, they will be unable to keep his Word. The Word was given to the Son by the Father, who has loved all of us from the foundation of the world. It is reminiscent of the twinkling of an eye that seems to contain more — far more — time than can be measured.

Their Savior and Lord reveals the work of the Holy Spirit. The Advocate, the Holy Spirit, is being sent by the Father in the name of the Son. The chief function will be to teach his disciples every-thing. Likewise, they will be reminded of all he has said to them. That is quite a tall order! While this precious Spirit would open the door to untold blessings, the abuse by the unscrupulous would wreak havoc among some of God's people. The purity of inspiration and guidance has been tested more times than anyone can count. Yet, our Lord's message is crystal clear. The Holy Spirit will be their teacher and act as a reminder of all Jesus has said to them.

Some view this promise as the creation of a divine pipeline to the Father and the Son. Through this conduit, the Master will continue to walk and talk with them. Others would even go so far as to call it a dispenser of practical truth for those adhering to the salvation of Jesus Christ. However we come at it or which descriptive phrases we use, one thing is sure and definite: They in the first century and all who follow have access to the guidance of our Savior and Lord. The provision has been made. You and I are the recipients. We are not neglected children who have to guess how to live our lives. Yet, dear friends, we do have to be receptive!

So much has been given to us. The Holy Spirit abides with us and provides for us. If we trust and obey, we are going to be happy in Jesus! The certainty of the promise is emblazoned in the Word of the living God. We might want to pause for a few minutes and begin to inquire just what more can we need. Our Advocate is permanently with us. Every day (and night) is a good one, filled with opportunities to serve God and all of humankind that touches our lives. What more can you and I possibly ask? The thrilling closeness of the Lord is beyond price tag. None of us may be saints or saintly but we know something about the riches of Jesus Christ.

Spiritually, we are only limited by our failure to listen and rejecting inspired powers of observation. Yes, it is possible to listen to hurting people and deal with intimate problems without gossiping! Yes, it is possible to have 20/20 vision and move to provide and/or enable healing to happen! Well, time is wasting, isn't it? We are behind and need to catch up. Our Lord has so many goodies in store for us and we nibble away at some stale carrot cake. Why are you and I so privileged? Well, we didn't earn any of it. It is all a gift from God. The secret is out (and it really wasn't much of one) that his will and ways are at work individually and collectively. Praise God from whom all blessings flow!

Their Savior and Lord leaves them his perfect peace and more. His good-byes are enshrined in the literature of the universe. They are forever relevant to all who would call themselves his disciples. A peace which passes all human understanding is given. It has a purity of purpose and perfection we can only kneel before in grateful expressions. We are in awe and earnestly hope it will descend upon us and never leave us. We learn, however, in our spiritual journey that we cannot contain or control it. Rightfully, like virtually everything the Master gives us, it is, in fact, a gift from God Almighty. Fortunately, for you and me, it is one that keeps on giving and we marvel at its tenacity.

We freely and openly admit that not all who call upon the name of Christ receive his peace that the world cannot give. Some seem to be afflicted at every turn in life. What went wrong? We are not to be judgmental and we are not to play the part of a guru dispensing esoteric wisdom. We are to be sympathetic and pray for the time they, too, will experience what we know in our lives. Truly, it is not because of our superior goodness. It is not because God just doesn't love them. Only the infinitely wise Creator of all has the answers. Let us humbly admit there are times we know little of that peace and we plead for its return. When it returns, how blessed we are!

As far as our hearts being troubled, we know plenty about that, don't we? Anxiety and even agony can smite us for days at a time. We have all wondered why. Some good souls will inquire day and night why this is happening. Again, what unassailable answer can we give? As we set our reason into motion, it is helpful to be reminded that our Lord's communication to us is in the form of a command: "Do not let your hearts be troubled." The clue presented is that you and I have a choice to make. Otherwise, he would have stated it differently. It is in our ballpark and we can choose whether or not to have a troubled heart. How like the Lord to show us that in this case we have freedom of will!

What is to be said about fear? The case is similar, as we notice the "Do not let them be afraid." A fearful heart is also a choice.

Some of us have the tendency to back away from such an understanding and attempt to figure out a way for it to be a gift like peace. Is this splitting hairs and seeking to know how many angels can stand on a pinhead or some such thing? Are we dealing with an almost trivial approach to the matter? Not if we believe in the wording of holy scripture, coming to us by the best translators the world has ever known. Please, however, do not be too hard on those who try to make the choice and seem never to get any place. Our limitations are always with us.

Our Savior and Lord wanted them ready to receive the Advocate. The groundwork was laid for the continuation and perpetuation of his life and teaching. He was confiding in them before he went. His death will not be the end. Even his resurrection will not be the end! The Holy Spirit would bridge the gap between his going to the Father and all future generations. They would not be left, so they have nothing upon which to believe. There would be no chasm. Yes, there would not even be a break in the ministry of the Christ destined from the beginning to come to us. Merely not being physically present will not jeopardize the Jesus movement.

Since they had been counseled to be ready, there should be no crisis in belief. He left nothing undone to maintain that continuity would be manifest to all believers. No one could accuse him of not planning ahead! His successor would be in place and all of the power and unlimited variations are to be enjoyed and enriched by his disciples. Is there thanksgiving in our hearts? If there isn't, there should be. Is there a sense of being at one with the Lord and drinking from his bottomless well of blessings? If there isn't, why not? We are privy to secrets hidden for the ages, as Saint Paul says, and now they have been revealed. For some of us, this is so sobering; we wonder why some have not seen it before. But let us not judge.

So much of this text seems fuzzy for so many people! Only God can know the real reasons for their confusion and hesitation. It is imperative that those who do understand, at least to some extent, not be in any sense condescending or self-righteous. If we are, then we may be met by more than fuzziness. The wrath of God might descend upon our big heads! With the priceless tool of prayer, we are moved to aid our brothers and sisters in understanding what

221

our blessed Lord intended. During prayer time, you and I shall also learn a thing or two. The Lord is so like that. You and I take dear ones to our sacred closets for quiet time in the Holy Spirit and we are taught new avenues of love.

Just to be honest, we would like to live on in our spirits also, wouldn't we? We desire — sometimes intently — for our loved ones through the generations to know us and what we have been about. At funerals, pastors pray that the memories left by the deceased will motivate better living in others. Yes, and some of us who have preached hundreds and even thousands of sermons want just a tidbit now and then to find a place in someone's heart and mind long after we are gone. Does this sound like an unworthy and perhaps unholy competition? Not on your life! For you see, dear friends, what Christians leave really should be a gift from the Holy Spirit.

It is a moment tantalizingly suspended between highly mystical phrasing and rationally stated commands. You and I can be emotionally exhausted by the heavenly strain placed upon us to understand the transition occurring long, long ago. We have had all this accumulation of the history of our faith to put these verses into perspective and some days we scratch our heads in bewilderment! We know to love him is to keep his Word, but then we fumble along, caught attempting to be in two places at the same time. Then, praise God, for some it dawns on them that Jesus has given us the answer in the Advocate or Holy Spirit.

Among the most touching and spiritually charged words in all of holy scripture are found here. We want his peace that the world cannot give! We do not want hearts that are troubled and afraid! If the Holy Spirit working in you and me can deliver all of that, how tremendously happy our lives should be. All of us have seen some evidence of the reality of such happiness from time to time. Oh, there is no perfection in the sense that there are those who are encompassed by these blessings all the time. It is painfully and incessantly an imperfect — even evil — world. Yet, colleagues in the cause of Christ, he has kept his word. It begins with love for him who first loved us. It is solidified by our consecration forever to him.

222

A Good-bye Topping All Others

Those bidding good-bye are around us all of our lives. Sometimes there are almost unbearable feelings and other times merely a shrug of the shoulders. We may sense terrible lostness. Occasionally, it may be a matter of saying under our breaths that it is good riddance. Perhaps most of us have been there and done all of that.

In the case of our dear Lord's ascension, we discover quickly that this is not a usual parting which is common to our experience. There is something very different here! We weren't there, of course, but it is a crucial part of the Lord's progression away from his followers to be with his Father.

Some professing Christians make very little out of this miraculous event. Some duly note it in the liturgical calendar and rather tip their hats. Still others underline it and emphasize it as an integral and necessary component to the gospel story. Fortunately, the latter has become a more prevalent view among many clergy.

We are called to look into this marvelous matter and make it come to life. We want, as nearly as possible, a complete story don't we? Now, our enthusiasm picks up and we look forward to more.

There was summarization to show fulfillment. He was brief — even terse — as he spoke of the Law of Moses, the prophets, and the psalms. Why should there be any dubious thoughts about his ministry? There it is for all to witness, especially his closest followers. From a rich background of his people everything he has done and said should be obvious. If one were to look carefully and with an open mind, there would not be much in the way of surprise. He called upon and commented about the law, prophets, and psalms. It is so hard for some to understand and accept the fact that his teaching is frequently reiteration.

If we could just come to terms in a positive way with our Lord's place in salvation history, how much more content some really good people would be! While Jesus Christ is the focus for us, that doesn't mean he came to us centuries ago separate and apart from other bright lights. Lofty thoughts and feelings are found throughout the Old Testament (Hebrew Scriptures). To believe and practice the New Testament is to acknowledge its dependency on what had gone on before. The entire and complete fabric is magnificent. The slighting of Moses, prophets, and psalms most certainly diminishes our needed understanding of our costly redemption.

It is crucial that we take note of "everything written about me." Otherwise, we can fall into the trap of subtlety separating the two testaments. The New Testament is the primary statement of fulfillment but it gains power and, to some extent, even prestige by carefully using the Hebrew Scriptures. Something new for Jesus invariably means some connection to those beacons who have come before him and who are also historical figures. While our faith has mystery, it likewise has some teachings so transparent we have to labor to misunderstand! Praises be to the living God for the light — often abundant — he grants to us.

There is no wasted space in these closing remarks. He reminds us that he has already spoken about such things. The foundation has been laid and it is time for him to go. On his Father's great board of historical happenings and movements, the schedule says it is just right for him to move into the heavenly realm. His birth, ministry, death, and resurrection are all there for them to see. The often-quoted phrase, "the time has come," indeed has come! The clinging to him no longer fills any purpose. The Holy Spirit will handle all their needs. The period of blissful and loving power is not gone, it merely begins to take on another form that will benefit all the world. Dejection is not at all appropriate. Thanksgiving is in order.

224

There is highlighting of his crucifixion and resurrection. Isn't it truly amazing how these two fit together in such a way that they are interlocked in one revelation of truth? While you and I separate them as two distinctly different incidents, they are one and the same powerful message. In the past, many Protestants have said Roman Catholics made entirely too much of the crucifixion and too little of the resurrection. Yes, and Roman Catholics maintained many Protestants made too much of the resurrection and mainly ignored the crucifixion. From ecumenical observations that appears to have changed for the good!

The Messiah is "to suffer" (crucifixion) and "to rise from the dead" (resurrection). As he prepares to ascend, our Lord does not deal with them by dividing the events. To have one is to have the other. Aren't we blessed and, in a way, relieved by this? As we reflect, how else can we have the doctrine and practical power to live out our faith? We would assuredly hate to attempt to live by the teachings of a dead Messiah. Why not live by Socrates, Plato, Aristotle, or some great philosopher? While we may be tempted to live in the basking light of him arising from the dead, how can we defend a salvation devoid of supreme sacrifice? Again, we detect it is not either/or but both/and.

Some would call it a trite reminder, but, it is nevertheless true the two provide us with the core belief absolutely necessary to the legitimacy of the Christian religion. Diminish one or the other and be prepared to deal with a religion weakened, weary, and worrisome. Who can defend a diminished doctrine devoid of earthly and heavenly power? There is a supernatural characteristic to our faith, which is simply a nonnegotiable. Much to the chagrin of some well-meaning people, they learn that the way to eternal life is found only in the twin towers of which we are speaking. Experience and history point out to you and me that the need to transcend orthodox belief can be very dangerous!

In the Christian context to love one another and to do unto others what we would have them do unto us is an ethical dilemma, unless we have accepted both cross and the crown. In reality to love the Lord our God with our whole heart, mind, soul, and strength and our neighbors as ourselves is a natural fruition of the two. The

225

ideal of pre-Christian teaching becomes reality with the power the two give us. Are we seeking to be too theological for our Lord's sheep and lambs? Not if we are totally serious about living a victorious Christian life! So, we are gently but sometimes firmly summoned to believe what our precious Master tells us to believe. Basic doctrine always does make a big difference in the way we go about being disciples of Christ.

There was proclamation of repentance and forgiveness of sins to go in his name to all nations, but it was to begin from Jerusalem. The Gentiles were to have full access, but it was to begin from the holy city of Jerusalem. In a way, these words helped us to stay honest. It was not to begin at Rome, Constantinople, New York City, or Nashville, Tennessee! At first, our dear Lord came to his own people. He ministered mostly to them. Paul, Peter, John, and others would take it eventually to every part of the world. Is it any wonder that sometimes our Jewish friends look at us in disbelief? Just maybe they are trying to convey to us that we have forgotten our roots. Yes, it behooves us to read the holy scriptures carefully.

Please note that there is no question about our having sins. We deal with them by repenting and receiving forgiveness. This revelation unquestionably does away with those who tell us there isn't such a thing as sins and why don't we just seek better adjustment and accommodation to our environment? Well, yes, such a frame of mind and behavior is all about us. Some of our best and brightest people do some of the best and brightest misleading! But let us be patient and compassionate. We are obligated, at least, for a time to hear what they have to say. The only perfection you and I can claim is most certainly found in our willingness to repent and receive forgiveness. There is cause to pause and give thanks.

Deeply ingrained in the fall of humankind is the penetrating reality that we are not what we were originally intended to be. However we tell the story or create the narrative, the fact of our being much less than our Creator intended is omnipresent. In his undying love, Christ preaches and teaches this to all of us. He gives us a peek at what we are intended by his healing, especially spiritual restoration. He provides a way out of our hopelessness and helplessness by the graces of repenting of our sins and receiving

226

his forgiveness. By extension we are moved into human interaction and apply these graces. To move away from our escape hatch is to delay the essential and perhaps to push us to the edge of hell.

Those in the first century and in the twenty-first century, plus all in between, are validators. As we look at ourselves and observe others in spiritually sensitized ways, our plight is ever with us. But let us not be downcast; after all, our glorious and satisfying getaway is also with us. Thus, sayeth the Lord! Knowing and thoroughly believing this ought to make us humble, sincere, and confident in the Lord. Daily confession of our sins of omission and commission is nothing more than good common Christian sense. A warm heart and willing spirit that is open to granting forgiveness to our comrades is nothing more than a reasonable expectation. The long-suffering Christ paid the price and continues to pay it from his heavenly throne.

There was confirmation that we were witnesses. We are led through his concise statement and then taken as far as Bethany, near the Mount of Olives, about two miles east of Jerusalem. His Word was spread among them and hopefully heard by most of his disciples. Soon they would receive power from on high. After all was prepared, the ascension occurred. Those who were present at these singular events and one-of-a-kind experiences were privileged in ways we have difficulty describing. Were all of his followers there? Not likely, and probably no chance whatsoever. Some activists might even want to shout the unfairness of it all!

With lifted hands, he blessed them and was carried into heaven. That miracle of the moment is one many of us would like to have attended. That's a healthy response and it should never provoke the slightest twang of envy. Once in a while, we run across people who say that if they had only been there, they would be able to believe. As we search our souls, maybe we discover a hiding part that wants the proof of a miracle before believing. If we could have been eye-witnesses, all doubt would be gone! Who are we trying to deceive? Remember Jesus fulfilled the need of doubting Thomas, but he called those blessed who have not seen but believe. Faith given to us by the grace of God and buttressed by much prayer and serious Bible study carries the day for most of us.

The ascending scene calls forth worship of him and a return to Jerusalem with great joy. So, our Lord puts the finishing touches to his ministry by an ascension which was unparalleled. In innumerable ways artists have tried to capture the momentous occurrence. It's fair to admit accuracy in all details will have to await another day and time. There are no living witnesses among us, but why should there be? They were told, and we as well, that the Holy Spirit would come to fill the bill. You and I are witnesses to that Spirit. Day after day we are reminded gently and at times harshly to be ever growing in the grace of our Savior and Lord, Jesus Christ.

After all had taken place, the disciples were found continually in the temple blessing God. It would not be possible for us to measure the intensity of those gatherings. It is not at all necessary for us to attempt to do so. What is necessary is for us to plead with our God this glorious episode be imprinted in us forever. We can appreciate it only with spiritual eyes and ears. But we can do that, so let us not feel slighted CNN or some other news media didn't take us there! All the disciples present on that day must have become incurable optimists. They were sons and daughters of the Father. His Son had been among them. An even more powerful outpouring of the Holy Spirit was at hand. It was a day like no other and the Father has not seen the need to repeat it.

We become aware quickly that Jesus places before us a concise statement. It is as though the heavy work is done and only a summarizing reminder is needed. So much is said in so little space. His threefold ministry of preaching, teaching, and healing has been accomplished. His holy sacrifice has been received by the Father and his resplendent resurrection is a matter of record. All are inscribed here below and in heavenly places. The essence of victorious living is in the gift of repentance and forgiveness. An outpouring of the Holy Spirit is only a brief time away. Yes, and with hands so preciously beautiful lifted, he was gone, leaving them with joy — mostly unspeakable!

Are you and I able to believe wholeheartedly everything that has happened? Are we then able to be radiant witnesses on behalf of Christ and the church? Herein, in these questions and their answers, lies the real conclusion. We are inspired to live out the revelation and pass it on to others. What a remarkably and truly wonderful job we have! It is our primary vocation in this life, whether we are clergy or laity. We are to be held accountable. If there is some fear in that, so be it. It is only a way of communicating the truth found in the holy gospel. There is a clarion call to give thanks and seek to be all we are asked to be by the Christ, no more and no less.

Call To Oneness

When, dear God, shall Christians all be one? It is a first-century inquiry. It is a here-and-now recurring question. Countless programs have been launched. Numerous proposals have been given. Only God knows how many problems have risen in our quest for Christian unity.

We live and minister in the twenty-first century in ways not that different from what our spiritual ancestors experienced. Have some things and relationships improved, especially since Vatican II? The answer without doubt is a resounding, "Yes" but, as we applaud, we are caught by recognizing that much has yet to come into place.

Chapter 17 of the Gospel of John or Jesus' "High priestly prayer" still calls out to you and me. The verses under consideration speak with majestic authority and demand to be heard until all precious parts of the puzzle fall into place. At times, the Holy Spirit grieves and groans in sorrow.

Our stance must always be never, never to give up. The world has been watching a long, long time and it continues to watch. Some of us yearn in nearly perpetual pain for the great day of days. We know it is to be but we do not know the final configuration. We must be patient.

The Father and Son are perfectly related in love. This is such a lofty idea and what are we to do with it? Perhaps our response is that God is God and there is no reason to take it as spiritual fact but more like a mystical moment that is unique to John's Gospel. In other words, any serious understanding is not necessary for the living out of practical matters in the Christian faith. If we do, we have missed truth intended for us and given in the holy scriptures as supreme revelation. After all, there were many writings competing to be in the New Testament and this gospel made it!

Love of this variety is so pure and noteworthy it tends at times to boggle the imagination of those claiming to be in a relationship with Jesus Christ. How do we attempt to understand in an elementary respect our quandary? We beg for our wills to have superimposed upon them the will of the Father. We may never have a rational understanding which satisfies us. It helps immensely to know there is a peace that passes all understanding. We enter another level of spirituality and begin to be gripped by the powerful love the Father has for the Son and vice versa. By way of a footnote, we must not allow our difficulties to tempt us into defeat.

The loving Father goes through the agony of the loving Son being killed like a common criminal and made even worse because of the indescribable humiliation for everyone present to view. The bond of love would not and could not break! Even a sense of being forsaken would offer only a brief look into the humanity of Jesus. If he were truly human, how could it possibly be any other way? Certainly one of the essentials of our faith is the acceptance that in order for our Savior and Lord to be powerfully valid he had to be fully a human being. The centuries-old problem of him just going through the motions — if it were true — would extremely diminish our religion. The supreme sacrificial lamb would be the Son of the Father!

Is our call to oneness one which self-destructs because many in our world see us as worshiping two gods? Our Jewish and Muslim friends have always had a problem with such mathematics. How can one plus one equal one? Perhaps we are straining to solve a problem which eludes solution. However, when we really allow our intellect to function under the guidance of the Holy Spirit, a blessed event is given birth. With God all things are possible. God chooses to come to us as Father and Son, perfectly related in love, with the Holy Spirit. They are one, united in love, that the most heinous satanic forces cannot destroy. Calvary proved it once and for all. As sons and daughters, we are to believe innocently and completely.

The Father and Son provide the model for disciples. The Father and Son are one. It only follows that disciples are to be one with each other. As they give evidence to the world, the world will know the Father has sent the Son to redeem it. It is a matter of depth and undisputed quality, isn't it? You and I can become very uncomfortable. It is to our advantage to keep at the task of synchronizing our wills with that of the Father. Love is in the air we breathe and it is intended to be so thrilling and satisfying that you and I are one, just as the Father and Son. We are not left without instruction and an inspirational sense of our expected pattern of living (and dying).

Those of us who have spent our entire ministries laboring on the behalf of Christian unity, accept the fact no amount of arranging and rearranging can bring about what Christ implores. The latest plan to bring churches together in an organizational framework in the long run may not model in love what we say we are about! Political tugs-of-war to see who controls what may break our hearts. However, we learn we are successful in our quest, as long as we do not lose sight of the vision and give up. The Holy Spirit gently reminds us to celebrate the oneness in love which already exists. It may be viewed as partial, but at least, it is that!

We are never defeated in our mandate, as long as we refuse to surrender. Love shall continue to abide, as we are open to configurations the Holy Spirit makes available. The leap from who and what we are to Christ's yearning victory remains in our midst but even that not so blissful predicament is accentuated by love! We must never dare to ask the practicality of being one on the Father and Son's terms. If we do that, it is like a growing subterfuge, awaiting the time to be expedited by the devil. Love will earnestly seek to save us and point to new avenues of growth on our becoming one. Yes, all that you and I are considering is serious business!

Holy Spirit, teach us to love one another in the model given to us. We are not so much afraid, as we are timid and distrustful. Take away our denominations — if he pleases. Allow us to fail if this is the road to full unity. Bring membership losses upon us — if it is a means for your will to be done. Call down fire from heaven — if this is the only phenomenon for your ways to prevail. Please, teach us to seize each and every opportunity to make for better spiritual relationships among us. We yield ourselves not out of exhaustion and despair, but because we seek to do right and to be right. Reassure us of your ongoing and undying love. We celebrate your holy presence among us!

The Father and the Son convey love with no beginning or ending. Even to make an attempt to speak of love "before the foundation of the world" is a very tall order! Nevertheless, our text tells us that is true of the Father/Son relationship. It moves us away from both the creation story and interpreting their relationship in the context solely of power. Creation and power are favorite tools philosophers and some theologians use to explain God's will and ways. John's Gospel wants you and me to know and believe that the eternal and everlasting link between Father and Son is love. It is a love that makes them one.

Christ earnestly seeks his followers to share in his glory and love. They were given to him by his Father. If you and I can be, at least, something like the relationship described, we enter a oneness that provides unlimited possibilities for Christian unity. Our personal identity is not obliterated. Indeed, Jesus and his Father are one but they remain separate and distinct. Perhaps this is much like a marriage of interdependence in place of either dependence or independence. We are one because both parties desire it be that way! Our faith is truly amazing and we don't realize it, until we grow far enough to deal with the issue at hand. Centuries have impressed upon us that love is the right way to go, now and forever.

So much love spills gloriously into the hereafter. Because of love, heaven becomes a realistic expectation. Simply to live indefinitely without that bond conjures up visions of boredom and lack of spiritual vitality. To live forever and flounder around the universe doesn't strike me as much of a way to be happy! Rule out the heavenly existence thoroughly imbued with love and what do you have? The key to our blissfulness is found in love, isn't it? This eternal virtue brings with it a solidarity. Every thing and

234

every one becomes as they were intended. We were originally made for heavenly perfection and we are not to back away in stubborn resignation.

When we tell the old, old story of Jesus and his love, we are also telling the story of the Father's love. It will be our theme in glory. We will be living in loving holiness and wholeness. In the meantime, we are to be faithful not just in a military sense but in a loving style of living. The intent is clear for this world and the one beyond. We are to be one in the Lord and one with one another. All of our aspirations seem to come together and we praise his name now and forevermore. Glory be to the Father, the Son, and the Holy Spirit. As it was in the beginning and prior to the beginning, is now, and ever shall be. The new commandment to love one another reflects an ever-existing bond between Father and Son.

The Father and Son instill love into Christ's holy church. It is always of the variety that seeks to unite and not divide. The only exception may be division which precedes a greater and more complete union. Sometimes denominationalism has its problems solved by dissolving! Who said the United Methodists, American Baptists, Disciples of Christ, Episcopalians, and others should continue indefinitely for the body of Christ to survive and grow? Could it be that love has its way by providing dissolution and wrecking crews? Experience has a way of showing us that the Holy Spirit can save us for better days by freeing us from institutions which bear little fruit.

For centuries, we have had dreamers point to the most complete configurations of the church, as it should exist in the world in which you and I live. We might quickly add that most, if not all, have been disappointed. The inspirational adjectives from what is popularly known as the Nicene Creed may be a major exception: "one, holy, catholic, apostolic." But aren't we astonished specifically that it makes no mention of love? Maybe we ought to send it back to the church fathers for review and possible editing! Perhaps there is room someplace for John 3:16. We can be certain whatever final form it takes, love will play a prominent part. The church devoid of love cannot be the church of Jesus Christ.

235

The call to oneness remains certain but the time for it to happen appears as elusive as ever. We may be assured the Holy Spirit is at work, coaxing and cajoling, or should we simply say inspirationally wooing? We may also be assured we will not be telling the Holy Spirit what to do and what not to do. As we have traveled the road of ecumenicity, hopefully we have learned that. If some have not, maybe that is why they become so disappointed and defeated. In a few cases, some of us can point out disillusionment. But let us not be downcast and doubt our God's Word to us! With chins up and head high we put failed attempts behind us and proceed to ask for more love and patience.

Every way you and I turn, love always is the answer. Love in Christ's holy church moves about in ways unknown to you and me. The ministry of ecumenism — perhaps like no other — shows us this. Just when we are ready to throw in the towel, we discover a new and unlikely dialogue is about to take place. Our Father has not forsaken his boys and girls! Our Savior and Lord has not stopped lovingly to be one, as he and the Father are one. The unity of Christ's people, so the world might believe, as an imperative, does not go away. We can avoid, evade, and reject but it absolutely refuses to go away. We are called to be patient and resilient, as the Holy Spirit independently moves about.

A few of us have traveled the country, and fewer still internationally, attending workshops and seminars on behalf of Christian unity. We have given speeches, chaired committees, contributed to dialogues, and written articles. We have been inflamed with passion for the unity of Christ's holy church. Unquestionably, progress has given us increased hope. Love of the Father, Son, and Holy Spirit was, and is, present. As an extension of divine love, we have sought to practice ecumenical discipleship. Our failures are there for others to view but so are our successes! We continue to pay a price for this discipleship but we do so in love for the Father and the Son. The Holy Spirit does not cease working.

As a backdrop of the unity for all Christians, we look worshipfully at the Father/Son relationship and catch a glimpse of what we are to be. While there is an incomplete view and some darkness, we are never left totally in the dark. Human loving persistence alone cannot take us where we are called to go. It can show other Christians and the world we are paying a price so that precious people may join us in the call to oneness. The key is the same as it always has been: love. What new tactic shall we use to improve our movement? In most cases the answer is "none." There is an old/new one that, in time, invariably becomes triumphant. It is a four letter word: love.

Sermons On The Gospel Readings

For Sundays
After Pentecost
(First Third)

Guided By
The Spirit

David R. Cartwright

The Day Of Pentecost
John 14:8-17, 25-27

A New Continuing

That first Pentecost was a grand and glorious day. It was a new beginning. On that special day, God's people were reborn through the outpouring of the Holy Spirit. It was an extraordinary event.

As Luke's Gospel reports it, all kinds of marvelous things took place on that day. As Jesus' disciples were all gathered in one place, there was first the sound of a mighty wind; then tongues of fire appeared and rested on each one of them. They were all filled with the Holy Spirit and began to speak in all kinds of languages, yet somehow they were all able to understand one another. More astounding than all this, was that barriers that had long existed between people of different nationalities were broken down that first Pentecost. Think of it, three thousand souls were added to the church that day! They were all of such a mind and heart that they shared what they had so that everyone's needs were taken care of. What a day to remember!

And to recover! For the experience of that first Pentecost 2,000 years ago was not meant to be the first and only one. It was meant to continue for years to come, right up to the present. But the only way the new beginning could remain a new beginning from generation to generation was for it to also become a new continuing.

Thomas Troeger's hymn for Pentecost catches the excitement of that first Pentecost and all Pentecosts to come, including this one today.

> *Wind who makes all winds that blow*
> *gusts that bend the saplings low,*

241

gales that heave the sea in waves,
stirrings in the mind's deep caves —
aim your breath with steady power
on your church this day, this hour.
Raise, renew the life we've lost,
Spirit of God at Pentecost.

The winds of Pentecost are still blowing if we have eyes to see it and ears to listen to it. If not — that is, if we are in a deep enough sleep — it's possible to miss it. I know, for I once slept through a tornado when I was in college. When I woke up the next morning, my roommate was furious at me for not getting up and seeing it through with him. When I asked him why he just didn't wake me up, he replied, "Well, I thought at least one of us should get some sleep." Needless to say, I long for those days when I could sleep that soundly, but there's a down side to being able to sleep like that. You miss all the excitement. The experience of Pentecost is no different.

Psalm 104 is a beautiful reflection on the majesty of God and of God's Spirit at work in renewing the earth. Indeed, the writer reminds us that all God has to do is to withhold his breath, to quit breathing his Holy Spirit, and in an instant everything would return to dust. But "when you send forth your spirit, they are created; and you renew the face of the ground" (Psalm 104:30).

Pentecost is still going on. The new beginning is still continuing, if we are attuned to pay attention to it.

The verses from the New Testament Lesson could well be called John's Pentecost story. In John's Gospel, Jesus promises a Pentecostal experience to his disciples. In the part of the lesson we heard this morning, the disciples have just learned that Jesus is going away. He's returning to the Father. Upon hearing this, they are quite distraught. Questions and thoughts race through their minds. Questions and thoughts like these: "How are we ever going to get along without him? What are we going to do? We're not ready for this. We're not up to this. You can't mean what you're saying, Jesus. How can we possibly make it without you?"

242

Jesus is quick to put all these fears to rest. To reassure them, he promises them that the Father will send them someone in his place. As it's translated in our version this morning, "... he will give you another Advocate, to be with you forever" (John 14:16). This word, "Advocate," is translated in many ways, depending on the Bible you look at. Some Bibles call Jesus the Advocate, a Comforter, others a Helper, still others, an Encourager. They all come down to this one truth: After Jesus leaves, his disciples are promised that they will continue to have someone on their side, someone who can help them.

A judge once said that he felt the best translation might just be a Defense Attorney: someone to speak on our behalf, and to argue our case.

When Jesus left this world, he did not leave us alone and without help. He promised that the Father would send us the best lawyer he could find to stand by our side and assist us.

Actually, when you come right down to it, the Holy Spirit is the form the Spirit of Jesus now takes in this world. The Spirit is the continued presence of Jesus in the church. As we read in John's Gospel, this is a Spirit of truth, of power, and of peace. These are three gifts of the Spirit in John's Pentecost story, and these three gifts correspond to three fears that surely must have been going through the disciples' minds and hearts.

- **Fear one:** How are we to know what we are to do now that we no longer have Jesus as our teacher?
- **Fear two:** How are we to find the energy and power to carry on his mission, if he's not there by our side constantly motivating us and encouraging us?
- **Fear three:** How are we ever to find a sense of peace and satisfaction in our work if we do not have him around to tell us that we're doing it right?

All of these fears and concerns are answered with one word. Advocate, Helper, Comforter, Encourager, Defense Attorney, the Holy Spirit, whatever you decide to call it, or better still, him. Jesus

243

promised his disciples that they would not have to do it all by themselves. They would find the truth they needed, the power they longed for, and the satisfaction they hoped for through the gift and presence of the Holy Spirit that would be with them forever.

In John's Gospel, the Holy Spirit does not just appear for a day and then leave. John goes out of his way to tell us that the Spirit remains or "dwells" with us, forever. We can always count on the Spirit to help us to do whatever it is we cannot accomplish on our own.

I believe it was Lloyd Ogilvie, now chaplain of the U.S. Senate, who once asked, "What are you and your church trying to do that you can't possibly accomplish without the work of the Holy Spirit?" That's a good question for us to ponder on this Pentecost Sunday. For the job of the church is a big one. It's no less than carrying on the mission of Jesus in the world. The church of Jesus Christ is charged with interpreting and continuing the mission of Jesus. The only way we can ever accomplish that enormous task is with the knowledge and power and help of the Holy Spirit. Jesus promised his disciples that the Spirit would be no less a help to them than he had been.

And so it continues on to this day. Or does it? That's the question we need to ask ourselves on this Pentecost Sunday. Is the Spirit still at work in the church today? The best way I know to answer that question is to put it like this: Can the world see the Spirit at work in us today? Can the world see the Spirit at work in the church? Can the world see the Spirit at work in our congregation? Do we show any visible evidence of being shaped by God's Holy Spirit as we go about carrying on Jesus' mission in the world?

Most times, when I'm called to conduct a funeral of a loved one from the church, I'm asked by the funeral director if I'd like to ride with them rather than to drive my own car. And most times, I take them up on the offer, for it's more relaxing not to have to worry about driving. I must say that I've had some interesting and informative drives out to the cemetery. One director told me about the effect God's Wind has on things that grow. It seems that over time, trees that have to stand out in the open become shaped in the direction the wind is blowing. Unless there are other trees around to block it from happening, a tree will eventually be shaped by the force and direction of the wind. Then, as living proof, the funeral director began to point out to me tree after tree that had all been shaped in this way, trees that I confess I had passed by many times, but had never really seen until then. Once this was pointed out to me, I began to see them everywhere. The cemetery was literally filled with them! All shaped by the Winds of God!

I leave you with this question. Like those trees in the cemetery, do we, as individuals, and as a congregation, show any evidence of being shaped by the Winds of God's Spirit? Is the new beginning Pentecostal experience a fresh, yet continuing presence in our lives?

The Holy Trinity
John 16:12-15

Guided By The Spirit

There are two main ways to go about teaching someone something. You can teach them what you think they need to know, or may need to know sometime later on. *Or* you can teach them what you think they're ready to understand at the moment. These two approaches are the basic ways of going about teaching.

But sometimes these two methods can come into conflict. I began my ministry as an associate minister in charge of youth and education. It was the typical associate position. It did not take me long to learn that youth and education is a big job all by itself. It was during this time that these two basic educational approaches became one live issue in the congregation.

The discussion centered around how much Bible could or should be taught to young children. There were those who felt that the Bible was basically an adult book. In their view, young children were not up to understanding much of what was going on in the Bible. This was certainly true with concerns such as Old Testament history. But more than this, these dedicated Christians felt that there were parts of the Bible that were not even appropriate for young children. They were referring to all that R-rated stuff, all the blood and gore, war and rumors of wars, that jump out at you page after page. "Tell them the stories of Jesus, and leave it at that," summed up the feelings of this approach to teaching the scriptures. These students of the Bible were quick to point out that even things like the Ten Commandments can be a little embarrassing when you try to explain them to four- and five-year-olds. How do you explain what not committing adultery means? Even in this modern world, children of this age are not ready for that lesson. How do you teach the Ten Commandments and leave one out? No easy task.

On the other hand, there was the other school of thought who felt that you needed to teach children not just what they were ready to learn, but what they might need to know later on that would prepare them for what they would surely encounter in this complex world of ours. Granted, children may not understand all that they were being taught, but later on with a little help, they may be able to piece it all together so that it makes sense to them.

A surgeon kidded his patient about the list of questions he brought in for the doctor to answer. After going through the list, the surgeon said, "Your questions are fine, but there are some things you need to know that you don't know enough to ask about." Then he went on to tell him some very valuable information that he did need to know, but because of his lack of expertise, he had no way of even knowing that he needed to know it. It's hard to ask a question about something that you know nothing about.

An experienced math and physics teacher once said that she has to deal with this all the time. She constantly tells her students that some of the things she's trying to teach them will not make sense until they know other things. When they get to those topics, it will all become clear why they needed to know them now. If you don't understand the basics of algebra, you will have no idea of what calculus is all about. A freshman student in an experimental physics course in college concurred when he took the course and then realized that it depended on a knowledge of calculus. But many in the class had not had calculus by that time. So the professor set up a lab to teach what was needed, but he was always getting ahead of the lab, so the students never had the information needed to do the problems until after it was needed. It was very frustrating indeed.

Scouting is based on the same basic teaching assumptions. All those skills and merit badges may be questionable to some scouts when they take them, at least to those scouts who are not in the mood to collect all those awards. But one day they might be called upon to use one of those skills, and then the skill would come in very handy. After all, the Boy Scouts' motto is "Be prepared." Being able to swim some day might not only save your own life, but perhaps the life of someone dear to you. It's too late to learn to swim when the boat has capsized.

A young adult in the church bragged to me not long ago that he had cooked pancakes at a church breakfast. When he was a teenager, he never showed the slightest interest in cooking anything. I said to him, "I didn't even know you knew how to make pancakes." He laughed, and replied, "I learned how on scout campouts." At the time, he felt he would never use that skill again. But you never know. You may be the very one the church needs to do that.

In this morning's Gospel Lesson, we see Jesus using a combination of both of these educational approaches, and maybe even another one in addition. Jesus tells his disciples, "I still have many things to say to you, but you cannot bear them now." Up to this point in his ministry, Jesus has told them a lot of things. He has taught them all kinds of things about who he is and how much God loves them and how they are to love one another and, eventually, extend that love beyond their little circle of friends. But there was simply not enough time to teach them everything he might have wanted to teach them. Besides, they were not yet ready for all that. One day they might be, but not now.

We can debate all day and into the night what these "many things" might be. They surely must have included a deeper understanding of some of the things that Jesus had already taught them. Whatever these "many things" were, there was no time to teach fully about them, and the disciples were simply not ready.

Jesus does not leave it at that. He goes on to tell them something else, something which must have been very intriguing the moment he said it, and is still intriguing today. Jesus says, "When the Spirit of truth comes, he will guide you into all the truth" (John 16:12). There was so much more that the disciples needed to know, and Jesus knew it. There was simply not enough time to teach them all that they would need to know in the future, but now that time is about to come. The Spirit will teach them. More to the point, the Spirit will *guide* them into these deeper meanings. "... for he will

249

not speak on his own, but will speak whatever he hears, and he will declare to you the things that are to come" (John 16:13b).

For one thing, right now, as Jesus is speaking to them, there's the matter of his upcoming death and resurrection. Obviously, as he's speaking, his death and resurrection have not yet happened. It will only be later that the disciples will be faced with coming to terms with what it means; what it means for them, and what responsibility they bear in it. As our African-American brothers and sisters have taught us, "They may be able to talk the talk, but can they also walk the walk?" After Jesus leaves them, the disciples will be called on the carpet and put on the hot seat for their association with him. Guilt by association, or accomplices in the crime, is the way we speak of it. But right now, as Jesus is talking to them, they do not yet know that. They will need the Spirit to give them the knowledge they will need when they need it. For them, the Christian life will become a way of life, and not just a nice Sunday school lesson or a soothing sermon.

Father Raymond Brown has described it this way: "The best Christian preparation for what is coming to pass is not an exact foreknowledge of the future but a deep understanding of what Jesus means for one's own time."[1] Living up to what you do know about the teachings of Jesus is the best way to know what to do with them tomorrow. I believe it was Mark Twain who remarked, "It's not the parts of the Bible that I don't understand that give me trouble, but the ones I do."

That little word, "guide," is an interesting word. The word as it's used in John's Gospel recalls how God led the children of Israel in the wilderness: a pillar of fire by night and a cloud by day. The children of Israel knew just what they needed to know, but only that. God filled in the details when they needed them. That's the third way that Jesus is talking about when he says the Spirit will guide them into all truth. In addition to teaching them when they are ready, or teaching them things they might need to know in advance, Jesus tells his disciples that they can depend on the Holy Spirit to give them the information they need when they need it.

One writer on this passage from John has an interesting take on the Spirit's role as guide. This writer says that the Spirit is "the

250

executor of Jesus' will."[2] Now, I've never been an executor of a will, but I have listened patiently to others who have been given this responsibility. And many times, as far as I can see, the job is a mixed blessing. At all times, it seems to be a difficult task. But it's a necessary task that has to be done if the family inheritance is to be passed on to the next generation.

The comparison is an apt one. This was the critical moment in the transfer of power from Jesus to his disciples. This is the decisive question. How will they know what to do after he leaves them? The Spirit will set out before them all that the inheritance means. He will spell out the legacy they are to live up to and to carry on.

Some of the disciples did not get it. Some of them resembled that television commercial where one of the relatives has the remote and is fast forwarding the video of their loved one's will to get to the part that's coming to him/her. We know for a fact that at least on two occasions a couple of the disciples were ambitious beyond belief. They couldn't wait to see what their position in Jesus' kingdom would be. They were ambitious beyond what was even respectable.

Not too long after Jesus' death, the early church found that they had some big problems on their hands. Could Jews be Christians without first being circumcised? Could Greek Christians eat meat sacrificed to pagan gods? Could Greek and Jewish Christians sit down and eat together? All of these issues were thrashed out under the guidance of the Spirit. Some of these issues were worked out better than others, and some were left for future generations to resolve. The problem was that Jesus had not given specific directions on any of these. Under the guidance of the Spirit, the church had to arrive at the truth.

We, ourselves, have some big issues that are equally difficult to resolve: the place of gays in the church, women's ordination, and married priests in some circles, stem-cell research, and beginning of life issues on the one hand and end-of-life issues on the other. These are some of the pressing issues that divide good Christians. This does not even speak of ongoing concerns such as war and capital punishment. As Christians, we need all the guidance of

251

the Spirit we can receive! Jesus did not speak specifically and directly on any of these issues, or at least, not all Christians agree that he did, or on what he may have implied by what he did say.

Yes, we still desperately need the Spirit to execute Jesus' will for our day and time.

On the church calendar, today is Trinity Sunday. Some denominations make more of this Sunday than others. Many have not always known what to do with the Trinity. One lesson on the Trinity that I see in today's Gospel Lesson is that the triune God — Father, Son, and Holy Spirit — is capable of doing what we call these days "multitasking." The Trinity tells me that this God of ours is a multitasking God. That's why God can give us the guidance we need with how to deal with these uncharted areas of ministry that Jesus left for us to decide. We will know what to do, when the Spirit tells us. Better still, we will know what to do, for the Spirit will guide us along the way. The one thing the Spirit will not do for us is to decide for us. As Christians, we still have a job to do. We have to let the Spirit guide us in executing Jesus' will. We can take comfort in knowing that the Spirit will be guiding us all the way.

And it all has to do with the multitasking way the Father, the Son, and the Holy Spirit goes about working out things. The Spirit extends the ministry of Jesus, allowing us to go beyond what he had to say when he was here on earth. In due time, the Spirit will unfold for us what it all means. Equally important, the Spirit will prevent us from going off the deep end, and coming up with all kinds of wild things that might capture our fancy.

This is the test. Wherever the Spirit leads, it is always consistent with what Jesus taught about God the Father when he was here on this earth. That's the standard and the measuring stick. "All that the Father has is mine. For this reason I said that he will take what is mine and declare it to you" (John 16:15).

As for us, on this Trinity Sunday, we can rejoice in knowing that the Holy Spirit not only gets the message onto the page for us to read, but also gets it off the page and into our minds and hearts. That's how we experience this multitasking, triune God when we're guided by the Spirit.

1. Raymond E. Brown, S.S., *The Gospel According to John* (xiii-xxi) (Garden City, New York: Doubleday & Company, Inc., 1978), p. 716.

2. Ernst Haenchen, *John 2*, (Philadelphia, Pennsylvania: Fortress Press, 1984), p. 144.

What Outsiders Can Teach Us

Those of us ministers actively engaged in congregational worship don't get many opportunities to visit other churches and to worship in different settings. We're pretty much committed to being in our own congregations for the better part of the year. Four or six Sundays at most is about all we have to experience how others go about it.

Actually, this pattern begins for most of us even before we're ordained. A colleague related that in divinity school he was a youth minister and only got a couple of Sundays off during the school year. He tried to make the most of every opportunity to visit prominent congregations in the area. Even though it's been more than forty years, he vividly recalled the first congregational visit he made. The service had just begun in this beautiful, historic New England meeting house. The minister got up and extended the welcome to those who were visiting. It was a greeting he's never forgotten. "We are glad that you are here. We have been here in this place for a long time. If you are of like mind and temperament, you may find yourself welcome. We know our faults. But in spite of them, we still try to be an outpost of the kingdom of God." Maybe the pastor was just having a bad day, or had gotten up on the wrong side of the bed. But if this was his usual way of speaking to visitors, it struck my colleague as odd. On the positive side, he was trying to see things from the visitor's viewpoint. He was brutally honest about the congregation. But needless to say, my colleague never went back. Given the limited opportunities for worship, he didn't want to waste it there. Outsiders have a lot to tell us about ourselves. But I'm not sure trying to outguess them is the way to go about it.

I took a sabbatical last year in England, and had several opportunities to encounter how some Brits view Americans. It had to do with 9/11. There was a quiet, but ever present, resentment among the English about how Americans seem to view the September 11 incident as an attack only on the United States. The English lost a lot of young people when the Twin Towers went down, as did many other nations. As they looked at it, September 11 was an attack on the whole western world, not just on America, where it took place. They thought that on the whole, Americans were oblivious to that. There has been an interesting bit of fall out, though. There are many English who have taken to wearing New York Yankees' hats out of respect for the city of New York and how they measured up to the nearly impossible task of making a comeback out of the rubble and rubbish of 9/11.

I also had an embarrassing moment one evening when I went out to eat at a local pub. I found that you never quite know what kind of pub it's going to be when you walk in the door. You have to sort of size it up. Some pubs are very nice, and family oriented; some are dives; and some are rather pricy. This one happened to be the local hangout for university students. It was loud, noisy, filled with smoke, and had people stuffed in the room tighter than sardines in a can. I instantly realized that I did not want to spend a moment longer there. So I headed for the door, evidently pushing a guy as I went by. The student looked me straight in the eye, and said, "Over here we say, 'Excuse me.' " I was mortified to death to be the typical ugly American. A lesson was learned that evening. You never do know what others have to teach you.

Today's scripture from the Old and New Testaments shows us how wide the circle actually is of those who believe in God. In fact, these scriptures tell us that those outside the faith may have more to say to us than we may think.

The verses from 1 Kings 8 are a part of the story of the dedication of the temple by King Solomon. The community is gathered for the dedication ceremony led by the king himself. The Ark of the Covenant is taken into the sanctuary. God's presence and approval of what was going on is signified by a cloud appearing in the holy of holies, the inner most part of the temple.

The verses from today's scripture are from Solomon's prayer of dedication. Taken together, these verses proclaim God as the one and only true God. "... there is no God like you in heaven above or on earth beneath, keeping covenant and steadfast love for your servants who walk before you with all their heart" (1 Kings 8:23). This part of the prayer recognizes the faith of the insiders, those faithful who make up the community of Israel.

The second part of the prayer goes on to acknowledge that there are those beyond Israel who also recognize God for who God is. "Likewise, when a foreigner who is not of your people comes from a distant land because of your name ... and prays toward this house, then hear in heaven your dwelling place, and do according to all that the foreigner calls to you, so that all peoples of the earth may know your name and fear you, as do your people Israel ..." (1 Kings 8:41-43).

There's an implicit recognition that while the temple is the central place for worship, the God of Israel also has relationships with people beyond Israel. That is, with non-Jews. The presence of these non-Jews at the temple tells the world how great God really is. In a word, outsiders can demonstrate to the insiders what the insiders have been saying all along: Our God is a great God. The prayer is that there will be a day when people of all nations will worship the God of Israel.

In Luke's story of Jesus healing the centurion's servant, we also see the principle of extending the boundaries at work. Or perhaps, it would be closer to the truth to say that we see the overturning of the conventional way of looking at things. After giving what's called in Luke "The Sermon on the Plain," Jesus enters Capernaum. The town will serve as his base of ministry. We're told that while Jesus is there, there's this centurion who has a slave. It is a slave that he values. But there's one problem. The slave is sick and at the point of death. From that little bit of information, we can glean a lot. Jesus is recognized as a master teacher. Later in the chapter, it's said that, "A great prophet has arisen among us!" (Luke 7:16).

Jesus is someone to be reckoned with — as is the centurion. A centurion was a Roman military officer in charge of a company of a hundred men. This man was probably not in charge of all the troops stationed at Capernaum, but he may have been in charge of some in the service of Herod Antipas, the local governor appointed by Rome.

That this man has a slave he values is revealing. Slaves were considered "living tools." Roman owners of slaves could treat them as they saw fit. They could punish them when they wished, and even kill them if they felt like it. Slaves were dispensable. The fact that this man cared enough about his slave to want to save him indicates that this man was a good man, even a compassionate one. So much so that when he heard Jesus was in town, the man went out of his way to see that his servant got the help he needed.

Interestingly, the centurion does not confront Jesus himself with his request. Later, we will find out why, but for now, the man uses the existing network he has with the local Jewish elders to get his wishes accomplished. He uses them to get Jesus to come and heal his slave. These elders are quick to do the centurion's bidding. They lose no time trying to convince Jesus, a Jewish teacher, to heal this slave, a non-Jew. In other words, to heal this outsider. Or in what was probably their evaluation, even less than an outsider, more like a nobody, a slave. The elders' appeal to Jesus is based not on the fact that the slave needs help, but because of the esteem they hold for his master. "He is worthy of having you do this for him, for he loves our people, and it is he who built our synagogue for us" (Luke 7:4b, 5). A little pressure is put on Jesus to ensure that Jesus will come across with the good deed. It's as if to say, "Jesus, you've got to heal the slave for this centurion, for we owe a great deal to him." We know for a fact that the Romans helped build many Jewish synagogues. The Romans felt it was in their interest to maintain good order and stability in the countryside.

Without so much as a question, Jesus goes with the elders to visit the centurion's house to see what he can do for the slave. "... but when he was not far off from the house, the centurion sent friends to say to him, 'Lord do not trouble yourself, for I am not

258

worthy to have you come under my roof; therefore I did not presume to come to you. But only speak the word, and let my servant be healed' " (Luke 7:6b, 7). The invitation is none other than for Jesus to heal the boy indirectly and from a distance.

Now the centurion appeals to what he judges to be a common bond that he and Jesus share.

"For I also am a man set under authority, with soldiers under me; and I say to one, 'Go,' and he goes. And to another, 'Come,' and he comes, and to my slave, 'Do this,' and the slave does it" (Luke 7:8). The centurion knows how Jesus must feel inside, being a man of authority himself. He is quite clear that he knows what it means to be under authority and to exercise it himself. He knows how to take orders and how to give them, something he feels that he and Jesus have in common.

When Jesus hears this, he turns to the crowd and says, "I tell you, not even in Israel have I found such faith" (Luke 7:9). Luke concludes the story with some crucial information. When the centurion's friends return home, they find the slave to be in good health.

What on the surface looks like a story about healing, turns out to be a story about faith, the extraordinary faith of an outsider. It's what I like to call the message in the miracle.

I find the contrasts in the story particularly enlightening. The Jewish elders judge the slave worthy of treatment. Jesus agrees, but for a different reason. The elders think Jesus should heal the boy because of the generosity of the centurion. But Jesus is willing to heal the boy because of the centurion's own personal faith and trust. The centurion shows himself to be one who trusts Jesus to heal his servant, even from a distance. The Roman officer does not feel he's worthy of having Jesus in his home. Actually, it's out of deep respect for Jesus that he does not want Jesus to enter his house. The centurion knows that for Jesus, a Jew, to enter the house of a Gentile, it would mean Jesus would instantly become contaminated or unclean. For this reason Jesus says, "I tell you, not even in Israel have I found such faith." Evidently, even Jesus was surprised to find such faith and compassion in an outsider like this Roman military man.

259

What can outsiders teach us? For one, they can teach us that we don't have a corner on the market. Whether it's in the church or in the world at large, because of all the power and wealth we have, Americans can get to feeling that we know it all and are the point of it all. But there are people of faith outside as well as inside the church. There are British men and women who are just as devastated by 9/11 as we Americans are.

Secondly, in much the same manner, we can learn from those outside that we are not the only ones God loves. I think of my aunt, Bessie Cartwright. Though not actually my aunt, she had the same name, and as she was a member of our church she adopted me, and asked me to call her "Aunt Bessie." One day, Aunt Bessie became quite concerned about her next-door neighbor who happened to be Jewish. Aunt Bessie was never one to let go of an idea once it entered her head. She always had to act on it. So she called up her neighbor on the phone and said, "Can I come over sometime and tell you about my Jesus?" Her neighbor replied, "Yes, if you will let me tell you about my God." Well, the day came when they had their religious conversation, each taking turns. Afterward, Aunt Bessie told me about it. She said, "You know, the more she talked about her God, the more her God seemed to be a lot like my Jesus." Aunt Bessie never tried that again. She and her neighbor remained good friends for as long as Aunt Bessie lived. That was the day she found that an outsider had a lot to teach her.

For us, here at the church, I think there's another small lesson that we can learn. Maybe it's not so little after all. Jesus treated the centurion no differently than he did the Jewish elders. He respected them both. He listened to what they each had to say, and he acted accordingly. In a word, he treated the centurion like he was already an insider. And in the process, Jesus healed a hurting boy, a boy who was not even a Jew, not even a Roman, but a slave, a nobody, but in Jesus' eyes, he was a boy who just happened to be a somebody. He was a fellow human being in need of help.

The moment the church stops acting like a club for the like-minded, and begins treating nonmembers the same as members, that's the day the church will really become an outpost for the kingdom of God. And when the church begins to act like this, those outside might just want to come inside.

Compassion Can Do
More Than You May Think

A teacher was fond of asking students in his counseling classes this question: "What can you know about a perfect stranger the moment you meet?" After the students had a go at the question, the professor shared his own answer, "You can bet that the stranger has just lost something." That person has just lost a job, a promotion, a loved one, a home, a car, a girlfriend, a boyfriend, their health, their zest for living, or God forbid, the very desire to live. Whatever it is, you can bet your life on it. The stranger before you has just lost something.

When you just heard that, your reaction may have been like mine. I thought to myself, surely that is too pessimistic a way to look at life. Surely, some of those strangers out there must have just found something. Surely, some of them are rejoicing over a new job, having graduated, having received a scholarship, or are looking forward to being married to a person with whom they wish to spend the rest of their lives. Maybe they have just moved into a new home or are off on a vacation of a lifetime. Who knows, one of those strangers might have just won the lottery. Why focus so much on the losses of life instead of the gains?

Well, maybe, because on the whole, in this life, there may just be more losses than gains, more sorrows than joys. Life can be very hard at times for some people, but as I pondered this question and its answer, I don't think that's what the teacher was thinking about. I've come to the conclusion that the reason the professor focused on the downside rather than the upside was because he knew that's the way we become more sensitive and compassionate. That's how we learn to understand what others are going through. When we focus on the good fortunes that come to others, it has a way of making us jealous and envious. But when we direct our attention to what others are having to go through, we open ourselves to becoming more sympathetic. If you're a teacher of counseling at a divinity school, it's a good approach. If your goal is to train pastors to help people, and to be ready to do it at a moment's notice, I can't think of a better way to go about it.

Certainly, we can learn this from the story in Luke's Gospel for today. Jesus has just arrived in a town called Nain, about 25 miles down the road from Capernaum where he had been teaching and healing. A large crowd together with his disciples has followed him here. Jesus is just outside the gate of the town when a large funeral procession goes by. We know it was large, for Luke tells us it was, but at that time all funeral processions were large. Back then, everyone in the town knew everyone else. Most everyone would have been there to pay their respects.

Most likely, there would also have been a group of professional mourners. It was their responsibility to play flutes and cymbals to work the crowd up into a frenzy. The women would be screaming loudly, shrill cries of grief. If you've never heard such Mideastern wails of grief, there's no way to describe it adequately. If you have, then you'll never forget it. The sound is piercing, and goes right through you.

The man who was dead, we are told, was the only son of a widow. Luke then adds this telling comment, "When the Lord saw her, he had compassion for her and said to her, 'Do not weep' " (Luke 7:13). Spontaneously and without so much as a thought, Jesus' heart goes out to this woman. Jesus knows that she has not only lost her only son, but also the sole means of support in her old age. Later, on the cross, Jesus will repeat a similar act of compassion with his own mother. He will turn to John, the disciple, and make sure that John will look after Mary when he's gone.

As the funeral procession passes by, so moved is Jesus that he touches the bier upon which the bearers are carrying the corpse. It was not probably the kind of bier that Luke had in mind. Luke is familiar with funeral customs in Greek and Roman culture. This bier, if you can call it that, was probably more like a stretcher or perhaps even a large woven basket. But that's not the point. Luke may have gotten the exact specifications wrong about the bier, but he didn't get the point wrong. Jesus was so moved to help this woman that he risked ritual contamination by touching the dead body of her son in an effort to revive him. But it was worth it. Besides, Jesus was never one to stand on ceremony. He says, "Young man, I say to you, rise!" (Luke 7:14b), at which the dead man sits up and begins to speak.

When this story is compared with other stories like this, or even with others in Luke's Gospel, what's remarkable is that there is no mention of faith as a requirement for the resuscitation to take place. Neither the faith of the mother, much less that of her dead son, is necessary for Jesus to perform the life-restoring feat. Just before in Capernaum, Jesus had healed the slave of a Roman centurion, apparently because of the trust the Roman officer had placed in Jesus. "Not even in Israel have I found such faith," said Jesus (Luke 7:9b). But here in this story, the good deed is done with no other motive or assistance whatsoever. Jesus' own compassionate heart is sufficient to perform the deed. The widow's son is restored to life simply because Jesus' heart went out to her.

In response to this unsolicited act of compassion by Jesus, fear, or more like it, reverent awe, filled the crowd. "And they glorified God, saying,'a great prophet has arisen among us!' and 'God has looked favorably on his people' " (Luke 7:16).

The words, "a great prophet," are code words for a prophet like Elijah. This story in Luke is based on one of the Elijah stories in 1 Kings. If there was one person Jesus patterned his ministry after, that person would have to be Elijah. I wish we had more time to trace the many ways Jesus' actions in the gospels have counterparts to those of the prophet Elijah in the Old Testament. The story we are looking at today is perhaps the clearest of all. Even some exact phrases have been carried over from the Elijah stories into Luke's Gospel account. When Luke tells us that Jesus gave him "back to his mother," that is the exact word-for-word phrase found in 1 Kings 17:23.

But this story of Jesus' raising the widow's only son is not just a rerun of what Elijah did long, long ago. Jesus is most certainly a prophet of the order of Elijah, but he's much more than that. In the Elijah story in 1 Kings, Elijah restores a widow's son. In this story, the mother is quite distraught. She accuses Elijah of somehow having a part in the death of her son. After all, she has welcomed the prophet into her home, and through the power of God, Elijah has provided for her and her son with enough to eat and more. She has been grateful, but now that her son has died, it's another matter. It has all taken place with the famous prophet under her roof. So she wonders if Elijah could have had a part in it. She says to Elijah, "What have you against me, O Man of God? You have come to bring my sin to remembrance, and cause the death of my son!" (1 Kings 17:18). Upon hearing this, Elijah is confused and bewildered. He takes the son up to a chamber and proceeds to revive him through the power of God. But first, Elijah himself has a few words with God about the unfairness of what has happened. In an act of what appears to be the transferring of vital life force from his body to the body of the young man, Elijah stretches himself out over the boy's body three times and cries to the Lord. "O Lord, my God, let this child's life come into him again" (Luke 16:21b). We're told that the Lord hears Elijah's prayer, and the boy is revived.

With Jesus, matters are much more simple. It's all done with dispatch. The word is spoken, and the deed is done. The son is returned to his mother. The mother does not even have to ask Jesus for her son's life. It all takes place simply because, "When the Lord saw her, he had compassion for her" (Luke 7:13).

The word for compassion Luke uses is the strongest word for sympathy in the Bible. In English, compassion literally means "with passion." Empathy is perhaps the word that comes closest today. However we speak of it and regardless of the words we use, it's a very strong and powerful word. So much so, that in this story it can bring life to the dead. Our lesson for today: Compassion can do more than you may think.

I recall a story I heard a long time ago, and since it has been a long time, the exact details are little fuzzy in my memory. As I recall the story, which is also supposedly a true story, it went like this: A prominent businessman was walking down the street of a large city on his way home from a meeting. It was night. Since his meeting had lasted later than it should, it was long after it was safe to be on the streets alone. By this time, there were all kinds of derelicts and people of questionable reputation on the streets. As he was walking by, the businessman happened to look down and see a man all curled up in the gutter trying to stay warm. The cool night air was progressively getting chillier and chillier. Something about this man made the businessman take another look at him, and then another. Finally, he walked over to get a good look. When he saw the man, and the look in his eyes, the businessman instinctively did what Jesus did with the widow who had lost her only son that day in the town of Nain. The businessman's heart went out to the man in the gutter. He bent down to him and said, "Whoever you are, you don't belong here!" The businessman took the man home with him to see if he could help him. As it turned out, the businessman was right. This man didn't belong there. He was a prominent physician who had taken to drink and had all but ruined his career. Just as Jesus had seen that the young man did not belong on the funeral bier, so the businessman saw that this man, whoever he was, didn't belong in the gutter. This story also has a happy ending. The businessman saw to it that the man got into a rehabilitation program and turned his life around. All because of that little word "compassion."

Compassion can do more than you may think. Especially if it's straight from the heart of Jesus.

Proper 6
Pentecost 4
Ordinary Time 11
Luke 7:36—8:3

The Extravagance Of Love

If there was anything Jesus despised, it was stinginess, especially the holding back of oneself. If there was anything he admired, it was extravagance, especially the extravagance of love.

There are really only two ways to live. You can live as if this is the last drop, and there won't be anymore; or you can live as if there is more where this came from. We can live out of scarcity, or we can live out of abundance. In the story from Luke's Gospel, we see these two approaches in conflict.

My Bible has this caption above the story, "A Sinful Woman Forgiven." But that's only half of the story. The story could also be labeled, "A Religious Man All Wrapped Up In Himself." This is one of the most beautiful stories in the New Testament. It's one of my personal favorites. It asks us to consider whether the cup of life is half empty or half full. The Pharisee views life as basically in limited supply. The woman, on the other hand, is a living example of the extravagance of love. We see in her the extent to which love will go, given the right circumstances.

Underneath it all, Simon — that's the name of the Pharisee — is really very stingy. He has gone to great lengths to cover it up. Even to the extent of throwing a banquet for a traveling rabbi named Jesus. It was common practice back then for important people to entertain other important people. I guess it still is today. Simon invites Jesus to his home for dinner. The invitation is not so much to enjoy Jesus' company as it is for Simon to look good in the eyes of the town. If Simon really wanted Jesus to be there because he wanted to learn more about what Jesus had to say, he would have observed the customary marks of hospitality and good manners current at the time. He would have washed Jesus' feet, given him a kiss when he arrived, and anointed his head with oil or perfume. Good manners dictated that these three be done for a guest. Streets were dusty and sandals let in the dirt and grit. It was simply good manners to see that a guest's feet were taken care of after the journey to the host's home. Providing water to calm and cool the feet was the thing to do. Traditionally, the host would place his hand on the shoulder of the guest as he came into the family residence, and give the guest a kiss as he did it. In most cases, especially on special occasions like the one in this story, a pinch of incense or a drop of rose perfume on the head would not only make the guest feel welcome and relaxed, but perhaps even special.

But Simon the Pharisee has other things on his mind. He's not interested in Jesus. He's only interested in the praise he will receive from his other guests as they congratulate him on opening his home to them so that they can get to know the traveling celebrity better.

That also explains why Jesus was there. It was not a trap as some have supposed. At this juncture, Jesus is still on relatively good terms with his opposition. No, it was not a trap, but more to show Jesus off and make Simon look good that accounts for Jesus' presence at the banquet.

There was an aunt who was very proud of her nephew who was in divinity school. So much so that she invited him to an outing to show him off to some of her new friends. She couldn't wait for the new doctor in town to meet her nephew who was studying for the ministry at a prestigious school. It didn't work, for the nephew rebelled at being used. It was not an enjoyable afternoon for either the doctor or her nephew. And it certainly didn't bring much glory to the school. The doctor probably went home thinking, "How did that fellow ever get into that school?"

Something like that, I think, explains Jesus' presence at the dinner. Once Jesus was there, Simon forgot about him and went on to other things. It was not so much what Simon did that was the problem, but what he did not do. He didn't even have the courtesy to observe basic good manners.

But the woman, a sinner at that, is another matter all together. Far from observing the customary social protocols, she throws caution to the wind and gives it everything she has. It's as if she has completely forgotten that there is anyone else there but her and Jesus. She didn't just say a couple of polite "Thank yous," and leave it at that. No, her actions were over the top.

Now remember that this woman is repudiated to be a sinner. Not even Jesus disputes that. The fact that she has her long hair down is a tip-off that she's a prostitute. In ancient Israel, Jewish brides bound their hair up at the wedding and never wore it down in public ever again.

But it's this woman who showers an abundance of love on Jesus that overflows to the point of being nothing but extravagant. Her generous actions cannot help but be contrasted with the inaction of Simon's stinginess. Simon is so wrapped up in himself that he can't see what's going on before his eyes.

We seem to know why Jesus was there, but why was the woman there? How do we explain her presence? It's difficult enough to explain why Jesus was at the dinner, but it's even harder to explain her presence. Again, if it were the custom for important people to invite other important people into their homes for a meal, it was also customary at the time to allow "whosoever would" to come and go at will. This gave the townspeople an opportunity to get their questions answered from the new budding teacher. It was kind of a Q & A session sprinkled throughout the meal. The homes of local, wealthy residents were especially set up for this. There would have been an open courtyard where people could come and go all evening long as time permitted. Even such a questionable person as the woman in the story would have had access to Jesus to ask him the burning questions on her heart.

But, of course, she was way beyond getting her questions answered. That had already taken place when she listened to Jesus preach to the crowds. We're not sure just what it was that Jesus had said that had meant so much to her, but whatever it was, she felt herself loved and forgiven. "Imagine, a person like me, a sinner, and one of the worst at that, a prostitute, is not beyond redemption, not beyond the realm of God's love." In fact, Jesus seemed to be saying that people like her were the very ones God was most concerned about. God was seeking and calling them back home.

Those like Simon, on the other hand, were beyond help. They didn't need God or anyone else, so assured were they in their own righteousness. "Those who are well have no need of a physician," is the way Jesus described them (Luke 5:31).

If Simon failed by what he did not do, this woman excelled in what she did. Jesus pointed out the difference to Simon, but first to press the truth home, Jesus told a little story about two debtors. One owed 500 denarii, the wages for about 500 days of work. The other owed 50 denarii, or the equivalent of fifty days of work. In a strange stroke of good fortune, when the creditor found that neither could pay, he cancelled both debts. Speaking directly to Simon, Jesus asks, "Now which one will love the creditor more?" (Luke 7:42b).

You can almost hear the agitation in Simon's voice when he replies. "I *suppose* the one for whom he canceled the greater debt" (Luke 7:43). Jesus says, "You got it, Simon."

If that were not enough, Jesus does not stop with this. He seizes the opportunity to apply the lesson in light of what the sinful woman has done in their presence. He says to Simon, "Do you see this woman? (That is, 'Can you *see* what she has done?') I entered your house; you gave me no water for my feet; but she has bathed my feet with tears and dried them with her hair. You gave me no kiss, but from the time I came in she has not stopped kissing my feet. You did not anoint my head with oil, but she has anointed my feet with ointment" (Luke 7:44-46). The precious ointment was probably from a phial, called an alabaster, which hung from around her neck, a common fashion at the time.

Jesus then goes on to drive his point home: "Therefore I tell you, her sins, which were many, have been forgiven; hence she has shown great love. But the one to whom little is forgiven, loves little." Then he said to her, "Your sins are forgiven" (Luke 7:47-48).

After this little lecture by Jesus, we do not hear another word from Simon. Simon has been put in his place and he knows it. And justly so. But you have to say this for Simon, at least now he has

270

the good manners not to publicly disagree with Jesus and to call his authority into question. Simon is not going to risk embarrassing himself by insulting the honored guest any more than he already has.

But those around the table were not so hesitant or silent. They began to ask among themselves a question. "Who is this who even forgives sins?" (Luke 7:49b). If these guests weren't ready to answer that question with their words, there was one in their midst who had already answered it by her actions. She had poured out her love and affection to Jesus for telling her that God loved her, too. She could not stop showing Jesus how grateful she was. Even Jesus had to take notice of how incessant her affection and gratitude was. It had gone on from the moment she arrived till the party was over — so extravagant was her love.

I'm sure we've all have had times when we have either been on the receiving end or the giving end of similar acts of love. As I was planning for my sabbatical in England, my wife, Susan, and I were trying to figure out just how much it was going to cost to live for almost three months in Cambridge. Even with the generous grant, things are expensive there. Added to that is the high exchange rate. At the time the U.K. exchange rate was about double that of the U.S. As we did our planning, it looked like we had enough money for everything we wanted to do except for a digital, single lens reflex camera that I had my heart set on. I resigned myself to using my old camera, which was certainly adequate enough, just not technologically up-to-date. Right before I was to leave for England, in an advance celebration of my birthday, which would take place while I was away, my wife surprised me with the camera. It was more than she should have done, and almost more than I could accept. It had been a long time since I had been showered with such a lavish, tangible display of love and affection. Her only remark as she gave it to me was this: "I didn't want you to go to England without it." I will cherish the gift for the extravagant love with which it was given.

To close, I say to you, as Jesus said to the woman, "Your faith has saved you; go in peace" (Luke 7:50).

Proper 7
Pentecost 5
Ordinary Time 12
Luke 8:26-39

What Happens When You're Not Prepared For What Happens

How do you handle what happens when you're not prepared for what happens? Well, sometimes not all that well.

I would like to call your attention to a recent movie, *Cheaper By The Dozen*, starring Steve Martin. There are numerous scenes in this movie that illustrate how one father tries to take care of things while his wife is away. This movie is about a father who has just gotten his dream job of coaching football at his college alma mater. But this job change calls for him, his wife, their twelve children — yes, twelve — to move from their beloved home and community in order for Dad to get his wish fulfilled. No sooner have they settled into their new home, than his wife, who has been writing a book on how to successfully raise twelve children, is off to New York City to clinch a deal to have her book published. She learns that the deal also involves obligatory cross-country tour engagements to promote it. Meanwhile, Coach/Dad is back home trying to handle this tribe and his new job at the university. The truth is, there is just too much going on for anyone to manage all this.

In a last-minute, desperate attempt to salvage everything, Coach/Dad comes up with a plan. He has the football team come over to his house for the briefing sessions and then takes the children who are not already in school to work with him at the university. Trying to work and take care of the kids at both home and school turns out to be another disaster. Things are so messed up, that Coach/Dad finally resorts to lying to his wife on the phone. He

273

tells her that he has everything under control, when actually everything is in utter chaos. Meanwhile, the university officials and local media representatives are raising the same question. Can this man coach two teams, the one at home and the one at the university? There's ample evidence that he cannot.

As I look back on my own fathering days, I don't believe I was ever in over my head as much as this dad was. But then, I didn't have twelve children and a wife on a book tour across the U.S. However, one day in particular does stand out in my memory. It was shortly after we had moved to Muncie, Indiana. My wife, Susan, was still teaching in Wabash, Indiana. I was in Muncie with our son, Chris, and our daughter, Megan. It was the first day of school for them. Chris was ten, and so he pretty much took care of himself. He knew what to do. Things were going okay for Megan, who was eight, until it came time to fix her hair. Susan had shown me what to do to make pigtails, but seeing it done and doing it was an entirely different matter. Finally, we all got off to Westview School for that first day. Let's just say that Megan's hair left a lot to be desired. When I picked her up later that afternoon, she was very excited and ran up to greet me and to tell me about her new teacher. I was shocked when Megan said to me. "My teacher said that she really liked my hair." I could hardly keep from laughing as I replied, "She must be some teacher!"

We all know what it feels like to be in over our heads. But I think the demon-possessed man in Luke's story probably knew it better than most, for he was literally in over his head.

What happens when you're not prepared for what happens? It can take various forms. In this healing story, we see a variety of reactions.

It all begins when Jesus arrives from the district of the Gerasenes. We're not exactly sure just where this village is. There's no real scholarly agreement on the exact location of the town, but wherever it is, Jesus has just arrived by boat on the Sea of Galilee. No sooner has Jesus stepped ashore than he's met with this man possessed by demons. By the time Jesus meets him, the man has been ill for a very long time. From all signs, the man was quite a case. The man had come to the point of no longer being able to live like a normal person in the village. For one thing, he lived in a graveyard, and ran around naked, yelling and screaming. To protect him from himself, and to protect the villagers from what he might do to them, the man had to be bound in chains and fetters. The man was so violent and strong that even the chains were not able to hold him. He could burst right out of them.

To put it mildly, the man was not prepared for a visit by Jesus and he asked him, "What have you to do with me, Jesus, Son of the Most High God?" (Luke 8:28). Or was it the demons who said that? It's not all that clear who's speaking. Most likely, it's the demons shouting through the man's voice, so in control are they of the man's interior being. It's apparent that the demons are threatened by the very presence of Jesus. The demons feel that Jesus is out to get them. "Don't torture me," they scream. The reason they say this is because Jesus had already commanded these unclean spirits to come out of the man.

Jesus stands out as the one person in the story who is prepared for whatever happens. Jesus knows the way to get the upper hand in this explosive situation. Once you know the name of the demons, you have them under your control. Jesus says to this demon-possessed man, "What is your name?" (Luke 8:30). The NRSV has the demonic reply, "Legion." I prefer another militarily descriptive word that William Barclay uses in his own personal translation: "My name is 'A Regiment' "[1] (Luke 8:30 Barclay). At the time of the Emperor Augustus, a regiment was made up of 6,000 troops.

A Catholic nun tells me about the time she came home from the grocery in Detroit, Michigan. Her apartment was in a rather rundown part of the city. As she was getting her groceries out of her car, this tiny, tiny, lady looked up and saw a gang of rough rogues headed toward her with what she felt was the intention to steal her groceries and make off with them. As they approached her, she looked them in the eye, and in a strong, confident voice, said, "Now, Tyrone, help me up the steps with these groceries!" One of the boys replied, "How did you know my name is Tyrone?" The nun exclaimed, "Ah, everyone in Detroit knows who you are.

Now you and your friends help me up the stairs with these groceries!" which they did instantly. When the nun was asked how she knew that the boy's name was Tyrone, she laughed and replied, "With that many boys on the streets of Detroit, I just knew that one of them had to be a 'Tyrone.' " Just by saying that name, she cast out her fear and their hatred. Just as Jesus did with the troubled man.

When the demons heard Jesus calling them by name, they were terrified and begged him not to send them to the abyss. The abyss is another name for hell or the place where nobody wants to go, not even demons.

Now, it just so happened that there was a herd of pigs nearby. The demons make the suggestion to Jesus that they be driven into the pigs instead of the abyss. Without so much as a hesitation, Jesus agrees. At their request, Jesus drives the demons out of the man's mind and into the herd of pigs. The Gospel of Mark says that there were 2,000 pigs. Luke is content to reduce the number to a more manageable "herd." Luke leaves the exact figure to our own imaginations. But, by driving the demons into the pigs, in an ironic twist, the demons get precisely what they were trying to avoid. When the demons took over the pigs, the pigs stampeded over the hill. They ran headlong into the deep blue sea and were drowned in the abyss.

Some people, when they read this story, become worried about the fate of the pigs. Other people become concerned about the loss of income to the pigs' owners. Still others are concerned about what this action says about Jesus. They don't think it reflects very well on him. But those kinds of questions push the meaning of the story too far. If you have to have an answer to those kinds of questions, I suppose, you might say that Jesus felt that the sanity of one man was worth the loss of all those pigs and whatever income they might have brought for the owner. But, as I say, that's not something Luke's story is interested in.

The incident did, however, create quite a reaction with the townspeople, especially those in charge of the herd. The herdsmen were certainly not prepared for what happened. They immediately ran away and told everyone else. Then the townspeople came out to see for themselves, and from their reaction, we see that they also

276

were not prepared for what they ran into. They were not prepared to see this previously insane and violent man, whom they feared so much as to put him in chains, now sitting quietly and in his right mind listening to every word Jesus had to say.

So startled were the townspeople that they asked Jesus to go away, immediately, and to leave them alone. All their lives, they had been dealing with this sick man. They may not have handled things the best way, but at least they felt they knew what to do while he was sick. Now that Jesus had come and stirred things up and healed him, they didn't know what to make of it, nor what to do about it. Of course, they could have rejoiced with the man and thanked Jesus for what he had done for him. But then, to have done that, they would have had to have been a lot more healthy themselves. They would have had to have been a lot better off in mind and body and spirit than they obviously were. Sick themselves, they could not deal with this new healthy one in their midst. Their natural response was to reject this new foreign element that had come into their lives, much as the body sometimes is inclined to reject a transplanted organ. They simply were not prepared to handle the man's being well. It required too much change on their part.

Family counselors see it from time to time. Sadly, if a family is too dysfunctional, when one family member begins to gain some measure of freedom and health, it often shakes the other family members up. Rather than undergo the change required of themselves, they unwittingly ignore or even refute that anything good is taking place in the person receiving counseling.

As for Jesus, rather than stay in what is evidently a hopeless environment, Jesus went away as they requested. He moves on to a town that will give a better reception to his ministry.

In gratitude for his new found peace of mind, the man healed of the unclean spirits begs Jesus to let him go with him. Jesus says, "Return to your home, and declare how much God has done for you" (Luke 8:39). And that's exactly what the man did.

So what happens when we're not prepared for what happens? In the movies, it all tends to end happily ever after, the so-called Hollywood ending. At least in *Cheaper By The Dozen* the ending is a little more realistic. This father comes to his senses when he

277

realizes what an impact fulfilling his dream has had on the rest of the family. Fulfilling his and his wife's dream has almost cost them their marriage and their family. That was the one thing he was not prepared for. He was not prepared for what his actions did to the rest of the ones he loved. At the end of the movie, like the demon-possessed man in Luke's story, Coach/Dad is now in his right mind. He now knows he prefers the name "Dad" to the name "Coach."

Sometimes, we're only prepared for what happens when we realize that we're not as well prepared as we thought we were. Then at other times, things turn out better than we may have expected. It certainly did that day for the man whose name was "A Regiment" when he met Jesus.

It even happened for one dad who was stumped with fixing his eight-year-old daughter's pigtails on the first day of school.

---

1. William Barclay, *The Gospel of Luke* (Louisville: Westminster John Knox Press, 1975).

Proper 8
Pentecost 6
Ordinary Time 13
Luke 9:51-62

Reactions To Rejection

Jesus knew what rejection felt like. When he preached his first sermon in his hometown of Nazareth, things went well in the beginning. But after he was finished, the people ran him out of town. They even tried to run him off a cliff, but he managed to escape. That was the first time Jesus experienced rejection for what he was trying to do for God, but it was not to be the last.

Many of us know how it feels, even though the circumstances may not be as dramatic. An excellent student minister was rejected by a search committee simply because he could not work full time. The church was in denial believing that they could support a full-time pastor. They did not extend the call, so both the church and the student minister missed out what might have been a good experience for both of them.

In the story from Luke's Gospel, Jesus is on a journey to Jerusalem. But rather than take the normal route most pilgrims took at the time, Jesus decided to go straight through Samaria. This was an unusual decision. Samaria was located in between Galilee in the north and Judea in the south. There had been a long-standing disagreement between the Jews and Samaritans. So the route Jesus took was not an easy shortcut. As a Jew, it placed him in the face of direct opposition. To be exact, religious pilgrims had long been hindered by the Samaritans for trying to pass through their territory on the way to Jerusalem. Jesus was almost certain to encounter hostility, and he did.

Why Samaria anyway? One possible answer would seem to be that Jesus was reaching out to them. He was trying to extend the olive branch of friendship as he moved on his way to the Holy City. Jesus was certain that God was calling him to go to Jerusalem to usher in the kingdom. Maybe he felt that the Samaritans were a test case. Perhaps, if they were to accept his graceful overture, it would be a sign to others that his mission was worthwhile, and might even turn out to be successful.

But the Samaritans wanted no part of it. If the Jews felt that the Samaritans were half-breeds, the Samaritans felt that the Jews were worshiping in the wrong place and using the wrong Bible. The Samaritans worshiped at the temple on Mount Gerizam, and they only recognized the first five books of the Hebrew Scriptures. The Jews, of course, felt that worship at Jerusalem was central, and they revered many more writings of the law and the prophets. This long-standing quarrel was not to be overcome in a day, and Jesus was to find that out. Nevertheless, he "set his face to go to Jerusalem." Evidently, the Samaritans could see it in his face. They could see his will and determination. As far as they were concerned, it would be over their dead bodies.

How did Jesus react to this rejection? It's hard to tell because even before he has a chance to act on his own, two of his disciples, James and John, decide to take matters into their own hands. When they saw that Jesus was not being well received by the Samaritan village, they asked Jesus if he would let them "bring down fire from heaven to consume them." They must have been thinking that Jesus would do what Elijah, the prophet, had once done in a similar situation. Little did they know just how far off they were from what Jesus had in mind. Luke tells us that Jesus turned and rebuked the disciples. What they wanted to do was not in accord with God's kingdom. Right there on the spot, Jesus met rejection with firmness toward his disciples on the one hand, and with respect and tolerance for his enemies on the other. And, he made sure that he taught his disciples a lesson. This was not the way to go about solving anything. It was to be the first of many lessons the disciples would have to learn as they made their way to Jerusalem. Had they been listening to what Jesus had been saying all along, they would have known what to expect. After all, Jesus was just putting into practice what he had taught earlier in the Sermon on the Plain. But as is so often the case, these disciples let their innate passions take over. So angry were they at the reception Jesus had received from the Samaritans that they were ready to let out all of that stored-up national hatred that was inside them.

I will show you a much better way, a way more like Jesus. There once was a man who ran for a local government position. He was well thought of and many felt he was a shoe-in. However, when the votes were counted, the race was very close, but he lost. Many were urging the candidate to ask for a recount. A recount was well in the realm of possibility, but as the candidate reasoned, the people had spoken and since the vote was so close he would not have the support he needed to carry out his duties, so he gracefully conceded the election. Many still say that he would have made the best elected official the town could have had. Such is one way to react to rejection.

As Jesus and his disciples went along the road, they began to collect a number of people who were interested in joining up with them. One person, in particular, was extremely enthusiastic about the prospects. This person ran up to Jesus all on his own and said, "I will follow you wherever you go" (Luke 9:57b). Jesus was never one to attract followers on false pretenses. Jesus always made sure from day one that anyone wanting to take part in his mission would know what they were getting into. So he said to this eager, would-be disciple, "Foxes have holes, and birds of the air have nests; but the Son of Man has nowhere to lay his head" (Luke 9:58).

There's a possibility that Jesus may have been speaking on more than one level. "Fox" was a derogatory word used for Gentiles. Jesus, himself, once called King Herod "that old Fox." Then again, maybe all that Jesus was asking the man to do was to take another look at Jesus. "Look at me. I have no job, no home, no family, no place to lay my head. Why, animals have more security than I do. Are you absolutely certain that you want this kind of life?"

Luke does not tell us what the man's reaction was, only that Jesus made it abundantly clear what was involved in being his disciple.

281

While the first seeker came of his own initiative, the next one was personally invited by Jesus to join the group. Evidently, the man was curious enough about what it might mean to give it serious thought, but he still had a few things that he felt he needed to take care of. Actually, he had one big one; he had to bury his father. Then, as now, seeing that your parents have a decent burial is an act of sacred trust. It is not something to be taken lightly. Likewise, Jesus considered following him to be equally important. No matter how you interpret it, Jesus' words may sound harsh and unkind. "Let the dead bury their own dead; but as for you, go and proclaim the kingdom of God" (Luke 9:60). Jesus put the choice clearly before the man as a matter of life and death. Again, Luke does not tell us what the man's reaction was to these strong words of Jesus. We can only infer that the man went away feeling rejected.

The third offer to follow Jesus is a combination of the other two. Like the first, this offer is a spontaneous gesture, full of enthusiasm. But like the second, it has some reservations. The man says, "I will follow you, Lord; but let me first say farewell to those at my home" (Luke 9:61). When writing this story, Luke may well have had in mind a similar occasion that took place between the prophet Elijah and his successor, Elisha. When Elijah taps Elisha on the shoulder, and throws his cloak over him, Elisha says in response, "Let me kiss my father and my mother, and then I will follow you" (1 Kings 19:20b). In this story from 1 Kings, Elijah gives his permission. He agrees that it's only right for the newly chosen prophet to say farewell to his family before he leaves to take up his new occupation. On the contrary, Jesus will not allow this man so much as a thought about all this. Jesus draws the line in the sand and tells the man that he has to make a decision then and there whether or not he's going to work for God's kingdom. "No one who puts a hand to the plow and looks back is fit for the kingdom of God" (Luke 9:62). Now, I'm not a farmer, but as a matter of fact, I know that it's impossible to plow a straight row if you're always looking back over your shoulder when you should be looking ahead. Or in more modern terms, it's difficult to arrive at your destination if you're always looking in the rearview mirror. Determination, not just enthusiasm is required to proclaim the gospel of Christ.

When we look at these stories about Jesus and rejection, we can see a common thread running throughout. Jesus knew how to accept rejection and move on. When faced with opposition, he went to another village and preached there. He did not just say, "I quit." Jesus found a way to move on. While the rejections we experience are rarely as intense as the ones Jesus had to face, nonetheless, in our everyday lives, each of us has to decide what we're going to do with the rejections that come to us. In a word, we have to move on. And when we do, we are following Jesus, whether we know it or not.

Ministering When
You're Not Welcome

Jesus knew what to do all the time, and he knew how to go about it. He knew how to serve God in good times and in bad.

In these scriptures from Luke, we continue to follow Jesus on the way to Jerusalem. But for now, the apparent destination of the trip has receded to the background. Something else has caught our attention. For one thing, Jesus' message of announcing the coming of the kingdom of God is being met with increasing curiosity. There is, at the same time, growing hostility to what Jesus has to say and an increasing acceptance of his message.

For this reason, the mission of Jesus must be enlarged. The scope of Jesus' work must be broadened. More workers must be recruited to get the good news out. So Jesus decides to appoint seventy (or 72 according to some sources) to share in the job. The mission will be the same mission that Jesus has had all along. But now, these new disciples will also announce the kingdom. The only difference is that now there will be more help to carry it out than Jesus and the twelve disciples could manage by themselves.

If it's the same mission, it's also the same strategy. Jesus sent these new missionaries in pairs to the very places he himself intended to go. He didn't just turn them loose and say, "Now sink or swim! Go find your own mission field." No, the way Jesus went about it is much like the way Donald Trump does with his apprentices. The apprentices' task, while daunting and always with a deadline attached to it, is also well-defined. Success or failure will readily be apparent, as is the way in which they have all worked together.

That's also the way we see Jesus going about it in this story from Luke.

Nor does Jesus sugarcoat the job. He does not stoop to doing what we in the church have sometimes been guilty of to get someone to take a position of leadership. Jesus does not say, "Oh, there's nothing to it. You'll love it!" Jesus wants his disciples to know what they're getting into. So much so, that in some ways it's a rather bleak picture that he paints for them. "The harvest is plentiful." That is, the time is ripe — but there's a catch — "but the laborers are few" (Luke 10:2). And those that do sign up for the job need to know that at times the working conditions are not all that good. They can be fraught with danger. It's not an easy task Jesus is calling for. "See I am sending you like lambs into the midst of wolves" (Luke 10:3b).

He does give them some advice, though, about how they are to go about it. They are to travel light. "No purse, no bag, no sandals" (Luke 10:4a). They are not to take anything that could hold them back. They are on an urgent mission, and they do not have the time to dillydally and engage in meaningless chitchat. "And greet no one on the road" (Luke 10:4b). In other words, let nothing distract you from the mission.

When I think about dillydallying on the job, I'm reminded of that precious scene in *Gone With The Wind*. You know, the one where Prissy has been sent to fetch the doctor to deliver Miss Melanie's baby. But the good doctor can't be worried with such. After all, it's in the middle of the Civil War, and he has more urgent matters to take care of, like binding up the wounds of the casualties. After hearing this from the doctor, you'd think that Prissy would rush right back to tell Miss Scarlet. But, no, she takes her own good time, meandering along the picket fences, singing as she goes. The click-clack of the stick in her hand along the fence serves as a percussion instrument to her voice.

During the building of an addition to a church, each morning when the pastor arrived, one of the construction workers wanted to talk about the Bible instead of doing the work he was assigned. After a few mornings of that, the pastor said to him, "I'd love to talk about the Bible with you, but not now when you're supposed to be working on this project. Make an appointment with me, and we can talk all you want." The worker never did. It was much more fun to talk on the job. It was a much more respectful way to goof-off. "That's not the way to go about the Lord's business," Jesus tells these seventy, and us.

What then are we to do? How are we to conduct ourselves? As we minister in the name of Jesus, we are to do as he did. We are to give everyone the benefit of the doubt. "Whatever house you enter, first say, 'Peace to this house!' And if anyone is there who shares in peace, your peace will rest on that person; but if not, it will return to you. Remain in the same house, eating and drinking whatever they provide, for the laborer deserves to be paid" (Luke 10:5-6). Likewise, don't go from house to house trying to find better accommodations. Eat what is set before you. Don't go off trying to see if you can find a better place to stay, one with a softer bed and more delicious food. Jesus is simply encouraging them to be good houseguests. Live on their terms. Don't make your host go out of their way for you. It's not bad advice for anyone at anytime, whether we're engaged in work for the church or not.

But what if the people do not welcome you? What do you do then? Jesus is just as specific in this case as he was before with those who were more accepting. The bottom line is to preach the gospel to them also whether they will accept it or not. Say the same thing to these people. "God's kingdom is coming." Then if they won't accept you, leave that place, and find one that is more receptive. A retired minister once put it this way, "Don't continue fishing in a pond where no one has caught a fish for years." The way Jesus put it was much more dramatic. "Wipe off the dust that clings to your feet." Leave the outcome to the judgment of God for their lack of hospitality and receptivity.

When I look at what Jesus is saying and what it might mean for us today, I hear Jesus telling me that how we carry out our mission matters. In the end, how we do it may matter as much as the mission itself. For that's what many times determines whether or not the message gets communicated.

James Dittes, who taught psychology and ministry at Yale Divinity School, once gave this advice to young seminarians, "When

287

you meet with opposition, just remember that resistance is a sign of vitality and an occasion for ministry. If people are not taking to what you are trying to do, that means that they are at least still alive. They are not dead yet. Dead people do not talk back." In our better moments, when we run upon an obstacle to what we've been trying to accomplish in our ministry, we tell ourselves, "This is a good sign. The congregation is not dead. Now, all we have to do is figure out what is the proper way to minister to these people."

In the materials many use in premarital counseling sessions prior to the wedding, there is a suggested exercise called "active listening" and "assertiveness." Active listening is an effort to hear what your partner is saying to you. It sometimes helps to be able to put into your own words what the other is saying. That way both you and they have a chance to check it out. Active listening involves putting yourself in their shoes and trying to imagine how you might feel if you were in their place. Assertiveness is a strategy to go out of your way to make yourself abundantly clear. One of the best ways to do this is to send "I messages" rather than "You accusations." An "I message" just states how things are from your end. A "You accusation" has a way of attacking the other person. It almost always raises anxiety, if not hostility. An "I message" says, "I get mad when that happens." A "You accusation" is more like, "You make me mad when you do that." See the difference?

Now, sometimes, there's a little resistance to this exercise, since from day one we've been taught that it's impolite to begin our sentences with I. Yet in interpersonal, especially intimate conversations, it's actually one of the best ways to communicate, if we do it properly, and it's not as easy as it may seem. Some of the "I messages" often heard in these counseling sessions go like this. "I see that it really upsets you when I leave my socks and underwear on the bathroom floor." Or, "I wish you would be a little more romantic." Which translated means, "I would really like for you to surprise me with flowers on my birthday or a surprise evening out just for the two of us." Things like that.

Jesus probably did not have had all this in mind when he sent the seventy out on their mission. But to be fair, I don't think he could have spent much time in psychological exercises that had

288

not yet even been discovered! But there was one thing that he did do that was psychologically sound. He told his followers in no uncertain terms that they should listen carefully enough to find out where the other person was coming from. In this way, the message they were trying to deliver might just get through. But then, if they were to run upon one of those impasses that we are bound to run upon from time to time, in the church and out of it, they were to move on and to be done with it. Have your say, and then leave it to the Holy Spirit to clean up the mess, is the way I'd put it.

What I find particularly intriguing about the instructions Jesus gives these new missionaries, is that while he gives them a pretty tough briefing session, outlining in detail all that could possibly go wrong and how difficult it was going to be, when the seventy return, they are ecstatic about what they have been able to accomplish. They have been successful beyond their wildest expectations. "The seventy returned with joy, saying, 'Lord, in your name even the demons submit to us!'" (Luke 10:17). When Jesus hears what they have to say, he takes this as a sign that God is having his way in the world. Satan is finally getting his due. And if these seventy think that they are successful now, it will be nothing compared with what they are going to experience later on. They will accomplish more than they may think or believe.

Most readers of these scriptures from Luke do not think Jesus really meant for us to become snake handlers. Some have tried that, of course. However, this is a symbolic way to indicate that the power of evil is being overcome through the mission of Jesus on earth, now as well as back then.

No sooner has Jesus recognized what the seventy have accomplished and rejoiced with them in their success, than he quickly realizes that now there's a potential new problem, one that may be even more difficult to deal with than handling snakes. And that is how to handle all this success. What do you do when you are successful? What do you do when the results come in far better than you had anticipated? Jesus knows and he tells them. Take care that you do not gloat! "Nevertheless, do not rejoice at this, that the spirits submit to you, but rejoice that your names are written in

289

heaven" (Luke 10:20). Don't gloat about what you have done, but give thanks that God approves of what you have done.

At the conclusion of a very successful capital funds campaign in a church, a wise leader from the congregation said to the pastor, "Isn't it amazing how much can get done when we don't care who gets the credit?"

So, how do you minister when you're not welcome (and when you are)? By following Jesus. By being utterly prepared for whatever comes. By being utterly prepared for the worst before you begin and utterly unselfish about taking credit for the success when it's over. Jesus knew that when we do that we are doing our part in bringing in God's kingdom on earth.

A Samaritan Took Care Of Him

The situation was this: A young Jewish lawyer wanted to reassure himself that he was doing the right thing. To help him, Jesus took the opportunity to tell him a story. The story was designed to set the young man straight.

The story begins the way a lot of stories begin. "A man was going down from Jerusalem to Jericho" (Luke 10:30). At this point, we aren't told anything about the man. Not his nationality or even his name is revealed to us. He was simply a man traveling down the road.

The road the man was traveling on remains, to this day, as one of the most dangerous roads in the world, the road from Jerusalem to Jericho. In a little less than eighteen miles, the road drops from 2,500 feet above sea level at Jerusalem to 770 feet below sea level at Jericho. For as long as anyone can remember, this road has been noted for being one not everyone should travel on, at least not alone, and certainly not at night.

Why the man was there all by himself, we can only surmise. Perhaps, he was with some others when the robbers fell upon him, and the others being faster, got away. We just don't know. What we do know is that the robbers stripped him, beat him, and went off, leaving him half dead.

Now this is an interesting predicament that Jesus has slipped into the story. The rules then and now are fairly clear about what to do with the living and the dead. We pretty well know how we are supposed to treat others; as we would like to be treated, right? We know how we are supposed to look after the dead, and if we don't, the funeral director and the minister can quickly fill us in. But what about the half dead? What about all those situations that are in between, that are on the borderline, grey, not black or white, the ones not easily found in the textbook? It was not just a coincidence, I think, that Jesus pointed out that the man was half dead. It raises all kinds of questions about how we are to react in situations where we are not sure what to do.

But in the characteristic way of telling a good story, Jesus first shows us some ways not to do it. The first way involves the religious community and one of its head leaders, a priest. "Now by chance," Jesus tells us, a priest was going down that same road, and when he saw the man, he passed by on the other side, evidently trying to avoid contamination by coming into contact with a dead person. This means that the priest must have assumed that the man was dead. At any rate, the priest did not get close enough to see what the real condition of the helpless victim was, for we're told that the priest passed by on the other side. Rowan Williams, Archbishop of Canterbury, has eloquently described it. "There is a gulf to be bridged, a wound that will not be healed until we have seen that it is bleeding."[1]

How many of us when faced with a situation that we feel might involve us deeper in matters than we want to be involved in at the moment, opt to pass by on the other side? We say to ourselves, "I think I'll sit this one out. I'll let someone else deal with it." Or as my parents' generation used to say, "Let George do it." We have other pressing concerns to take care of. No doubt the priest was on the way to a church meeting that couldn't possibly go on without him. We all know about that. But Jesus won't let us off the hook, will he?

Once when a pastor was visiting the hospital and standing by the receptionist counter, a group of ten to fifteen burly men came in together. They were dressed in black leather jackets, had long hair, and they were dripping to their waists in chains of one size or another. The pastor's first reaction was that of the priest's. He wanted to get out of there as fast as he could. For some reason, the pastor felt threatened. How the elderly lady at the receptionist desk must have felt can only be imagined, both of them were outnumbered.

But then the pastor noticed that one of the men had a bouquet of flowers in his hand. They had come to the hospital for the same reason the pastor had come, to visit one of their friends! But because they looked different than the pastor did, he wanted to pass by on the other side.

Then, Jesus tells us that a Levite came by. That is, a kind of assistant priest. He also came upon the place, saw the man, and he, too, passed by on the other side. Probably, because he had been taught by the priest what to do, or perhaps, he was close enough to observe the priest and follow his example. The point is that the two who might have been expected to do something chose not to. Neither the senior minister nor the associate seemed to want to be bothered. They had more important things to do. They were probably on the way to a meeting to figure out how to help needy people. They couldn't see the opportunity before them. But then, can we? That's the question Jesus leaves us with, isn't it?

"But a Samaritan!" And with those words Jesus turns the tables upside down. Jesus knew that this was the least acceptable individual from the young Jewish lawyer's point of view. Samaritans were outcast, despised, and considered subhuman. Everything about them was detestable even the way they worshiped, especially. They even went to the wrong church! But "a Samaritan" is just the one Jesus centers his story around to show us what we ought to do in these half dead, ambiguous situations that life continually confronts us with.

What's simply amazing, when you look at it from the Samaritan's point of view, is that he would have been brought up to be just as prejudiced as the priest and Levite and the young lawyer. The Samaritan also would have been trained in the law. He also would have known how to use the same scriptures to justify his position. Had he chosen to pass by on the other side of the road like the other two did, it would have been understandable. No one would have thought much about it, least of all the priest and the Levite. In fact, they might have respected him for it. For after all, the man was living up to the religious principles of purity he claimed to believe in.

293

But, as the story tells us, this is not what happened. No, "this Samaritan," who was also on a journey, came upon the battered man by the side the road. When he saw him, he was moved to pity, or "had compassion," as another translation states it. Evidently, the Samaritan had allowed himself to come close enough to find out that the man was still partially alive. And having determined that, he then went over to him, bandaged his wounds, and poured oil (which was to encourage healing) and wine (which was believed to relieve the pain). Then the Samaritan set the man on his own beast. Notice that little word, "own." He didn't call a cab or a camel, but put him in his own car and took him to the local Motel 6, and made provisions for him there.

The next day, the Samaritan took out some money from the ATM machine and paid the innkeeper to take care of the man until he came back. As he's leaving, the Samaritan says to the manager of the motel, whom he may have known from previous associations, "If it takes more than that, I'll take care of it when I return. You have my word on it."

This Good Samaritan is not only good; he's amazing! "Good" is not a good enough word for it. Not only is he the least likely one to offer help — remember, he, too, had to overcome his own inner resistance to do it, for he, too, had been carefully taught what to do and not to do in these situations — but somehow — we call it the grace of God — this man had learned to rise above his restrictive upbringing and see that some things were not as simple as he had thought they were. This was a real person lying there in the ditch; someone who needed help. It didn't matter who he was, what color he was, how much he made or didn't make, what gender he was, or what sexual orientation he might claim. The only fact that mattered at the moment was that the man needed help.

We face the same dilemmas every day, don't we? With many issues from birth to death and before and beyond. Genetic malformation, stem-cell research, cloning, abortion, homosexuality, AIDS, to extend life or terminate it. It's not always crystal clear what to do in these half dead or half alive situations. "What would Jesus do in these borderline situations?" we ask ourselves. The parable of the Good Samaritan answers clearly and unambiguously: Jesus would offer help!

So how did the Samaritan take care of the man? If we can determine that perhaps we can find out what we ought to do. First, he used what he had. He dipped into his own resources, the oil, wine, money, even the donkey he was traveling on, and graciously — there is no better word to describe it — used it all for the one in need.

But he did not let it go at that. He saw that the man would have what he needed when it came time for him to leave. In other words, he saw to it that there were others who could pick up where he had to leave off. Since he was not able to stay with the man until he was brought back to health, the Samaritan did the next best thing. He wrote a check to the innkeeper to cover whatever the man needed. And if, as it turned out, that was not quite enough, he would settle up when he returned. Then the Samaritan went on his own way to take care of whatever it was he had to take care of, confident in his own heart that he had done all that he could do. That's a good feeling, to be sure. It's one of the best there is in these kinds of situations. It is satisfying to feel that you have done all that you could possibly do.

That was the situation and how one man chose to respond to it. But what about today? What is our situation today? Anything like that? If you're beginning to think that there are more problems like this that we have to deal with every day, you're right. Recently, there have been more disasters, both natural and human. Sometimes they seem to come at the rate of one or two a day. The truth is, we have more opportunities all the time to try to be a good neighbor by following Jesus' example of the Good Samaritan.

In the summer of 2005, the G8 Economic Summit was held in Edinburgh, Scotland. Hundreds of thousands of protestors gathered to express that the starving in Africa and India must be addressed. The fact is, the United States is the nation giving the largest amount of money, but the smallest percentage of aid. Even before the summit began, there had been some overtures of help, such as the move to cancel some of the debts incurred by the poorest nations. Fifty-nine billion dollars in aid to Africa and Palestine was pledged by the G8 nations.

The call is still to be a good neighbor by following Jesus' example of the Good Samaritan.

Whatever we do, we can do as the Samaritan did. We can give out of the resources we have, and then rest in the assurance that someone else, someone in a better position perhaps than we are, will be able to take care of it.

Sometime back, there was a news broadcast in which a reporter in Rwanda was shown on television looking up at the sky. The reporter remarked that he had just spotted the first airlift relief aid to this war-torn country. The only problem with that report was that churches had been working in that area for more than 100 years, day in and day out. No one ever saw fit to take notice of it long enough to flash it on the screen.

But, let's not go overboard, not just yet. For there's still one character in the story that we haven't checked in with yet. And that's the response the rich, young lawyer had after he heard Jesus' story. Going back to the man's original question, "And who is my neighbor?" (Luke 10:29). Jesus takes a twist on his question and asks the young man, "Which of these three, do you think, was a neighbor to the man who fell into the hands of robbers?" (Luke 10:36). The man's answer is revealing. On the surface it's right enough. The man answers, "The one who showed him mercy" (Luke 10:37). Nothing wrong with that; or is there?

You see, old ways die hard sometimes. The young man still cannot quite bring himself to say outright, "The Samaritan is the neighbor, for he's the one who took care of him." I can see that word "S-a-m-a-r-i-tan" stuck there, right about where his Adam's apple would be. Yes, let's give the young man credit. He got the right answer out. But he couldn't let himself feel it, not just yet. He wasn't quite ready to let himself be changed by what he had learned. He had learned it in his head, as we say. He just hadn't let his heart find out about it yet. The young lawyer protected himself from really being changed by not giving the credit to where credit was truly due. Make no mistake about it, it was a Samaritan who took care of him.

296

So, I think the words of Jesus, "Go and do likewise" (Luke 10:37b), must have stung the young man's ears, even as the word "Samaritan" could not pass his lips.

Oh, well. Let's not be too hard on the poor guy. We all have a way to go, don't we? God will not be satisfied until we all become more compassionate. And that's our hope. For when we are compassionate, when we get close enough to feel another's pain, close enough to see that they are bleeding, all these other things have a way of taking care of themselves.

---

1. Rowan Williams, *Resurrection: Interpreting the Easter Gospel* (Cleveland, Ohio: The Pilgrim Press, 2002), p. 74.

Proper 11
Pentecost 9
Ordinary Time 16
Luke 10:38-42

How Not To Become Distracted

We live in what has been called the "Information Age." We have more information at our disposal than any generation before us. We are flooded with bits of information, or should I say "bytes"?

I think a much better description of our time would be the "Age of Distraction." Everybody and everything are out to get our attention. And one way to do that is to distract us from whatever we may have been doing or are trying to do.

A case in point, I particularly dislike the scroll at the bottom of television newscasts. I can barely concentrate on what the broadcaster is reporting, because the latest news is being run across the screen at the same time. I have an elderly friend in New Jersey who says she's tempted to send her doctor's bills for her high blood pressure to the television station because of these scrolls. Of course, you can say that she doesn't have to watch that. You can always change the channel. Like that would help.

Pop-up messages on the computer screen is another needless bother, if you ask me. I know some of those messages are supposed to be for my benefit. But I'd rather not be interrupted when I'm trying to concentrate on sending an email to a friend or at work on a sermon.

Cell phones are the worst of all, for they are almost universal. A church hit a new low during a Palm Sunday processional when a member of the choir was seen answering a message on the cell phone as the choir made its way to the chancel during the opening hymn. A minister experienced something similar during a wedding rehearsal. As the minister was explaining the ceremony, the groom's cell phone went off. He turned to his bride and said, "It's for you." Now, even at wedding rehearsals, the minister has added a new item to the list of reminders about gum chewing and such. "Turn your cell phones off. We are about the Lord's business here." There have been many newspaper articles confirming what we have all suspected; that using cell phones while driving is definitely contributing to more accidents on the highway.

The sad thing is that since we are so bombarded with so many messages from so many sources that those sending them constantly have to up the tempo and increase the volume to enable the messages to get through. Even ambulances are having to change their sirens because we have become so numbed to their presence. New Zealand must be heaven in this regard. Flashing lights are enough to alert these good people to let the medics through. It's good to know that there is still one place in the world where you can quietly get somebody's attention.

All this can become rather personal. For one reason or another, we can become more distracted than usual. We flit from one thing to the next before we've finished the first. Sometimes it's even difficult to accomplish simple things like making a cup of coffee. We don't even seem to be able to go through the process without stopping in the middle and doing something else that has caught our attention. We find ourselves doing things like forgetting to pour the water through the filter because the trash caught our attention and we took care of that instead.

I am beginning to think that our whole house is becoming infected. Is distraction contagious, like measles? I suspected as much when Higgins, our West Highland terrier, began to stop everywhere on walks, sniffing this and that, something the dog rarely did before. I found myself constantly giving him the command, "Leave it." Now, there had always been some things that were sure to grab the dog's attention, such as the voices of little children or little furry animals such as squirrels and rabbits. The terrier was at their mercy. But, recently, the list of things cluttering up our dog's life seems to have been growing as long as my own.

How not to become distracted is not just a title for a sermon, but a very much needed way of survival for us right now. I wish I

300

had the definitive answer to all this. I'm not sure I do. But, if not the answer, I do plan to give us some hope by the end of this message. I not only want to help myself, but all who are within hearing distance, as well. I don't think for a moment that we're alone in this problem. We all live in a world where it's getting easier and easier not to concentrate and ever harder to focus our attention.

We all have this problem. The scripture is today's Gospel Lesson from the common lectionary. The lesson was chosen a long time ago, but as it turned out, it could not have come at a better time. This scripture speaks as if it had been written for us personally this morning. God must have sent this text into our life. We desperately need to hear what it has to say.

Jesus is visiting in the home of Mary and Martha, sisters of his good friend, Lazarus. (We learn that from the Gospel of John.) Their home is in Bethany not far from Jerusalem. It was probably not the first time Jesus had been in their home. But it would be near to the last. Unknown to his hosts, Jesus is on his way to Jerusalem to be crucified. No doubt he was tired from the journey and looking forward to spending some quiet time with his closest friends. Most of all he was looking for a warm welcome. And a warm welcome is exactly what he received.

Let us pause for a moment over this and take full notice that it was Martha who welcomed Jesus into her home. Martha was the perfect hostess. And before we get too far into the story, and learn too much about her to prejudice our feelings about her, I want us to remember that it was Martha, not Mary, who was the first to welcome Jesus that day.

But then in an effort to be the perfect hostess, Martha became distracted with many tasks. So much so that she felt called upon to ask Jesus for a little understanding. After all, her sister, Mary, was not all that much help. Mary had decided to take her place at Jesus' feet and listen to what he had to say. To put it mildly, Martha is rather put out about all of this. She wants Jesus to side with her. "Lord, do you not care that my sister has left me to do all the work by myself? Tell her then to help me" (Luke 10:40).

I'm sure we've all had moments like this when we thought we were left with the short end of the stick. It can happen at home

301

after a party when everyone goes to bed and we're left with loading the dishwasher. Or even here at the church, when the work force dwindles after the program is over and everyone is on the way home. It's the Marthas of this world who are left to put out the trash and turn out the lights. It's easy to get to feeling that you are put upon because you feel others are not pulling their weight. They have left you to move the piano back into place all by yourself.

My mother came from a long line of women who never sat down at a family meal. These Southern women were servers, and that was that. They were not comfortable being included in the dinner conversation. They were always on guard duty, worried that someone might not have that extra piece of fried chicken or pecan pie they had their heart set on.

On the other hand, her father, my grandfather, used to say that help is no help if those giving it do not do it exactly the way you want them to. As a teenage grandson in charge of mowing the lawn, I disagreed. Each and every Thursday during the summer, unless it rained, we had an argument about this philosophy. My grandfather thought I should mow the lawn over a three-day period of time. "It's too big a yard to do in a day!" he would say. I would stand my ground and tell my grandfather I was glad to mow it, but I didn't want to spend parts of three days doing it. That was just too much intrusion into my life. So as I was mowing one day with my grandfather following me around saying, "You're going to kill yourself if you continue to do this," I replied, "Just let me do it my way!" Now that my grandfather is dead, I miss those sparring matches we used to enjoy every Thursday in the summer!

Like Martha, my grandfather had definite ideas about how he wanted to be helped. Though to tell the truth, in some respects, Martha had a better case than my grandfather did. He was not satisfied to get the help he needed. It had to be his way or no way. Whereas with Martha, her sister, Mary, was simply nowhere in sight. Or worse yet, she could be seen through the kitchen doorway sitting in the living room at Jesus' feet listening to his every word. Can't you just hear Martha muttering under her breath, "I wish I had the time to sit and listen to our honored guest? But

302

someone has to do the work. And you certainly can't count on Mary to do it."

Of course, what's so troubling to the many Marthas of this world is that Jesus seems to side with Mary. For centuries, readers of this story have tried to soften the blow and say that this is not really what Jesus meant. What he meant to say was something like this. "There are different ways to serve the Lord. We all have various talents to offer. We need both Marys and Marthas in the church." And we do. It's just that this is not the scripture to support that. There are others, to be sure, but this is not one of them.

What I do not want us to overlook, however, is that Jesus is just as concerned about Martha as he is Mary. But not in the way Martha may think. Jesus is more concerned about Martha's spiritual welfare than her expertise in hospitality. So he gently chides her, "Martha, Martha, you are worried and distracted by many things; there is need of only one thing. Mary has chosen the better part, which will not be taken from her" (Luke 10:42).

There seems to be a kind of play on the fact that Martha is busy serving up many tasty dishes for Jesus who may have been too tired to eat them. One simple dish may have been more suitable at the moment. Martha is not only guilty of busyness, but of not being able to size up the situation. Like my grandfather, Martha thinks that she knows what's best for others, whether it is or not. Sometimes we miss the boat in the way we try to help others because we insist on doing it in a way that we ourselves would like. As I read the story, I'll bet Martha is busy fixing the kind of dinner that she would like someone to fix for her someday: three meats, four salads, five vegetables, and six cakes and pies. Now that's a meal fit for an honored guest like Jesus! The problem is that all Jesus may have had a hankering for that evening was crackers and a bowl of soup.

In contrast, Mary has chosen "the better part." Just what is this better part? Mary has decided not to miss out on what she can learn from Jesus while he's in their home. She sits at his feet and listens to what he had to tell her. She's bent on gleaning all she can from the time she has with Jesus. Rather than being distracted by all these other things, she sits in raptured attention, hanging on his every word.

I have come to learn that there is one thing that will capture my dog's attention, and that is a nest of field mice outside the family room sliding glass door. Higgins will sit for an hour glued to the spot waiting for the mouse to appear. There's almost no way to get his attention away from it. Even his treat of choice, Pupperoni, won't do it, he's so focused.

How do you not become distracted? By being focused like Mary at the feet of Jesus or a West Highland terrier lost in a world of his own waiting for the mouse to appear out of the hole. It's like the Danish philosopher, Soren Kierkegaard, said: "Purity of heart is to will one thing." And one thing only.

Back when our daughter, Megan, was in high school, she was trying to write a paper for her English class. She was experiencing what is known as "writer's block." I watched her pace up and down the family room, working herself up into quite a frenzy. Finally, she came over to me and said, "Dad, I just can't think of anything to write. How do you do it week after week?" I looked at her and said, "Well, first of all, I've found that it's helpful to sit down in front of the typewriter." She replied, "Oh, Daddy, that's no help!" I said, "You asked me for my advice, and I gave you the best I had." Not too much time went by before I saw her sitting down at the typewriter working away on what turned out to be a prize-winning essay. It worked.

The only way Mary could learn what Jesus had to say was to sit down and give him her undivided attention.

I'm afraid in this confusing world of ours, focusing is becoming a lost art. Sometimes it's helpful to see something in the extreme to get a better idea of it. In the movie, *Aviator*, Leonardo DeCaprio stars as Howard Hughes, the genius, and as the film has it, a genius afflicted with OCD, Obsessive Compulsive Disorder. Dr. Jeffery Schwartz from the Westwood Institute for Anxiety Disorders in California served as a consultant on the film. Dr. Schwartz has come up with a treatment for OCD that involves what he calls "mindful awareness." There are four steps to the treatment, but the step he calls "Refocus" seems to me to be the key to getting back on track.[1]

In one scene of the movie, Hughes is in the middle of a big business deal. He becomes distracted by a piece of lint on the jacket of a client's suit. The business deal cannot proceed. It comes to a standstill as Hughes insists that the piece of lint be removed. Had Hughes been able to refocus his attention and bring it back to matters at hand, the deal would have proceeded normally. It's amazing that Hughes was as successful as he was, given all the mental torment he went through.

The better part Mary chose was to be able to focus on what really mattered at the moment. To sit at the feet of Jesus and learn from him. That's something that will last long after the meal is over and the dishes have been done and put away. It's something we need to learn today as never before. Our well being depends on it; maybe even our sanity. I venture that's why Jesus is so insistent on it.

---

1. Jeffery M. Schwartz, Westwood Institute for Anxiety Disorders, Dr. Jeffery Schwartz' Four Steps from his book, *Brain Lock* (New York: Regan Books, 1996), p. 4, www.hope4ocd.com/foursteps.

Sermons On The Gospel Readings

For Sundays
After Pentecost
(Middle Third)

Only The Lonely

Ron Lavin

Dedicated to

Diane Wilkinson

Kathy Shutt

Dodie Andersen

Rod and Caroline Anderson

and other Christians
who have inspired me with their spiritual growth
and selfless service

Foreword

The preaching of Ron Lavin changed my life. Ron was the senior pastor at King of Glory Lutheran Church in Fountain Valley, California, from 1993 to 1999. As a member there I heard him preach week after week. Ron brought renewal to my worship experience. I was not aware of the need for renewal until I heard his sermons. They hit home. Each week God's Word spoke directly to me. The sermons also spoke effectively to my wife, Caroline. She took notes on Ron's sermons each week. She refers to these notes often. I hope these sermons speak to you, as well.

In my previous church associations I had volunteered as a teacher of junior and senior high school Sunday school classes and served as an advisor to youth groups. By the time I reached King of Glory, I was weary of volunteer work. I just wanted to rest. Slowly, I eased back into teaching youth classes.

When Ron arrived in 1993, he saw potential in me. He encouraged me to get more deeply involved in leadership at King of Glory. He talked to me about serving as a candidate for the congregational council. I was elected. He also encouraged Caroline and me to teach an adult class on spousal relations. Then, he asked me to teach a Bible class on Genesis. I was petrified

Ron's sermons on prayer challenged me to think of prayer as talking to a friend and turning decisions and fears over to God. On the first day of my Genesis class, I was well prepared, but in a total panic. My hands were perspiring and I knew that I wasn't capable of teaching forty to fifty adults, most of whom knew much more about the Bible than I knew. It was raining heavily. I secretly hoped no one would show up. Caroline knew that I was panic-stricken. She said, "Why don't you ask God to help you with the class and give you peace?" I began talking to God in prayer. I told him how scared I was and that I wasn't capable of conducting this class. I

309

asked him to speak through me. God answered my prayer. The class of fifty responded positively to my teaching. I grew spiritually as I heard the Word preached at church and used my gifts for God's work.

My four years on the council were also years of growth. I was elected vice-president, then president of the congregation. Ron and I worked closely together on personnel and financial matters. We also worked on long-range planning. All of this was preparation for my election to the executive committee of the Pacifica Synod. Eventually, I was elected vice-president of synod.

Ron may not realize how great an impact he and his sermons had on my life. I am glad to write this "Foreword" and share with him and you how God's Word inspired me.

Ron has been retired from parish ministry for seven years now. Caroline and I get together with him and his wife, Joyce, each month for fellowship and mutual ministry. My friend continues to encourage me to talk to God in prayer and step out in faith. For that I will be grateful all of my life. Welcome to a series of sermons that may touch your life, too.

Rod Anderson
Vice-President, Pacifica Synod
Evangelical Lutheran Church in America

Preface

The sermons in this book are all based on texts from the Gospel of Luke. Luke was a doctor (Colossians 4:14). He was concerned about those who were ill and hurting. He was a Gentile. He knew that many Jews considered Gentiles as permanent outsiders. He was a historian and the author of Acts. He had a sense of God working in history. He recorded the missionary work of the early church, especially with those who were hurting. Outsiders play a big part in the story of Jesus and Luke helps us understand that Christianity is inclusive of the lost and lonely.

Special features in the Gospel of Luke include:

- Jesus' relationships with people,
- prayer,
- miracles,
- angels,
- women, and
- Jesus' compassion for the poor, the despised, and the displaced.

When you are poor, despised, or displaced, you may discover your need for God more readily than someone who is rich, successful, and well placed in the power structure. When you are humbled by the circumstances of life, you may discover that your basic loneliness is for God.

Those who are lonely for God are particularly important in the Gospel of Luke. This group gave rise to the title of my sermon on Luke 14:1, 7-14. The inciting incident for Jesus' emphasis on those who are lonely for God and know it is a banquet at a Pharisee's house. In this context, Jesus told the parable about arrogant fools who chose places of honor at a party, only to be told to take lesser places. In addition, Jesus told the guests that when they gave their social gatherings, to include those who could not invite them back. He told them to invite

- the poor,
- the crippled,
- the lame, and
- the blind.

Those lost souls, by society's standards, could not afford to throw parties and invite their hosts back. In other words, when we are talking about kingdom values, we need to keep in mind what other people need, not what they can do back for us. Jesus was saying, "Invite the lost and lonely." The lost and the lonely were precisely the ones Jesus invited into the kingdom.

All of us are lost before God and lonely for God, but not all of us realize and confess this condition. We were created by God and we long for God. We too easily fill the void in our hearts and souls with idols like money, possessions, or power. Some, like the Pharisees and Sadducees, even replace their hunger for God with an excessive emphasis on religious rules and regulations.

In Luke 14, and elsewhere in the gospels, we see Jesus confronting the false gods the scribes and Pharisees have created to fill up the holes in their souls. Jesus also exposes the reason for their inordinate emphasis on religious rules. Of course, these respected religious leaders didn't like having their illusions exposed. Of course, they fought back. "They watched him closely" (Luke 14:1). In other words, they sought to trap him.

Luke 11:53-54 reports "... The scribes and Pharisees began to be very hostile toward him and to cross-examine him about many things, lying in wait for him, to catch him in something he might say." Tension — confrontation — drama — conspiracy — the plot thickens as hypocrisy is exposed.

Jesus continually pointed out that the scribes, Pharisees, and Sadducees were hypocrites. A hypocrite is someone who looks good on the outside, but inwardly is filled with evil. A hypocrite may look religious, but has lost his way in relationship to God. A hypocrite is someone who fills the loneliness in his or her soul with devotion to something other than the one true God, but pretends to be godly. Hypocrites don't like it when their flaws are exposed.

Jesus repeatedly pointed out that his kingdom is for those who know they are lost and lonely and are willing to hear the good news that God loves them anyway. The lost and lonely frequently responded positively to Jesus' words because they knew they had no real fulfillment elsewhere. That's true for all of us, but when we have apparent fulfillment in the world, we may avoid real fulfillment which is only known by returning to God.

That's why Jesus said that prostitutes, tax-collectors, and sinners entered the kingdom of God before the so-called righteous. By confronting the hypocrisy of the religious leaders of his day, Jesus made enemies of those who thought of themselves as his judges. A judgmental spirit is evidence of self-righteousness. Jesus attacked self-righteousness because it is a barrier to faith.

No wonder the religious leaders grumbled and murmured against Jesus (Luke 15:1). No wonder they resented it when Jesus told them three stories about the lost and lonely being found by God (Luke 15:2-32). No wonder they were shocked when Jesus said, "... There will be more joy in heaven over one sinner who repents than over ninety-nine (self) righteous persons who (think they) need no repentance" (Luke 15:7, parenthetical insertions mine).

Jesus challenged the powerful, but welcomed sinners who acknowledged their low estate and underdogs who recognized their situation. The Gospel of Luke is sometimes called, "the good news for the underdog." Luke shows Jesus' love for the poor. Jesus said in the Beatitudes, "Blessed are the poor" (Luke 6:20). He added, "The poor have the good news preached to them" (Luke 7:22).

In the parable of the rich man and Lazarus, it is Lazarus who goes to heaven when he dies. The rich man finds himself in hell (Luke 16:19-31). This is a major reversal of what was expected in the society in which Jesus lived. In my sermon on that parable, I will try to show that Jesus was open to both rich and poor, but it is clear that poor people were much more apt to say, "Yes," to the invitation to come into the kingdom of God than their rich neighbors. Many of those who thought they were secure in their personal wealth or position were not open to Jesus' invitation to seek first the kingdom of God. They didn't notice the poor and they didn't notice God who made himself known in his Word.

There's no virtue in being poor. Having little of this world's goods and power doesn't guarantee status in the kingdom of God. The poor can fill their loneliness for God with resentment and hatred. On the other hand, the rich and successful often cover their longing for God with the world's goods and power. They find it hard to bow down before the mighty God in repentance.

Jesus is a friend of outcasts and sinners precisely because they have so little and know it. They are physically and spiritually lost and lonely. Only the lost and lonely, who know their condition, listen. Unless you listen, you can't hear the good news. Spiritual loneliness can lead to spiritual fulfillment. Loneliness is not all bad. It can be the very door which opens to the kingdom of God.

Henri Nouwen, the Roman Catholic spiritual writer, described spiritual loneliness in positive terms. He wrote: "... The more I think about loneliness, the more I think that the wound of loneliness is like the Grand Canyon — a deep incision in the surface of our existence which has become an inexhaustible source of beauty and self-understanding."[1] Nouwen added, "The Christian way of life does not take away our loneliness; it protects and cherishes it as a precious gift."[2]

Without the awareness of our human loneliness, we too easily fall into the demonic trap of following false gods. False gods like money, success, and power deceive us and fill us with illusions that initially may satisfy but eventually deeply disappoint us. Contrary to the world's illusions, "the painful awareness of loneliness is an invitation to transcend our limitations and look beyond the boundaries of our existence."[3]

This group of sermons is an invitation to look at human loneliness as a prelude to God's call. Martin Luther put it this way: "It is God's nature to create out of nothing; if you are not yet nothing, God can't make anything out of you."

314

Only those who are spiritually lonely and know it let Jesus address their condition with God's answers for their condition. Only the lonely acknowledge that no love, or friendship, or marriage can fill the void in the human heart. Only the lonely accept Jesus' insistence that all idols mislead and no human community can completely heal our wounds.

Only those who are spiritually lonely and know it face their loneliness instead of fleeing from it. Only the lonely see the limits of the pleasures of this world. Only the lonely see the illusions of this world for what they are: false ideas that cause misery if we devote ourselves to them as ultimate goals. Work is necessary and good; it may even be a way to use your God-given gifts in a meaningful way, but work is not the ultimate goal of life. Play is good for body and soul, but play is not the ultimate goal of life. Family is high in the constellation of values, but it isn't the highest value. Nothing calms our raging spiritual loneliness except the Lord.

Only the spiritually lonely are willing to lose something of themselves as they listen to the painful loneliness of others. Only the lonely are compassionate like Jesus instead of practicing what they will say next while others speak. Only the lonely listen and hear what others are really saying instead of what they seem to be saying. Only the lonely who are in touch with their loneliness exchange stories in depth with those in pain.

Only the spiritually lonely can enter solitude and then come out of solitude for service. Only the lonely who are in touch with their loneliness discover that being is more important than doing and thus refuse to sell their souls to a wide variety of graders in this world.

Facing our loneliness is the one thing needful and the hardest thing of all. The avoidance of loneliness is epidemic and chaotic. Chaos is catching and we easily succumb.

There is an alternative. We can face our loneliness and see it for what it is — a prelude to ultimate fulfillment in God. When we face our loneliness, we can help others face the loneliness that haunts them. Henri Nouwen speaks of Christians as wounded healers whose own wounds can be a source of healing and whose hospitality means that they pay attention to the pain in others.[4] The

315

Christian who is lonely and knows it is much more likely to be a part of the healing process than someone who is preoccupied with his or her own ideas, success, or values. Jesus went to a lonely place, a place of solitude, in order to be empowered for ministry.[5] So can we.

This sermon section is about Jesus Christ who is more than a spiritual leader who taught his disciples to go deep before going out; more than a moral teacher; more than a good man, more even than the best man who has ever lived. Jesus was more than a story-teller — though he was a great storyteller; more than a miracle worker — though he worked miracles; more than a healer — though he healed many hurting people. Jesus Christ claimed to be the Messiah, the Son of God, the one through whom we receive the forgiveness of sins.

None of the world's religious leaders made such a claim. Mohammed, Buddha, and Socrates never claimed to be God. Jesus claimed divinity. Either he was deluded or deliberately deceived his followers. Either he was a mad man with an ego out of control, or he was what he claimed to be — God incarnate. There's no middle ground. This book attempts to present the Lord Jesus Christ as he presented himself — the Son of God, the Lord of all, and the Savior of the world. When on earth, Jesus, who was both God and man, made disciples. He still does.

This group of sermons focuses on Jesus' disciples going into solitude for spiritual strength and coming out of solitude for self-less service. The first sermon in this book is about prayer; the last sermon is about living our faith. The inciting incident for the first sermon is the plea of the apostles, "Lord, teach us to pray" (Luke 11:1). The inciting incident for the last sermon is the plea of the apostles, "Increase our faith" (Luke 17:5). These heartfelt requests are heard yet today.

My thanks go to the many Christians who have taught me about solitude and selfless service. Thanks to the disciples who have taught me the counterpoint between getting in touch with one's own lone-liness before God and then getting in touch with the loneliness of others. The sermons in this section are all about living in the ten-sion between prayer and action.

1. Henri Nouwen, *The Wounded Healer* (Garden City, New York: Doubleday and Company, 1972), pp. 85-86.

2. *Ibid.*, p. 86.

3. *Ibid.*

4. *Ibid.*, pp. 90-91.

5. Henri Nouwen, *Out of Solitude* (Notre Dame, Indiana: Ave Maria Press, Seventh Printing, 1978), pp. 18-25.

Abba, Your Kingdom Come

The provoking incident for Jesus teaching his followers what to pray and how to pray is that the apostles watched Jesus and listened to his prayers. Nobody had ever prayed like this. His prayers were uniquely personal and profoundly humble. The apostles wanted to know more about prayer. So do we.

"Lord, teach us to pray," they said (Luke 11:1). We have the same plea today. There is a vague sense that we don't pray enough, nor with as much focus as we should have. There is a longing among Christians today to be more effective at prayer.

In Luke 11:1-13 Jesus teaches the content of prayer (vv. 1-4), the necessity to be persistent in prayer (vv. 5-10), and the encouragement to believe that God is faithful in answering prayer (vv. 11-13). We will focus here on the content of Jesus' prayer, but first let's look at the need for persistence in prayer and God's faithfulness in answering prayer.

Jesus' illustration of a man requesting bread at midnight from a friend is intended as an encouragement to pray persistently to God. If a friend will rise and give you bread at midnight, *how much more so will God answer prayers?* Persistent prayers are different than parachute prayers. Parachute prayers spoken only in emergencies are not based on a long-term relationship with our Heavenly Father. Parachute prayers are superficial at best, manipulative at worst. Parachute prayers are the opposite of persistent prayers. Our part of the formula for effective prayer is persistence and faithfulness in offering prayer. God's part is faithfulness in answering prayers.

God is faithful to those who persistently ask, search, and knock persistently. God promises to respond by giving us those things we really need instead of those things we think we need. As Jesus says in Luke 11, God doesn't give us snakes and scorpions. He gives us answers. Sometimes God's answer to prayer is "No." Sometimes God's answer to prayer is "Yes." Often God's answer to prayer is "Wait." Waiting is the school in which we learn to submit to God's reign and control. The Lord's Prayer is all about God's reign over us for our own good.

We approach God in prayer as our loving Father and as the Lord of the universe. The prayer "Abba, Your Kingdom Come" picks up both ends of paradox of the king of the universe being our Father. The Lord's Prayer as we know it includes some material not found in Luke 11:1-4. Here we will deal with only these four verses.[1]

Abba, Hallowed Be Your Name

The first word in the Lord's Prayer is "Abba." "Abba" is the Aramaic name used by a Jewish child for his or her father. Aramaic is a Jewish dialect spoken by the Jews in Jesus' time. Literally, "Abba" means "Daddy." It is a term of affectionate intimacy. No one before Jesus dared to think or teach that we could approach God in such an intimate way. That's one of the reasons the apostles were stunned by the way Jesus prayed. He talked to God like a son might talk to his Daddy. Jesus not only prayed this way; he expected his disciples to pray this way, too.

A little boy was standing on the banks of the Mississippi River waving and shouting at a steamboat that was going by. He was beckoning the steam boat to come to shore. A stranger came by and said, "That's foolish young man. The boat will never come ashore because of your request. The captain is too busy to notice your waving and shouting." Just then the boat turned and headed for shore. The little boy grinned and said to the stranger, "The captain is my daddy."

The captain of the universe is our Abba. He pays attention to our petitions because he loves us. The first word in the Lord's Prayer encourages us to believe in the affectionate intimacy of the Lord of the universe, but that doesn't mean we should take God for granted.

The first petition of the Lord's Prayer provides the corrective for those who forget that our Daddy is also the Lord of the universe. "Hallowed be your name" is a reminder that we are called to be humble before the ruler of all things. The Lord's Prayer calls us to be uniquely personal and profoundly humble before our God.

God's name is holy. We pray in this petition that we might make it holy in our lives by our words and deeds.

When Moses received the call of God to go back to Egypt and lead God's people out of bondage, he resisted. He felt unworthy. He was sure that his words would have no power. When God assured him that he had made his tongue and that his brother, Aaron, could be his spokesman, Moses agreed to go. "But the people will ask me, 'Who sent you?' " Moses said. "Whom shall I say sent me? What is your name?"

The name God gave to Moses was "YHWH." In ancient Hebrew, there were no vowels. Moses and the people of God were so fearful of mispronouncing and/or misusing this name that they used the name "Elohim" instead. The Hebrews wrote the name, "YHWH," but didn't use it in speech. When Hebrew scholars added vowels to the language, it was uncertain which vowels to use and where to place them in this word. That's how the name "Jehovah" came into use. Scholars today tell us that the more likely pronunciation is "Yahweh."

The point of this little excursion into God's name is that his name was so holy that the ancient Jews didn't pronounce it all. Compare that with the way people use God's name in vain today! The first petition in the Lord's Prayer is a helpful corrective for the disrespect shown to God in our time.

Your Kingdom Come

The kingdom of God is God's reign over us for our own good. To pray this petition means that we recognize that God is in control of our lives. The control issue is a major issue for all of us.

In our time, we have remote controls for television sets, for VCRs, for tape recorders, and for DVD players. Button, button, who's got the button? We have it. We have remote controls for garages, gates, and car doors. Button, button, who's got the button?

We have it, right? The trouble is that we tend to think that we have the button on the remote control device for life. Not so! Button, button, who's got the button? To confess Jesus as Lord and recognize that he rules over us means that we believe God has the remote control button for life. That's what the kingdom of God is all about.

The kingdom of God doesn't come in fullness until the end of time when God shall reign forever and ever and every knee will bow before the Lord Jesus Christ, but the kingdom came to earth in a special way in the person of Jesus. In other words, the kingdom of God is a future event, but it came near when Jesus appeared on earth in the past. Jesus said, "The time is fulfilled, and the kingdom of God has come near; repent and believe in the good news" (Mark 2:15). While the kingdom of God won't come in fullness until the end of time, Jesus encouraged his followers to start living as if it had already arrived.

In addition, the kingdom of God comes today. The kingdom will come in fullness at the Second Coming of Christ; it came as a preview of coming attractions in the First Coming of Jesus and it comes in the present wherever Jesus comes today. Jesus is present in Word and sacraments. The kingdom of God breaks into Christian fellowship today as a foretaste of the ultimate reign of God.

To pray, "Your kingdom come," means that we acknowledge God's rule over us. We do more than acknowledge it; we agree to it. By nature, we fight this rule and have done so from the beginning of time. God said, "Don't." Eve said, "Why not? I will. Join me, Adam." Adam easily agreed. That's called the Great Rebellion. We have been rebelling ever since. We don't want anyone to rule over us, even when the Ruler is our Abba who seeks to rule us only because he knows what is good for us better than we do.

The prayer petition, "Your will be done on earth as in heaven,"[2] drives home the point that the issue of the control button is a matter of the will. To pray "Your kingdom come" means that it is our intention to bend our will to the will of the one who made us, and to do it gladly, not with clenched teeth and frowns. We don't always know the will of God completely, but to the degree God reveals it in his Word, we are invited to agree to his control like the angels do it. The angels do the will of God gladly.

322

Give Us This Day Our Daily Bread

This petition of the Lord's Prayer clearly means that we should be grateful for the food which comes to us daily from God and to offer what we call "grace" at all our meals. But there may be more here than gratefulness for food.

Alternatively, this petition may be translated, "Give us our bread for tomorrow" or as New Testament scholars Johoiachim Jeremias and John V. Taylor suggest, "Give us tomorrow's bread today." In other words, this petition about bread is about the kingdom bread that we need to sustain us if we are to be the people who try to live under God's reign. The Aramaic word *machar* (tomorrow) from an ancient manuscript suggests this translation and connection with the kingdom of God.

Tomorrow's bread is the bread of the coming kingdom of God. This bread comes to us in Word and sacraments as we meet in Christian fellowship. It is like the manna from heaven given to the ancient Hebrews as they crossed the desert on the way to the promised land. Our spiritual journey is like that of the ancient Hebrews. We are no longer in Egypt, but we have not yet reached the promised land. We are wanderers in the wilderness of life. The wilderness is a place where we need to be sustained so that we can continue the journey toward heaven. God sends "tomorrow's bread," manna from heaven, to sustain us.

Forgive Us As We Forgive Others

Forgiveness of sins is a sign of the breakthrough of the kingdom of God. Jesus not only taught his followers that they should forgive their enemies. He lived his teaching, saying from the cross, "Father (Abba), forgive them for they don't know what they are doing."

In the parable about the prodigal son and his father (Luke 15:11-32), forgiveness is offered *before* repentance is made. That's a kingdom of God way to do things. We aren't responsible for someone else saying, "I'm sorry." As Christians, we are responsible for a willingness to forgive *even before* those who have hurt us see the error of their ways and repent. As Christians, we are responsible for a willingness to forgive even if there is no repentance on the

323

part of those who have hurt us. In a sense, it isn't our responsibility to forgive others. Our responsibility is to be willing to forgive and to offer forgiveness.

That's the way God treats us. Kingdom of God people try to do things the way God does them. God is willing to forgive us when we hurt him. Therefore, we should be willing to forgive those who hurt us. If we are not willing to forgive those who offend us, even when from our point of view, *they don't deserve it*, that's a signal that we don't understand that we have been forgiven, *when we didn't deserve it*. In other words, our promise to be willing to forgive is attached to the prayer petition about forgiveness. "We will try to do for others what you, our Abba, have done for us."

This revolutionary idea about God who is more willing to forgive than we are to seek forgiveness, and the promise to forgive as we have been forgiven, greatly upset the Pharisees and other religious leaders who first heard these words. They saw that Jesus was saying that God is like that father in the parable who offers forgiveness *before* the lost son returned and that we are called to imitate God's ways.

Do Not Bring Us To The Time Of Trial

"Do not bring us to the time of trial" (NRSV) is a better translation than "Lead us not into temptation" (KJV). God tempts no one to sin. In my opinion, the best translation of this petition is: "Save us from the great ordeal."

The Lord's Prayer begins with the term of affectionate intimacy, "Abba." That means that we can endure anything if our Daddy is close by. Jesus went through the great ordeal when he cried out, "My God, my God, why have you forsaken me?" This is the only place in the recorded prayers of Jesus that he doesn't call God, Abba. On the cross Jesus was bruised for our iniquities, bereft because of our sins, and forsaken.

In this petition, we pray that we never have to go through what Jesus went through on the cross: the feeling of utter forsakenness. In Christian history this state of utter loneliness is called "the dark night of the soul." God loves us. He is our Abba. We learn to accept that love and love him back. God guides us. We learn to follow that

324

guidance. Then when we really need God and pray to him to help us or someone we love because what is happening is far beyond our control, sometimes God seems to be asleep. Worse yet, God seems not to care. That is the great ordeal. Some Christians don't go through the great ordeal. Some go through it, get to the end of their rope, tie a knot, and hang on by their fingernails and just barely get through it.

Because the great ordeal is the territory of the evil one who seeks to separate us from God, we pray we will be saved from going there. Because Jesus went there, apparently lost the battle with the evil one, but then conquered all the powers of evil in his resurrection, if ever we find ourselves in the great ordeal, we are called to remember that Jesus got through it, conquered the evil one, and is calling us to overcome the temptation of feeling forsaken. Persistence at such times is difficult but essential. God is listening, even when he doesn't seem to care.

We want to have more effective prayer lives. Luke 11:1-13 gives us our Lord's instructions about how to do that. Having affectionate intimacy with our Abba and profound humility before the King of kings and Lord of lords, we are called to pray with persistence, overcoming the illusion that God doesn't care. We are called to believe that God is answering our prayers, even when he seems not to be listening or when he answers them in ways we don't understand.

With the apostles, we ask, "Lord, teach us to pray."

---

1. The Lord's Prayer as we know it includes some material not found in Luke 11. For further exposition of all verses of the Lord's Prayer, see *Abba (Another Look At The Lord's Prayer)* by Ron Lavin, CSS Publishing Co., Lima, Ohio, 2003.

2. Some ancient authorities include this phrase in the Lord's Prayer (Luke 11:2). In the Gospel of Matthew it is also included (Matthew 6:10).

Proper 13
Pentecost 11
Ordinary Time 18
Luke 12:13-21

You Fool!

The incident stirring up this text is the request of someone in the crowd who asked Jesus to judge between on older brother and himself regarding an inheritance. The real problem isn't the request which Jesus refused, but the greed lying beneath the surface of the request which Jesus addressed with a parable about a rich fool who went to hell.

In Jesus' day, the oldest brother got the inheritance when his father died. He was then expected to take care of the rest of the family. This procedure protected the family farm from being divided into such small portions that it wouldn't do anyone any good. Apparently, the man who approached Jesus was dissatisfied with this arrangement and wanted Jesus to tell his older brother to give him his half of the inheritance. Jesus looked deeply into the heart of the man making the request. What did he see there? He saw greed and told the man, "Take care! Be on guard against all kinds of greed; for one's life does not consist in the abundance of possessions" (Luke 12:15).

Then Jesus drove his point home with a parable. The parable is about the temptation to succumb to the attractive distraction of devoting oneself to possessions and missing the call of God to have right priorities.

The man who asked Jesus to judge between himself and his brother and the farmer in the parable Jesus told had the same problem. They embraced the temptation of gathering possessions out of greed.

327

The rich farmer in the parable made wise business decisions and seeing the crops come in with abundance asked himself, "What shall I do to store all my crops?" What's the problem with that? He decided to build bigger and better barns. So, what's the problem? To his own soul, he said, "Soul, you have ample goods laid up for many years; relax, eat, drink, be merry." That's the problem. He embraced the voice of greed and ignored the voice of God. The day was coming when he would die and have to face God. That day was coming sooner than he thought, but like a lot of folks, he lived as if he'd never die. Like him, we are caught between the voices of good and evil.

A story is told about a man who described the human predicament in terms of two dogs. "We have two dogs in our hearts," he said. "One dog is called Good; the other dog is called Evil. They fight all the time."

A friend asked, "Which one wins?"

"The one I feed," the man replied.

The greedy man in our text and the greedy farmer in Jesus' parable both fed the wrong dog. They fell into the trap of feeding the dog which urged priority to the trivial pursuits in this life to the neglect of eternal pursuits.

It's like someone got into the window of life and moved the price tags on the items displayed there. The expensive eternal pursuits like prayer, church, worship, and selfless service got cheap price tags while cheap items like the possessions of this world got expensive price tags.

When we seek possessions as the ultimate goal of life, possessions turn around and possess us. An old fable about a fly and a strip of flypaper illustrates the point. The strip of flypaper looked so appetizing that the fly decided to claim it for himself. After chasing away all the other insects that threatened to share his find, he landed on the flypaper and happily announced, "My flypaper." Then he proceeded to partake of the tasty feast he found there. When he tried to walk around, he found he was stuck. Then he tried in vain to fly away. Completely exhausted, he gave up. Then the flypaper proudly exclaimed, "My fly!" When possessions become our highest priority, they possess us. How foolish.

Shortly after Jesus told the parable about the rich, but foolish, farmer, he spoke about the dangers of worrying about the things of this earth, but forgetting about the higher priority of heaven. He said:

> *Consider the lilies, how they grow: they neither toil nor spin; yet I tell you, even Solomon in all his glory was not clothed like one of these. But if God so clothes the grass of the field, which is alive today and tomorrow is thrown into the oven, how much more will he clothe you — you of little faith! And do not keep striving for what you are to eat and what you are to drink, and do not keep worrying. For it is the nations of the world that strive after all these things, and your Father knows that you need them. Instead, strive for his kingdom, and these things will be given to you as well.*
> — Luke 12:27-31

The foolishness of setting the wrong priorities can lead to eternal death. Setting the right priorities leads to eternal life.

E. Stanley Jones pointed out that whatever gets our attention gets us. If we focus on our problems and glance at God, our problems get us. If we focus on possessions and glance at God, our possessions get us. But if we focus on God and glance at our problems and the need for possessions, God gets us. It's a matter of setting the right priorities. Too many of us major in minors. That's what Jesus means by striving for the kingdom. Accepting God's reign over us in love is the highest priority we have.

Striving for the kingdom doesn't get us there. We get into the kingdom only by the grace and mercy of God, but if the kingdom is not our focus, we won't hear the call of God to come to him. When greed gets our attention, we miss the invitation to the abundant life in the hereafter as well as in the here and now. We miss the opportunity when God comes to us.

A rich man who was an inactive member of a church responded to the pastor's invitation to return to regular worship: "I'm never coming back to church again. I'm through with religion."

"Why is that?" asked the pastor.

"I was in Alaska on a fishing expedition and I got lost. I prayed to God to save me. I told him that if he got me out of my predicament I'd give the church a bundle of money, but he never showed up."

"But you're here," replied the pastor. "You didn't die. What happened?"

"Oh," said the rich man, "an Eskimo came along and rescued me."

Greed and possessions can blind us to the coming of God. When we are focused on something other than God, God can present himself and not be seen. Have you seen any Eskimos lately? Is something obscuring your view? Possessions can be attractive distractions.

A rich woman, let's call her Betty, lost her husband. She had been away from church for many years. She felt isolated and lonely in her grief. It seemed that God had forgotten her. She went to a grocery store, but found she wasn't particularly interested in buying groceries for one. She wasn't hungry. The pain of losing her husband was still too raw. This grocery store held many memories.

Her husband often went shopping with her. He'd pretend to go off and look for some special food, but she knew what he was up to. She'd see him walking down the aisle with three yellow roses in his hands. He knew she loved yellow roses.

Her heart was filled with grief. She wanted to buy a few items and flee. Shopping for one took time, more time than shopping for two. She looked for a small steak, feeling lonely and forsaken, even by God.

Suddenly a woman came up to her. She was blonde, slim, and lovely in a soft green pantsuit. She picked up a large pack of T-bones, dropped them in her basket, hesitated, and then put them back. She turned to go and once again reached for the pack of steaks. Then she saw Betty watching her. She smiled and said. "My husband loves T-bones, but at these prices ... I just don't know what to do."

Betty responded, "My husband passed away eight days ago." Trembling, she added, "Buy him the steaks and cherish every moment you have together."

The woman placed the steaks in her basket and wheeled away.

Betty rolled her cart to the other side of the store to the dairy products, trying to decide what size milk to buy. Then she looked down the aisle. First she saw the green suit, then a package in the woman's arms, then a bright smile on her face. Her eyes held Betty's eyes which soon filled with tears when she saw what the woman was carrying.

"These are for you," the woman said, placing three beautiful long-stemmed yellow roses in Betty's arms. "When you go through the check-out line, they will know that these are paid for." She reached over and kissed Betty's tear-stained cheek, smiled, and left.

Betty wanted to tell the woman what she had done, but couldn't speak. "How did she know? How could she know what this meant to me?" Betty thought. Suddenly, it dawned on Betty that she wasn't alone. God had not forgotten her. "That woman was my angel," she said out loud.

Seen any angels lately? Anything obscuring your view? Possessions can be attractive distractions which keep us from seeing God at work.

That's why the first lesson for today (Ecclesiates 1:2, 12-14, 18-23) says, "Vanity of vanities, says the Teacher, vanity of vanities! All is vanity." Possessions can only temporarily fill the void in our hearts which God alone is intended to fill.

That's why the second lesson for today says, "Set your minds on things that are above, not on things that are on earth" (Colossians 3:2). Setting our minds on the things of the earth eventually, if not immediately, disappoints. After all, we can't take possessions with us when we die. As a creed, greed is seriously flawed.

That's why Jesus said to the young man who wanted him to judge in his favor and fill his heart with possessions, "Take care! Be on your guard against all kinds of greed; for life does not consist in the abundance of possessions." We can try to fill the void in our lives by seeking success, but, in truth, only God can fill that void. All substitutes fall short and then come crashing down on our heads when we die.

That's why the focus of the farmer in Jesus' parable was so tragically dislocated. He was caught in the illusion of success. He thought he'd made it, only to discover that he had been seeking the wrong things in life. At best, God was on the periphery of his life. Success and possessions were in the middle. He was caught in the trap of giving his life to the attractive distractions of this world and neglected to focus on the world to come. The pursuit of possessions is trivial when compared to the striving for and receiving of the blessings of the kingdom of God. That's why the rich farmer was pitiful. That's why he was foolish.

The parable of the rich, but foolish, farmer ends with a poignant reminder for all of us. At the end of life we'd like to hear God say, "Well done, good and faithful servant. Enter into the joy of your Master," but if, like the farmer, we set the wrong priorities we may hear these words:

"You fool."

"Tonight, you fool."

"Tonight your soul will be required of you."

"Tonight, you fool."

"Tonight. Tonight. Tonight."

Proper 14
Pentecost 12
Ordinary Time 19
Luke 12:32-40

Ready Or Not, Here I Come

When you were a child, did you play the game, "Hide and Go Seek"? The person who is "It" closes his or her eyes, counts to ten, and then searches for the other children who are hiding. "1-2-3-4-5-6-7-8-9-10. Ready or not, here I come!"

Something like that is going on in our text. The master is off to a wedding banquet. His servants are at the family farm. Some are alert, ready for his return; some are not ready. The countdown has begun. No one knows exactly when the master will return. At the end of our story, Jesus says, "You ... must be ready, for the Son of Man is coming at an unexpected hour" (Luke 12:40).

Clearly, Jesus is talking about his Second Coming. Clearly, Jesus is speaking of his return at the end of the world. Clearly, we must be ready to meet him when he returns in power and majesty. We don't know when that will be, but we are called to wait with patience and act with faithfulness, like good servants. The countdown has begun.

We live between the lightning and the thunder. The First Coming of Christ is like the lightning. We wait; then comes the thunder. When we see the one, we know the other will follow. The countdown has started: 1-2-3-4.... The Second Coming of Christ is like that. We know it's coming, but we don't know when it will arrive. Between the lightning and the thunder we are called to wait with patience and faith and act with faithfulness and obedience to the master's teaching. The countdown has begun for the Second Coming.

In addition, the countdown has begun for our death. At death, as well as at the Second Coming of Christ, we must be ready to meet the Lord face-to-face. We don't know when we will die, but we are called to wait patiently and act faithfully in this in-between time.

In this in-between time, before the Second Coming of Christ and before we die, the servants of God are called to wait with faith. That means that we believe what the master said. We trust him. We trust his Word. We are called to treasure his Word. Jesus said, "Where your treasure is, there your heart will be also" (Luke 12:34).

The world may live in fear because the people of the world don't know what is happening, but we, the disciples of Christ, have been told what is coming at the end of time and at the end of our time. Therefore, we can be ready to meet Christ with faith and hope in our hearts. Jesus said, "Do not be afraid, little flock, for it is your Father's good pleasure to give you the kingdom" (Luke 12:32).

"Ready or not, here I come" Jesus said. Death sometimes comes unexpectedly.

A couple from Minneapolis decided to go to Florida to thaw out during one particularly icy winter. They planned to stay at the very same hotel where they spent their honeymoon twenty years earlier. Because of hectic schedules, it was difficult to coordinate their schedules, so the husband left Minneapolis and flew to Florida on Thursday with his wife scheduled to fly down the next day.

The husband checked into the hotel. There was a computer in his room, so he decided to send an email to his wife. Accidentally, he left out one letter in her email address and without realizing it, sent the email message to the wrong person.

Meanwhile, somewhere in Houston, a widow had just returned home from her husband's funeral. He was a minister of many years who was called home to glory following a sudden heart attack.

The widow decided to check her email since she was expecting messages of condolence from relatives and friends. After reading the first message, she fainted. The widow's son rushed into the room, found his mother on the floor and was amazed by what he saw on the computer screen.

To: My loving wife
Subject: I've arrived

*I know you're surprised to hear from me. They have
computers here now and you are allowed to send emails
to your loved ones. I've just arrived and have been
checked in. I see that everything has been prepared for
your arrival tomorrow. Looking forward to seeing you
then! Hope your journey is as uneventful as mine was.*

P.S. It sure is hot down here!

The widow wasn't ready for that message. It was a mistake.
The time will come when we get the message saying that the time
has come for us to die. It won't be a mistake. We are called to be
ready for this time by having faith and hope in Christ.

Harry Andersen was ready. He had terminal cancer, but kept
his sense of faith and hope alive. His pastor could tell he was
ready because they talked about Christ's death and resurrection
and what this event means for us when we die. Harry showed no
fear since he believed the promises of God. In addition, a sign of
Harry's faith and hope was expressed in the humor he shared with
his pastor.

After scripture reading and prayer, Harry told the pastor the
story of a man who was dying of cancer. He was bedridden on the
second floor of his house. He could smell the aroma of chocolate
chip cookies baking in the oven downstairs. He loved chocolate
chip cookies. As a matter of fact, they were his favorite. He forced
himself to get out of bed and crawled to the flight of steps leading
downstairs. Each step brought new pain to his body, but he had to
have some of those chocolate chip cookies. When he got to the
bottom of the stairs, he crawled to the kitchen table and reached up
for a cookie.

Suddenly, his wife appeared out of nowhere and slapped his
hand with a spatula.

"Why did you do that?" he cried out.

"Those cookies are for your funeral reception," she said.

Harry Andersen laughed out loud as he told the story. The pastor rolled on the floor with laughter at the unexpected ending. Then Harry said, "That's just the kind of thing my wife would do."

Just then Harry's wife walked into the room. "I wouldn't do that," she said smiling at the pastor, "but there's something else I'd like to do at Harry's funeral."

"What's that?" asked the pastor.

"I'd like to pass out plastic forks to everyone as they arrive for the funeral."

"Plastic forks?"

"Yes," she said. "I love the story about the woman who went to many church potlucks and always rejoiced when she was given a new plastic fork at the end of the meal. That meant that homemade pie was being served for dessert. When she got the fork, she always said, 'The best is yet to come.' "

A few weeks later, Harry died. As the parishioners arrived at the church door, they were each given a plastic fork. When they asked the reason for this unusual gift, they were told that they would hear more about it later. The title of the pastor's funeral sermon was, "The Best Is Yet To Come." He explained that Jesus died for us that we might be forgiven and go to heaven. "It is the Father's pleasure to give you the kingdom" he said, quoting Luke 12:32. Then he told the story of the woman who loved homemade pie at the end of church potlucks and he pointed out that Harry was being buried with a plastic fork in his casket because when we have faith and hope in the Lord in this life, the best is yet to come.

Harry was ready to meet Jesus. Some people aren't. Their hearts are set on the treasures of this world instead of heaven. They don't wait patiently for the Lord with faith and hope. They don't act faithfully with their eyes focused on the Lord, their lamps lit and dressed for action (Luke 12:35).

It's always good to check the context of a sermon text. Both the front side context and the back side context of this parable add meaning to our story. The front side context (Luke 12:13-31) is about a rich, but foolish, farmer who believed in and sought possessions in this life as if they were the ultimate goal of life. The

336

back side context (Luke 12:41-48) is about a servant who mistreated his fellow servants because he didn't think he'd ever have to face the absent master again. This evil servant lived as if he were the master, eating and drinking excessively. He was saying, "The master is away, I can do whatever I wish."

Jesus said, "... The master of that slave will come on a day when he does not expect him and at an hour that he does not know ... and will put him with the unfaithful" (Luke 12:46). There is punishment for evil deeds.

In other words, we are not just called to believe in the master. We are not only called to realize that we will face him again at the end of time or at the end of our lives, whichever comes first. In addition, we are also called to act on these beliefs. We are called to be "dressed for action and have our lamps lit" (Luke 12:35). We are called to make faith active in the way we live for God and people. Sometimes there are demonic factors that seem to make it nearly impossible to put our faith into action. These factors can be overcome, but not if we keep them secret. Secrets make us sick. Secrets have to be revealed before anything can be done about them. The beginning of forgiveness is to bring secret sins out of hiding.

A woman named Mary came to her pastor for counseling one day. After the preliminaries, Mary confessed that she had done many things in her past that made her feel ashamed. "My behavior has not been that of a Christian," she said. Then she went on to explain that she had had sex many times before she was married and had committed adultery after she was married. "I've tried to confess my sins to God," she said, "and I know the Bible says that he forgives me, but I just don't feel forgiven. My marriage is falling apart. I feel guilty about the past, fearful of the future, and inhibited in the present."

The pastor prayed privately, "Lord, help me to find some way to help Mary." When Mary finished her story, the pastor asked her to stand in front of a crucifix he had on his wall. "That's where you're headed when you die," he said. "One day, you will see Jesus face-to-face."

"Yes," she said, "I know, and I'm not ready."

"Right now, you are burdened by your past," the pastor told her. "It's like you are carrying a bag of rocks on your back." He walked over to the corner of the room where he recently had placed a bag of rocks he had taken from church property during a church clean-up day. He hoisted the heavy bag onto Mary's back and asked her to grab it. "You are carrying a bag of rocks from your past," he said. "That's the guilt you feel for what you've done. The reason you feel stuck in the present is because of that guilt. Your fear of the future also makes you feel stuck in the present. Do you want to continue carrying this bag of rocks?"

"No," Mary said. "It's heavy."

"Then let Jesus have it. He died on the cross to take your bag of rocks from you. You can't carry those rocks. He can. Your only job is to let him have your bag of rocks and not pick it up again."

The pastor took the bag of heavy rocks from Mary's back. "That's what the forgiveness of sins is like," he said.

A week later, Mary told the pastor, "For the first time in my adult life, I feel free to live my faith with faithfulness. It's like a new world."

"It is a new world," the pastor responded. "It's called the kingdom of God. When you gave your bag of rocks to the Lord, you got a foretaste of what it will be like when you go to heaven."

Together they turned to Luke 12:32. "Maybe you'd like to read it out loud," the pastor suggested.

Mary read, "Do not be afraid, little flock, for it is your Father's good pleasure to give you the kingdom."

"You are ready to meet the Lord," the pastor told her.

Jesus told his followers that he would return. He told them to be ready for his return at the end of time. He also urged us to be ready for *our* end time, when we die and come before his throne of grace. He doesn't ask us to be perfect. He asks us to wait with faith and hope and act faithfully with obedience to what he has taught us. He wants us to be ready.

In the child's game of Hide and Go Seek there's a countdown. There's also a countdown in life.

"1-2-3-4-5-6-7-8-9-10. Ready or not, here I come!"

Family Ties And Good-byes

If ever we needed to strengthen the institution of family, it's today. Many forces of evil are pulling the family apart. Ethical relativism, which teaches that there are no absolutes, not even God, is increasingly popular. Immorality abounds. Listening and hearing one another seems to be a lost art in many homes. Spouses often seem to be going in opposite directions. Parents and children have a hard time communicating. Many modern homes are little more than large telephone booths where arrangements are made to leave.

At first glance, our text appears to compound the problem of the divided family. Jesus says, "I came to bring fire to the earth, and how I wish it were already kindled! ... Do you think that I have come to bring peace to the earth? No, I tell you, but rather division! From now on five in one household will be divided, three against two and two against three ..." (Luke 12:49-52). That doesn't seem to be a way to focus on good family relationships!

It gets worse: "They will be divided: father against son and son against father, mother against daughter and daughter against mother, mother-in-law against her daughter-in-law and daughter-in-law against mother-in-law" (Luke 12:53). It seems at first glance that this fire Jesus advocates is all about destruction and division. In fact, one of the primary purposes of fire is to cleanse and purify. Divisions may come, but God's first purpose in sending fire to families is to cleanse and purify people's lives and relationships. Before looking at the family good-byes that may be involved when one person comes to faith and other family members don't, let's look at God's intention of establishing family ties.

339

God created male and female and established marriage and family. God said, "It is good." Family ties are more than human contracts; they are part of God's order.

Psalm 68:6 (NIV) says, "God sets the lonely in families." Our most fundamental loneliness is only fulfilled by a relationship with our Maker, but we have a loneliness for human contact as well. In other words, it's God's intention to give us a preview of fulfillment as members of his eternal family by placing us in loving family relationships in this life. The Bible speaks of the relationship between God and human beings in terms of a groom and bride (Revelation 21:2). Family ties are good when we see these ties as a foretaste of the ties we will have in heaven with God and his heavenly host. God works to establish these human ties, to strengthen and purify them.

Family ties are strengthened and purified when the members of the family remember the order of creation: God first; family second; work third. When this order of creation is followed, families come closer to one another. When this order is upset and something other than God is in first place, there is disharmony and division.

For example, Carol had a low self-image and an inferiority complex. She was sure no man would ever propose marriage to her, but when Harry did, she jumped at the proposal and said, "Yes," immediately. She dedicated herself to making Harry happy. He didn't pray, so she stopped. He didn't go to church, so she didn't go, either. Carol had gone to church as a child and loved it, but her children seldom attended because Harry said that churches were just after your money and were worthless. She had been raised as a Christian, but her faith began to fade as she was away from the Christian fellowship, the Word and the sacraments. Carol was overdependent on Harry. He was number one in her life. The weather forecast for Carol's life was blizzards with no sign of sunlight in sight.

Harry devoted himself first, last, and always to his work as a television anchorman. He was successful and rich and he wanted to keep it that way. He said he believed there was a God, but he was a practical atheist. He lived as if there was no God. He neglected God. He also neglected his family. The weather forecast for Harry's life and afterlife was: "Tornado coming. Beware." Blinded by his drive for success, Harry reversed the order of creation. He made work first; family second; and God third. Of course, he didn't believe in the order of creation, so this reversal and its destructive end was not apparent to him. He died of a sudden heart attack at age fifty.

Carol was devastated. She had built her life around Harry. Now he was gone. Grief threatened to ruin the rest of her life. Depression gained a foothold and threatened never to let go. Fortunately, a friend invited Carol to a grief recovery class at her church. There Carol learned that grief is a natural reaction to the death of a loved one, but if a person stayed in that state of depression for a long time, that was a sign that something was wrong in the relationship. One woman in the group confessed that she stayed depressed after her husband died for over a year and the reason was that she had made her husband the number one thing in her life. It suddenly dawned on Carol that that's what she had done, too. "It helped me when I got back to church and got my priorities straightened out," the woman said. "God is the only number one that works."

Carol asked her friend if she could go to church with her the next Sunday. There she found a welcoming fellowship and a pastor who helped her feel that she was once again a part of the family of God. Grief, like a blizzard, passed through but did not stay permanently in Carol's life. As Carol got back to the order of creation with God first, family (her two children) second, and work third, her life was integrated. She found peace.

Harry had been a good provider, and the insurance money helped to keep Carol's family going, but after six months with no paychecks, Carol realized she needed to get back to work. She talked to some of the people where Harry worked. They found a place for her. In the next two years, she got three promotions. Her confidence level rose.

She met a man named Stan at church. After nine months of dating, Stan proposed. Carol went into this marriage with her eyes wide open. "I love you, Stan," she said, "but I love God more." "I understand," he said. "That's the way it's supposed to be." At age 49, life began again for Carol.

Family ties are strengthened when family members love and respect God above everything else and have love and respect for one another. Absolute obedience belongs only to God, but we are called to honor those over us in the Lord (parents) and be honorable to those under us in the Lord (children). Spouses are guided in their relationship by Jesus' words, "Just as I have loved you, love one another" (John 13:34).

By the time she got married for the second time, Carol's children were 24 and eighteen. Harry Jr., the oldest, was a senior in college. Mary, the youngest, was just graduating from high school. They had never respected their mother because she was too easy on them. Their father had made all the decisions as they were growing up. There was another problem. Harry, Sr., was an alcoholic. Family members were ashamed of his condition, so they kept it a secret.

Harry, Jr., and Mary didn't oppose their mother's marriage to Stan, but they weren't too excited about it, either. They said, "We'll be gone soon. She can do as she pleases."

One day when Carol tried to correct Mary for staying out beyond the agreed upon time of return from a date, Mary flew out of control, showing major disrespect for her mother and cursing her out for "never letting me do what I want." Stan decided that he had seen enough of this kind of behavior, so he went to Mary's room, knocked, and entered. She was crying. He listened to her sobs; then he listened to her side of the story. When she was done crying and feeling sorry for herself, Stan said, "In our religion we teach respect for parents as one of the basic teachings for the family. You may not agree with your mother, but you've got to get your act together and show her more respect." He turned on his heels and walked out the door.

It didn't change Mary right away, but little by little she came to realize that her lack of respect was hurting everyone, including herself. Two years later, when she and her fiancé decided to get married, she attended the pastor's class at her mother's church, and heard the Ten Commandments explained. When it came to the fourth Commandment, "Honor your father and your mother ..." Mary realized that she was going to have to show more respect for her mother and stepfather if she ever expected her children to honor and respect her. Mary and her new husband joined the church. Family ties got stronger for Mary.

That was not the case with Mary's brother, Harry, Jr.

Harry, Jr., called "Junior" by his family, respected neither his father nor his mother. In his opinion, his father had been a drunk; his mother a weakling. He didn't know Stan and he didn't want to know him. He had his own life now. He worked as a weatherman for a small television station hundreds of miles from where his mother lived. He hardly ever came home. When he got married, he and his wife ran with a crowd that went to a lot of parties where there was alcohol and drugs. He was a weatherman, but he could not forecast what was coming to his own life. His mother phoned him and sent him letters encouraging him to come back to the faith and find a church like she and Mary had. It was all to no avail.

Family ties are strengthened when each member of a family makes a commitment to Jesus Christ as Lord and Savior. When one or more family members are unbelievers, barriers go up, divisions spread, and estrangements happen. That's what Jesus means when he talks about family good-byes.

Stan and Carol had made a commitment to Jesus Christ as Lord and Savior. Mary and her new husband also made that commitment. By taking seriously that Jesus is number one in life, family is in second place, and work is in third place, these four had a unity to their lives that was absent from the lives of Junior and his wife. Unless, or until, Junior and his wife come to faith in Jesus Christ, they will continue to be outsiders. It isn't so much that Christians separate from outsiders; outsiders separate from those who are Christians. Carol continued to invite Junior and his wife to come home for a visit, but the answer was usually that they were too busy to make the drive and they didn't want to stay at the house. What was Carol's alternative? Keep on inviting them. Keep praying for them. "But they are adults and must make up their own minds," Carol thought. A voice in her mind responded, "Look for openings."

When Junior lost his job because of his drinking and taking drugs, Carol was there, offering a listening ear and urging her son to get help with his drinking problem. When Junior was divorced by his wife, Carol was there. "If you turn your life over to God and get to an AA group, you will get help," she said. He turned a deaf ear to his mother.

When Junior began to live on the streets, and occasionally showed up at Carol's house, she always let him stay as long as he didn't drink. As soon as he began to drink again, she and Stan told Junior he'd have to go. "We won't tolerate intolerable behavior," Stan said, "because to tolerate intolerable behavior is to encourage intolerable behavior."

"You sound like a preacher," Junior said. From that point on, Junior didn't call his stepfather Stan. He'd call him Preacher, and then he'd snicker.

The final family good-bye came when Junior got drunk and started throwing things at his mother's house. The police were called. Junior was locked up. When he was finally released, he took off, leaving this note for his mother and Stan:

> *Dear Mom and Preacher,*
> *I'm leaving town. Don't expect to see me again. I'm sick and tired of all this talk about the Lord and church. I'm not going to listen to your sanctimonious talk about my drinking problem, AA, and going to worship. I've had enough of it. When you count the members of the family, count me out. Good-bye.*
> *Your former son,*
> *Harry, Jr.*

The gospel of Jesus Christ is good news, but when someone is locked into their sins, they may see it as bad news. The fire of the gospel is intended to cleanse family relationships. On some occasions, the fire of the gospel is too hot for certain family members to handle. They flee from the family that embraces the gospel. They say, "Good-bye."

Jesus had serious trouble in his own family. Maybe that's why he spoke so strongly about what happens when family members reject the gospel. In Luke 4:16-30 we read that when Jesus preached in his home town of Nazareth there was great conflict.

We pick up the story with the hometown folks being very proud of the local boy's popularity. Jesus' sermon in his hometown synagogue went well. He read from a passage in Isaiah:

The spirit of the Lord God is upon me, because the Lord has sent me to bring good news to the oppressed, to bind up the brokenhearted, to proclaim liberty to the captives, and release to the prisoners....

As he rolled up the scroll of scripture and sat down, all eyes were upon him. What would he say next?

"Today this scripture has been fulfilled in your hearing," he said.

The crowd was excited. Comments were made: "Dramatic." "Dynamic." "Such a preacher." "A little exaggerated, but he's young." "He'll learn not to be so personal." "What does he mean that the scripture is fulfilled today?"

Then someone added, "Isn't this Joseph's son?" That got some murmuring started. There was a buzz in the air. Jesus recognized it for what it was. He addressed it directly.

"Doubtless you will quote to me this proverb, 'Doctor, cure yourself!' And you will say, 'Do here also in your hometown the things that we have heard you did at Capernaum.' "

The murmuring increased. If you had been there, maybe you would have heard whispers like this: "How could he have heard what we were saying? We are too far away for him to hear. Is he a mindreader? Who does he think he is?"

With authority Jesus rebuked the crowd; "Truly I tell you, no prophet is accepted in the prophet's hometown." That comment turned the crowd into a mob. "Why is he blaming us?" "What did we ever do to him?" "Is Joseph's son suddenly condemning his friends?"

We pick up the story in verse 29. "When they heard this, *all* the synagogue were filled with rage" (emphasis mine). In the account of the same story in Matthew 13:54-58 and Mark 6:1-6, we are told that Jesus' brothers and sisters were in the synagogue that day. Listen to what happened next. "They got up, drove him out of town,

345

and led him to the brow of the hill on which their town was built, so that they might hurl him off the cliff" (Luke 4:29).

Did Jesus' own brothers and sisters participate in this threat of death? We aren't told, but we are told that they were there. We don't read anywhere that they protested this treatment of their brother. Was there leftover bitterness and resentment because Jesus had left the family to become an itinerate preacher? Possibly so. Wasn't the oldest son supposed to take care of the family when the father died? Yes, he was. Why didn't Jesus fulfill his duty as the oldest son? Good question. Was there jealousy in the family because of Jesus' popularity? Quite possibly. What we know is that there was conflict in Jesus' family and the conflict was about who he was and what he was teaching.

On another occasion, Jesus was told that his mother and brothers and sisters were present in a crowd that had gathered. Jesus replied, "Who are my mother, brothers, and sisters? Those who do the will of God are my mother, brothers, and sisters" (Matthew 12:46-50). That comment must have added fuel to the fiery family conflict.

This conflict in Jesus' family was eventually resolved. We don't know all the details of the reconciliation, but we read in Acts 1:13-14 that the group that met for prayer in the upper room after Jesus' resurrection included Mary and Jesus' brothers. We are told elsewhere that Jesus' brother James became the head of the church in Jerusalem (Acts 15:13). Apparently because of the crucifixion and resurrection, family good-byes became family-of-God ties. When his family realized that Jesus had come back from the dead, they accepted him as Lord and Savior. Accepting Jesus as the resurrected Lord can do that. Believing in the resurrected Lord can work reversal of family good-byes and establish new family ties.

If ever we needed family ties to be established and strengthened, it's today. Faith in the crucified and risen Lord Jesus Christ will do that.

Will Harry, Jr., ever find saving faith in the resurrected Lord? Will he put aside his resentments and bitterness? Will he conquer his addictions? Will he forgive his father for being an alcoholic?

Will he forgive his mother for being weak? Will he take responsibility for his own life and quit blaming other people for what goes wrong in his life? The truth of the matter is, we don't know the answers to these questions.

Harry, Jr., is still out there somewhere. Junior, if you read this sermon or hear it, please consider again the open invitation to come home to the family of God and rediscover the wonder of your family. Your mother and stepfather, your sister and her family are waiting. So is God, your Father.

Proper 16
Pentecost 14
Ordinary Time 21
Luke 13:10-17

Cured Cripples And Crabby Critics

Have you ever been crippled by something that happened to you? At age seventeen, Joni Eareckson, dove into the Chesapeake Bay, hit the rocks, and was paralyzed for life. She lives in a wheelchair today. Physically, she is still crippled by the accident, but she has overcome the excruciating mental and spiritual pain of her situation. Faith in Jesus Christ made a major difference in her life.

Ron Heagy, a football player from Oregon, broke his neck in the Pacific Ocean in California when he dove into a sandbar. Like Joni, Ron is physically crippled for life. Like her, he had to overcome resentment that threatened to cripple him mentally and spiritually. Like her, Ron found strength to overcome his painful and debilitating physical handicap by a strong faith in Jesus Christ. Cripples are still being cured today.

The woman in our text had been crippled for eighteen years. She was bent over, unable to stand up straight. She was in a synagogue praying when Jesus noticed her. He looked intensely at her and then said, "Woman, you are set free from your ailment" (Luke 13:12). Cured, she stood up straight and praised God. A simple, straightforward healing of a cripple, a miracle in a synagogue.

The congregational president of the synagogue was upset by Jesus' miraculous healing of the crippled woman. He was angry. He was critical of Jesus and the people who sought him out for healing because it was done on a sabbath day. Healing was work, he reasoned. Healing should not take place on a sabbath day, a day devoted to rest and worship. "You've got the other six days to do

349

your work of healing," he was saying. "You don't need to heal on the sabbath."

The synagogue leader got caught up in religious rules and regulations and lost track of the bigger picture. He is one of thousands of crabby critics who unwittingly get in the way of the work that God is doing. Crabby critics often miss miracles.

A seminary professor addressed the question of miracles like this: "Since God exists, miracles are possible. Since God is love, miracles are probable. Since God became a man in Jesus Christ, miracles are to be expected. Miracles happen. Cripples are still being cured even today."

Jesus healed a handicapped woman in a synagogue almost 2,000 years ago. He called the synagogue president and his friends hypocrites because they allowed for work with animals, but not healings of people. Those are the facts of the story, but what difference does all this make today? This story makes a difference because Jesus Christ continues to heal handicapped people today. The handicaps he heals are not all of the physical variety.

Betty was crippled by divorce. Jack, her husband of ten years, left her for another woman. Jack said, "You chased me away by your criticisms. You always found what was wrong with me. You never showed any confidence in me." That confrontation turned Betty's crabbiness into bitterness. "It just isn't true," she told everyone who would listen to her. "It's all Jack's fault."

Betty projected her troubles onto others. She blamed everyone but herself. She had a low self-image, but the way it expressed itself was by crabbiness and the appearance of superiority. Family and friends began to shun her.

Joanne was crippled by the death of her baby, Amy. The doctor called it "sudden infant death syndrome." Joanne called it unfair. Understandably, she cried against God. Who else could she blame? "Why did you let this happen to Amy?" she screamed. Her neighbor was a pastor. He cried with her for thirty minutes. Then in the midst of their tears, he thought of something. "There's another question," he said. "No one can answer the question about why this happened, but the Bible gives us an answer to the question, 'Where was God when this happened?' "

350

Joanne stopped crying for a moment and asked, "Where was he?"

"He was with Amy," the pastor said. "And he's with you now. God is always with those who suffer. That's why we call Jesus the suffering servant. What Amy went through, God went through first. God experienced the grief you are experiencing now before you experienced it. As there was a pillar of cloud by day and a pillar of fire by night before the Hebrews as they traveled through the wilderness, so God is out in front of us as we make our pilgrim journey through life."

"I never thought of it that way before," Joanne said. She calmed down, but she remained crippled by the sudden loss of her daughter. Two weeks later, her pastor friend said, "I'm going to the hospital to visit a patient. I'd like you to come along." Together they visited Steve, an eighteen-year-old young man who had been diagnosed with terminal cancer. Steve told Joanne that he had been bitter about his cancer until he was confronted by a Christian who asked him directly if he was ready to die and face God. When he thought about it, Steve said, he realized that although he was a pastor's son and had been in church all his life, he had never accepted Christ as his Lord and Savior.

"My cancer hasn't been cured," Steve said, "but Christ has cured me in another way. He has changed the way I think. I'm going to die, but now I'm ready." Through Steve's influence, Joanne came to see that she could accept what she couldn't change — Amy's death. But she saw that she could change something else — her bitter attitude toward God. The pastor read some Bible verses and the three of them prayed.

As the pastor and Joanne reached the door, they turned to say their final good-bye to Steve. "Just a minute," he said. "There's something else I wanted to tell you, Joanne. When I see Amy soon, I'll tell her, 'Hello,' from you and I'll tell her how much you love her."

On the way home Joanne said, "Pastor, now I know what you mean by saying that God is out in front of us, suffering as we suffer. That young man, Steve, was a spokesperson for God, wasn't he?"

The pastor replied, "Steve is crippled by cancer, but not by the bitterness he originally felt about his cancer."

Joanne said, "Now I know why you wanted me to meet Steve."

Three weeks later, Joanne attended Steve's funeral at the church served by her pastor friend. "That was a real celebration of life," she said. "Now Steve is cured of his cancer as well as of the bitterness he originally felt."

"I can only say, 'Amen,' to that," the pastor responded.

Joanne was not crabby. Her baby had died. She had every right to feel and express her grief in negative terms. On the other hand, when she met Steve, she came to see that her negativism, especially toward God, wasn't doing anyone any good. Steve showed Joanne a different way to think about life, death, and heaven. In a sense, he confronted her illusion that she and Amy were somehow singled out for divine punishment.

John was a crabby critic. He criticized his wife, children, and business associates. As a matter of fact, John was critical of everyone he met. He looked for negatives and found them. His attitude crippled him. Eventually, John was fired from his job. John blamed everyone but himself. "It's my boss' fault. It's the fault of the sales department. It's my assistant's fault." John was crippled by his attitude. After hearing this repeated blaming of others for a week, John's wife finally confronted him. "It's nobody's fault but yours that you got fired. It's your drinking that is behind your problems. You are an alcoholic, and you'd better admit it if you are ever going to be anything but a cripple as a human being."

John stormed out of the house and went to a tavern and got drunk, pouring out his troubles to the bartender at the tavern he regularly frequented. After he left drunk, the bartender said to another patron, "That guy is a real loser. All he ever does is complain, complain, complain."

John's wife divorced him. His children seldom talk to him today. He's alone and remains uncured. He's in and out of Alcoholics Anonymous (AA) — mostly out — and doesn't accept the AA message of taking responsibility for your own behavior. At this point in time, John is still a crabby critic and a cripple. He has been

352

repeatedly confronted, but he has not allowed the confrontation to change his attitude.

On the other hand, Betty (mentioned earlier as a crabby and critical person) changed when a Christian friend gave her a straight-forward talk a year after her divorce. "You are probably right about the complaints you're making about your ex-husband, Jack, but your complaints are getting you nowhere. It's time to get on with your life. Right now, most of your friends don't want to be around you and hear all the negative stuff you have to say. You say that you believe in Jesus Christ as your Lord and Savior, but you have failed to integrate that faith into your life. I love you, but you need to know that you will continue to be a hypocrite until you start to put your faith into action and do something positive to get yourself out of the hole you've dug for yourself by your crabbiness."

"Wow," Betty said. "I never thought about it that way before. I guess I've been president of the 'Poor Me Club.' Let me think about what you said. Right now I'm a little shaken up by it."

Later, Betty told her friend that her tough talk was the turning point in her decision to turn the page and start her life again. "As a matter of fact," she said, "I'm now part of a divorce recovery group at church called 'Second Chance.' "

There are people who are physically handicapped. All of us, at one time or another, are mentally and spiritually handicapped by self-defeating feelings of self-pity and resentment.

Joni Eareckson (now married with the last name Tada) says that at age seventeen she wanted to commit suicide when she realized that her paralysis was a permanent condition. Since she had no use of her arms or legs, she asked a friend to assist her in taking her life. The friend refused.

Joni was bitter and filled with resentment. From a human point of view, who could blame her? Yet, she says that her attitude crippled her as much or more than her accident. Feelings of helplessness and depression gained control until she turned her condition over to Jesus Christ.

Today, Joni is a painter, an author, and a speaker on overcoming handicaps through the power of Jesus Christ. Billy Graham says, "Joni's life has been a remarkable portrait of Christian faith and God's grace in the face of trial and hardship ... Joni is an extraordinary person, yet her real strength and creativity come from a vital relationship with Jesus Christ."[1]

Over three million copies of her book, *Joni*, have been sold in over forty languages. She reaches people with all kinds of handicaps and urges them to depend on the Lord to change their attitude. In addition to writing books and giving inspirational and motivational talks around the country, Joni is a painter. With the brush coming out of her mouth, she paints beautiful pictures.

Joni is also the president of JAF Ministries, an organization that accelerates Christian outreach in the disabled community. She strives to pass on encouragement to other people with all kinds of disabilities: physical, mental, and spiritual. "Our attitudes make the difference," she says.

Ron Heagy, the young athlete who broke his neck with a dive in the Pacific Ocean, had been able to bench-press 300 pounds. After his accident, he couldn't lift a finger, yet he went on to graduate and get a master's degree in social work from San Diego State University. He was totally paralyzed from the neck down so he had to write with a pen in his mouth, or by typing on a computer keyboard with a pointer in his mouth. Ron now heads up an organization called "Life is an Attitude." He is a motivational speaker for Wheels for the World and a disability consultant. Like Joni, Ron believes that all people who have self-pity and resentment are seriously handicapped.

Tom Landry, the former football coach of the Dallas Cowboys, says, "Ron Heagy's success story is one of a kind. His determination, positive attitude, pleasing personality, and tremendous sense of humor are an inspiration to everyone he meets."

Life isn't easy. Bad things happen to good people. We are tempted to give up or give in as we face physical, mental, and spiritual suffering. Faith in Jesus Christ can make a major difference, especially when other people around us multiply our misery by what they say and do. Crabby critics, demons, are still within us and around us today. Joni had to face them. So did Ron. So do we. Even when we try to do something good for someone, there are people who put wrong interpretations on our actions. Take heart,

354

the same thing happened to the Lord Jesus Christ. Through Jesus' example and the power of the Holy Spirit we can be overcomers, people who live not just under the circumstances, but above them.

In the Bible, we find encouragement for having an attitude of gratitude, overcoming our own handicaps and helping others overcome their handicaps. The Apostle Paul says in 2 Corinthians 4:8-10, 15-16:

> *We are afflicted in every way, but not crushed; perplexed, but not driven to despair, persecuted, but not forsaken; struck down, but not destroyed; always carrying in the body the death of Jesus, so that the life of Jesus may also be made visible in our bodies ... so that grace, as it extends to more and more people, may increase thanksgiving to the glory of God. So we do not lose heart. Even though our outer nature is wasting away, our inner nature is being renewed day by day.*

In other words, in spite of crabby critics within us and around us, and handicaps of our own that we can't overcome by mere human effort, we don't collapse because there is power in Jesus, the healer and suffering servant.

---

1. Joni Eareckson Tada, *Joni* (Grand Rapids, Michigan: Zondervan Publishing House, 1976 and 1996), Foreword by Billy Graham.

Proper 17
Pentecost 15
Ordinary Time 22
Luke 14:1, 7-14

Only The Lonely

There are three words I hope you will take home from church today. The words are "Only The Lonely." As you think about these words, the assurances of God's Word will comfort and strengthen you. But I'm getting ahead of my story. Before we get to these three words, we need to look at the full text of Luke 14:1, 7-14. That involves looking at three other words: humility, hospitality, and hope.

Humility

The inciting incident in our story is that guests at a party started to take places of honor. Jesus told them a parable about a wedding banquet where people who took places of honor were told to go to lower places. Disgraced, they moved out of the top spots. On the other hand, those who took low places were told to go up higher.

Jesus said, "... All who exalt themselves will be humbled, and those who humble themselves will be exalted" (Luke 14:11).

The first lesson for today, Proverbs 25:6-7, adds to this emphasis on the need for humility. "Don't put yourself forward in the king's presence." Those who put themselves forward are taking a step backward in their spiritual lives. Boastfulness, arrogance, and rudeness are unveiled as demonic means to self-destruction.

The Pharisees in our text were boastful, arrogant, and rude. They thought of themselves more highly than they ought to think and in addition saw themselves as Jesus' judges. You can make a case for the theme of the story of Jesus going to a leading Pharisee's house being the entrapment of those who tried to trap Jesus. After all, verse 1b says, "... they were watching him closely." In addition to their other faults, the Pharisees were judgmental.

According to Luke 14:2-6, the host Pharisee and his friends tried to point out the errors in Jesus' ministry since he healed a man with dropsy on the sabbath day (Luke 14:2-6). Jesus' response was quick and stinging. He asked them what they would do if a child or an animal fell into a well on the sabbath. Wouldn't they rescue the child or animal? Of course they would. In other words, Jesus trapped the Pharisees in their own traps. He popped their preconceptions about their self-importance. He showed them that they were on a staircase to nowhere.

Some years ago, the *Chicago Tribune* ran an article and a picture about a fire that had taken place at the Glenview Naval Air Station. The damage exceeded $10 million. The picture of the disaster featured a circular iron staircase which had survived the fire, but ended up detached from everything. The title under the picture was "Staircase To Nowhere." That's what Jesus was saying to those who exalted themselves. "You are on a staircase to nowhere."

Exalting yourself keeps you out of the kingdom of God. Scheming for places of honor reveals a fatal flaw in character. Elbowing your way past others shows that there is inordinate, sinful ambition in the heart. Self-seeking, the malady of the Pharisees in our story, is also the malady of many people today.

In the secular "Me Generation" you frequently hear phrases like this:

- "If you don't push yourself forward, nobody will."
- "Those who do not step forward, should step aside."
- "Move over, here comes Number One."

You can make a case for the theme of this passage being the need for humility. The parable Jesus told the Pharisees, is all about taking lower rather than higher seats at banquets. That will preach. In addition, you can make a case for this passage being about the need for hospitality.

358

Hospitality

Jesus said, "When you give a luncheon or a dinner, do not invite your friends or your brothers or your relatives or rich neighbors, in case they may invite you in return, and you would be repaid. But when you give a banquet, invite the poor, the crippled, the lame, and the blind. And you will be blessed, because they cannot repay you, for you will be repaid at the resurrection of the righteous" (Luke 14:12-14).

In other words, "Don't get trapped in the game of social reciprocity." Social reciprocity means expecting to be repaid for your invitations by invitations in return. When you do good in order to get back in kind, you are on a stairway to nowhere.

Henri Nouwen says that genuine hospitality means "paying attention to the guest."[1] Social reciprocity means paying attention to ourselves instead of our guests. When we ask questions about the other person's life, sometimes we don't really listen to the answers. We are practicing what we will say next. This self-centeredness is the opposite of genuine hospitality.

The second lesson for today is about hospitality. "Do not neglect to show hospitality to strangers for by doing that some have entertained angels without knowing it" (Luke 13:1). Hospitality means making strangers' needs more important than your own. When we do that, we often receive back much more than we expect.

Abraham saw some strangers approaching his tent. He told his wife, Sarah, to prepare a meal while he talked with the strangers and made them feel at home. As they talked, one of the men said that Abraham and Sarah would have a child. They were old, very old, so when Sarah overheard the prediction, she laughed. Nine months later, a child was born to Sarah and Abraham. They named him "Laughter," the English translation of the Hebrew name, Isaac. After long-suffering and frustration as a childless couple who had been told they would be the father and mother of a great nation, joy came to Abraham and Sarah because of their hospitality to strangers. These strangers turned out to be angels from God. Abraham, who sought to give, received more than he gave.

Hospitality, really paying attention to the needs of strangers, often results in unpredictable blessings coming back to the one

359

who offers hospitality. Of course, if you show hospitality in order to get a blessing, your hospitality is fake and no blessings come to you. Hospitality, with no view toward reward, is a major theme of Luke 14.

Like humility, the theme of hospitality will preach.

But there's another theme hiding in verses 12 through 14. As an extension of the parable about taking high and low seats at a banquet, Jesus focuses on the kinds of people who should be invited to a banquet. These are the lowly, undeserving people Jesus invited to the banquet of the kingdom of God: "... When you give a banquet, invite the poor, the crippled, the lame and the blind. And you will be blessed, because they cannot repay you...." Those who are named here are the lost, the lonely, and the hopeless souls of society.

Hope

Signs of the saved include being humble, showing hospitality to strangers, and offering hope to the seemingly hopeless.

Often it is helpful to consider the context of a Bible passage. That's the case here. Right after the parable about seeking honor at a banquet comes the parable about inviting people to that banquet (Luke 14:15-24). The social etiquette of the time meant that many people were contacted far in advance of the banquet. Many agreed to come. As the date for the dinner approached, a servant of the host would go to those who had agreed to come to the banquet with news of the exact time they should arrive. That's when the excuses started.

One man said he had a real estate deal that was important and he couldn't come. Another said he had just purchased oxen for his farm and he couldn't come. A third said he had just taken a wife and he couldn't come. These excuses sound reasonable to us, but the pricking point of the parable is that these excuse-makers did not put a priority on the host and his invitation. They did good things, instead of the one thing needful. That's what was happening as Jesus announced the coming of the kingdom of God. Many were choosing good things over the best thing. Many were making excuses. Some still are. There is nothing more important than God, but some people make something else more important. There are consequences for such bad choices. If we think something is more important than the kingdom of God, others take our place at the kingdom banquet.

When the excuses were made, the host told his servants to invite the seemingly hopeless souls of society. Notice, the invitation in the second parable goes exactly to the same people Jesus named in the first parable: "the poor, the crippled, the blind, and the lame." In addition, in the second parable Jesus urges that the tramps of his day, living in the bushes of the lanes and the roads, be "compelled" to come in. The word, "compelled," used here doesn't mean physically forced. Rather, it means urgently invited.

The point of this parable is the answer to the question: "Who should be invited?" The answer is surprising. Everyone! Anyone who is willing to come!

Who are these seemingly hopeless people Jesus wants us to include in our understanding of the kingdom of God? Are they really the derelicts of society? Yes, but more. Are they the handicapped? Yes, but more. Are they the nobodies who have been humbled by what has happened to them in life? Yes, but more. Are they the strangers like Abraham's visitors? Yes, but more. Are they the lost and lonely? Yes, they are, and we are all lost and lonely.

We are all lost and lonely. That ought to bring us to humility. In other words, we can't get into the kingdom on the basis of our achievements. It's not a matter of achieving, but receiving. Bishop William Temple observed that all we bring to our salvation is the sin from which we need to be saved. Our contribution is acknowledged sin. God's contribution is everything else. Sometimes only the lonely get it.

We are all lost and lonely. That ought to bring us to hospitality. In other words, since we have been invited into the kingdom, not on the basis of our worthiness, but on the basis of God's grace, we should offer hospitality to strangers on that same basis. God's grace offers us space; therefore we need to make space for others. Sometimes, only the lonely listen to what God tells them.

We are all lost and lonely. Thus we are all hopeless when it comes to the ultimate relationship of life: the relationship with God.

361

There is hope for the hopeless because Jesus died on the cross to give us the status of the children of God. But only those who acknowledge their loneliness, who stop pretending that all is well and take off the masks of self-satisfaction are willing to follow the instructions God gives in his Word. Sometimes only the lonely hear that Word.

Only the lonely repent. They have tried other methods of self-improvement that fail, other religious exercises that frustrate, and other means of trying to attain peace, only to discover that these are limited at best and totally self-defeating at worst. When they see that all these methods are hopeless, they turn back to God.

Only the lonely realize that they are not worthy to come to the Master's banquet. As soon as people think they are deserving, they miss the invitation. As soon as people take comfort in their own prosperity, they miss the wealth of the kingdom. When people cover up the hole in their souls with the things of this world, with success, or wealth, or notoriety, they forget that the hole in their souls was put there by God who alone can fill it.

Only the lonely realize that their spiritual emptiness can only be filled by the one who made us. The fantasies and illusions about happiness which are nurtured by the world's standards are only discovered for what they are by those who find their loneliness remains when they attain what they have sought. Those who hunger for the things of this world and then get what they want, no longer want what they get. They want more. That's why greed rules today.

Only the lonely make their own wounds a source of healing for others. Therefore, they invite strangers into their hearts as well as into their homes. This invitation is an offer of care more than cure. This is an invitation to intimacy and wholeness. Only the lonely understand the depths of loneliness others feel. They are the only ones who are willing to listen and hear the depths of others' longings.

Only those who are lonely and acknowledge that no one in this world can satisfy their hunger, stop playing the world's games. They know that life is not a large scoreboard where the most points measure our worth. They refuse to sell their souls to the people of this world who think they can give out grades.

Loneliness in itself is not a good thing, but all of us have a hidden loneliness which can be the very stuff out of which God makes us into the children he wants us to be. When we are lost and lonely, and know it, we are in the proper place to turn control of our lives over to God. That's what accepting the invitation to come to the kingdom banquet means — accepting that God is in control.

Only the lonely who acknowledge that they are hopeless as to their own power in their search for God, discover that God is seeking them.

Only the lonely hear the call of God: "Come up higher."

Only the lonely.

Take those three words home from church today.

---

1. Henri Nouwen, *The Wounded Healer* (Garden City, New York: Doubleday and Company, 1972), p. 91.

Counting The Cost
Of Discipleship

The best thing to say to a pastor after you hear a sermon that moves you is not, "That was a good sermon." That's a little better than saying, "That was a lousy sermon," but in saying, "That was a good sermon," you may be missing the point of preaching. The point of preaching is for the listeners to put the Word of God into action.

Soren Kierkegaard, the Danish theologian, says that the role of listeners in a devotional address is not that of an audience at a play. The pastor's role, he says, is not that of an actor on stage. The pastor is like a prompter in the wings who is trying to help the actors on stage say and do the right things according to the script. The people are on stage. God is the audience. In other words, God will judge the pastor on how well he/she follows the script. God will judge the hearers on how well they act out the script on the stage of life.

Something like that is happening in our text. After giving his hearers some harsh and hard challenges regarding discipleship, Jesus says, "Let anyone with ears to hear listen" (Luke 14:35). In the Hebrew tradition, to listen and hear means that we don't just appreciate an idea or how it is presented, but put that idea into action. Jesus, who was a Jew, challenged his hearers to make their faith active in discipleship. In Jewish thinking, to have ears that hear means action.

Jesus calls his hearers to count the cost of discipleship. He uses three illustrations: "hating" family, building a tower or an army, and retaining "saltiness." These ideas are challenging enough. When

365

you add to this formula that Jesus is not satisfied with his hearers just agreeing with him, but expects them (and us) to put his words into action, the revolutionary nature of Christian discipleship is revealed.

To understand this difficult verse (Luke 14:20) about hating family, it is helpful to look at the historical setting of the text. First, Jesus was on his way to Jerusalem where he would face a cross. Large crowds were gathering. Many people in the crowd thought Jesus was going to establish a worldly empire of power and glory. They were wrong. Many were not interested in being disciples of the way of the cross.

In his book, *Imitation of Christ*, Thomas à Kempis puts it this way: "Jesus has many lovers of his kingdom, but few followers of his way." In today's terms, Jesus has many admirers who think of him as a great teacher or wonderful leader, but are not committed to him as Lord and Savior. Being an admirer costs nothing. Discipleship means adjusting all other loyalties. Discipleship means change in behavior. On his way to the cross, Jesus said that being a disciple means picking up your cross and following him. To believe in Jesus as Lord and Savior costs a lot. Jesus was separating the admirers from the disciples as he approached the cross.

Second, Jesus was a Jew. That's another historical factor in understanding the harsh words about hate in Luke 14:26. If you don't enter a Hebrew way of thinking, you can't understand this verse as Jesus intended it to be understood. In Hebrew thinking there is often exaggeration for emphasis. Consider Jesus' story of a man with a tree growing out of his eye looking for a speck in his brother's eye (Matthew 7:3). Jesus could have said, "Stop all that judgmental thinking." Instead he used an exaggerated picture to get his point across.

Third, Jesus spoke these words in Greek. The thought patterns were Hebrew, but the language to convey the thoughts was Greek. An additional factor in trying to get at what Jesus really meant is that we have the words in English. That complexity of translation makes it more difficult to know what Jesus was really saying.

The original Greek word used here is *misei* from the root word, *miseo*. *Miseo* literally means to regard with less affection, to love less, or to esteem less. It doesn't mean animosity, ill will, or revenge, which our English word, "hate," suggests. *Miseo* doesn't mean that the object is detestable or repugnant. Having *miseo* toward someone doesn't mean that he or she is an abomination. It just means that by comparison, someone or something is less important than someone or something else.

For example, consider two other scripture passages where the word, *miseo*, is used. In both passages, the topic is discipleship. In both cases, comparisons are made.

1. "Those who love their life lose it, and those who hate (*miseo*) their life in this world will keep it for eternal life. Whoever serves me must follow me, and where I am, there will my servant be also. Whoever serves me, the Father will honor" (John 12:25-26).

2. "No one can serve two masters; for a slave will either hate (*miseo*) the one and love the other, or be devoted to the one and despise the other. You cannot serve God and wealth" (Matthew 6:24).

In both cases, the sense of disciples loving one thing more and one thing less is the point Jesus is making by using the word *miseo*. In Luke 14:25-26, Jesus is saying that the cost of discipleship is to love God more than anything else, even family and self.

The parallel passage about discipleship in Matthew 10:37-38 emphasizes the same point about comparison. "Whoever loves father or mother *more than me* is not worthy of me; and whoever loves son or daughter *more than me* is not worthy of me and whoever does not take up the cross and follow me is not worthy of me" (emphasis mine).

Counting the cost of discipleship means loving God more than family or self. The first commandment takes priority over all other commandments. "I am the Lord your God. You shall have no other gods before me." To love the Lord our God is the highest priority in life, even higher than loving our families or ourselves. Jesus doesn't diminish the importance of family life by prioritizing love of God as the first priority. As a matter of fact, four chapters later, in Luke, Jesus emphasizes the importance of family by quoting the fourth commandment, urging his disciples to honor their fathers and mothers (Luke 18:20). Placing anything other than God in first place results in disaster. Family members all die. If God is in first place, we will grieve, but grief will not hold us forever. Only God is forever. That's why God is the highest priority in life.

Jesus compares discipleship to loving family and self. He also compares discipleship to building a tower and building an army.

How is discipleship like building a tower or building an army? How do these comparisons relate to our lives?

An incomplete tower is a commentary on poor planning. We aren't all in the building trades, but all of us are aware of the need to plan whatever we build. Planning without action results in frustration, but action without planning results in misdirected energy and failure.

Bob and Lucille Carlson were wealthy by most standards. Bob was a successful dentist. They had a big, beautiful house and two luxury cars. Their pastor, who was a good friend, asked them about their wealth and discipleship. "We have been blessed, to be a blessing," Bob said. "We are tithers. We give ten percent of our income to the work of God through the church. We give offerings above the tithe to special needs. But that isn't enough. We know that if Christ called for it, there is no possession we would not be willing to give."

When a building fund for a new church building came along, the Carlsons gave a large gift to the fund. They also put the church in their wills. They counted the cost of discipleship. Their planning reflected their attitude of generosity. Jesus' illustration about the building trades is about counting the cost of discipleship.

Jesus also draws a picture of discipleship from the military. To be a soldier means getting into battle, risking your life. In other words, Christianity isn't lived in a vacuum. There are struggles and conflicts. Our hymn, "Onward Christian Soldiers," reflects the fact that we must fight when demonic forces attack us in life. A Christian must be willing to do spiritual battle for Christ. That's a high cost.

Soren Kierkegaard said that there are a lot of parade-ground Christians who wear the uniforms of Christianity, but few who are willing to do battle for Christ and his kingdom. When it comes to doing battle for the Lord, too many church members are just sitting on the premises instead of leaning on the promises of God.

On Easter, in the days of Communist domination in Russia, a Communist leader made a scathing speech to a large crowd against God and faith. Then he ended by saying, "Can anyone here answer me?" There was an awkward silence. The consequences of standing up to the Communist leader were apparent to all. A young Orthodox priest rose and mounted the platform.

"I'll give you just five minutes to answer my speech," said the Communist.

"I don't need five minutes, just five seconds," said the priest. He then turned to the crowd and in a loud voice said, "Jesus Christ is risen."

With one voice, the crowd responded, "He is risen, indeed."

That was doing battle for Christ in a war zone.

Being a disciple of Jesus Christ means counting the cost of having faith. Being a disciple also means faithfulness. That's what Jesus' illustration about salt is all about.

Jesus said to his disciples, "You are the salt of the earth" (Matthew 5:13). Here in Luke 14:34 he warns his followers not to lose their saltiness.

In the ancient world, salt was both a preservative and an additive. Salty Christians are called to preserve eternal values. In the midst of changing value systems and raging immorality today, Christians are called to hold on to the biblical teachings that God intended for all time. For example, the Ten Commandments don't go out of vogue just because so many people ignore them or marginalize them. Jesus' words about the greatest Commandment of loving the Lord our God and our neighbors do not expire in modern times just because so many people are selfish. Salty Christians are called to preserve God's eternal truths.

Salty Christians are also called to add zest to life. The picture of a Christian in the minds of many unchurched Americans is of a stodgy, judgmental, and self-righteous person who seldom, if ever, has fun. On the contrary, faith frees us from those things which keep us from genuine joy. Unless or until you come to faith, you

369

are less than you were created to be. When you come to faith, you can be yourself.

In addition to being a preservative and an additive, in ancient society salt was also a fertilizer. It made things grow. That, too, is the call of God for us to be Salty Christians, and help others grow in the faith. This third use may be the one Jesus had in mind when he told his disciples not to lose their saltiness. "Salt is good; but if salt has lost its taste, how can its saltiness be restored? It is fit neither for the soil nor for the manure pile; they throw it away" (Luke 14:34-35). In other words, it isn't enough to come to faith. The call to discipleship is a call to be faithful as well.

William Arndt says,

> *Salt can actually lose its character of saltness. In Pal-*
> *estine one can see lumps of it, which through exposure*
> *to the air ... have lost the character and virtue (of salt).*
> *Salt which has lost its saltness is fit for nothing, not*
> *even for the lowliest service imaginable. Food that has*
> *deteriorated can at least be used as fertilizer, but not*
> *savorless salt. The use of salt for manure is a well-at-*
> *tested practice for Egypt and Palestine, both in ancient*
> *and modern times.*[2]

We started out this sermon with an admonition not to regard the preacher as an actor on a stage and the congregation as an audience that either likes or doesn't like what he says. We began by advocating that people stop saying, "That was a good sermon," to the pastor if the sermon hits home. After all, all of us are on the stage of life. God is the audience. The pastor is just a prompter who is trying to get us to say and do those things that the script calls for.

What should we say if a sermon really hits home? How about a simple, "Thank you." The pastor is just a prompter back in the wings helping actors who are on the stage of life. He/She tries to keep the actors on script. He/She is a messenger for the king, reminding us what to do. If a messenger gave you a message from the king of the universe, you would thank that messenger. More importantly, in your prayers you would want to thank the one who sent the message.

"Let anyone who has ears to hear listen" (Luke 14:35).

---

1. The Gospel Reading for Proper 18/Pentecost16/Ordinary Time 23 is Luke 14:25-33. I have included verses 34 and 35 because, in my opinion, these two verses are critical for understanding the text.

2. William Arndt, *The Bible According to St. Luke* (St. Louis: Concordia, 1956), pp. 345-346.

Proper 19
Pentecost 17
Ordinary Time 24
Luke 15:1-10

Only The Lost And The Least

A woman approached her pastor with a question: "Where is the lost and found department in our church? I've lost my glasses and I just can't see well."

The pastor replied, "We don't actually have a lost and found department. You might check the secretary's desk. Maybe you'll find your glasses there." After the woman left, the pastor rethought his answer. "Actually, the whole church is a lost and found department. The business of the church is to find the lost."

The incident that gave rise to Jesus' parables of the lost sheep and the lost coin (Luke 15:1-10) was the attitude of the Pharisees and the teachers of the law. They grumbled when they saw tax collectors and sinners being welcomed by Jesus.

Jesus didn't approve of the behavior of tax collectors and sinners, but he demonstrated God's welcome to all people who repent. The religious leaders regarded tax collectors as the least worthy members of society. After all, in Jesus' time, tax collectors were Jews who were traitors. They collected money from fellow Jews to give to the Romans. In the process they lined their own pockets by taking extra for themselves. Tax collectors were the scum of society, the least important people around.

The religious leaders saw common people as sinners. The religious leaders considered themselves better than the common folk spiritually, morally, and economically. Sinners were regarded as hopeless, lost souls.

373

Like the woman with lost glasses, these religious leaders didn't see very well. They were shortsighted. Jesus told them parables about the lost sheep and the lost coin to correct their lack of vision.

The word, "lost," is generally used in two ways. The word may describe someone who sins and is separated from God and people by that sin. The word may also be used to describe someone who is confused by his or her surroundings (geographic, mental, or spiritual) and can't find his or her way home. The Bible uses the term "lost" both ways.

Jesus welcomed tax collectors and other bad people who had broken the commandments of God and the laws of the land. He didn't welcome them because he approved of their behavior. He welcomed them because he saw what the religious leaders of his day didn't see; their need.

Looking down on notorious traitors, cheats, and other evildoers is understandable but dangerous. It's understandable because we don't want to promote or approve of evil people doing evil deeds and not facing justice for their deeds, but it's dangerous because before God, a self-righteous, judgmental attitude is as bad as the deeds of evil people. The human malady being addressed here is self-righteousness, expressing itself through grumbling (or murmuring in some translations). Looking down on people can say more about ourselves than about them.

Gert Behanna, who came to Christ late in life after she had devoted herself to riches, booze, and drugs, said that we have to be careful about looking down on people. "I've recently discovered a new sin. I found myself looking down on people who look down on people."

Looking down on what we consider to be inferior human beings is dangerous. The same self-righteousness that damages the souls of those who consider themselves morally superior people can infect the souls of those who consider themselves the economic upper class. Jesus hits these attitudes of superiority to the lost right between the eyes.

The second use of the term, "lost," has to do with drifting off in the wrong direction because of being inexperienced or naive, like a child who doesn't know better. In Matthew 18:2-3, 10-14, the parallel passage to Luke 15:1-7, the context of the parable of the lost sheep is Jesus welcoming a child.

> *He (Jesus) called a child whom he put among them (the disciples who asked about who was the greatest in the kingdom), and said, "Truly I tell you, unless you become like children, you will never enter the kingdom of heaven."*
>
> *Take care that you do not despise one of these little ones; for I tell you, in heaven their angels continually see the face of my Father in heaven. What do you think? If a shepherd has a hundred sheep, and one of them has gone astray, does he not leave the ninety-nine on the mountains and go in search of the one that went astray? And if he finds it, truly I tell you, he rejoices over it more than over the ninety-nine that never went astray. So, it is not the will of your Father in heaven that one of these little ones should be lost* (parenthetical statement mine).

It is dangerous for a child to wander off because a child can't protect itself from dangers. Someone or something can take advantage of a wandering child. A child can't adequately defend itself against dangers. In like manner, it's dangerous for a sheep to wander off because it is vulnerable to being attacked by wolves, or being turned over on its back. A sheep turned over on its back is totally helpless, unable to right itself without help. A little sheep can lose its footing and fall off a mountain to a shelf below and there die from exposure to the elements of nature.

That's why the good shepherd leaves the 99 sheep and goes out after one lost sheep. A sheep can be lost as it drifts away from the shepherd and the flock. So can human beings.

In the Old Testament Lesson for today, Exodus 32:7-14, we hear about the lost Hebrews in the wilderness. They wandered off from God and from their moral traditions. They were lost in the wilderness.

Moses was sent by God to go down to Egypt and say to Pharaoh, "Let my people go." The Hebrews were slaves in Egypt. They yearned for freedom and a return to the land of their forefathers. Moses was called by God to lead the people through the wilderness back to the promised land. As slaves, the Hebrews were hopeless and lost. Freed from slavery, they were lost in a different way.

Because of their disobedience and rebellion, the Hebrews were lost in the wilderness as they traveled toward the promised land. They complained and murmured against Moses and God. God, through Moses, sought to save the lost Hebrews. They were lost both in the spiritual sense and the sense of wandering in the wilderness.

Like the ancient Hebrews, we are lost spiritually on our journey in the wilderness.

Like them we are lured away from God by attractive distractions and false gods. Like them we easily get diverted by wrong turns on our journey toward the promised land. Like them, we need to hear and heed the Word of God to get back on the path that leads to eternal life. We need to be found and saved.

It is encouraging to hear that God seeks the lost. It is also encouraging to hear that God seeks the least. One sheep seems considerably less important than the 99 that do not wander off, but God thinks otherwise.

God is a seeker. He searches until he finds the lost and the least. That's the point of the parable of the lost sheep. That's also the point of the parable of the lost coin.

To a rich, powerful person, one silver coin, a drachma, may have seemed like very little, but to a common laborer, a drachma was one day's full labor, and therefore very important. To the religious leaders who were in the upper class, a drachma might have seemed like it had little worth, but to a common housewife, a lost drachma, was worth a tedious search. Jesus said, God is more like the common laborer and common housewife than like the rich and powerful upper class.

In the parable of the lost coin, Jesus was saying that each individual, created in God's image, is worthy of God's attention. God focuses on each of his children because he loves every one of us as if there is only one of us.

A pastor was making a home visit to one of the families in his church. "How many children do you have?" he asked the woman of the house.

"There's Mary, Johnny, Betty ..." she started.

"I just want their number, not their names," the pastor said abruptly.

"They don't have numbers. They have names," the parishioner replied crisply.

The woman was a lot closer to the kingdom of God than the pastor. God loves each of us as if there were only one of us.

One tradition says that Palestinian women received ten silver coins (drachmas) when they got married. Besides their monetary value to a poor family, these coins held sentimental value like that of a wedding ring.

A man was playing on his church's baseball team when, suddenly, he looked and saw that his ring finger was bare. He had lost his wedding ring. The game stopped. An extensive search was made, but the ring couldn't be found. When he got home that night and told his wife, she was terribly upset. "How could you have lost that ring?" she said bitterly. "How could you? That ring was one of our most precious possessions."

"You're right," he replied. "I really feel bad about losing it. We searched for two hours, but just couldn't find it. I posted a notice at the ball field. Maybe someone from one of the other teams will find it."

Two days later, the manager of another baseball team found the ring in the dust. He returned it to the owner. The husband and wife went out for dinner that night and celebrated the restoration of the lost ring.

As the husband and wife rejoiced in finding his wedding ring, so the woman in the parable rejoiced in finding her lost coin. In the same way, the angels in heaven rejoice over one sinner who repents. God grieves over every lost soul and celebrates when a lost soul returns to him.

As God rejoices over each sinner who returns to him, so we should seek out and witness to the lost, rejoicing in their return. As God cares for the least, we, too, should care for the needy, the

377

hungry, the thirsty, the sick, the prisoners, and those with other overwhelming needs. Jesus said, "Anything you did for the least of my people, you did for me." As Max Lucado puts it, "The sign of the saved is their love for the least."[1]

Jesus' concern for the lost and the least is revolutionary. It turns the value system of the world upside down.

A Sunday school teacher asked her class, "What is the last book in the Bible?"

Johnny, a ten-year-old boy answered, "The book of Revolution."

"That's Revelation, not Revolution," she replied as the bell rang and the class left.

The following Sunday, the teacher said, "I've been thinking all week about Johnny's answer. The last book of the Bible is Revelation, but it is a kind of revolutionary book. As a matter of fact, the whole Bible is revolutionary. Does anyone know who wrote the last book of the Bible?"

Johnny's hand went up. "Was it Saint Paul Revere?"

Johnny was wrong about Saint Paul Revere but, in a certain sense, he was right about the Bible being revolutionary. Love for the least and the lost flies directly in the face of the way many people think.

Christianity offers a revolutionary reversal of values. Saint Paul the Apostle, the premier missionary and theologian of all time understood this transvaluation of values in the light of his own sin. In our second lesson for today, Paul said, "The saying is sure and worthy of full acceptance, that Christ Jesus came into the world to save sinners — of whom I am the foremost. But for that very reason I received mercy, so that in me, as the foremost, Jesus Christ might display the utmost patience, making me an example to those who would to believe in him for eternal life" (1 Timothy 1:15-16). In other words, Paul saw himself as one of the lost and the least because of his sin.

In that respect, we are like him. If we don't see our sin as more offensive than the sins of others, we haven't understood our sin at all. The primary comparison is not between you as a sinner and me as a sinner, but between me as a sinner and God as the righteous

378

one. We are called to compare ourselves to God. That eliminates self-righteousness and arrogance.

A pastor explained Jesus' love for the least and lost sinners to a successful and arrogant businessman. The man replied, "If that's what Christianity is all about, I want no part of it. I am a self-made man. When I do something for someone, I expect to be paid back in kind. These people you talk about — the lost and the least — they're just lazy. They can't pay back their debts. They aren't worthy of our attention."

"Since God gives them attention, we have no choice but to do the same," the pastor replied. "Since God made it his business to find the lost and the least, that's what the church must do, too. The church is one big lost and found department."

The self-righteous businessman was like the Pharisees and scribes in our story. He was spiritually shortsighted. He didn't see that we should look at the need for God in everyone's life. The lost and the least have the same need for God that all of us have.

The distressed, displaced, and despised of this world may be better in touch with their need for God than the successful. The down-and-out may be more open to the call to repentance than the up-and-out.

In addition, whatever we do — or don't do — for the lost and the least, we are doing — or not doing — for God. Christianity is all about finding and welcoming the lost and the least.

---

1. Max Lucado, *And the Angels Were Silent, The Final Week of Jesus* (Portland, Oregon: Multnomah Publishers, 1992), p. 142.

A Puzzling Parable
With A Sharp Point[1]

A young boy used to describe foods like spinach by saying, "I hate it." His wise mother responded, "Don't say you hate it. Just say, 'I'm not very fond of it.' " She also taught her son that when he really liked some food to say, "I'm really fond of this." The boy said, he was "really fond" of cookies, candy, and cake. His mother told him, "Too many cookies, too much candy, and cake can be bad for you. You can be very fond of the wrong things."

Something like that is going on underneath the story of the shrewd manager. The topic is not food, but money. This parable is a puzzle. It is a mystery in many respects. How could a shrewd manager who cheats his master be held up as an example?

One of the first clues to unraveling the mystery of the dishonest money manager is found in verse 14, "The Pharisees who were lovers of money, heard all this and ridiculed him" (NRSV). The King James Version describes the Pharisees this way: "They were covetous." The Phillips translation (a paraphrase) describes the situation like this: "Now the Pharisees, who were very fond of money, heard all this with a sneer."

Here we have a clue to help us unravel the mystery of this parable. The wise mother's advice to her son was: "You can be very fond of the wrong things." The Pharisees were very fond of money. The parable about the inordinate love of money disturbed the Pharisees because they were very fond of the wrong thing. No wonder they sneered.

The sneer of the Pharisees is a clue to getting at the heart of this parable. The sneer comes because the Pharisees try to justify themselves before the eyes of men, forgetting that God knows what is in the heart (Luke 16:15). Jesus' parable is about money. The Pharisees loved money too much. Mammon was their god. By focusing on money, they had missed the real focus of life which is God himself. "No slave can serve two masters for a slave will either hate the one and love the other, or be devoted to the one and despise the other. You cannot serve God and wealth" (Luke 16:13).

That statement is the one that gave rise to sneers and ridicule. In trying to interpret a puzzling parable, sometimes we should look for a clue at the end of the story. At the end of this parable Jesus shows that money can be a distracting attraction in life, causing us to miss the meaning of life. The meaning of life is to be found in our relationship with God. It's not money that is the problem, but an inordinate focus on money that can be our undoing. "... What is prized by human beings is an abomination in the sight of God" (Luke 16:15b). Elsewhere the Bible puts it this way: "... the love of money is the root of all kinds of evil" (1 Timothy 6:10). Not money, but being overly fond of money, is the root of the problem of the Pharisees in our story and the root of the problem many people have today.

What we have here is a reversal of values. What is highly valued among people is possessions, land, honor, and money. What is highly valued in the kingdom of God? A relationship with God and relationships with people that include gracious acts toward them, faith in them, love for them, and forgiveness of them when they offend us — these are the things Jesus says have real value. Money is not meant to give us superiority over people, but is to be used to help people. Using one's possessions for people is called good stewardship. Understanding the biblical concept of stewardship is a big clue in solving the mystery of this puzzling parable.

When we think about stewardship, it is always helpful to think of the heroes and heroines of the faith who set good examples by the way they used money and possessions to meet the needs of people. Saint Francis of Assisi and Mother Teresa of Calcutta come to mind. There is also a little old lady in Lebanon, Indiana, who is worthy of our consideration.

Ada Gleb was a widow who lived in a run-down house on the south side of town ("the other side of the tracks"). Her clothes were clean, but certainly not fancy. She drove an old car. She never talked much about stewardship, but her actions spoke louder than words. She put faith into action by using money for God's work and for other people.

When her new pastor, right out of seminary, arrived in Lebanon, he was faced with a task of trying to build up a very small congregation that worshiped in a run-down garage. Most of the members were not rich by the standards of the world. Ada Gleb was one of the poorest of the poor, but she was one of the top givers in the congregation. When her pastor asked her about her giving, she humbly said that as a little girl she had learned to tithe, to give ten percent of her income to the Lord through the church off the top, before bills were paid. She didn't have much income now, she said, mostly Social Security money, but she was glad to share it with her church.

Her pastor, who had a very small salary, decided that if Ada could tithe on her little income, so could he. The seminary had taught him very little about personal stewardship. "Professor" Ada Gleb was his teacher.

The church grew and held a building fund drive for a new church building. Ada's pledge was one of the largest in the congregation. "How can you do that?" her pastor asked. "No problem," Ada responded, "I'll just take the money out of my savings account each month. Don't be so surprised, pastor. Maybe you've never heard the principle I learned as a child: 'You can never out-give God.' " "Professor" Ada taught the pastor a great principle about Christian stewardship. He raised his giving from ten percent to eighteen percent that year.

After several years, the pastor moved to another church. When Ada died, she left him $1,000 from her small estate. He still had a small salary and was tempted to use the money for his family's needs, but something else seemed more in harmony with Ada's lifestyle. A recent high school graduate from his church had just been thrown out of her home by her father and had come to live

383

with the pastor, his wife, and their three small daughters. The student had no money for college. In Ada's name, the family gave the money to the young woman who went away to college and eventually earned a doctor's degree in biology.

"Professor" Ada was fond of the right things. She was fond of God and his church. She was fond of people who needed the gospel and who had physical needs. She helped people with money. That is a clue to unravel the mystery of the parable of the shrewd manager.

Jesus said, "... I tell you, make friends for yourselves by means of dishonest wealth so that when it is gone, they may welcome you into eternal homes" (Luke 16:9). In heaven, should God ever ask for testimony on behalf of Ada Gleb, there will be a pastor's family, a woman with a doctor's degree, and many others who will gladly speak up.

It's possible to be "really fond" of the right things in life. It's also possible to be "really fond" of the wrong things. That brings us to another clue to solving the mystery of the puzzling parable with a sharp point. A good question to ask about all the parables is, "What is Jesus trying to do here?"

In many of his parables, Jesus is trying to upset the equilibrium of his hearers. That's certainly true with this parable. Jesus is trying to work a reversal, upsetting his hearers with a big kingdom surprise. He is trying to pop preconceptions that will only get his hearers into trouble. He's doing it on purpose. He wants to help his hearers think about their value systems. People have trouble making changes in their lives, especially big changes. Change isn't easy. One man described change like this: "I don't have any problems making changes in my life as long as I don't have to act differently." Ugh.

The nature of Jesus' parables is to serve as wake-up calls to people who are missing the purpose of life. The parables of Jesus are like a bucket of cold water thrown in our faces to wake us up to what life is really about.

The parables of Jesus are not moral example stories. If this parable of the shrewd manager was a moral example story, we'd be in real trouble. The hero of this parable is an unjust rascal who is trying to save his own neck by working a compromise settlement with his master's debtors. Where is the integrity in his actions? Where is the moral example for our young people? Why should we hold up a man who is "cooking the books" and then wiggles out of his troubles by compromised settlements? What is Jesus' point?

Jesus tells the story of the shrewd steward who "cooked the account books" not because the man is a good moral example, but because he wants to tell us about real vales in the kingdom of God compared to the false values of this world. In a parable, the thing to look for is the point of tension to which the parable is addressed.

Here, that point of tension is a distorted view of money and possessions. We are stewards, not owners. If we think of ourselves as owners, our possessions will possess us. "You cannot serve God and mammon," Jesus says.

In addition to the point of tension in the Pharisees' lives 2,000 years ago, the parable is aimed at points of tension in our lives today. The parables of Jesus are stories to remember. If we let them do their job, they will come rushing out of the past and wake us up today. If we really listen to what Jesus is saying, we actualize the past and experience the power and presence of the Lord today. In order to understand this parable we need to "stand under" the lordship of the storyteller and hear the words as if we are hearing them addressed to us today. To hear a parable of Jesus in the right way, we must hear it from the inside, as participants.

In his book, *How to Preach a Parable*, Eugene Lowry says that in order to understand a parable we must look for the itch before we can feel the scratch. We must sense the tension before we can receive relief from the tension. We must place ourselves in the puzzling setting before we can see the resolution to the puzzle. Lowry calls this "finding the focus of the story."[2]

All this talk about participation and finding the focus notwithstanding, what do we do with the steward who is a rascal, making deals with shady debtors and a master who commends the shrewdness of his steward for the deals he makes? What's the sharp point Jesus is trying to make?

The sharp point of this parable is that the master commends the use of money for people, instead of for pride, power, position,

and possessions. In other words, the value of money and possession comes to a dead end when we die. The sharp point of this
parable is that money and possessions will do us no good when we
arrive at eternity and face the judgment of God.

Helmut Thielicke, puts it this way:

> *It is made perfectly clear to us that one day every one*
> *of us will be left destitute. The day will come when we*
> *shall stand naked before God, unable to answer him*
> *once in a thousand times. We shall be stripped of all*
> *things in which we put our confidence here below. We*
> *shall stand before the throne of God without title, with-*
> *out money, without home, without reputation — in ut-*
> *ter poverty.*[3]

That's the sharp point of this powerful parable. One day we
will have to face God. We can't fool God. He knows our motives
and our actions. God knows our hearts (Luke 16:15). He also knows
all about our checkbooks. He knows whether we have used money
to help people or for self-aggrandizement and power over people.

The Bible tells us two things about this judgment. First and
foremost, God is very fond of us. He desires to save us, not send us
to hell. "God ... wants everyone to be saved and to come to the
knowledge of the truth" (1 Timothy 2:4).

Second, the Bible tells us that God is not mocked. What a man
sows, he shall reap. God isn't fooled.

One day we shall all stand before the throne of God in utter
poverty. In that place where money is neither received nor spent,
where all values have been turned upside down, and the importance of relationships with God and people will be clear, will there
be someone who will come forward and say for you, "He (She) is
very fond of you Lord. Out of gratefulness for grace, he (she) used
the resources of this world to glorify your name and help people."

The parable of the bad man's good example is about a steward
who is a rascal in many respects, but does one thing right. He is a
servant who is left in charge of the estate of the absentee landlord.
Guilty of embezzlement, he is hardly a hero. Yet, he did one thing
right. He used money for people. Jesus is not urging us to be like

this bad man, but to be wise in this one way. Using our money and possessions for people can make an eternal difference.

This parable about judgment day is a warning and an invitation. The warning comes in the words of the wise mother quoted at the beginning of this sermon, "You can get into big trouble if you are really fond of the wrong things." The warning is that whether or not we acknowledge Jesus as Lord in this life, we will have to face the fact of judgment in the next life. The warning is that whether or not we see Jesus' lordship extending to the use of all things in this life — including money — we will have to face the facts on judgment day.

The invitation is to come into the wide-open arms of Jesus and place our faith in him as Lord and Savior. The invitation is to connect faith and life, to make faith active in love. The invitation is by the power of the Holy Spirit to follow Jesus' example of selfless service to people. If we accept Jesus as Lord and Savior and put our faith into action in all areas, including the use of money, on judgment day we can hear his greeting, "I'm very fond of you. I died rather than give you up. Enter into the joy of your Master."

---

1. This sermon, in a slightly different form, was previously published in the book, *Stories To Remember*, by Ron Lavin, CSS Publishing Company, Lima, Ohio, 2002, pp. 115-124.

2. Eugene Lowry, *How to Preach a Parable* (Nashville: Abingdon Press, 1990), p. 33.

3. Helmut Thielicke, *The Waiting Father* (New York: Harper and Brothers, 1959), p. 102.

Proper 21
Pentecost 19
Ordinary Time 26
Luke 16:19-31

Welcome, Rich And Poor

Can you name some disillusioned people you've met in life? How about a woman who is so badly hurt by her husband committing adultery with a younger woman and then divorcing her, that she wants nothing to do with men? How about a child who believes in Mom and Dad, only to discover that they have frequently lied to him? How about the students of a beloved teacher who find out that their teacher is a pedophile who is going to prison for his sexual molestation of children? How about parishioners who love their pastor, only to discover that he has been cheating on his income tax for years?

We could go on with many illustrations about disillusioned people in the negative sense of that term. That's how we normally use the word "disillusioned." We normally think of it in terms of disappointment, unmet expectations, hurt, and sorrow. Something just didn't work out the way it should have worked out.

On the other hand, one of the definitions of the word, "disillusioned," is "freed from illusions." Illusions are false ideas. There is a positive use of the word "illusions" which should be considered. By telling the truth, the prophets freed people from their illusions. Moses disillusioned the Hebrews about the false gods they worshiped. Jesus went about telling parables that burst the bubble of many misconceptions people had about life.

In the story of the rich man and Lazarus there are at least three illusions. Jesus exposed them and freed people from the demonic power of their false ideas about riches and happiness, heaven and hell, and the Word of God.

389

While Jesus often uses illustrations of rich land owners, wealthy hosts at banquets, and powerful lords of servants as stand-ins for God in his stories, he never suggests that these people are happy because of their riches, possessions, or power. As a matter of fact, frequently, as in the parable before us, Jesus shows that riches and power can so distort a person's life that they miss the obvious: love for God and neighbors.

Self-absorbed, the rich man in Jesus' parable missed the point of life — living for God and other people. He didn't even give poor Lazarus the scraps from his succulent feasting. Dives (a name which means "rich" in Latin) ignored the Word of God. He took notice of the social register. He paid attention to the list of "Who's Who in Jerusalem." He focused on the power of money in human affairs and liked the fact that many envied his riches. He didn't notice the Word of God, which teaches that riches and possessions have dangers, as well as opportunity, associated with them and that riches can keep you out of heaven if you have the wrong attitude toward them.

The Word of God doesn't teach that money is the root of all evil, but that the love of money is the root of all evil (1 Timothy 6:10). That verse is in our second lesson for the day. Paul urges his young protégé, Timothy, to help his rich church members and friends not to be haughty and not to set their hopes on the uncertainty of riches but rather to focus on God and be generous with their resources (1 Timothy 6:17-19).

A rich businessman in Muncie, Indiana, had family members who encouraged him to attend worship at the local Lutheran church. He attended and said that he liked the new pastor. When the pastor invited him to come to a pastor's class for instruction about the Christian faith, he decided to try it. When the pastor explained the nature of salvation by grace through faith alone and that our good works don't get us into heaven, the businessman began to back away. He said, "I follow the philosophy of business — that is — you get rewarded for your hard work. You mean to tell me salvation is free?"

"Free, but not cheap," the pastor replied. "Jesus paid for our salvation by dying on the cross. We are saved by his grace, not by our good works."

The rich man stomped out of class saying, "I'll never join this or any other church. I'm through with religion."

The pastor lost track of the businessman for a time, but two years later, the man's family phoned and told the pastor the man had died. If the man didn't learn the truth about God and salvation before he died, like Dives, he had to face it after he died.

Everyone dies and must face God. If we don't get the point of life while we are alive, we will have to face it after death.

The Word of God teaches that the point of life is that God so loved us that he gave his only begotten Son that we might have eternal life. We are called to love him back with our hearts, minds, and souls, and to love our neighbors as ourselves.

Dives may have been a big man in town and even a big donor to charities in town, but he didn't pay attention to God, and he didn't notice Lazarus, the needy man right outside his door. Dives tried to live as a good citizen. He may have gone to the temple for worship. He probably thought that he would be rewarded in heaven. But, like the Pharisees to whom this parable was addressed, Dives didn't pay enough attention to the Word of God which teaches that God is our help, our only hope for salvation.

The name "Lazarus" means, "God is my help." Unless we make that discovery, we are not the people we were created to be. When we come to Jesus Christ by faith, we become the people we were created to be. Real happiness means fulfillment of God's purpose for us.

Illusion number one is that money brings happiness in this life and a free pass to heaven in the next. The second illusion Jesus addresses in this parable has to do with heaven and hell

First, Jesus points out here and elsewhere that there is an afterlife. Life is not just a matter of the here and now. The hereafter is a major category addressed in many of Jesus' parables and teachings. The kingdom of heaven is an overriding teaching of the Bible that corrects a secular view of reality that insists that when you die, that's all there is.

In modern times, many people live as if there is no eternity and no eternal consequences to their actions. Ethical relativism is running rampant today. Ethical relativists teach that there are no absolutes. That means that God and his law are not absolutes. That means that the Son of God is not an absolute. That means that there is no Lord over us. In the minds of many today, there is no heaven and no hell, no afterlife.

It was a very hot day in Dallas, Texas. The air conditioner at Christ Lutheran Church was broken. The pastor got into the pulpit and preached this ten-word sermon: "Hot, isn't it? Hell's like that. Don't go there. Amen."[1]

If we believe this parable, we have no alternative but to face the consequences of whether we have faith in the Lord Jesus Christ or not. Heaven and hell are eternal realities. Consult the Word of God. Pop, there goes a misconception about eternity.

This parable shows that there is no direct connection between financial success and prosperity in this life and heavenly reward in the next life. If anything, those who have many possessions may find it hard to accept the basic premise of faith, that Jesus is Lord and Savior. The rich often try to find salvation elsewhere.

Jesus said that it is as hard for a rich man to enter the kingdom of God as it is for a camel to go through the eye of a needle. The "Eye of a Needle" was a small place in the bottom of the wall in Jerusalem where the only way to enter was to kneel down. That kneeling down and accepting Jesus as Lord of all is difficult for wealthy men and women. The principles of success in this world and the principles of eternal status are not the same. Pop, there goes another misconception about eternal life.

In this parable, Jesus teaches that heaven is not exclusively for poor people or rich people. Poor people don't go to heaven because they are poor any more than rich people go to hell because they are rich. Salvation is dependent on whether or not we believe and follow the Word of God which teaches the lordship of God over us for our own good. We know that Lazarus went to heaven because he bowed before the God who helps us. We know that the rich man went to hell because he refused to accept that lordship of God over his life, but we are also told that the wealthy man's wealthy brothers have the same opportunity that Dives had when he was alive. They have Moses and the prophets. In other words, they have the Word of God. So do we. They had an opportunity to believe in the Son of God for salvation. So do we.

A story about a wealthy man and his son may help to illustrate the importance of the place of the Son of God in salvation. The father and son loved to collect works of art. They had everything in their collection from Picasso to Raphael. The would often sit together and admire the great works of art.

When the Vietnam conflict broke out, the son went to war. He was very courageous and died in battle while rescuing another soldier. The father was notified. He grieved deeply for his only son. About a month after the death, just before Christmas, there was a knock at the door. A young man stood at the door with a large package in his hands.

He said, "Sir, you don't know me, but I am the soldier for whom your son gave his life. He saved many lives that day and he was carrying me to safety when a bullet struck him in the heart. He died instantly. He often talked about you and your love of art." The young man held out a package. "I know this isn't much. I'm not really a great artist, but I think your son would have wanted you to have this."

The father opened the package. It was a portrait of his son, painted by the young man. He stared in awe at the way the soldier had captured the personality of his son in the painting. The father was so drawn to the eyes that his own eyes welled up with tears. He thanked the young man and offered to pay him for the picture.

"Oh, no, sir," the young man said. "I could never repay your son for what he did for me. It's a gift."

The father hung the portrait over his mantle. Every time visitors came to his home, he took them to see the portrait of his son before he showed them any of the other great works he had collected. The man died a few months later. There was to be a great auction of his paintings. Many influential people gathered, excited over seeing the great paintings and having an opportunity to purchase one for their collections.

On the platform sat the painting of the son. The auctioneer pounded his gavel. "We will start the bidding with this picture of the son. Who will bid for this picture?"

There was silence. Then a voice in the back of the room shouted, "We want to see the famous paintings. Skip this one."

The auctioneer persisted. "Will someone bid for this painting? Who will start the bidding? $100? $200?"

Another voice shouted angrily, "We didn't come to see this painting. We came to see the Van Goghs, the Rembrandts. Get on with the real bids!"

But still, the auctioneer continued. "The son! The son! Who'll take the son?" Finally, a voice came from the very back of the room. It was the long-time gardener of the man and his son. "I'll give $10 for the painting." Being a poor man, that's all he could afford.

"Ten dollars is the bid. Won't someone bid $20?"

The crowd was becoming angry. They didn't want the picture of the son. They wanted the more worthy investments for their collections. The auctioneer pounded the gavel. "Going once, twice, sold for $10."

A man sitting in the second row shouted, "Now, let's get on with the collection!"

The auctioneer laid down his gavel. "I'm sorry," he said. "The auction is over."

"What about the other paintings?" a woman asked in a shrill voice.

"I'm sorry. When I was called to conduct this auction, I was told of a secret stipulation in the will. I was not allowed to reveal that stipulation until this time. Only the painting of the son would be auctioned. Whoever bought that painting would inherit the entire estate, including the paintings. The man who took the son gets everything."

God sent his Son 2,000 years ago to die on the cross for all of us. Much like the auctioneer, our message today is: "The Son, the Son. Who'll take the Son? Whoever takes the Son gets everything, including heaven."[2] That flies in the face of the popular belief that if we are good, we go to heaven.

Pop, there goes another misconception about eternity.

That brings us to the third major illusion Jesus addresses in this parable.

394

Dives neglected the Word of God in life. In hell, Dives asked that someone from eternity be sent to his brothers that they may not make the same mistake he made of seeking mammon instead of God. Many people want miracles.

"If God appears on a cloud and with a megaphone announces that Jesus is Lord and Savior, then I'll believe," said Fred, the town atheist with a sneer. "God is not on trial," replied his friend who was a Christian. "The question is not 'Is there a God, but is there a Fred?' You will never be fully Fred until you return to your Maker with faith in the Lord. You don't need a miracle; you have the Word of God. That's all any of us need." He spoke in the spirit of Luke 16:19-31.

There are many illusions about the Word of God today, but one of the most serious ones is that we need more than God's Word for life. Jesus speaks directly to this illusion when he says, "If they do not listen to Moses and the prophets, neither will they be convinced even if someone rises from the dead" (Luke 16:31). Shortly after saying these words, Jesus rose from the dead. Through his resurrection, many have come to faith, but the truth of the matter is that he has come back from the dead and still many do not accept him as Lord and Savior.

Today, many people still live in the land of illusions, believing in mammon instead of God, creating idols instead of following the Lord Jesus Christ, stubbornly clinging to their misconceptions. Still others find faith and fulfillment when they cross over into the land of the living by faith in Jesus Christ.

An anonymous author described his journey from the land of illusions to the reality of the kingdom of God like this:

I Met The Master Face To Face
I had walked life's way with an easy tread
Had followed where comforts and pleasures led
Until one day in a quiet place
I met the Master face to face.

With station and rank and wealth for my goal
Much thought for my body but none for my soul

I had entered to win in life's race
When I met the Master face to face

I had built my castles and reared them high,
With their spires had pierced the blue of the sky
I had sworn to rule with an iron mace
When I met the Master face to face.

I met him and knew him and blushed to see
That his eyes full of sorrow were fixed on me
And I faltered and fell at his feet that day
While my castles all melted and vanished away.

Melted and vanished and in their place
Naught else did I see but the Master's face
And I cried aloud, "O make me meet
To follow the steps of your wounded feet."

My thought is now for the souls of men
I have lost my life to find it again
E'er since one day in a quiet place
I met the Master face to face.

— Anonymous

The poet wrote, "My thought is now for the souls of men." In other words, he now is about the business of disillusioning people, freeing them from their illusions about God, eternity, and life.

---

1. Adapted from an article in *The Joyful Noiseletter*, a publication of The Fellowship of Merry Christians.

2. An anonymous story.

Faithquakes

A woman who went through her first earthquake in California said, as it was happening, "I think a train just hit our apartment building. I think our foundation is gone. We better pray."

A faithquake is something like an earthquake. Something comes along and shakes us up. Something shakes our very foundations. Through the foundation-shaking event, we want to know more about God and faith.

Something like that is going on in our gospel. The apostles cried out, "Increase our faith" (Luke 17:5). In the front side context of this verse we hear the foundation-shaking words of Jesus about forgiveness which prompted this cry for more faith.

"Be on guard! If another disciple sins, you must rebuke the offender, and if there is repentance, you must forgive. And if the same person sins against you seven times a day, and turns back to you seven times and says, 'I repent,' you must forgive" (Luke 17:3). These words about forgiveness were a faithquake for the apostles. They were all shook up when they heard them. "We just don't have enough faith to understand what you are saying," they were saying as they pleaded for more faith.

Even if we've heard these words about forgiveness many times before, these words shake us up, too. Questions abound. "Seven times a day? Are these repeated sinners really repentant or are they just saying the words? Are they going to change their ways? How can we forgive that often?"

The problem of offering repeated forgiveness is compounded when we hear Peter's question in Matthew 18:21-22: "... Peter came

397

and said to him (Jesus) 'Lord, if another member of the church sins against me, how often should I forgive? As many as seven times'? Jesus said to him, 'Not seven times, but I tell you, seventy-seven times.' "

Peter thought he was being generous. The rabbis of his time taught that under certain conditions of repentance you might forgive a person as many as three times. Peter thought he'd be commended for more than doubling that amount. He was all shook up when Jesus told him, "Not seven times, but seventy-seven times." Other translations say, "Not seven, but seventy times seven." Whatever the numbers, Peter must have felt that he was experiencing something like an earthquake when he heard the words. His foundations were shaken.

Our foundations are shaken, too, as we hear about forgiveness. Strained relationships in families, with friends, and at church make the task of forgiveness seem impossible, especially when we know what the numbers "seven," "seventy-seven," and "seventy times seven" mean.

The numbers "seven," "seventy-seven," and "seventy times seven" have nothing to do with arithmetic. Seven is the perfect number in the Bible. Seven is the number of days in creation. Seven means "whole" or "complete." Seven came to be the number which the Hebrews associated with being like God.

In our story, the use of numbers means that we should act like God acts, willing to restore someone who has sinned against us over and over again. If there is repentance and forgiveness, reconciliation is possible. The key word here is "if." "If" is the biggest little word in the English language. "If ... he sins ... and if he repents" is the key which opens the door to the forgiveness factor.

Consider three elements in the forgiveness factor. The first is that repentance must be present for forgiveness to take place. Often when people say, "I'm sorry," they mean, "I'm sorry I got caught" or "I'm sorry it happened." That's not repentance. In the Greek New Testament, the Greek word for repentance, *metanoia*, means "turning around." That's different than "I'm sorry I got caught," or "I'm sorry it happened."

There are two sides in any conflict. Both must be willing to do something. The person who sinned must be willing to repent. The person who is sinned against must be willing to forgive.

Second, Jesus is addressing the situation of the "offendee," as well as the offender in these words about the willingness to forgive. In other words, we are called to be like God when our brothers and sisters hurt us, offend us and sin against us. We are called to be willing to forgive, no matter how many times the sins take place. Careful now, this is a revolutionary concept. It's an earth-shaking approach to human relations, a faithquake.

Third, being willing to forgive doesn't mean that there are no consequences to our sins because God and other people are willing to forgive us. Concretely, if a murderer repents and expects to get off "scot-free" because he is genuinely sorry for his sins, he has not properly distinguished between the law and the gospel. The gospel tells us that God is willing to forgive us and therefore we should be willing to forgive one another. The law tells us that there are consequences to our sins.

A murderer told a pastor, "I have been converted. I have accepted Jesus Christ as my Lord and Savior. I have repented for my terrible sins and I hope that God will forgive me and that someday I can go to heaven. But I know I must pay the penalty for my sins. My hope is that I will not die in the electric chair, but that I will be allowed to pay my debt to society by a life-long sentence in the penitentiary." This murderer distinguished properly between the law and the gospel.

The wife of an alcoholic who continually refuses to face the reality of his actions may be doing him more harm than good. When you tolerate intolerable behavior, you encourage intolerable behavior. Confrontation must take place when there are repeated patterns of sinful behavior. In Matthew's Gospel, right before Jesus tells us to be willing to forgive again and again, he prescribes the method for Christians to confront one another after repeated sin. "If any member of the church sins against you, go and point out the fault when the two of you are alone. If the member listens to you, you have regained that one. But if you are not listened to, take one or two others along with you, so that every word may be confirmed by the evidence of two or three witnesses. If the member refuses to listen to them, tell it to the church; and if the offender refuses to listen even to the church, let such a one be to you as a Gentile and a tax collector" (Matthew 18:15-17).

Having a willingness to forgive means being like God. God's arms are wide open for the sinner to return, but God is not mocked. What a man sows, that shall he reap. Many who sin repeatedly are never willing to repent. The way is wide that leads to destruction and many go that way. They bring judgment on themselves by an unwillingness to repent.

We can't control what another person does. We can't make someone else repent. We can only control our own attitudes. When we are offended, the best thing we can do is to be willing to forgive, to offer forgiveness, instead of holding a grudge, living in bitterness, or clinging to resentment. When grudges are held, bitterness, and resentment are like seeds in a garden of discontent. Whether forgiveness ever takes place is dependent on a willingness to forgive by the offended person, and a willingness to repent by the offender. When we are unwilling to forgive, we make the other person's problems, our problems.

The willingness to forgive and the willingness to repent are both part of the faith factor.

The apostles said, "Increase our faith," because they were all shook up by Jesus' words about forgiveness. They realized how far from God they were. They sensed they needed to be closer to God if they were to act like God acts in offering forgiveness to sinners. They experienced a faithquake.

The faith factor means that we change our orientation from the ways of this world to the ways of God's kingdom. Sometimes it takes another person's strong words about what is really important to wake us up. That's what happened to the apostles. Having to face our sins helps us see the need for our Savior.

The faith factor means that we give up control of our lives to the Lord Jesus Christ. We seek to do what God wants us to do, instead of stubbornly clinging to what we want to do. Submitting to Jesus Christ as Lord is the one thing needed and the hardest thing of all.

The faith factor means that we seek to act the way Jesus acted. Since he forgave people, we are called to forgive. Since his arms were always outstretched to sinners, we should also be willing to forgive.

On a small commuter plane from Chicago to Rochester, Minnesota, a pastor sat next to a young business executive. As they talked, the pastor realized that the young man was living a totally secular life. The businessman indicated that all he wanted out of life was a better position with his company, more money, and more things. He also said that he'd like to get even with some executives who had put him down on numerous occasions. "I'd like to really stick it to them," he said.

"Tell me more," the pastor said. The young man explained that in business it's every man for himself and that some of the executives from his company had told lies about him in order to promote themselves. "It's a dog-eat-dog world," he said, "but I can never forgive them." Then the young man asked a question: "What do you do for a living?"

"I'm a pastor and church consultant," the minister replied. There was an awkward silence from the young secularist.

"My grandmother was a Christian," the young man finally replied meekly. "My mother taught me about Christ and faith, but frankly, I haven't been a practicing Christian. I haven't been in church for years."

Suddenly, a snowstorm came up and the voice of the flight attendant reminded the passengers to tighten their seatbelts. Then the flight attendant did something strange. She came down the center aisle, bent down, and with a screw driver lifted a small section of the carpet. Then she manually opened a trap door.

"What are you doing?" the young business executive screamed.

"I'm just manually checking to see if the landing gear is down," she said.

After she went to the cockpit, the voice of the pilot came over the loud speaker. "The flight attendant has not been able to manually determine if the landing gear is down. The electronic landing gear check isn't working. It's frozen. Don't worry, we think everything is okay." After a long pause, the pilot announced, "We will land in a few minutes."

The young businessman turned to the pastor and said in a trembling voice, "I'm scared. Do you think we're going to make it?"

"I don't know," said the pastor. "Is there anything I can do to help you?"

"I don't want to die. I'm too young. Tell me, what do I need to do to be saved?"

"Believe in the Lord Jesus Christ with all your heart, soul, mind, and strength," the pastor said. "Trust him for your salvation. He is your Lord and Savior. He will forgive you, as he promised."

"I believe," the young man said, "I trust him."

Just then the plane set down on the runway without a problem. There was a collective sigh from the passengers

"Wow," said the young man. "That was a close call."

"Maybe that was your wake-up call," the pastor said. "God bless you. Remember, you have been forgiven and don't forget to pass it on."

The young man smiled.

The pastor smiled back. In his mind he questioned, "I wonder if the emergency really woke him up? Will this young man's faithquake stick?"

When he got to the church where he was preaching that Sunday, the pastor checked on the texts for the day. He was preaching on Luke 17:5, "Increase our faith." The first lesson was from Habakkuk, "The righteous shall live by their faith" (Habakkuk 2:4). The second lesson included this verse: "I am reminded of your sincere faith, a faith that lived first in your grandmother Lois and your mother Eunice and now, I am sure, lives in you" (2 Timothy 1:5).

Sermons On The Gospel Readings

For Sundays
After Pentecost
(Last Third)

Father,
Forgive Them

John Wayne Clarke

Gratitude — A State Of Mind

Today's Gospel Reading reminds us once again that Jesus' journey has a destination. He is moving, slowly but surely, toward the holy city. Today we watch and listen as Jesus comes into Bethany, and his journey toward Jerusalem comes ever closer.

Geographically, Jesus is probably somewhere between Samaria and Galilee. The miracle that happens here is not in keeping with his other miracles. The miracle has an unusual skew to it. We have learned to expect Jesus to heal someone and for that healing to happen while Jesus is present. Not here! The lepers who are the object of this remarkable healing are told to do something a bit unusual. You see, Jesus did not heal these people on the spot. Jesus does something that seems a bit out of character, he tells these poor souls to go and show themselves to the priests. It is not really so strange because the instructions are in keeping with the Levitical instructions found in Leviticus 13:1-2, "The Lord spoke to Moses and Aaron, saying: 'When a person has on the skin of his body a swelling or an eruption or a spot, and it turns into a leprous disease on the skin of his body, he shall be brought to Aaron the priest or to one of his sons the priests.' " Jesus, in instructing these ten lepers does so with the intention that they will be healed before they reach their destination.

It is important here for us to pause and understand what it meant to be a person in the time of Jesus who had such a disease. In our world, we may make an analogy by looking toward the AIDS pandemic. People with AIDS are, in many instances, shunned by family and friends. But as horrible as that may be, it pales in comparison to the way lepers were treated in the time of our Lord.

These poor souls were forced to stand at a distance from Jesus or anyone else. They had to announce their sickness and they had to do so loud enough so that no one would accidentally rub up against them or touch them in any way. Again we see the biblical instruction, "the person who has the leprous disease shall wear torn clothes and let the hair of his head be disheveled; and he shall cover his upper lip and cry out, 'Unclean, unclean' " (Leviticus 13:45). We can only imagine the way these poor people were treated. And, of course, if *they* were treated poorly you can be sure their families suffered, as well. As is usually the case, discrimination casts a long and broad shadow.

Now, imagine that you have suffered with this disease and Jesus recognizes your plea for healing and mercy. You are healed; a miracle has happened in your life, your life has quite literally been restored. Do you not think that gratitude would be a natural by-product of this miracle? Wouldn't you be terribly disappointed if nine out of ten of those healed simply walked away without so much as a "thanks"? And who is it that takes the time to acknowledge this wonderful miracle?

All of the lepers must have believed that Jesus was capable of performing this remarkable healing. But the only one who takes the time to personally come back and thank Jesus, is a despised Samaritan. It is the Samaritan who has the genuine faith.

Two men were walking through a field one day when they spotted an enraged bull. Instantly, they ran for the nearest fence. The raging bull followed in hot pursuit, and it was soon apparent they wouldn't make the fence. Terrified, the one shouted to the other, "Put up a prayer, John. We're in for it!" John answered, "I can't. I've never made a public prayer in my life." "But you must!" implored his companion, "the bull is catching up to us." "All right," screamed John, "I'll say the only prayer I know, the one my father used to repeat at the table: 'O Lord, for what we are about to receive, make us truly thankful.' "

The Samaritan who returned must have understood that genuine faith involves the recognition that God's mercies are undeserved.

Gratitude, therefore, is an essential part of true faith. If there is one shortcoming that is most evident in our world today, it is that people, not all, but many suffer from a condition of ingratitude. God does so much for us. Our indebtedness to God is enormous and yet we rarely offer thanks for what God has done in our lives. In fact, most professing Christians don't even offer thanks over their meals much less offer thanks over all that God does in their lives. We are much like the little boy who was given an orange by a man. The boy's mother asked, "What do you say to the nice man?" The little boy thought and handed the orange back and said, "Peel it."

For a child of God, thankfulness is not confined to a day or a season, it is an attitude that we should have every minute of every day. To magnify this point, I want us to examine the account of the ten lepers in Luke's Gospel and see some important truths concerning an attitude of gratitude.

When we compare our concepts of the Christian life to those of Jesus, we often discover how narrow and limited we are. We live in a time of indifference. We have come to a point in our lives where if a sister or brother offends us, we simply cut them off. Society has taught us that it is easier to cancel our responsibilities than to relate to them. Why respond to his or her desire for reconciliation when we can simply move on with the crowd and not be bothered?

What this shows, of course, is our inability to grasp the importance of what God can do in our lives and in the lives of those we love. Our ideas about the possibilities of faith are shoved to the side and we miss the wonderful opportunity to be in relation with Jesus in showing an attitude of gratitude for all the gifts we are so fortunate to have received. We do not really believe that God can move mountains. We have learned to fly over them, drive over them, or simply remove them! You see, Jesus sets before us a whole new world of wonder. It is a world of new life, and endless possibilities. If we posses even a small amount of the faith of the Samaritan leper, there is no telling what we may experience.

One of the problems with this faith scenario is that it places us at the feet of the Master. It means that all of our bragging will have to be put in the closet. We often act as if we feel that we are doing

407

God, and the church, a big favor by gracing them with our presence. We want to be recognized for the things we do for God. After
all, without us, the church would fold up like a cheap tent. We fail
to remember what we learned in Sunday school as children; that it
is impossible for us to do enough for God — impossible!

We have already established that these lepers were in an unap-
proachable position. Here are these men living shut-out lives. But
we have good news. The good news is that although the Levitical
Law says one thing, Jesus says something quite different. What the
law declares out of bounds, Jesus declares within bounds. When
the law passes on the other side, Jesus makes it a point to make
contact and listen. Jesus came to show us a better way to live life.
He went this way on purpose because even in the awful position
we sometimes find ourselves, Jesus is able to reach us and to save
us. My family can't help me, my friends can't help me, the church
can't help me, but Jesus can, and while we stand afar off from him,
he does not stand afar off from us. When they could not get to
Jesus, Jesus got to them. When they could not come to him, he
came to them, and we come to understand he will come to us, as
well.

Our reading shows clearly that all ten of the lepers were in the
same position. They all wanted to be healed of this hideous disease. They all prayed and they were all healed. Yet, only one out of
ten bothered to show gratitude for a new life.

It is really important to understand how important it is to show
in a concrete way that we acknowledge that without God our lives
are empty. The Samaritan sets a wonderful example for us all. He
saw a reason to praise. He saw that his life was forever changed for
the better. He understood that nothing he did or could do would
have ended with the same results. He saw a change that only Jesus
could have made possible. He saw an opportunity to praise God
and he seized it. Many see their need to pray but don't see their
need to praise. I don't know how it happened; the Bible does not
allow us to peek into the life of this man. We are not told what it
was about him that pulled him at that place at that time to go back
to see Jesus. Maybe as they walked toward the priest's house he
began to notice his skin losing that scaly, white appearance. Or

maybe they passed people who would ordinarily have turned away in disgust, but now they did not. I really don't know how he came to the conclusion, but when he saw that he was healed he stopped going in one direction, turned around, and began moving in a new direction. He began a new journey of faith and it led him back to Jesus Christ. He had reason to praise God. They all had reason to praise God, but only one saw it.

In a little church, there was a father and mother of a young man killed in a military battle. One day, they came to the pastor and told him they wanted to give a monetary gift as a memorial to their son who died in battle. The pastor said, "That's a wonderful gesture on your part." He asked if it was okay to tell the congregation, and they said that it was. The next Sunday he told the congregation of the gift given in memory of the dead son. On the way home from church, another couple was driving down the highway when the father said to his wife, "Why don't we give a gift because of our son?" And his wife said, "But our son didn't die in any conflict! Our son is still alive!" Her husband replied, "That's exactly my point! That's all the more reason we ought to give in thanks to God."

We too often build fences around forgiveness, faith, duty, and gratitude. In passages like this one, Jesus encourages us to remove those fences in order to achieve the possibilities of the Christian life.

Jesus continued his journey toward his triumphant entry into Jerusalem. This miracle is one more step in that journey. Today, each of us is asked to join in this journey of faith. Like the Samaritan, we seek him out and ask for healing, and like the Samaritan we have the unique opportunity to say thank you by dedicating our life to his.

What will you do this day? Will you join the nine who walked away, or join hands with the one who was healed, and seek a new direction for your life?

Amen.

Lean On Me

One of the tangible benefits of reading the Bible is that we discover that God calls people to service in areas they may not have thought possible. People often discover that with God's help they are able to reach deep within themselves and find strength they did not know existed.

Back in the '60s, Bill Withers sang, "Lean on me when you're not strong, and I'll be your friend, I'll help you carry on." For most of us, it is not until we find ourselves unable to carry on that we discover that with God we can carry on and we can excel because in Jesus we have a friend that will carry us when we can no longer carry ourselves.

This chapter of Luke is marked with important transitions. Jesus is embarking on a preaching ministry that will carry him into a variety of settings. The section we are dealing with is one of those teaching gems that Jesus so carefully scatters throughout his ministry. It is followed up later with four very important miracles. But, as always, it is just as important to understand the story that comes before the verses we are dealing with.

The preceding conversation is about the eschatological, or end, times. Jesus is speaking about the coming of the kingdom. He tells them they will need to live life without him, but they must carry on the work of the kingdom, regardless of his absence. The days would come when they would wish for his coming, and Jesus warned them not to be influenced by false stories and rumors.

We all know how easy it is to be led astray. Sometimes out of fear, sometimes out of our own greed, and, occasionally, because

411

we want something to be true, because it will make our lives easier, if only for a moment. It is within this context that our Gospel Lesson for today takes shape.

Later, in this same chapter, come the following helpful words as we continue our journey, "What is impossible for mortals, is possible for God" (18:27).

These eight verses tell about a widow who comes to an unrighteous judge for help against her adversary. Jesus tells the story in just eight verses and so it is fair to assume that there is plenty to the story that we do not know.

We don't know if the widow had money or not. Probably she didn't. So she requested legal help from an unrighteous judge, and she wanted him to give her case favorable consideration without any financial reimbursement at all.

The point of the story is that this woman didn't become discouraged when the judge turned her down. She kept coming back again and again, until finally, the judge just threw up his hands and said, "Yet because this widow keeps bothering me, I will grant her justice" (v. 5). Just to get rid of her, I am going to do what she asks me to do. Do you see the end time theme here?

All of us who claim the name, Christian, will be tested. To be a Christian in this world means that there will be times when you will feel like the woman in our lesson for today. You may feel defeated momentarily, but you will not take that defeat as final or authoritative. You will look to the cross, you will remember the promise, and you will go once again in front of the judge and you will demand justice! You will do that because you know that as it said in the preceding verses, Jesus, whether standing in front of you, or living within you, is present and can be counted upon.

The parable teaches us, and indeed urges us, not to lose faith in God if God seems to delay in the execution of justice. The parable forces us to ask ourselves the question, "When the end comes, will all of humankind have lost heart?"

In our linear world, we sometimes get caught up in the technology of the here and now. We sometimes succumb to the notion that we have control of the world and control of our lives. But the truth of the matter is that the Bible teaches us that history does not go in circles. The Bible teaches us that time is moving ahead, like it or not. Time is proceeding toward a goal. Not just some random event, not some cosmic happening; no, time is moving toward a goal. That goal has been carefully planned and determined by the sovereign will of God.

The widow in our parable has no visible means of hiring a competent attorney to plead her case. We are so used to seeing high-profile people with high-profile representation. From O. J. to Michael Jackson, we see that wealth can purchase the very best legal minds. Our lesson drives the point home that it is not money, nor who the attorney is — it is who Jesus is that matters!

As was mentioned earlier, this parable is told in the shadow of the closing verses of chapter 17. Within our story this morning, we see the importance of persevering in prayer. The argument is this: If an unrighteous judge will give a fair judgment in the case of a helpless widow in whom he has no interest, how much more will our God answer the unwearied cry for justice from those people who remain true to the faith?

It is important to remember here that the person in our parable is identified as a widow. Remember the "then and there" of our parable. A widow in this time in history was a defenseless human being. They were as a class of people without rights. It is one thing to stand before the judge as a person of privilege, it is quite another to stand there as someone who has no status in the world! Her persistence is our example.

Throughout his ministry, Jesus cautioned his followers not to be misled. No person or group of people will have special, inside information denied to others. The coming of the Son of man is like "lightning." "For as the lightning flashes and lights up the sky from one side to the other, so will the Son of Man be in his day" (Luke 17:24).

In our world today, there are countless people who are like the widow in this parable. We identify with her because of some of the reasons already mentioned but for other reasons, also.

I imagine that when this parable was being told and retold over the centuries, it took on a different form and shape depending upon the circumstances of those who told it. If your life was easily identified with the life of the widow then it is fair to assume you would start with her. If you know what it feels like to be in a situation where you are without any strength, you are the widow. If you know what it feels like to have to go back again and again into the same ugly situation, then you can walk a mile in her shoes. The fact is that the widow was not going to allow that judge to sleep at night until she was granted justice.

In fact, that widow became a model for the early Christians. She was the perfect example of the need for prayer to be without ceasing. She showed that prayer is not a last resort; it is a daily Christian nutrient. We need it, it makes us strong. Her life is an example of a strong faith lived out as a witness to the world.

It is surely fair to say that for some, the judge was the story, not the widow. It is funny isn't it, how several people can see or hear the same story and come away with different perceptions of that story?

If you are an attorney, you may see this parable in an entirely different light. You may think that the judge was not at all ruthless. One of the primary responsibilities of a judge is to see to the protection of the weakest people in our society. It is the judge's job to lift the burden from the weakest and most vulnerable. I will admit, however, that in this case it would be pretty hard to erase the fact that it seems this judge has a well-earned reputation of being corrupt. It seems more honest to admit that the only way to reach this judge was by the insistence of this widow not being denied.

Her example helps us to understand how important it is to set goals and not be defeated at the first sign that things may not go as easily as we may have hoped. One of the clear lessons from the parable is that when you are making plans, especially plans for God's kingdom, you need to set realistic goals.

I like a story that is told about Henry Kissinger. One of his aides came with a report that Kissinger had requested on a conflict in Africa. He laid the report on Kissinger's desk.

Kissinger didn't pick up the report, but instead, looked up at his aide and asked, "Is this your best effort?" The man answered,

"Well, sir, there are some other things that I wanted to check out, but there wasn't enough time."

So Kissinger said, "Take it back, rework it, and then bring it back to me."

The man took it back and, for two weeks, labored over the report. Finally, he brought it back and gave it to Henry Kissinger. Once again, without looking at the report, Kissinger asked, "Does this represent your best effort?"

The man thought for a moment and said, "Well, some things aren't too well documented. I could spend some more time in research." Kissinger said, "Take it back, work it over, and bring it back when it represents your best effort."

A week later, after working almost day and night, the aide brought in his report and laid it on the desk. For the third time, without looking at the report, Kissinger asked, "Does this represent your best effort?"

"Yes, sir," said his aide, "it represents my best effort." Kissinger replied, "That is all I ever wanted. I will be pleased to read your report."

The actions of the widow in our parable say to the judge and to anyone who will listen that I am giving all that I have here and I can do no less. I believe that is all that God asks of any of us. Do your best. Try your hardest. God wants the very best for all of God's children and expects the very best in return. There is the wonderful saying, and I do not know who said it, but it is so appropriate, "God does not make junk!" You and I are made for a purpose and to not stand up and do the very best with what we have is simply not acceptable to God.

Bruce Larson tells about an elder in his church who had an incredible faith. He said that this elder would sit in church board meetings and listen to all the plans and dreams and proposals presented. Then he would ask questions.

After he was satisfied, he would always say the same thing. He would say, "Why not? If it is for Christ and his kingdom, why not?" In fact, his words were so predictable that some of the board decided to see how far they could go and still get the same response.

415

They came up with a lavish proposal, an idea that seemed totally ridiculous. There was no way in the world that they could ever raise enough money. No way that they could ever work hard enough to see this proposal accomplished in the church.

But, they presented it, and this elder listened. He asked his questions, and when they were through, he said, "Why not? If it is for Christ and his kingdom, why not? If we are doing this for Christ, and God is a part of it, why not?"

If it is for Christ and his kingdom, why not?

You know that every church needs someone like the elder in our story. Every church needs someone who is willing to stand before the judge and not back down because it seems he or she has insufficient funds to do the job. We need people who are not afraid to trust in God, even and especially when it seems fruitless to do so.

The two characters in our parable belong together. They represent persistence in prayer and confidence that prayer will be answered. There is no good reason for anyone here this morning to pray without at least an inkling that the prayer will be answered. Otherwise, our petitions to God fall on deaf ears and our lives are worthless and have no value in God's sight.

The fact is that anything worth achieving will take a certain amount of sacrifice. The attaining of lofty goals always requires emptying yourself of yourself. Prayer, that act of standing before the judge and airing your petition, is a very human form of humility. It is a good practice because it places us in a position of understanding that we must from time to time rely on something and someone other than ourselves.

Jesus is saying, "Christianity is all about selling it all, giving it away, coming empty to Christ, and then letting him fill us with himself. Before we can ever realize the blessings that Jesus is so anxious to give, that must take place in our lives."

The first lesson for us to learn today is that if we are really going to do things for Christ, set lofty goals. "If God is our partner, why not?"

The second lesson is about commitment — commitment of ourselves and commitment of all the material things that God has given to each of us.

James Byrnes, who was Secretary of State under FDR, said that the difference between successful people and average people can be summed up in three words. Here are the three words, "and then some." He said, "Average people do what is expected. Successful people do what is expected, and then some." Our widow did what was expected, and then some.

Most people are perfectly happy to attend Sunday worship, have some time at fellowship, and then go home. But our widow reminds us that we should not be happy to come to worship and then fellowship and then go home. No, we should demand more of ourselves and of our church.

Christians come to church. Successful Christians, who are successfully living the Christian life, come to church, and then some.

Average Christians give. Successful Christians give, and then some. Average Christians pray and read their Bibles. But successful Christians read and pray, and then some.

The widow only asked for justice and that is what God grants. The parable this morning is not telling us that God is some sort of super discount store that will give us whatever we ask as long as we are as vigilant as the widow before the judge. Rather, the lesson this day for you to take with you is that if what you seek is within God's character, you will persevere over all the evil judges in the world. But, if our prayer is not based on our life-long commitment to Jesus Christ, then we can expect things not to go well in court.

Once again, let me say that God wants some "and then some" Christians who are willing to sell out to God no matter what the cost.

Amon.

Proper 25
Pentecost 23
Ordinary Time 30
Luke 18:9-14

Prayer — What's In It For You?

The Gospel Lesson for this day is the familiar story about the tax collector and the Pharisee. As usual Jesus uses a colorful juxtaposition to gain our attention. A tax collector, hated by many, reviled by most, and the so-called religious Pharisee. It is easy to visualize the scene. The Pharisee looks very religious. He wears religious garments. He sounds religious. He does religious things. He feels entitled to special treatment because of his religious position in his society. He may even believe that God smiles upon him for being such a religious person. Sounds like a few pastors I know!

The other guy, the tax collector, could be wearing the very latest fashion and it would not make one bit of difference in the way people looked at him. No matter how hard he tries, he is not going to be well respected in the community.

The obvious thing about this reading is that both men pray. The difference is in the way they pray. One prays filled with pride and spirit. However, that spirit and pride is in himself! The other prays with a sense of humility. When you look at this reading you get a real sense that the tax collector is fully aware of his status, not only to the general public, but more importantly, to his standing before God.

One of the primary ways that Jesus taught his disciples was to speak to them in parables.

He was able to help them better understand day-to-day living through the use of these colorful stories. Neatly woven within these stories were the fundamentals of life that we all live with each day. Jesus, however, was able to weave these tales in a way that touched

419

each life then, and touches each life today. When we listen today with ears of faith, we are likely to find our own life within the life of the parable told by Jesus to his disciples so long ago. One theme that often finds its way into these stories is that there have always been those who place themselves on a higher level than the rest of us, even on a higher level than God!

In many ways, the ancient Pharisee was a religious icon. As a group, the Pharisees held sway over a great many people and institutions. Then, and now, we must always be careful about who we put on a pedestal, because it is likely they will fall from grace when the going gets tough. And, in a direct parallel to our world today, the Pharisee stands in opposition to anyone who does not follow the party line. They were in our common language today, fundamentalists. There was no room for any interpretation of the law, unless by the scribes and that interpretation needed to meet with the approval of the Pharisees. Although they, like later Christians, believed in the resurrection of the dead, the similarities pretty much end at that point of agreement.

Much like strong religious figures of our own time, the Pharisees and their scribes enjoyed a good deal of popular support. In one way, this is surprising, since the Pharisees kept pretty much to themselves. They always seemed to be ready to criticize others for not keeping the laws, and they often looked down on those who showed no interest in God's Law. Pharisees observed the law carefully as far as appearances went, but their hearts were suspect. Their motives were questionable because they often wanted to heap praise upon themselves, or at the very least have the appearance of holiness to all who would pay attention. As I said earlier, they very much mirror some of the stronger political and religious figures of our own time. They had the kind of power that the Christian church once had in America. Their voices were heard as authoritative, and what they said had great influence within the society of that time. We see the same kind of power exhibited by religious figures in the Middle East today. One look at the news will tell you that the modern-day Pharisees can incite violence or peace by a mere word. They can, and often do, use their positions for political and monetary gain. History tells us that the power of God in the hands of the self-centered was dangerous then, and it is today.

People often raise questions about religious institutions. Why do denominations exist? There are, of course, many answers to such a question, but one clear answer is summed up in one word, "accountability." Without accountability we run the risk of becoming corrupt by our own sense of pride or arrogance.

It really should not be surprising to any person living in today's world that so many people believe that the only person they can trust is themselves. The Bible tells us to trust God, but somehow we manage to find flaws in that logic. When people heap praise only on themselves and do not recognize the activity of God in their lives, they become full of themselves to the point of being a danger to themselves and those around them. The idea that salvation can only come by our trust and faith in God leaves power-hungry people anxious and misguided. And anxious and misguided people are not likely to humble themselves even before the Creator of all that is. Many have turned down the invitation because they fail to trust God. If you find that you have wandered down the wrong paths in life — if you will carefully search your past — you are likely to find that you trusted in yourself and not in God.

Self-righteous people, like the Pharisees in our parable, are likely to attack your character if you question what they say. Some within the Pharisaic community believed they were so holy that they felt they would become infected by the presence of others. Most people, if they take the time to think about it, will discover that those people that are righteous (in themselves) do not live by the Word of God, nor do they feel that they need it. These people have not submitted themselves to the righteousness of God, but have rewritten God's laws of righteousness to fit their own lifestyles.

Our world today glorifies those that proudly justify themselves. We watch television shows that are geared to the success and riches that people have acquired by their own devices. We even enjoy watching some of the rich and famous as they fall from grace because it seems to us that they probably deserve whatever bad thing is happening to them. And why do we enjoy watching such a thing?

421

We enjoy it because whether we admit it or not, we want what they have. If we can't have it, we enjoy watching them pay a high personal price for success. It is funny, many reach for the stars without ever giving serious consideration to who created the stars and put them in their place. The success of advertising campaigns that promote, youth, money, sex, and success point to a very basic problem in our world. There is nothing wrong with being attractive, youthful, or rich. There is something terribly wrong when those attributes are used to the detriment of others.

The problem for people who lift themselves above the God that created them is that they place themselves in a no-win situation. The Bible for them becomes a book full of nice stories and wise tales that tells about a time long, long ago. Nothing more — nothing less.

Now I know someone out there is thinking that they don't fit this job description — don't fall into this category. Let's take this discussion a little further. If you take a close look at biblical history you will find that there were at least three different kinds of Pharisees. There were what we can call the Cultural Pharisees — those that just couldn't stand others because the others didn't look as good as they think they looked. There were the Societal Pharisees — those that looked down their noses and the only time they would help someone is when recognition was bestowed upon them, making them look superior to the one receiving the help. Then there were the Intellectual Pharisees — those that thought they knew everything, and that no other person could add anything to their knowledge that would increase their own intellectual ability. Now, before you get all comfortable, thinking that you do not fall into any of these categories, ask yourself:

- Do you like the ability to correct others?
- Do you enjoy putting yourself in a position of superiority over others?
- Do you often see the wrong in others, but not in yourself?
- Do you feel that you have to fix others (even if they do not think they need fixing) just because you can?
- Do you feel that you are closer to God than anyone else?

- Do you pray to glorify God, or do you pray to glorify yourself?
- Do you want recognition for everything that you do?
- Do you have a tendency to criticize others, no matter what the situation?

Just in case there are some Pharisees here this morning, I want you to know that Pharisees, tax collectors, and the rest of us can be redeemed. The message for us, today, is that Jesus will hear your prayer and he will make your life worthy of his attention. Jesus can take you and mold you into the instrument of love you were meant to be. He has already set the example and has allowed us a peek at what it is we are to be. He has allowed us to understand how it is we are to live life and why we are to live for him. This is good news!

We all need to remember the simplicity of the prayer the tax collector offered that day. He said simply, "God, be merciful to me." You see, the important thing about this parable is to see the position the tax collector places himself in. He puts himself in a posture of contrition; it is a position with which most are unfamiliar. Unlike the Pharisee, the tax collector understands that he is in danger of putting himself in a place of divine displeasure. In order to close the gap he perceives between himself and God, he throws himself in the everlasting arms. The message seems clear for those who will hear it. Those everlasting arms will not let go, not now, not ever!

We all need to take the "I" out of our prayers and put in the "You." Remember the closing verse of our Gospel Lesson for today, "... for all who exalt themselves will be humbled, but all who humble themselves will be exalted."

Amen.

A Tax Collector Becomes Rich

This chapter of Luke brings us ever closer to the end of Jesus' public ministry. Jesus enters Jericho, just fifteen miles or so from the holy city of Jerusalem. It is here that Jesus transforms the life of Zacchaeus, the tax collector. This is one of the few stories that is peculiar to Luke and is a wonderful human-interest story. The fact that Zacchaeus is willing to climb a tree to see Jesus is a clear indication that he really wanted to see and meet the carpenter from Nazareth. His eagerness to see Jesus is rewarded in a very special way. Jesus makes himself a dinner guest at Zacchaeus' home. As you may well imagine, this did not sit well with the local folks who viewed tax collectors with more than a little dislike. These guys were really hated for what they did for a living. Moreover, it is precisely that fact that makes this encounter so very special.

The second verse of our reading says that Zacchaeus was, "A chief tax collector and was rich." The use of the word "chief" is also unique to this gospel. It more than likely carries the connotation that he was a commissioner of taxes. That may look good to someone in today's world, but not in the time of our Lord. Being the chief collector would be like being the chief executioner or chief thief! Nevertheless, it also brings some clarity to the statement that Zacchaeus is about to make. Being a man of some stature, at least in the eyes of those who coveted his money and position, he was not used to humbling himself in front of anyone.

There is a story about a local fitness center that was offering $1,000 to anyone who could demonstrate that they were stronger than the owner of the place. Here is how it worked. This muscle man would squeeze a lemon until all the juice ran into a glass, and then hand the lemon to the next challenger. Anyone who could squeeze just one more drop of juice out, would win the money.

Many people tried over time — other weightlifters, construction workers, even professional wrestlers, but nobody could do it.

One day, a short and skinny guy came in and signed up for the contest. After the laughter died down, the owner grabbed a lemon and squeezed away. Then he handed the wrinkled remains to the little man.

The crowd's laughter turned to silence as the man clenched his fist around the lemon and six drops fell into the glass. As the crowd cheered, the manager paid out the winning prize and asked the short guy what he did for a living. "Are you a lumberjack, a weightlifter, or what?"

The man replied, "I work for the IRS."

The point, of course, is that certain people and institutions do carry at least the appearance of unbridled power. Those that take our money usually fall within that category. It is not uncommon, even in today's world, for people to distrust and even revile the IRS. That fact makes what happens in our lesson today even more important. Jesus and his association with Zacchaeus marks the last recorded incidence of Jesus' openness to the religious outcasts of his day. He had demonstrated repeatedly that the least of these really are important to God. He has walked, talked, and touched all those who were deemed unclean by the authorities in his time.

Jericho was an important border town and it was a center of commerce for that region. As such, it required someone to collect the revenue that was owed the government. It was customary for towns, especially border towns, to have what we would call "toll booths" to tax those coming and going from the city. Of course, for us, a toll booth is on a highway and we are paying to travel on that road. Zacchaeus was collecting customs on goods traveling the Jerusalem highway. Sort of a "sales tax" on goods that were going to be sold or traded.

Some of the most honest people in the world have a hard time paying their taxes. It just sort of rubs people the wrong way to give away that which they have worked hard to earn. It would not be

426

human not to be a bit tight with your money. I have a buddy who always starts preparing his taxes on April 14 every year and stays up all night to get them finished. I think he likes the adrenaline rush!

It is tough to be honest during tax time, isn't it? Here's an actual letter that was received by the IRS a few years ago: "Enclosed you will find a check for $150. I cheated on my income tax return last year and have not been able to sleep ever since. If I still have trouble sleeping, I will send you the rest."

Zacchaeus was an enthusiastic tax collector. In fact, he was so enthusiastic that he figured a way to skim a few bucks here and there from those who paid up as they were expected to do. He was like our friend in the joke; he could squeeze that lemon for all that it was worth. The real problem here is that he was, in effect, stealing from his neighbors. He stood on top of the collection pyramid, stuffing his pockets with shekels before he sent the required taxes to Rome. If Rome charged a five percent tax, he may have collected ten percent from the people.

Is it any wonder that people were really uncomfortable with Jesus inviting himself to share the evening meal with this guy?

We are not privy to the initial reason that Zacchaeus was drawn to Jesus. Maybe it was strictly curiosity, maybe something much deeper. However, what we do know is that when they met, Jesus had a profound effect on this man's life. In fact, Jesus transformed his life forever.

Put yourself in Zacchaeus' shoes for a moment. You have become one of the most hated people in town. People avoid you like you are a leper. Most people, if given the chance, would do you serious harm! It is into this atmosphere that Jesus comes and makes friends with Zacchaeus. Of course, his actions raised eyebrows. What on earth was Jesus thinking? Didn't he know who this guy was? Didn't he know that just by being in his home he was labeling himself as a friend of the friendless? Of course, he knew! In addition, we should remember that this is not the first time that Jesus has done something like this. Early in his ministry, he brought on the wrath of the religious elite when he associated with tax collectors and sinners. "The Pharisees and their scribes were complaining to his disciples, saying, 'Why do you eat and drink with tax collectors and sinners?' " (Luke 5:30).

One of the interesting things about our reading is the way in which Zacchaeus approaches Jesus. You get the sense that he did not just want to know who Jesus was. He wanted to see who Jesus was. He wanted to figure out what it was that made Jesus different from everyone else. News traveled fast and he had probably heard of the healing of the blind beggar. Now this healer was walking through his town. He may not have fully understood what was going on in his heart, but he had a desperate need to get to Jesus. Like many before and after him, he probably couldn't explain what it was that seemed to pull him in Jesus' direction.

The story of Zacchaeus and the encounter with Jesus once again illustrates the complete and total freedom with which Jesus welcomed people. He could welcome and relate to anyone. In our world, filled with differences of race, class, economic power, and religion, is it any wonder that this story should be taken seriously today? You can bet that everyone was critical of Jesus going to this man's house. But Jesus teaches us today that we are not to give in to the temptation of making decisions based on acceptance by any one group of people. Jesus teaches us again today that we are to be about the business of tearing down walls, not putting them up.

There have always been those who think they want to get to know more about Jesus. They are drawn to him, intrigued by him, and probably a bit confused by him. People today speak of being "born again" as if they had somehow found something new. It is not new. It is not even miraculous. Jesus has come to us and shared our common lot. He is available; he is not on a mountaintop far away. You do not need to climb a tree to find him.

That which drew Zacchaeus to Jesus is the same thing that draws us to him today. Jesus erased the notion that good people associate with good people and bad people with bad. He made it acceptable to not make those distinctions. How wonderful is that? Look around you and you will see that principle in practice. Many of you know each other well. Some of you know each other only from church on Sunday. But here you are drawn together by the same thing that caused a despised tax collector to climb up a tree just to get a glimpse of Jesus. That is one of the most intriguing things about church. We are the sum of our parts, but our parts do not all come from the same factory. We are not all alike, but we share a common bond and that bond is Jesus Christ our Lord.

Zacchaeus did not allow anything, not the crowd or his condition, to stand between him and his desire to see the Lord Jesus. What about you? Do you care enough about the condition of your soul to pay whatever price is necessary to be right with God? Are you willing to turn from that little petty sin? Are you ready to walk away from the crowd in order to see Jesus? Are you ready to run to him?

In verse 5, we see that while Zacchaeus may have been searching for Jesus, Jesus was also looking for him. "When Jesus came to the place, he looked up and said to him, 'Zacchaeus, hurry and come down; for I must stay at your house today.'"

We are not told why Jesus noticed Zacchaeus. We really do not know why he stopped.

We do know that he stopped, looked up, called him by name, and told him that he must come to his house. Again, we see that while Jesus has set his face toward the cross, he stops and ministers to a searching sinner. He knew right where Zacchaeus was because he knew all about him — and he was filled with compassion toward him.

This is how it always happens. Jesus makes the first move by coming to us and offering life through himself. We would never be able to come to Jesus unless he came to us first.

Zacchaeus didn't waste any time getting out of the tree and neither should we. Zacchaeus came down right away and welcomed Jesus joyfully and with great excitement. He got way more than he asked for. He just wanted to get a closer look at the Savior, but now the Savior was coming over for dinner!

Friends, let's learn from this example: When people encountered Jesus, they broke out into joyful praise! That should be reflected in our daily lives and when we gather together for corporate worship.

Notice that when Zacchaeus is finished at the table he pushes himself away from the table and says to Jesus, "Look, half of my possessions, Lord, I will give to the poor; and if I have defrauded anyone of anything, I will pay back four times as much" (Luke 19:8b). Is that not exactly what each of us should be offering our Savior? He has given us his all; do we dare give anything less?

"For the Son of Man came to seek out and to save the lost." In case you are wondering, it is time now to come down from the tree. Jesus is waiting with arms open wide. Pretty terrific stuff, isn't it? You know it is! Praise God!

Amen.

Putting Eternity To The Test

Today's Gospel Lesson is one that is troubling if you care about fairness. By that, I mean, would you deliberately try to fool someone just to see if you could get that person in trouble? I am not talking about getting a brother or sister in trouble, because that is almost part of growing up. I mean really getting someone in hot water. Would you do that?

Our reading presents us with the Sadducees posing a hypothetical case intended to make the resurrection appear foolish. We must keep in mind that the Sadducees were the aristocratic party among the Jews. They were not as numerous as the Pharisees, but they held the highest offices. They did not believe in the afterlife and lived their lives for this world and this world alone.

To put this reading in context, it is important to remember that the Sadducees accepted as their scriptures only the first five books of the Hebrew Scripture. They said that they found no evidence of the resurrection in those five books, so they rejected the idea. They put a question to Jesus that was designed to show how mistaken the whole idea of the resurrection really was. They used as their argument, what was known as Levirate marriage. This was the practice whereby if a husband died without leaving any children, the wife would then be married off to the brother assuming a brother existed. The brother of the one who died had the responsibility to raise up heirs for him. It is important to notice that Jesus does not become involved in a game of Bible bingo here. He is not going to be pulled into an argument over the authority of scripture. Rather, Jesus plays their game by quoting scripture that the Sadducees did consider authoritative. He uses a passage from Exodus, "He said further, 'I am the God of your father, the God of Abraham, the God of Isaac, and the God of Jacob.' " In other words, he teaches them that the question they pose is irrelevant to their argument. Implicit in his quoting from the book of the Exodus is the reality that Abraham, Isaac, Jacob, and Moses all dwell with God in eternity.

Jesus always took the time to teach that all of life is under the direction of God. Everything we do should be seen in light of God's activity in the world. We cannot remove ourselves from God's presence, so all of our life is lived within that presence.

One of the most pressing questions any of us have in life is what happens after our life is over. We don't like to think about it, of course, we need to be concerned about living the life we do have. But, nonetheless, each time someone we know dies, that nagging question raises its ugly head. Jesus teaches us over and over again that what we do with our life today, will indeed have an effect on what shape our life will take when we die.

Can we really know anything at all about our future? The Sadducees say, "No," but the resurrection says, "Yes." There are plenty of fortune-tellers who make a fair amount of money telling you what your future is going to be. They can do it with cards, by reading the lines on your palms, or looking into the ever-present crystal ball. But what is the truth? What about my future life here on earth? There are certain things that we do know, because God has seen fit to reveal them.

But before we can understand our earthly future, we first have to ask, "What will happen to me when I die?" Job asked, "If mortals die, will they live again?" (Job 14:14). You see our eternal future directly affects our earthly future. So we start with Job.

If you think about it, the question posed by Job is really not a difficult one to answer. The question is not so much, "If we die." We are going to die, that is a given. And maybe that is one of the problems we need to face in our country. We do everything possible to deny the reality of death. We use language that hides death. We say things like, "They have gone on to a better place," or "They have passed away." We have people die in hospitals, we have funeral homes deal with the bodies for us, and we pay money to make our dead look like they are alive. Many people shield their children from funerals and, for some, the subject of death is a forbidden conversation. Is it because we don't want to face the reality of our own death? In the end, that attitude will show itself to be silly, won't it? We may even take the time to cover the earth that will cover our coffin with a cloth to make it look nicer! One of the first things we need to do to overcome the misgivings of the Sadducees is admit that death is inevitable. You see, the Sadducees, and many people today are living for death.

In Jesus' day, there were no fancy funeral parlors. The body was anointed, if the family had the money, but generally death was quite stark and quite painful. There were no hospitals where people went to die. There was no special make-up to make the dead look like they were only sleeping. Death was stark and it was unavoidable. Death and questions about it were right out in the open. In particular, within the Jewish faith, there was a great debate over Job's question. The Sadducees believed that there was no life after death. The entire spiritual realm of angels and heaven, hell and Satan were nonexistent to them and irrelevant because they rejected the resurrection. The Pharisees, however, believed in all those spiritual things including a resurrection to eternal life. Yet both claimed to believe in scripture as God's Word. You see, it's not only today that people can read the very same words and come to all kinds of different conclusions about what is true.

The Sadducees were all about death. But the true God is all about life. We must agree that we do not possess adequate knowledge or language to describe what the resurrection will be. The fact is that we do not know. Jesus' teaching is that God's future cannot be understood as an extension of our present existence. It is not the case that we can simply assume that the life we live now will be the life we have in eternity. All we can be certain of is that the resurrection entails transformation — transformation into the hands of God. That should be all anyone really needs to understand.

Paul gets it in the proper perspective in Romans 6:23: "For the wages of sin is death, but the free gift of God is eternal life in Christ Jesus our Lord." Then, again, in 1 Corinthians 13:12: "For now we see in a mirror, dimly, but then we will see face to face. Now I know only in part; then I will know fully, even as I have been fully known. And now faith, hope, and love abide, these three; and the greatest of these is love."

One way to look at these verses is to understand that with God, every generation is present tense and once God is your God, that fact remains for eternity. When Jesus comes, he connects himself to the great "I AM," by proclaiming for all to hear, "I am the resurrection and the life. Those who believe in me, even though they die, will live, and everyone who lives and believes in me will never die ..." (John 11:25-26). Yes, we will die. But for the Christian, death is not the end. It is merely the door through which we enter into the ultimate glory of our God.

Just imagine that. The promise is astounding, but Jesus makes the promise and as far as I can determine, Jesus keeps his promises! You and I get to share in the glory of God. Death is no longer an issue of concern or worry. In fact, many people who truly believe in the resurrection understand that a funeral is to be a celebration of life; not a proclamation of a life lost, but of a life lived!

The resurrection puts us all in a very special place. It says to us that since we do not need to worry about our eternal life, we can concentrate on living the life we have now to the glory of God. If ours is the God of the living, then God has called us to live. We have been created for life, not death. That is not a denial of the physical limitations that our finite human body has, it is a declaration that until that body ceases to function, we are to live for God. That means that our faith is an active faith, and a lively faith seeks to do God's will.

We are called to take what we have been given and share it in love with all who will listen. There are people all over the world that have never heard the gospel promise. There are many reasons why people do not listen or are prevented from hearing the old, old story.

By God's grace we are, as Jesus told the Sadducees, "God's children," "children of the resurrection" who "can no longer die." All of that is ours because our God is Yahweh, the one who is, who is always with us, who is giving us the gift of salvation by grace

434

through faith alone, who is hearing the cries of those souls that do not yet know him and who is therefore empowering us to share the wonders and the joys of being "resurrection children."

Beginning today, may we live and serve our living God through a life lived with purpose and direction. A life lived without dread of dying, but with the hope of living eternally. When we no longer worry ourselves over our deaths, our lives will take on new energy and a vital new direction. We will see the world in which we live with resurrection eyes, eyes that see God at our side in every challenge, struggle, and pain. We see through eyes that see Abraham, Isaac, Jacob, Moses, and all of our fellow believers alive and active before God's throne. We see through eyes that see them and hear them singing with us, "Holy, Holy, Holy, Lord, God Almighty"; eyes that see Jesus in every challenge and opportunity to come. We see through eyes that understand "Now he is God not of the dead, but of the living; for to him all of them are alive" (v. 38), for in him alone we have life and we live and we serve in his "resurrection eyes."

Amen.

The End Of Time

No reading of Luke is complete without coming to realize that Luke is concerned that the world understands that Jesus is the hope of the world and that any teaching that leads away from that fact is a false teaching. No matter what, no matter when, Jesus will be there to give us life.

In our own time, there have been those who have predicted that the end was near because of some tragedy that has shaken our world. The terrible tsunami was such an event. Over 200,000 people were dead in minutes. Some doomsday people took from that awful event that God was getting ready to shut down planet earth. There is nothing new in people claiming such knowledge. It happened in the time of Jesus and it will happen again in our time, as well.

In the world in which Jesus lived, there were certain events that seemed to foretell the end of the world. Just such an event was the destruction of the temple in 70 A.D. To some people that event signaled the time when Jesus would come again and the end was near. Luke is careful to teach that the end of the world is not going to be connected with any event we can orchestrate.

Jesus uses the story of the temple being destroyed to make an important point. History tells us that on a clear day the temple in Jerusalem was visible from miles away. The reason it was so easy to see was that it was constructed of huge pieces of white marble and when the sun struck it just right it almost looked like a snow-covered mountain. Not unlike our own capital building, the temple was a visible reminder of stability and strength. Anyone who had ever seen it knew that it was always going to be standing as a witness to the greatness of God. The huge marble pieces would stand the test of time and would always remind the Jewish people of the permanence of their place in the promised land.

Our text today tells us that the disciples asked Jesus a very human question. If what Jesus has taught them is true, namely that the temple itself will fall, when will this catastrophic event take place? Hey, wouldn't you want to know? Of course you would, so would I. We would want to know because we would be afraid that when it happened, we would not be ready and we might die! We, like the disciples, would have been scared to death! Remember that temple meant as much to the disciples as it did to anyone else.

Every church, from time to time, needs to "clean the rolls." It is always a difficult task and one without many rewards. Sometimes it is hard to hear why people stop attending worship and why they stop supporting the church in other ways, as well. Generally churches have by-laws or a constitution to guide them in this process. There are several ways to approach the job. One is to send out a letter asking the member what he or she intends in terms of continuing or not continuing as a member of the church. That is the easier choice. The second way is to send volunteers out to visit these folks, talk with them, and personally invite them to come back. As is often the case, the volunteer visitors will discover that most of the people visited had found other things to do on Sunday morning. It is surprising just how much routine determines the things we do. Sometimes a person no longer attends worship simply because they changed their Sunday morning routine. They got used to watching the early morning news shows or something similar. Another common response is, "We came to church when our children were involved. When they outgrew Sunday school, we stopped coming," or "I enjoy going to church on the really big days, like Christmas and Easter. Compared to those days, other services are a little bit dull." But likely, the most difficult thing to be told is that the church is no longer relevant to that person's life. That means the church has failed this person in some way. Worse yet, it means the church didn't even recognize the problem before the missing member stopped attending.

438

In this day and age of terrorist attacks, of planes falling out of the sky, of not knowing what the future may be, we would be well served to be diligent in ensuring that our members feel the real need to be a part of the worshiping community. It would be truly terrible if our church members, or anyone for that matter, felt as if the only thing to do was sit back and wait for the end of time to happen. Imagine waiting for the temple to be destroyed without so much as seeking an understanding of why. The disciples, at least, were not afraid to ask.

One of my favorite movies was *The Poseidon Adventure* from 1972. You might remember that a cruise ship was turned upside down by a big wave. Everything was turned upside down. Reality was turned "upside down." The way out was up to the bottom and back to the front. The survivors had to go to the bottom of the boat, which was now the top, to get out. A whole group of people were not willing to follow the lead of the pastor to crawl up a Christmas tree to get out of the ballroom, to safety. He said: "Everybody is dead who was above us when the ship turned over. Now they're underneath us. It's up to us to get out of here."

The people who waited for help drowned, but those who were willing to risk, to have faith eventually were saved. Not all, but most. The pastor was indeed the Christ figure for those people. They eventually trusted in him and were saved. So for us it is no different, "But not a hair of your head will perish." Jesus says, "By your endurance you will gain your souls. By your endurance you will gain your lives. By your faith in me you will be free. The world may be falling apart around you, but having faith in me will save you."

We live in a very confusing and, it seems at times, broken world. We live in a world where there is suffering, pain, and sorrow. We live in a world where competing religions threaten to undo our ability to live together in peace. Things are not as they once were. The world is not simple and it is not innocent. The days of *Leave it to Beaver* are not even known to our current generation. Our young people today know only a world where terrorism and indifference pervade our world. They have every right to question where history is going. We dare not miss the opportunity to help them, like

439

the disciples, learn that they do not need worry about the end of the world. If you live life not worried about the end of the world, you will live life to its fullest now and that will help everyone.

In the mainline church, we have sometimes avoided talk of the Second Coming. However, today we are faced with a new kind of indifference. It is a feeling of hopelessness that threatens the very foundation of our world. Now, as it was over 2,000 years ago, the ultimate answer is to be found in Jesus Christ.

There is no need for us to be afraid! Christian people have nothing to fear about the end of time. Christian people have nothing to fear about death or the end of the world. In our suffering and pain, we have nothing to fear. We will not be immune to the pain of this world. Christians are not set apart from the world, but experience all the harsh realities of this world. Someone said: "Whatever the future may hold, God can be trusted to see you through. In the meantime, demonstrate your faith and faithfulness by doing whatever it is God is calling you to do."

"I have met with but one or two persons in the course of my life who understood the art of Walking, that is, of taking walks — who had a genius, so to speak, for sauntering." Henry David Thoreau wrote these words because he was concerned, more than a century ago, that Americans were so busy making a living that they didn't know how to enjoy life.

As we live out our days and await eternity — whenever it may come — why not spend every day trying to experience in some way the joy of living, no matter how many days we may have to live? Let's ask ourselves: How is it with sauntering — with the joy of living — in our time? In our place? Perhaps we need to slow down in order to keep moving.

We know that Jesus' words in verse 18 cannot mean that Jesus' followers will not be harmed by their enemies. Some of them we know, were beaten, thrown in jail, and killed. But Jesus affirms for us that the ultimate security of his disciples is in God's hands. The people who persecuted the disciples and other Christians in the early years of the church failed to understand that in the end, God will fashion eternity. That is why we can take great comfort in Jesus' words, "By your endurance you will gain your souls."

440

Hope for the future, hope for today, is worth living for. Making each day count even if it is just taking a walk. We cannot fear the future, because that is in God's hands, we cannot fear today, because that is in God's hands, too. So live for the moment and wait. Wait for the coming not with fear, but with hope. We wait planning our lives, living our lives, hoping our lives will mean something to those around us.

The following story came to me on the internet. It was from an anonymous source, but nicely sums up today's Gospel Lesson.

> *The pickle jar, as far back as I can remember, sat on the floor beside the dresser in my parents' bedroom. When he got ready for bed, Dad would empty his pockets and toss his coins into the jar.*
>
> *As a small boy, I was always fascinated at the sounds the coins made as they were dropped into the jar. They landed with a merry jingle when the jar was almost empty. Then the tones gradually muted to a dull thud as the jar was filled. I used to squat on the floor in front of the jar and admire the copper and silver circles that glinted like a pirate's treasure when the sun poured through the bedroom window.*
>
> *When the jar was filled, Dad would sit at the kitchen table and roll the coins before taking them to the bank. Taking the coins to the bank was always a big production. Stacked neatly in a small cardboard box, the coins were placed between Dad and me on the seat of his old truck.*
>
> *Each and every time, as we drove to the bank, Dad would look at me hopefully. "These coins are going to keep you out of the textile mill, son. You're going to do better than me. This old mill town's not going to hold you back."*
>
> *Also, each and every time, as he slid the box of rolled coins across the counter at the bank toward the cashier, he would grin proudly.*
>
> *"These are for my son's college fund. He'll never work at the mill all his life like me."*

*We would always celebrate each deposit by stopping
for an ice cream cone. I always got chocolate. Dad always got vanilla. When the clerk at the ice cream par-
lor handed Dad his change, he would show me the few
coins nestled in his palm. "When we get home, we'll
start filling the jar again." He always let me drop the
first coins into the empty jar. As they rattled around
with a brief, happy jingle, we grinned at each other.*

*"You'll get to college on pennies, nickels, dimes, and
quarters," he said. "But you'll get there. I'll see to that."*

*The years passed, and I finished college and took a
job in another town.*

*Once, while visiting my parents, I used the phone in
their bedroom, and noticed that the pickle jar was gone.
It had served its purpose and had been removed. A lump
rose in my throat as I stared at the spot beside the dresser
where the jar had always stood. My dad was a man of
few words, and never lectured me on the values of determination, perseverance, and faith. The pickle jar had
taught me all these virtues far more eloquently than the
most flowery of words could have.*

*When I married, I told my wife, Susan, about the
significant part the lowly pickle jar had played in my
life as a boy. In my mind, it defined, more than anything else, how much my dad had loved me. No matter
how rough things got at home, Dad continued to dog-
gedly drop his coins into the jar. Even the summer when
Dad got laid off from the mill, and Mama had to serve
dried beans several times a week, not a single dime
was taken from the jar.*

*To the contrary, as Dad looked across the table at
me, pouring catsup over my beans to make them more
palatable, he became more determined than ever to
make a way out for me. "When you finish college, Son,"
he told me, his eyes glistening, "You'll never have to
eat beans again ... unless you want to."*

*The first Christmas after our daughter, Jessica, was
born, we spent the holiday with my parents. After dinner, Mom and Dad sat next to each other on the sofa,
taking turns cuddling their first grandchild. Jessica*

began to whimper softly, and Susan took her from Dad's arms. "She probably needs to be changed," she said, carrying the baby into my parents' bedroom to diaper her.

When Susan came back into the living room, there was a strange mist in her eyes. She handed Jessica back to Dad before taking my hand and leading me into the room.

"Look," she said softly, her eyes directing me to a spot on the floor beside the dresser. To my amazement, there, as if it had never been removed, stood the old pickle jar, the bottom already covered with coins. I walked over to the pickle jar, dug down into my pocket, and pulled out a fistful of coins.

With a gamut of emotions choking me, I dropped the coins into the jar. I looked up and saw that Dad, carrying Jessica, had slipped quietly into the room. Our eyes locked, and I knew he was feeling the same emotions I felt.

Neither one of us could speak.

— Author unknown

That pickle jar was, and is, a symbol of hope in their world. Where is your pickle jar?

Amen.

The Freedom To Interpret

Reformation Sunday is one of those unique times in the church year when we take a moment to remember a movement that changed the religious landscape forever. It is within this landscape that we find John and his gospel message this day. How does this story of Jesus and Abraham relate to Reformation Sunday?

First of all, it is important to see that Jesus' followers would be encouraged by this passage because it places them in the position of seeing that Jesus had faced what they were facing; some members of their churches had defected and had begun turning away or, in fact, betraying other Christians to persecution. Now, why would they do that? Well, look again at verse 31, "Then Jesus said to the Jews who had believed in him, 'If you continue in my word, you are truly my disciples; and you will know the truth, and the truth will make you free.' "

What were the reformers looking for? They were looking for the truth! They were looking for freedom. They were worried that the truth they had learned and lived with was being changed by the powers that be and that truth was no longer the word Jesus had taught. The Greek concept of what constitutes truth emphasized the importance of reality. The Hebrew Scriptures translated "truth" in a way that allowed the word to be married to the ideas of character, integrity, or even faithfulness.

It is critical here to see the importance of Jesus' use of the name of Abraham, because Abraham's name was filled with character, integrity, and faithfulness. Jesus understood that he and his follower's use of Abraham shows that they understand that the truth is for everyone, even those who had been subjected under the yoke of at least four different kingdoms: Babylon, Persia, Greece, and Rome.

Here the word, "truth," must be sitting next to the word, "freedom." The Jewish folks listening would understand freedom in a political sense. But, here, Jesus is speaking about a freedom that lives within a person. A slave is one who finds herself mastered by sin. A follower of Jesus finds himself mastered by Jesus himself. Looking at this idea strictly from a political or even philosophical sense, one can see how a very personal feeling of freedom comes with receiving the Word who has become flesh!

And so, using Abraham as the ultimate model for Jewish piety and hospitality is a way of insuring that all people understand that the truth, in this case Jesus, has the power to set all people free. In this way, truth and freedom are Jesus Christ himself!

Any reading of history will show us one thing for certain. You can kill people, but you cannot kill their ideas when those ideas are based in truth. Jesus wanted us to know the truth. The reformers wanted us to know the truth. The truth the reformers sought to infuse the population with was the truth of Jesus Christ, and the power of that truth to bring about freedom.

Luther presented 95 particular reasons why the truth was more important than anything else. He nailed those truths to the door of the Wittenburg church. Later, other reformers, like Zwingli and Calvin, spoke eloquently from their pulpits and wrote voluminously why the truth would set people free. Their ideas were all based on Jesus' life of truth and the reality that Jesus was in himself, the truth, the way, and the life. They understood, as should we all that truth, especially truth that resides in the person of Jesus Christ is a truth that cannot ever be defeated!

The Catholic church of the time was clinging to power and using that power to influence people; not so much with the Word as with the power of that Word which was held by only a few. The reformers were determined that the truth, that is the Word, would not be held by any one person or group, it would be for all people, even those once held in captivity. It is through the tenacious and

446

steadfast use of God's Word that the Reformation took hold and moved forward.

The encyclopedia says about the Reformation: "but the force of the Reformation did not end then. It has continued to exert influence to the present day with its emphasis on personal responsibility and individual freedom, its refusal to take authority for granted, and its ultimate influence in breaking the hold of the church upon life and consequent secularization of life and attitudes." The reformation was a fluid movement that understood that people are fickle, but there is perfection in Jesus Christ.

One lady must have been desperate. She decided to write a letter to Dear Abby. Her letter read: "Dear Abby, I am 44 and would like to meet a man my age with no bad habits." She signed her name, "Rose." Abby replied: "Dear Rose, so would I." There's more truth to Abby's answer than her typical pithiness conveys. "So would I" — meaning that perfect people are not easy to come by. I hope we can all find ourselves within that letter. Perfection is a difficult thing to define, let alone live. In fact, I honestly believe we know we will never attain it.

Military officers have an interesting saying — whenever they commit a serious gaffe — when they seriously mess up, often they say, "I fell on my sword." Meaning, "Boy, did I ever goof." The person who falls on his or her sword has self-destructed or done something that obviously reflects badly on them.

Jesus, and through him the reformers, want us all to know that the truth may elude us from time to time. The freedom that can be found in Christ may also elude us from time to time. But, Jesus will not elude us, and therefore, his truth and freedom, although sometimes difficult to find, will be there when we need it most.

Having this truth will not make us perfect. We will from time to time, at least figuratively, have to fall on our swords, too. We make mistakes and then say, "I'll never do that again!" In the guilt and shame that follows, we think or say aloud once more that we will "never do that again." But, because we are frail human beings, not a lot of time passes before we find ourselves once again, saying, "I'll never do that again, really!"

447

Going back to verse 31, "Then Jesus said to the Jews who had believed in him, 'If you continue in my word, you are truly my disciples; and you will know the truth, and the truth will make you free.'"

One of the single most important things about freedom in Christ is that it allows us to continue the Reformation each and every day. The Reformation is not something that happened and then died. The Reformation still is ongoing because the truth is ongoing. It is a truth that emphasizes personal responsibility, individual freedom, which by extension means using that freedom to protect the freedom of others, and refusal on our part to ever take freedom or authority for granted, and truth and freedom mean never ever taking the Word for granted!

Sometimes it is easy to overlook the fact that the word, "Protestant," comes from two Latin words which mean, "To be a witness." And so, our freedom in Christ calls us to witness to personal responsibility, to witness to the life-saving and life-changing power of freedom, again, not taking that freedom for granted and always bearing witness to the grace and peace of the God who fashioned us to be free in the first place.

You see, there is a common thread that all of us share — people of all tribes and nations, races and tongues all suffer from this — we fall. At the time of the Reformation, people often failed at being who they knew they should be in Christ. We're all in that same briar patch — we're fallen. The good news is that God is willing to forgive when we confess.

But there's another problem. We forget. We have a tendency of not remembering. You see, it's not a pleasant thing to be reminded that our very nature is flawed. Paul's words, "All have sinned," burns within us. Nobody likes to hear this. And, like memories of a bad dream, people ignore this fact, set it aside, have selective amnesia. That is what was going on in today's Gospel Lesson.

The Reformation is a vivid reminder that from time to time we all need to read once again our Gospel Lesson for today. It is a familiar scene. Jesus is doing what he does the best, he is teaching. His lesson is not all that difficult to learn, yet for thousands of years we have been either refusing to hear it, or we demand a right to change it. He tells some of his Jewish followers that if they continue in his Word, they will be truly free. But they react in almost shock. They denied that they were ever slaves in the first place. "We're Abraham's descendants," they said. "We've never been slaves," they claimed. "How can you say that we need to be set free?"

Talk about short memories. What about all of that exodus stuff? What about the parting of the Red Sea and Pharaoh's army chasing their ancestors through the desert? That whole "Moses-leading-them-out-of-slavery-in-Egypt-thing" was central to their faith. But all of a sudden, they get amnesia. And what about the Romans that were parading up and down their streets? What about the Roman Prefect, Pontius Pilate? How could any Jew ever forget about all that stuff?

My sisters and brothers in Christ, Reformation Sunday presents us with a lesson that we all need to learn. It is the lesson, or better yet the picture, of Jesus handing the truth to his disciples. It is the picture of those same disciples handing that truth onto Paul and to other followers after them.

And then those followers who remained true and focused on freedom in Christ handed that same truth onto Wyfliff, Huss, Calvin, Luther, Zwingli, and those that followed them. It was, and is, freedom to be the people that we have been created to be. Not people who will be told how to read the Word, and then how to use and live that Word. It is freedom to interpret that Word within the context of our own lives and world.

Brothers and sisters in Christ, the Reformation must continue today. The church is called to participate in the Reformation every day as we continue to make a great effort to learn what it means to be the people of the Word. The struggle must continue today and every day or we run the risk of becoming just another group of people who refuse to hear that, "If you continue in my word, you are truly my disciples; and you will know the truth, and the truth will make you free."

Amen.

449

What Price Must We Pay?

Today's Gospel Lesson mirrors the Sermon on the Mount that is found in Matthew 5-7. The sermon is directed at the disciples. It explores some of the things that will be expected of the twelve in the days and years ahead. It delineates the kind of outlook they should have as well as the kind of life Jesus expects them to live. Both Luke and Matthew start out with related materials. They both present us with what we have come to know as the Beatitudes and both end with the parable of the two foundations.

The verses presented here in Luke provide us with an astounding idea. That idea is simple; the value of your life will not be determined by how many years you live. It will be determined by how you used the years you were fortunate to live. I use the word, "astounding," in the sense that the normal life span for a male in the time of Jesus was under 35 years of age. So, it was easy to think that how long you lived was the single most important factor in life. And, although longevity has its place, longevity without value attached to it, means very little. On this day that we celebrate All Saints, it is astounding that there were those in the early church and in later times, who clearly understood the price, and were willing to give life itself to live the life Jesus directed them, and for us to live.

It is always tough to be asked the proverbial question that no one really wants to answer, and that question is, "If you died right now, what donation would you have made to life itself? Would you die knowing you really made a contribution to those around you? Have you been a grabber for yourself or a giver to others?" Many people have lived a long time without making any difference in the world. Sadly, every child of God has gifts to be shared, but not all come to understand how important it is to share those gifts with others.

Most of the time we live our lives inclined to believe that the demands of the gospel are that we remain good people and try to be fair in our dealings with the world. Our reading today throws a major curveball at all of our assumptions about living the life Jesus wants for us to live.

Let us retrace some of what has already happened to this point in Luke's Gospel. Jesus chooses twelve of his disciples for a special role. We can say, with some authority, that he chose twelve because that number represents the twelve tribes of Israel. By choosing these twelve Jesus was saying that they represented for him the new Israel. With something new, comes some new ways of living life. New values are outlined in this passage, new ideas that carry the power to transform the world. Powerful ideas that may at first seem radical, but with strong determination can bring about the kingdom that Jesus wants us all to share. The saints who have come before us had the determination to incorporate those ideas into their lives.

At its foundation, these ideas teach a new way of giving. They show us that giving is as much about attitude as it is about what is actually given. Jesus turns the world's ideas of what it means to be happy upside down. The very ones who the world has designated as poor and out, are the ones designated by Jesus as the rich! Wait, what does that mean? How can being poor, make a person rich? That just does not make any sense and it is an affront to our senses to be told otherwise. No money, no food, no friends, but blessed — Please!

Before we get upset about being poor but blessed, we have to read the rest of the story, "But woe to you who are rich, for you have received your consolation. Woe to you who are full now, for you will be hungry. Woe to you who are laughing now, for you will mourn and weep. Woe to you when all speak well of you, for that is what their ancestors did to the false prophets."

These verses should never be read quickly, never read without prayer, and never read without looking in the mirror. Jesus is saying you're blessed or you're happy when you have very few finances, very little food, and few friends, and you're in trouble if you have a lot of finances, food, or friends. You ask, "Wait a minute, is Jesus anti-rich and pro-poor?" Fair question, but the answer is, "No." In fact, it has little to do with what he is teaching. Jesus is trying to get the point across to those listening, and to those of us listening today, that all the wealth in the world will be of little use if you do not use what you do have for God's good purposes. It all seems rather self-evident when you think about it. We all know deep down that how we live our lives always has an impact on those around us. That does not only mean family, it means all those around you. When looked at that way, you begin to realize that you contain within you the gifts to help change the world! You can be a "saint" of the church just like those who have come before. That is phenomenal, is it not?

If you hoard the things you have, and don't pass on to others the good gifts you have received, then you will get back exactly what you have given! Enjoy what you have today, because you are never going to have more than what you have right now. Go ahead and eat the food. Go ahead and enjoy the friends, because that's the limit to all that you are ever going to have, because you're not a giver in life. There is usually something deeper in what Jesus is teaching. In this case it is values. Jesus is teaching about values. He's talking about priorities. A plaque that hangs on the wall of the kitchen in a small church in Perry, Maine, has the following sentiment, "Only one life twill soon be past, only what's done for Christ will last." Do our lives indicate that we recognize the truth in these words?

There is the story of vandals who broke into a hardware store and, for several hours in the early predawn morning, did their work. The doors opened the next morning at 7:30 a.m. as usual and, surprisingly, everything seemed to be in good order. No one knew that the vandals had been there until they went to purchase goods. The intruders had switched all the price tags. Hammers were $.07 a piece, and bolts were $6.95. Screwdrivers were $1,995 and small televisions were $2.95. Everything looked the same on the outside, but the value placed on items had been changed.

It seems to me that these verses from Luke's Gospel ask us to redo the price tags of our lives. Jesus teaches us that all of our old ideas about what we value are now being challenged. The fundamental value that we have placed on things in our lives and in the world around us has been switched. Jesus wants us to understand that values are what shape us, mold us, drive us, and define us. Today we live in a society that tells us on bumper stickers that, "He who dies with the most toys wins," and that is a problem. The choice is, "Am I going to be a giver or a taker, am I going to be a consumer thinking of number one first and foremost, or others?" Jesus wants us to be sure that we know that it has nothing to do with the amount of assets or possessions we have. People will say, sure I'd be a giver if I had something to give. You have something to give, my friend. Quit using that excuse. God has given you talents, God has blessed you, God has made you unique and you have gifts to give. The issue is not do you have anything to give — the issue is, "Are you a giver or a taker?"

Our nation has been built on encouraging people to stand on their own feet. You know, the whole notion of rugged individualism that has been fostered by so many for so long. Needless to say, this societal value works against the sense of community that Jesus worked so hard to instill in the disciples and through them to us. Christians are not to be rugged individualists but community-minded sisters and brothers in Christ. As Christians we are to be steeped in biblical values, just like the ones outlined in Jesus' sermon from our text today. We are to be people who give ourselves to communal accountability and discipline when needed, and to seek the very best we can for the body of Christ, the church. We are to do this even at the expense of our own wealth, whatever that wealth may be.

A number of years ago, in Anchorage, Alaska, there was a big earthquake. A lot of damage was done. Calls poured into the governor's office. He went on television to reassure the people that the government was doing all it could to meet the thousands of request that were pouring in. As governor, he felt a tremendous load of responsibility. Loss of life, damaged buildings, ruined pristine forests, and more. He understood the insistence that something needed to be done. He ended his television spot with some encouragement he had received. He had received a postcard from a ten-year-old boy. It had two nickels stuck to the back of it with scotch tape. The words were written, "Use this wherever it's needed. If you need more let me know." Two nickels, a million dollars, it's all in the attitude. It has nothing to do with your finances.

What price must we pay to be true to our Bible lesson today? First of all, Jesus indicated that givers live on a higher level than most people. He tells us that there are two roads to travel. You can take the low road or the high road. The high road is traveled by people that give in life. Remember what Jesus said, "But I say to you that listen: 'Love your enemies, do good to those who hate you, bless those who curse you, pray for those who abuse you. If anyone strikes you on the cheek, offer the other also; and from anyone who takes away your coat do not withhold even your shirt. Give to everyone who begs from you; and if anyone takes away your goods, do not ask for them again. Do to others as you would have them do to you' " (vv. 27-31).

Christianity and Christian conduct emphasizes what you do. Jesus describes the givers. They pray for those who abuse them, bless those who curse them, go the extra mile, and turn the other cheek. In other words, Christianity is not a bunch of don'ts. The Pharisees were all about doing things according to the law. There were all kinds of things they did not do. Jesus says its not only what you don't do that matters, it is what you do that matters more. You see, Jesus wants us to know that Christianity is leaving the past and doing something today. The Lord begins to tell us what the things are that we are to do. There is something else about this high road we are to travel and that is that the givers who travel it do more than expected. The Lord is talking about an unnatural way of living. He's talking about us living in a place where we do more than what's expected. This is what grabs the world. The world sees us as Christians being givers and going the second mile, and turning the other cheek, and blessing those who curse us. They see that and say wait a minute, I do not understand these people. They always take the high road. It's the high road that will change our society. Jesus says one more thing a little later in this chapter, he says, "... do good, and lend, expecting nothing in return" (v. 35b). You see, the world looks at us and sees that we do good and that we ask for nothing in return. Notice that Jesus did not say, "If you become this kind of giver, you will have nothing in return," he tells us to expect nothing in return.

Let us quote verse 31 one more time, "Do to others as you would have them do to you." All of the previous verses are summarized in this one verse. In fact, living this one verse will bring about the reality of the totality of Jesus' sermon to us this morning. Treat the world the way you wish to be treated. Pretty simple, really.

John D. Rockefeller, Sr., was a millionaire at age 23. At the age of fifty, he was a billionaire. He was the richest man in the world, but he was a miserable, rich man. At the age of 53, he was eaten up with physical diseases and ulcers. He was a grabber, not a giver. He was always trying to get more money and he was a greedy man. Greed had so consumed him, that at the age of 53, the doctors told him he had one year to live. Just one year.

Here's a billionaire, the richest man in the world, and all he could eat that year, all that his stomach could handle was milk and crackers. Milk and crackers. The man could go out and buy any restaurant in the world, buy it; he could have any food before him on the table, but it wouldn't do him much good. It was in that year, that Rockefeller began to look at his life. He said, "I have all these possessions and I've never been a giver."

That's when he decided to become a giver. He gave to churches, to hospitals, to foundations, and to medical research. Many of the discoveries we've had in medicine have come from money provided by the Rockefeller Foundation. That man who had only one year to live at age 53, began to live, and began to give, and do you know what happened to him? He started releasing all of the internal negative things that were killing him. He got rid of his stress, his tension, and his ulcers, and he lived to the age of ninety, a saint to many.

Have a good celebration of All Saints, and remember, "Do to others as you would have them do to you." It's the saintly thing to do!
Amen.

Father, Forgive Them!

Each of the gospel accounts of the crucifixion has its own peculiarity. Luke presents the trial of Jesus in a way that points fingers directly at the Jewish leaders involved. Luke goes out of his way to make sure we understand that the Jewish leaders are the ones who frame the charges against Jesus. It is they who insist he be crucified. Luke also is careful to make sure that we understand that the Roman governmental officials find no reason for Jesus to be prosecuted. It is important to recognize that it is only in Luke's Gospel that Jesus goes before Herod. Even the centurion who is in charge of the crucifixion exclaims that Jesus is innocent. Most scholars agree that Luke is presenting the facts this way to communicate to all who will listen that Jesus and his followers were no threat to the establishment of the day, the Roman government. These verses should never be understood in a way that would cause anyone to blame the death of Jesus on the Jewish people.

Luke has set the stage for us to understand just how important it is to comprehend Jesus' words of forgiveness. We may rightfully ask, "How can he forgive these people who are in the process of ending his life?" And, one of the most critical things for all of us to grasp is that unless Jesus does what he does, the cross stands for nothing!

When tragedy strikes, it is often hard to trust in God. We give God lots of lip service when a child is born or some other wonderful things come into our lives, but we are equally quick to condemn God, or at the very least ask, "How God, could you let this happen?" It is an accusation more than a question. If you are a God of love how can this happen? There are no easy answers, but it is into this milieu that we find ourselves in the accounts of the crucifixion and in the presence of Jesus' act of forgiveness. We learn by observation of this horrific act that Jesus is the supreme example of innocent suffering. His witness to us is that even there, even at the point of torture and death, when he should feel most vulnerable and exposed, he shows us that God's love never takes a vacation. His example is our good fortune in understanding that there is one reality that remains when all seems to be darkness, and that is, in the end, God prevails even over death!

H. G. Wells wrote a story titled, "The Country of the Blind." In it, he tells about a hidden valley shut off from the rest of the world by very high cliffs. That valley was inhabited only by blind people, and no one there had ever been able to see.

A lost and weary traveler stumbled into this country of the blind, and stayed with them for a while. As he lived among them, he found himself falling in love with a blind maiden, and began considering the possibility of marriage.

However, the blind people thought that this man who could see was strange. They felt that his mind was cluttered and confused, distracted by his ability to see. They insisted that if he wanted to continue living among them, he would have to have his eyes put out and become as blind as they.

For a while, the man thought that he would be willing to do that, but one morning he got up and saw the beauty of the sunrise, the mist rising from the valley floor, the dew glistening on the petals of the flowers, and he realized that he could not stay in the country of the blind. He climbed out of the valley and returned to the world of sight.

The way in which Jesus forgave allows us to see the true light. It also allows us to see Jesus not only as the suffering servant, but as Christ the King. Who but a servant and king could understand the relevance of true forgiveness? When Jesus came into our world, he saw things that the world was unable to see. He viewed the world from more than one vantage point. He saw the world both as a carpenter from Nazareth and as the King of kings. He lived and did things that the rest of humanity could not grasp. He thought

458

thoughts that the world had never thought. He did deeds that the rest of the world could not do. And our world could not stand that. It tried to pull him down to its own level, but Jesus refused to be a part of the darkness of this world.

Unlike the character in H. G. Wells' story, Jesus did not run away from the darkness. Instead, he conquered it. The place where that victory took place is a hill called Calvary, Golgotha, the "place of the skull," on an old rugged cross. As Jesus hung on that old, rugged cross, as he prayed to his Father to "forgive them, for they know not what they do," he revealed that there are no limits to God's willingness to forgive and pardon. Because we are all frail, we tend to strike out when we are hurt. But, when we pay attention to our lesson for today we learn that even when we strike out in anger or fear, the cross of Christ calls us to pull back and reassess our feelings. We are to be examples of forgiveness, even and especially when it is hardest. Jesus has shown us that there is nothing we can ever do to put ourselves beyond his healing reach.

One of the remarkable things about what is happening on the cross is the very fact that Jesus is praying. What a place to pray! We pray in church, we pray when we prepare for bed, we pray at the table before a meal, but on a cross?

I think most of us would agree that if you found yourself on the cruel cross you would curse the cross not pray on it. You would scream out your hate and indifference. You would cry. You experience pain on crosses. You certainly don't pray to forgive others while hanging on a cross.

Historically, we discover that the Romans worshiped revenge as one of their gods. They were constantly waging war on countries that had done them wrong, seeking revenge. For them revenge was a tool in the art of warfare. Revenge was sweetest when you conquered a people and enslaved them in your service. You used them to build your roads and cities. You exploited them for whatever you could get from them and out of them, but you didn't pray for them.

Who thought up the cross? Who thought about a person having nails driven into his hands and feet, watching him die a slow

459

death that drags out over hours and sometimes days? What kind of twisted mind thought up something like that?

Crucifixion was accomplished by nailing or tying the arms and legs of the victim to the cross. The agony was planned, you were supposed to suffer and become an example to anyone who harbored the thought they might just try to start an insurrection against Rome. Death actually resulted from exposure, shock, and eventual suffocation, when the body was so exhausted that breathing in that position was no longer possible. Yet, Jesus prayed to forgive them!

I wonder how many times he prayed it. Did he pray it when they beat him with the cat-o'-nine-tails? Did he pray it when they thrust a crown of thorns upon his head, put a purple robe around his shoulders, and mocked him by saying, "Hail, King of the Jews"? Do you suppose he prayed that prayer as he was carrying his cross up the hill? Did he pray it as they were driving nails into his hands and feet? Did he pray it as he was hanging there, his life's blood dripping to the ground? Do you suppose he prayed that prayer when he looked into the angry faces shouting, "If you really are the Son of God, come down from the cross"? How many times did Jesus pray that prayer?

God hangs on a cross! Jesus clearly identified in death as he had in life with the regular folk of his time. He hung on the cross and in that suffering he did in death what he did in life. Born homeless, for a short time a refugee in Egypt, and then, a brief ministry, a rabbi who socialized with the outcasts of his day. Jesus forever stands as the servant of the poor and the downtrodden. But, just as clearly he stands as Christ the King who welcomes all into his kingdom, even those who would kill him!

Some have suggested that Jesus was praying for a "blanket pardon for all the people who participated in his crucifixion. He was just going to forgive everybody who had anything to do with it." I don't believe that, because God never forces forgiveness on anybody. God is not going to walk up to a cursing, mocking priest shouting "Crucify him! Crucify him!" and say, "I'm going to forgive you whether you want to be forgiven or not."

Sisters and brothers in Christ, the death of Jesus on the cross is not a matter of an angry God requiring a perfect offering or sacrifice; a case of one member of the Trinity being sacrificed for another. Nor does it represent some kind of an agreement between God and Satan. The cross is at the center of Christian faith now and forever because the cross is a window into the heart of God. It reveals the overarching, all encompassing, never-ending love of God. The empty cross that stands in most Protestant churches is a visible reminder to all Christians of the victory of the Resurrection in which we all will share one day.

When Jesus prays for forgiveness he is saying to anyone who will listen that the kingdom is near and that all of God's children are invited to enter. That kingdom is present and made available wherever right relationships are being entered into. The kingdom is present wherever justice and mercy are being shown, and membership in this kingdom is not granted because you deserve to be allowed in, but because God offers membership as a free gift. You see, the forgiveness that Jesus prayed about from the cross is not dependant on priests or others acting as mediators. It has been pronounced by Jesus as free and available to any who seek or ask for it. It does not require you to sacrifice anything other than your ego. Who but a servant and king could offer such a gift? You and I are here today because the prayer that Jesus prayed 2,000 years ago is still being honored by God in heaven. That's why the sun shines on the good and the bad. That's why the rain falls on the just and the unjust.

For 2,000 years, his disciples have been going into the world telling people that God paid the price on Calvary's tree for their sins. For 2,000 years they have been inviting people to come and be forgiven of their sins.

Maybe we'll have another 2,000 years to preach the message. Maybe we won't. Right now, though, that prayer is still being honored. Right now forgiveness is still offered. God will never force it on you, but God offers it, makes it available, and paid the price for it. It is ours for the taking.

Amen.

A Breadbasket Full Of Goodies

In this the sixth chapter of John's Gospel, Jesus begins to withdraw to the east side of the Sea of Galilee. He has fed the 5,000, and he has walked on water. The press of the crowds had become all consuming and he needs some solitude to prepare himself for what lay ahead. Considering that the crowds that followed him more than likely knew of the feeding of the 5,000, and some may even have heard of the miraculous walking on water, it is difficult to explain why in these verses, they would doubt anything he had to say — but they do. It is like the saying that if it seems too good to be true, it probably is too good to be true. For many, Jesus is just too good to be true. He has already handed out a basket full of goodies, yet people want another example of his power.

Notice in our reading that in the dialogue between Jesus and the crowds, Jesus uses the word, "work," in a crafty way. I use the word, "crafty," only to highlight his teaching skills. You see Judaism stressed the importance of righteous works, but Jesus signals out one work: faith in him. Another example would be the way that Jewish teachers would stress Abraham's "work" of faith in God. Jesus puts the emphasis on one "work," that "work" being himself.

The crowds, like all of us, want more. They want Jesus to perform some kind of magic act to prove that having faith in him will be worthwhile to them. John uses the word, "sign," in place of what we may call miracle. They want Jesus to prove that he will be at least as good a leader and provider as Moses was, if not a better one. After all, it was Moses who made manna come down from heaven, so what can Jesus do to top that? Jesus is quick to correct

463

the people and remind them that Moses did not provide anything himself, but that God provided them all the manna they needed. The people really wanted Jesus to be the new Moses, but they wanted more than just a biblical leader. They wanted Jesus to be the new Moses that was both a religious and a political leader. Jesus is not going to fall into any sort of trap here. He is not the new Moses, he is the realization of what Moses and the people have wanted all of their lives. Jesus is quick to point out that what he is speaking about will fill them for eternity, no quick fixes here. "Do not work for the food that perishes, but for the food that endures for eternal life, which the Son of Man will give you" (v. 27). Implicit in these comments is the fact that if you want to be a follower of Jesus, you will have to do something. You will have to put your faith (work) in Jesus. You will have to understand that it is by this faith that you will be made full. No amount of good luck will fill you, at least not with the food you need for eternity.

The story is told of two old friends who bumped into one another on the street one day. One of them looked forlorn, almost on the verge of tears. His friend asked, "What has the world done to you, my old friend?"

The sad fellow said, "Let me tell you. Three weeks ago, an uncle died and left me $40,000."

"That's a lot of money."

"But, two weeks ago, a cousin I never even knew, died, and left me $85,000 free and clear."

"Sounds like you've been blessed...."

"You don't understand!" he interrupted. "Last week my great aunt passed away. I inherited almost a quarter of a million."

Now he was really confused. "Then, why do you look so glum?"

"This week ... nothing!"

Gratitude is something that you only feel when a gift is truly appreciated. When you look at how much we have in the way of material blessings in America is it any wonder that an attitude of gratitude is sorely missed? We watch hot dog eating contests where people eat so many hot dogs they often need to throw up. We are then able to change channels and watch children dying by the minute in the Sudan or some other poverty-stricken country. The sadness

464

is that we can switch between these two contradictory scenes almost without notice. We need the Hebrew Scripture and the heavenly manna it provides. But, we need equally to understand that manna without Jesus is never enough to fill our lives.

When we fill our lives with both, we are then ready to proclaim to the world that there is more than enough of Jesus to go around, and then, through him, more than enough gratitude to be shared with the world. When that gratitude becomes a part of our lives, we will no longer be able to watch people dying while others gorge themselves. We will, with Jesus by our side begin to understand that our breadbasket full of goodies needs to be equally distributed all over God's good creation.

In this season of Thanksgiving, maybe we should be revisiting why we feel entitled to have as much food and other goods as we feel we want, needed or not.

Once again turning to our text for today, these Jewish listeners were trying to grasp what Jesus was teaching them, he made a historical connection for them referring back to the manna from heaven that God provided for the Israelites when they were wandering in the wilderness for forty years. Again, demonstrating that God met their needs when they needed it. Jesus, the rabbi, maneuvers the discussion in a way that helps them to understand that things of a spiritual nature are important, but that he, Jesus is the Bread of Life. With a belief in Jesus, they would never be hungry, at least, not in things of eternal significance.

There is no clearer picture in scripture of what humankind must do to be fulfilled. Our lives will always be empty without the life-saving presence of Jesus. We come into a right relationship with God through Jesus. Once in that right relationship, we will begin to see that we are filled with his presence and because of that, we will be able to see the world and all of the good and bad things in our world with new clarity. More importantly we will know how vital it is that we do something about the injustice that we see around us every day.

How sad it is when we as wayward children put other "needs" ahead of this need for the Bread of Life made known in the person of Jesus Christ! Jesus Christ is the only real need that we have to ve a life of eternal blessing. Yet, we pursue cars and homes and all manner of expensive toys and in the process neglect the importance of returning thanks to the giver of all good gifts for the only thing that really matters for eternity. It is sort of like going into the public library and seeing all the books. You can look at all that knowledge, but unless you take down a book and read it, you can only guess what knowledge is contained between its pages. You literally have to take that knowledge inside yourself in order to gain anything from it. Same thing with Jesus. You need to take him into your life in order to show the benefits outside of your life.

Friends, we have been blessed by God in ways too many to number, and yet we often feel just like the people in our text for today. We, too, want Jesus to give us one more thing. We want one more demonstration of his power. It is almost as if they, and now us, are viewing Jesus' ministry as a biblical magic show. They wanted yet another demonstration of his power so "then they would believe." It seems to me that it was well past time for them and it is definitely past time for us to believe in him and in the Father who had sent him.

Maybe circumstances in your life have left you unable to see the many wondrous things God has done and continues to do in your life. Maybe the pain of life has overwhelmed you to the point where you don't see anymore how blessed you truly are. Maybe Thanksgiving is a time of sorrow for you because this is the first year without the person you loved. Maybe it is just that life has gotten away from you with the busyness that is so much a part of all of our lives. Maybe you are lucky enough to be in that category of people who have been so blessed, that even those blessings don't look all that good anymore.

How, then, can we overcome our mind-set of apathy and move toward a true spirit of thanksgiving in a culture that teaches us to enter into the rat race and compete for status with a world of unthankful people. I don't pretend to have all of the answers, but I do think we need to recognize God's blessing in all of their many manifestations and give thanks to God even and most importantly when it seems impossible to do so.

An anonymous email provides the following suggestions. Make an effort today to recognize the blessings you've come to take for granted. Focus on what you have rather than on what you don't have, and see if it doesn't improve your attitude.

A few suggestions:

- Be thankful that you don't already have everything you want. If you did, what would there be to look forward to?
- Be thankful when you don't know something, this gives you the opportunity to learn.
- Be thankful for the difficult times. During those times you grow.
- Be thankful for your limitations, because they give you opportunities for improvement.
- Be thankful for each new challenge, because it will build strength and character.
- Be thankful for your mistakes. They will teach you valuable lessons.
- Be thankful when you're tired and weary, because it means you've made a difference.

It's easy to be thankful when things are good. It is easy to see the world through rose-colored glasses when your life is rosy. But, a life of true fulfillment can come to those who are also thankful for the setbacks. As hard as it may be, find a way to be thankful for your troubles, and learn from them so they can become your blessings.

As we look around us at the land of plenty that we live in, it is my prayer that we will see through new eyes each day the ways that God has blessed us and never take God or those blessings for granted. When we internalize those blessings we will be happy to spread our breadbasket full of goodies throughout the world. This year, as we celebrate Thanksgiving, may we each see God for who God really is and see ourselves as who we really are: People who have been blessed beyond our wildest dreams. We have been given the Bread of Life; we know this bread and have had our only lasting hunger satisfied. May we now be truly thankful to the God who deserves our thanksgiving!

467

Lectionary Preaching After Pentecost

The following index will aid the user of this book in matching the correct Sunday with the appropriate text during Pentecost. All texts in this book are from the series for the Gospel Readings, Revised Common Lectionary. (Note that the ELCA division of Lutheranism is now following the Revised Common Lectionary.) The Lutheran designations indicate days comparable to Sundays on which Revised Common Lectionary Propers or Ordinary Time designations are used.

(Fixed dates do not pertain to Lutheran Lectionary)

Fixed Date Lectionaries *Revised Common (including ELCA)* *and Roman Catholic*	Lutheran Lectionary *Lutheran*
The Day Of Pentecost	The Day Of Pentecost
The Holy Trinity	The Holy Trinity
May 29-June 4 — Proper 4, Ordinary Time 9	Pentecost 2
June 5-11 — Proper 5, Ordinary Time 10	Pentecost 3
June 12-18 — Proper 6, Ordinary Time 11	Pentecost 4
June 19-25 — Proper 7, Ordinary Time 12	Pentecost 5
June 26-July 2 — Proper 8, Ordinary Time 13	Pentecost 6
July 3-9 — Proper 9, Ordinary Time 14	Pentecost 7
July 10-16 — Proper 10, Ordinary Time 15	Pentecost 8
July 17-23 — Proper 11, Ordinary Time 16	Pentecost 9
July 24-30 — Proper 12, Ordinary Time 17	Pentecost 10
July 31-Aug. 6 — Proper 13, Ordinary Time 18	Pentecost 11
Aug. 7-13 — Proper 14, Ordinary Time 19	Pentecost 12
Aug. 14-20 — Proper 15, Ordinary Time 20	Pentecost 13
Aug. 21-27 — Proper 16, Ordinary Time 21	Pentecost 14
Aug. 28-Sept. 3 — Proper 17, Ordinary Time 22	Pentecost 15
Sept. 4-10 — Proper 18, Ordinary Time 23	Pentecost 16
Sept. 11-17 — Proper 19, Ordinary Time 24	Pentecost 17
Sept. 18-24 — Proper 20, Ordinary Time 25	Pentecost 18

469

Sept. 25-Oct. 1 — Proper 21, Ordinary Time 26	Pentecost 19
Oct. 2-8 — Proper 22, Ordinary Time 27	Pentecost 20
Oct. 9-15 — Proper 23, Ordinary Time 28	Pentecost 21
Oct. 16-22 — Proper 24, Ordinary Time 29	Pentecost 22
Oct. 23-29 — Proper 25, Ordinary Time 30	Pentecost 23
Oct. 30-Nov. 5 — Proper 26, Ordinary Time 31	Pentecost 24
Nov. 6-12 — Proper 27, Ordinary Time 32	Pentecost 25
Nov. 13-19 — Proper 28, Ordinary Time 33	Pentecost 26
	Pentecost 27
Nov. 20-26 — Christ The King	Christ The King

Reformation Day (or last Sunday in October) is October 31 (Revised Common, Lutheran)

All Saints (or first Sunday in November) is November 1 (Revised Common, Lutheran, Roman Catholic)

U.S./Canadian Lectionary Comparison

The following index shows the correlation between the Sundays and special days of the church year as they are titled or labeled in the Revised Common Lectionary published by the Consultation On Common Texts and used in the United States (the reference used for this book) and the Sundays and special days of the church year as they are titled or labeled in the Revised Common Lectionary used in Canada.

Revised Common Lectionary	Canadian Revised Common Lectionary
Advent 1	Advent 1
Advent 2	Advent 2
Advent 3	Advent 3
Advent 4	Advent 4
Christmas Eve	Christmas Eve
The Nativity Of Our Lord/ Christmas Day	The Nativity Of Our Lord
Christmas 1	Christmas 1
January 1/Holy Name Of Jesus	January 1/The Name Of Jesus
Christmas 2	Christmas 2
The Epiphany Of Our Lord	The Epiphany Of Our Lord
The Baptism Of Our Lord/ Epiphany 1	The Baptism Of Our Lord/ Proper 1
Epiphany 2/Ordinary Time 2	Epiphany 2/Proper 2
Epiphany 3/Ordinary Time 3	Epiphany 3/Proper 3
Epiphany 4/Ordinary Time 4	Epiphany 4/Proper 4
Epiphany 5/Ordinary Time 5	Epiphany 5/Proper 5
Epiphany 6/Ordinary Time 6	Epiphany 6/Proper 6
Epiphany 7/Ordinary Time 7	Epiphany 7/Proper 7
Epiphany 8/Ordinary Time 8	Epiphany 8/Proper 8
The Transfiguration Of Our Lord/ Last Sunday After The Epiphany	The Transfiguration Of Our Lord/ Last Sunday After Epiphany
Ash Wednesday	Ash Wednesday
Lent 1	Lent 1
Lent 2	Lent 2
Lent 3	Lent 3
Lent 4	Lent 4
Lent 5	Lent 5
Sunday Of The Passion/Palm Sunday	Passion/Palm Sunday
Maundy Thursday	Holy/Maundy Thursday
Good Friday	Good Friday

Resurrection Of Our Lord/ Easter Day	The Resurrection Of Our Lord
Easter 2	Easter 2
Easter 3	Easter 3
Easter 4	Easter 4
Easter 5	Easter 5
Easter 6	Easter 6
The Ascension Of Our Lord	The Ascension Of Our Lord
Easter 7	Easter 7
The Day Of Pentecost	The Day Of Pentecost
The Holy Trinity	The Holy Trinity
Proper 4/Pentecost 2/O T 9*	Proper 9
Proper 5/Pent 3/O T 10	Proper 10
Proper 6/Pent 4/O T 11	Proper 11
Proper 7/Pent 5/O T 12	Proper 12
Proper 8/Pent 6/O T 13	Proper 13
Proper 9/Pent 7/O T 14	Proper 14
Proper 10/Pent 8/O T 15	Proper 15
Proper 11/Pent 9/O T 16	Proper 16
Proper 12/Pent 10/O T 17	Proper 17
Proper 13/Pent 11/O T 18	Proper 18
Proper 14/Pent 12/O T 19	Proper 19
Proper 15/Pent 13/O T 20	Proper 20
Proper 16/Pent 14/O T 21	Proper 21
Proper 17/Pent 15/O T 22	Proper 22
Proper 18/Pent 16/O T 23	Proper 23
Proper 19/Pent 17/O T 24	Proper 24
Proper 20/Pent 18/O T 25	Proper 25
Proper 21/Pent 19/O T 26	Proper 26
Proper 22/Pent 20/O T 27	Proper 27
Proper 23/Pent 21/O T 28	Proper 28
Proper 24/Pent 22/O T 29	Proper 29
Proper 25/Pent 23/O T 30	Proper 30
Proper 26/Pent 24/O T 31	Proper 31
Proper 27/Pent 25/O T 32	Proper 32
Proper 28/Pent 26/O T 33	Proper 33
Christ The King (Proper 29/O T 34)	Proper 34/Christ The King/ Reign Of Christ
Reformation Day (October 31)	Reformation Day (October 31)
All Saints (November 1 or 1st Sunday in November)	All Saints' Day (November 1)
Thanksgiving Day (4th Thursday of November)	Thanksgiving Day (2nd Monday of October)

*O T = Ordinary Time

472

About The Authors

Gary L. Carver has been the pastor of First Baptist Church in Chattanooga, Tennessee, for more than twenty years. His sermons and articles have appeared in a variety of publications, including *Lectionary Homiletics*, *Preaching*, and *The Abingdon Minister's Manual*, and he is the author of *Acting On The Absurd*, *Distinctively Different*, and *Out From The Ordinary* (CSS). Carver is a graduate of Samford University (B.A.) and Southern Baptist Theological Seminary (M.Div. and D.Min.), with additional graduate study at Candler School of Theology and Harvard Divinity School.

Tom M. Garrison is the pastor of Sun Lakes United Church of Christ in Sun Lakes, Arizona. He has also served as pastor of congregations in Alabama, Georgia, Tennessee, Pennsylvania, and Nova Scotia (Canada), and has also taught ministry and homiletics at Southern Christian University (Montgomery, Alabama) and Atlantic School of Theology (Halifax, Nova Scotia). Garrison is a graduate of Alabama Christian College (B.A.), Southern Christian University (M.A. and M.Div.), and Columbia Theological Seminary (D.Min.). He is the author of *A Call to Love* (CSS).

Donald Charles Lacy is now retired after more than four decades serving United Methodist churches in Indiana. He is the author of ten books, as well as more than 1,000 smaller pieces, several of which appear in his recently published *Collected Works* (Providence House). Lacy's sermons have appeared in many outlets, including *Great Preaching 2001*, *Keeping the Faith: Best Indiana Sermons* (2003), and *The Minister's Manual 2004*.

David R. Cartwright served for 22 years as the senior minister of Hazelwood Christian Church (Disciples of Christ) in Muncie, Indiana. He is a graduate of Washington University, Yale Divinity School, and Christian Theological Seminary.

Ron Lavin is the award-winning author of more than twenty books, including *Turning Griping Into Gratitude*, *Way To Grow!* and the popular *Another Look* series (CSS). He is the former Pastor-Director of Evangelical Outreach for the Lutheran Church in America, and pastored five thriving congregations, all of which grew substantially under his leadership. Lavin is a popular speaker and church consultant on the dynamics of small groups and evangelism.

John Wayne Clarke is an ordained minister in the United Church of Christ who currently pastors First Congregational Church in Meriden, Connecticut. He is the author of *What Good Is Christianity Anyhow?* and *A Quest for Silence*. Clarke is a graduate of Bangor Theological Seminary and Providence Theological Seminary (Otterburn, Manitoba, Canada).

Title: Sermons On The Gospel Readings, Series II, Cycle C

ISBN: 0-7880-2399-3

INSTRUCTIONS TO ACCESS PASSWORD FOR ELECTRONIC COPY OF THIS TITLE:

The password appears on the reverse side of this page. Carefully cut the card from the page to retrieve the password.

Once you have the password, go to

http:/www.csspub.com/passwords/

and locate this title on that web page. By clicking on the title, you will be guided to a page to enter your password, name, and email address. From there you will be sent to a page to download your electronic version of this book.

For further information, or if you don't have access to the internet, please contact CSS Publishing Company at 1-800-241-4056 in the United States (or 419-227-1818 from outside the United States) between 8 a.m. and 5 p.m., Eastern Standard Time, Monday through Friday.